CHINA'S SPECIAL ECONOMIC ZONES: POLICIES, PROBLEMS AND PROSPECTS

China's Special Economic Zones

Policies, Problems and Prospects

EDITORS
Y.C. Jao C.K. Leung

CONTRIBUTORS
C.H. Chai Thomas Chan C.Y. Chang E.K.Y. Chen
Steve Chin D.K.Y. Chu Karl Herbst Y.C. Jao
R.Y.W. Kwok K.C. Lam C.K. Leung T.W.C. Lo
K.K. Shum L.T. Sigel Victor F.S. Sit

HONG KONG OXFORD NEW YORK
OXFORD UNIVERSITY PRESS
1986

Oxford University Press

Oxford New York Toronto
Petaling Jaya Singapore Hong Kong Tokyo
Delhi Bombay Calcutta Madras Karachi
Nairobi Dar es Salaam Cape Town
Melbourne Auckland

and associated companies in
Beirut Berlin Ibadan Nicosia

First published 1986
Published in the United States
by Oxford University Press, Inc., New York

Library of Congress Cataloging-in-Publication Data

China's special economic zones.
Includes bibliographies and index.
1. Free ports and zones — China. I. Jao. Y. C.
II. Leung, Chi-Keung. III. Chai, C. H.
HF1418.C515 1986 382.7'1'0951 86-5159
ISBN 0-19-583799-1 (U.S.)

Printed in Hong Kong by Liang Yu Printing Factory Ltd.
Published by Oxford University Press, Warwick House, Hong Kong

Preface

THE idea of this book was first conceived in July 1983. Several authors of the present volume were also contributors to another book, *China and Hong Kong: The Economic Nexus*, published by Oxford University Press in 1983. Because of the favourable response to that book, it was suggested that we might consider a project on China's Special Economic Zones (SEZs). After some consideration, we felt that, despite a burgeoning literature on the SEZs, there was still a lack of studies from a multi-disciplinary, multi-dimensional perspective, which were accessible to the general public. Accordingly, we approached and invited a group of scholars, based in Hong Kong and Australia, to participate in the project.

Nearly all the contributors to this volume have, individually, visited the SEZs and undertaken field research there from time to time. However, a collective field trip to Shenzhen and Zhuhai, comprising most of the authors, was made in June 1984. A seminar, jointly sponsored by the Centre of Asian Studies of the University of Hong Kong and Zhongshan University was held in Zhuhai on 12–13 June 1984. Seventeen scholars from China, Hong Kong and Australia attended. Marked by frank exchanges of views and lively discussions, the seminar proved to be most valuable to the project. We wish to record here our warm thanks to our Chinese colleagues for their friendly co-operation in providing highly useful information on various aspects of the SEZs.

Since our project was launched in early 1984, the pace of economic reforms in China has quickened noticeably. It is physically impossible for us to undertake an in-depth study of all recent developments, such as the opening up of 14 coastal cities and the whole coastal area, the special treatment given to Hainan Island, the emergence of 'development zones' in the hinterland, and so on. Our focus is on the four established SEZs, especially Shenzhen. We are acutely conscious, nevertheless, of the fact that the SEZs are but part of China's continuing process of modernization and reform, and can only be properly viewed in that perspective. Hopefully, the latest developments will be more adequately studied on another occasion.

University of Hong Kong — Y.C. Jao and C.K. Leung
February 1985

Contributors

C.H. Chai
Lecturer in Economics, University of Hong Kong

Thomas Chan
Research Officer, Centre of Asian Studies, University of Hong Kong

C.Y. Chang
Lecturer in Government and Public Administration,
The Chinese University of Hong Kong

E.K.Y. Chen
Director, Centre of Asian Studies, and Reader in Economics,
University of Hong Kong

Steve Chin
Research Officer, Centre of Asian Studies, University of Hong Kong

D.K.Y. Chu
Lecturer in Geography, The Chinese University of Hong Kong

Karl Herbst
Formerly Lecturer in Law, University of Hong Kong;
now Attorney-at-Law, Morrison & Foerster, Hong Kong

Y.C. Jao
Reader in Economics, University of Hong Kong

R.Y.W. Kwok
Professor of Urban Studies and Urban Planning
and Director, Centre of Urban Studies and Urban Planning,
University of Hong Kong

K.C. Lam
Lecturer in Geography, The Chinese University of Hong Kong

C.K. Leung
Reader in Geography, University of Hong Kong

T.W.C. Lo
Lecturer in Marketing, The Chinese University of Hong Kong

K.K. Shum
Lecturer in Economic History, University of New South Wales

L.T. Sigel
Lecturer in Economic History, University of New South Wales

Victor F.S. Sit
Senior Lecturer in Geography, University of Hong Kong

Contents

Tables

Figures

1. Spatial Redeployment and the Special Economic Zones in China: An Overview

C.K. LEUNG

Introduction

The establishment of the special economic zones (SEZs) in China has been closely watched and intensely debated. Domestically, Chinese scholars, with few exceptions, have spared no efforts in delineating the functions and characteristics of the Chinese SEZs and similar creations in other parts of the world, such as export-processing zones and free trade zones, or in justifying and rationalizing the existence of the SEZs on Chinese soil.[1] The latest and perhaps the only major controversy within China concerning the SEZs is whether or not progress in the Shenzhen SEZ has been the result of a 'transfusion' from the rest of the country, a point on which even the provincial and central leadership do not seem to be in total agreement.[2] Outside China, most of the studies on the SEZs are concerned with various practical aspects of their development, for example, infrastructure, land use, the investment environment, costs and finance.[3] While they generally welcome the SEZs as being innovative, some point to the possibility that the new reforms in general and the SEZs in particular could be early signs of China's turning capitalist or giving up socialism.[4] Indeed, most outside critics, taking the SEZs merely as an economic phenomenon, argue from a structural perspective that they represent a violent departure from past policies and hence constitute a serious challenge to accepted ideology.

From a spatial perspective, however, it seems that there has been a general consensus that China's experience of, and strategies on, what may be called rural or peripheral development[5] have been reasonably successful, especially during the first twenty-five years of the People's Republic. Policies introduced since the mid-1970s favouring a reorientation towards coastal or 'core' development strategies represent China's new drive towards further technological and economic expansion. In other words, in the light of a changing set of national priorities, the re-emphasis on the coastal area and the establishment of the SEZs can be viewed as the result of spatial redeployment for modernization.

Development Strategies and Spatial Redeployment

Spatial Imbalance and Development Strategies

For a long time, pronounced spatial inequality within China has been noted, and has undoubtedly been one of the major considerations in the development process and in the formulation of development strategies in China.[6] Briefly, before 1949, more than 70 per cent of China's industries were concentrated within a narrow coastal belt stretching from the Northeast to Guangdong, heavy industries mostly being found in the Northeast and light industries in a few major cities along the coast in the East and South, namely, Shanghai, Tianjin and Guangzhou. Vast inland areas, particularly the peripheral and minority regions in the North, Northwest, and Southwest, were practically devoid of any modern industry.[7]

Since the establishment of the People's Republic, development strategies have been generally designed to correct this imbalance and to disperse modern industries to the interior. In short, between 1952 and 1978, the cumulative total capital investment ratio between inland and coastal areas, excluding those not regionally classified, was 1:0.74.[8]

Within inland China, development strategies have not been unselective. Thus, during the First Five-year Plan (1953–7), new industrial bases were erected in Wuhan, Baotou, Lanzhou, Xi'an and Taiyuan; and during the Second Five-year Plan (1958–62), the Great Leap Forward movement not only further dispersed large major industrial undertakings to the Northwest and Southwest, but also led to the emergence of backyard furnaces in rural areas throughout the country.[9] More specifically, so far as the construction of the railway system is concerned, development up to the early 1960s was clearly concentrated in environmentally 'hostile' and geopolitically sensitive regions, or in economically underdeveloped regions possessing a low output of grain, a low population density, and limited cultivated land, namely, Xinjiang, Yunnan, Guangxi, Nei Monggol, Ningxia, Gansu, Qinghai, Guizhou, Shaanxi and Xizang. In other words, it was the 'extra-ecumenical' area or the 'periphery' of China that was emphasized.[10]

After the Sino-Soviet split and a short period of adjustment in the early 1960s, spatial priorities shifted away from the 'periphery', much of which lies within a short distance of the land frontiers.[11] It now transpires that the so-called Third Front, as a part of inland China which had had some major industrial undertakings right from the beginning of the First Plan, became the overwhelming focus of national reconstruction after 1965 through the Third and Fourth Five-year Plans (1966–70 and 1971–5). The Third Front is an area away from the coast and the land frontiers that consists of Sichuan, Guizhou, Yunnan, Shaanxi, Gansu and the western parts of Henan, Hubei and Hunan.[12] The fundamental ideology behind its construction was the preparation for a supposedly imminent and total third world war, and the guiding principles for construction emphasized 'mountainous, dispersed, and tunneled' locations for protection. The sense of insecurity and urgency behind this policy was only too obvious.[13]

Table 1.1 shows that of total capital investment, the inland area as a whole accounted for nearly 70 per cent during the Third Plan and for well over half up to the late 1970s. Although the proportion of capital investment in the 'extra-ecumenical' area, especially for the first two planned periods, cannot be ascertained due to a lack of data, that for the Third Front, which somewhat overlaps with the former area, rose sharply during the Third Plan to an all-time high of 53 per cent of total capital investment, more than

Table 1.1 The Distribution of Total Capital Investment by Selected Areas (percentage)

Area	1952	I FYP[1]	II FYP	1963–5	III FYP	IV FYP	1979	1982	1983
Coastal[2]	—[5]	46.65	44.13	—	31.51	42.53	47.89	50.84	49.31
Inland[2]	—	53.35	55.87	—	68.49	57.47	52.11	49.16	50.69
'Extra-ecumenical'[3]	—	—	—	—	—	—	—	17.60	18.15
Third Front[4]	23.9	30.60	36.90	38.2	52.70	41.10	34.70	25.65	24.03

Notes: 1. FYP = Five-year Plan.

2. The division of coastal and inland areas has not been entirely consistent. The coastal area originally referred to the eastern littoral provinces and municipalities, namely, Beijing, Tianjin, Shanghai, Liaoning, Hebei, Shandong, Jiangsu, Zhejiang, Fujian, Guangdong and, more recently, Guangxi. The remaining provinces and autonomous regions are thus defined as inland. However, the coastal area includes Anhui according to Liu Zaixing, *Zhongguo gongye buju xue* (*A Study of Industrial Locations in China*) (Beijing, People's University of China, Department of Planning and Statistics, 1981), p. 60, and Suen Jingzhi, *et al.*, *Zhongguo jingji dili gailun* (*Introduction to the Economic Geography of China*) (Beijing, Commercial Press, 1983), p. 40; or it may include Jiangxi *instead* of Hebei according to Liu Guoguang, *Zhongguo jingji fazhan zhanlue wenti yanjiu* (*A Study of the Problems of China's Strategies for Economic Development*) (Shanghai, People's Press, 1984), p. 264. The present chapter adopts the original and more geographical definition.

3. The 'Extra-ecumenical' area comprises Gansu, Guangxi, Guizhou, Nei Monggol, Ningxia, Qinghai, Shaanxi, Xinjiang, Xizang and Yunnan.

4. The Third Front consists of Gansu, Guizhou, Henan, Hubei, Hunan, Shaanxi, Sichuan and Yunnan.

5. A dash indicates that the data are not available.

Sources: Data for the years 1952–79 are calculated from Liu Zaixing, 'Lun sanxian jianshe' ('On Third Front Construction'), in *Gongye buju cankao ziliao* (Beijing, People's University of China, 1984), pp. 104–19; Liu Zaixing, *Zhongguo gongye buju xue* (*A Study of Industrial Locations in China*) (Beijing, People's University of China, Department of Planning and Statistics, 1981), pp. 64–6; and Suen Jingzhi, *et al.*, *Zhongguo jingji dili gailun* (*Introduction to the Economic Geography of China*) (Beijing, Commercial Press, 1983), pp. 93–5. Data for the years 1982–3 are taken from State Statistical Bureau, *Zhongguo tongji nianjian, 1982* (*Statistical Yearbook of China, 1982*) (Hong Kong, Economic and Information Agency, 1983), p. 336, and *Zhongguo tongji nianjian,. 1983* (Hong Kong, Economic and Information Agency, 1984), p. 316. All figures exclude investments not regionally classified.

three-quarters (77 per cent) of all inland capital investment or two-thirds greater than that for the entire coastal belt.

With some allowance for a time-lag, Table 1.2 reinforces the pattern of spatial priorities depicted in Table 1.1. Between 1952 and the early 1980s, as a result of capital investment priorities approximately 10 per cent of the total gross value of industrial output (GVIO) shifted from the coast inland. In particular, the share of the 'extra-ecumenical' area nearly doubled to 10.13 per cent, and that of the Third Front grew by half to 23.76 per cent. In absolute terms the 'extra-ecumenical' area grew 32 times and the Third Front 29 times between 1952 and 1983, compared to the coastal belt's mere 16 times and the nation's 18 times. In other words, the former two have grown roughly 70 per cent faster than the nation as a whole and twice as fast as the coastal area. More importantly, the period of sustained high growth as reflected by the GVIO for the 'extra-ecumenical' area came to an end by the mid-1970s, whereas that for the Third Front did not end until the early 1980s.

Consequently, between 1952 and 1979, there existed a long contiguous belt along the eastern coast in which all the provinces (Guangdong, Fujian, Jiangxi, Zhejiang, Shandong, Hebei, Anhui and Jiangsu) remained relatively static, that is, merely maintained their shares of growth; while the three Northeast provinces, as well as the municipalities of Shanghai and Tianjin, experienced a substantial decline in their relative shares of the nation's industrial output. (Beijing, the national capital, was an exception. It doubled its share.) By contrast, provinces and autonomous regions west of this belt in the interior achieved either huge increases in their shares (from Guangxi in the south up through Hunan, Hubei, Henan and Shanxi north to Inner Mongolia, and westward to Shaanxi, Gansu, Ningxia and Qinghai), or at least above national average increases (Sichuan, Guizhou, Xinjiang and Yunnan). Others that had never had any industries began to industrialize and accounted for some share of the national output (Xizang).[14] In other words, spatial deployment up to the end of the Fourth Five-year Plan (1975) deliberately avoided the entire coastal corridor where heavy and light industries were traditionally concentrated.

Economic Efficiency and Spatial Redeployment

There is no doubt that the adopted strategies have successfully and speedily spread development to the interior of China. Not only does inland China as a whole now account for over 40 per cent of total GVIO, an amount which is still rising as is shown in Table 1.2, but also the successive sets of strategies have brought the most remote and backward regions of China into motion with the rest of the economy. For example, in terms of GVIO per capita, the 'extra-ecumenical' and Third Front areas used to have only one-third of the national average and between one-fifth and one-quarter of that of the coast in 1952, whereas in 1983 they averaged roughly 60 per cent and over 40 per cent of those of the nation and coastal area respectively (Table 1.3). Moreover, during the same period, about 2 per cent of the total population shifted inland from the coast, particularly to the 'extra-ecumenical' area, which

Table 1.2 The Gross Value of Industrial Output by Selected Areas

	1952		1957		1974		1979		1982		1983	
	Million *yuan*	Per cent	Million *yuan*	Per cent	Million *yuan*	Per cent	Million *yuan*	Per cent	Million *yuan*	Fer cent	Million *yuan*	Per cent
National	33,770	100	69,798	100	344,965	100	—[1]	100	557,745	100	616,441	100
Coastal	23,467	69.49	45,293	64.89	230,022	66.67	—	60.7	333,356	59.77	366,748	59.49
Inland	10,303	30.51	24,505	35.11	114,943	33.33	—	39.3	224,389	40.23	249,693	40.51
'Extra-ecumenical'	1,968	5.84	5,342	7.65	33,945	9.84	—	10.5	55,974	10.04	62,435	10.13
Third Front	5,081	15.05	13,371	19.16	62,577	18.14	—	23.0	131,090	23.51	146,408	23.76

Note: 1. A dash indicates that the data are not available.

Sources: Data for 1952 and 1974 are taken from R.M. Field, N.R. Lardy and J.P. Emerson, *A Reconstruction of the Gross Value of Industrial Output by Province in the PRC: 1949–73* (Washington, DC, United States Department of Commerce, July 1975); data for 1957 are taken from 'China: Gross Value of Industrial Output, 1965–77' (Washington, DC, Central Intelligence Agency), Research Paper ER78–10355, June 1978; data for 1979 are taken from *China, Socialist Economic Development* (Washington, DC, World Bank), Vol. II, 1983, Table 2.5, p. 145; data for 1982 are taken from State Statistical Bureau, *Zhongguo tongji nianjian, 1983* (*Statistical Yearbook of China, 1983*) (Hong Kong, Economic Information and Agency, 1984); and data for 1983 are taken from State Statistical Bureau, *Zhongguo tongji nianjian, 1984* (*Statistical Yearbook of China, 1984*) (Hong Kong, Economic Information and Agency, 1985).

Table 1.3 The Gross Value of Industrial Output Per Capita by Selected Areas (*yuan*)

	1952	1957	1974	1979	1982	1983
National	57.96	107.96	379.41	—[1]	555.85	603.93
Coastal	93.77	163.95	585.08	—	807.16	871.63
Inland	31.00	66.18	222.73	—	380.06	416.19
'Extra-ecumenical'	20.92	50.26	227.52	—	297.67	326.39
Third Front	22.04	52.48	178.75	—	340.03	373.97

Note: 1. A dash indicates that the data are not available.

Sources: See Table 1.2. Population figures for 1952, 1957 and 1974 are taken from John S. Aird, *Population Estimates for the Provinces of the PRC: 1953–1974* (Washington, DC, United States Department of Commerce, February 1974), Tables 1 and 2; those for 1982 are taken from the *1982 Population Census of China (major figures)* (Hong Kong, Economic Information and Agency, 1982).

gained more than 2.5 per cent to account for 18.74 per cent of the total population in 1983. This means that the gap in terms of GVIO per capita between the inland and the coastal areas could have been even narrower had it not been for the population transfer, assuming the same distribution of total GVIO.

Nearly a decade ago, when it was observed that spatial priorities since 1949 had been placed on inland China in general and on the 'extra-ecumenical' area in particular, the question was raised as to 'how much regional imbalance ought to be eliminated before a reversion of policy should set in, or more directly, at what stage a primary contradiction will be viewed as secondary and therefore no longer requires the most urgent, and in many cases very expensive on a short and even medium-term basis, action program'.[15] This question may never be answered precisely, but it is clear that development strategies have not remained static;[16] indeed, spatial priorities shifted from the most backward 'periphery' to the not-so-backward Third Front of inland China from the mid-1960s, and have noticeably been reoriented towards the 'core' or coastal area since the mid-1970s.[17]

Summing up developments up to the mid-1970s, Chinese scholars have almost unanimously pointed out the problems of over-emphasis on the inland area and the lack of promotion of regional advantages in the past.[18] It is said that in spite of heavy investment in the inland area over the past thirty years, the total GVIO of the area in 1979 amounted to only two-thirds that of the coast, a pattern which has essentially remained unchanged in the 1980s, as can be observed from Table 1.2. It is estimated that investments in the Southwest and Northwest industrial regions during the period were three times that of Shanghai, yet the revenue they produced in the form of tax and profit was less than half that of the municipality; and that on the basis of coal consumption for every 10,000 *yuan* of gross industrial value produced, the coast was approximately seven times more economical than the inland area.[19] Moreover, the cumulative investment-output ratio for the

Third Front was only 0.256, or 2.8 times lower than that for the coast.[20] From Tables 1.1 and 1.2, it can also be seen that in terms of ratios of capital investment to GVIO in 1983, the coast was still 1.5 times more efficient than inland China, and 2.16 and 1.22 times more efficient than the 'extra-ecumenical' area and the Third Front respectively.

Clearly, therefore, the reorientation towards the coast since the mid-1970s has been based primarily on considerations of economic efficiency. Even though signs of further dispersion, the promotion of small-scale industries resembling the Great Leap Forward, and continued emphasis on the Third Front did emerge during the first three years of the Fifth Plan (1976–80),[21] they were soon rectified at the Third Plenary Session of the Eleventh Central Committee of the Chinese Communist Party in 1978, which adopted the policy of readjustment.[22]

Table 1.1 shows that the coast began to gain in its share of capital investment during the Fourth Plan and reached an all-time high, accounting for more than 47 per cent of total capital investment, by 1979. Its share continued to grow and accounted for approximately half of total capital investment in the early 1980s, while that of the Third Front dwindled to less than a quarter, roughly the same proportion as in the 1950s. Thus the reorientation towards the coast since the mid-1970s should not be regarded as an abrupt or deviant move, but instead should be seen as part of a continuous dialectical process of spatial deployment to best serve changing national priorities. For as early as 1956, it had already been fully recognized that the emphasis on the interior must be changed, that China would suffer if insufficient attention was paid to the old industrial bases, that is, the coastal area, and that unless the advantages of industrial production in the coastal area — inertia, high technology and quality — could be harnessed and further developed, the industrialization of the interior was well-nigh impossible.[23]

The Spatial Characteristics and Implications of the Special Economic Zones

The Four Modernizations and the Open-door Policy

Similarly, the seemingly 'abrupt' establishment of the SEZs since the late 1970s is misleading. For Chinese attempts at modernization have an equally long and consistent history. The SEZs as a component of the open-door policy — the backbone of Chinese modernization — are the not unnatural outcomes of a shift in emphasis to the coast.

Elsewhere, it has been shown that the first vision of a modernized China can be traced back to the early 1960s, when it was envisaged that by the end of the projected Fourth Five-year Plan, that is, 1972, the modernization of industry, agriculture, science and culture, and defence could be realized.[24] This wish was repeatedly expressed at the Third and Fourth National People's Congresses in 1964 and 1975 respectively, though the date for the realization of the so-called Four Modernizations was pushed forward to

1980. It was at the Third National People's Congress that the need for 'correctly handling the relationship between self-reliance and international co-operation' and for pursuing a 'technological revolution' was first mentioned.[25] After the deaths of Zhou Enlai and Mao Zedong, the goal of the Four Modernizations was formally written into the new constitution of the Chinese Communist Party, which was passed at the Eleventh National Party Congress on 18 August 1977, and again incorporated into the new constitution of the People's Republic of China, which was passed at the Fifth National People's Congress on 5 March 1978.[26]

Therefore, at the Third Plenum of the Eleventh Central Committee of the Chinese Communist Party in December 1978, when the emphasis of the Party's work was formally placed on economic and social rather than political development, an all-out effort geared at socialist modernization and construction was launched, which came to be known first as 'readjustment' and more recently as 'system reforms'.[27] It was, however, not until the Fourth Session of the Fifth National People's Congress in November–December 1981, when Zhao Ziyang, then Premier of the State Council, made his report on government work, that the new policies finally came to be explicitly defined. In his report, he outlined ten principles as the concrete embodiment of the policy of 'readjusting, restructuring, consolidating, and improving', and clearly stated, among other things, that China will 'persist in an open-door policy'; that she will give prominence to the development of consumer goods and service-oriented industries; that she will carry out a technical transformation; and that she will actively and steadily reform her economic system.[28] In the words of some Chinese scholars, the new policy called for a change of strategy from one of isolation and self-reliance to that of the open door, and a change in the economic system from one based on egalitarianism, over-centralization to the exclusion of the market mechanism, and collectivism to one allowing the co-existence of a variety of different economic and management structures, and of centralized and decentralized or planned and market-oriented systems, while still insisting on the dominant role of state enterprises.[29] In short, the impetus behind policies to promote foreign investment and technology came from the long-standing drive towards socialist modernization and the SEZs are simply the first test of the feasibility of such policies.

Unfortunately, data on capital investment in the SEZs or even in the provinces of Guangdong and Fujian are incomplete and thus do not permit a more detailed examination of the extent of spatial emphasis. However, a number of features may help to demonstrate the point. First, available data show that between 1981 and 1983, capital investment in Guangdong and Fujian increased from 3,179 million *yuan* and 869 million *yuan* to 3,841 million *yuan* and 1,183 million *yuan* respectively, or by 20 per cent and 36 per cent in two years respectively.[30] Second, according to the Deputy-Governor of Guangdong, capital investment in Shenzhen alone accounts for at least 1,640 million *yuan* per annum, nearly half that for the whole province.[31] Third, it has been calculated that the national average investment for each additional urban inhabitant stands at well above 10,000 *yuan*. Since standards in the SEZs are much higher and hence investment per capita must be higher than the national average, it is estimated that investment in Shenzhen during the first twenty years will approach 21,000 million *yuan*.[32] Fourth, taking the example of Shenzhen, investments from state, provincial, and city government sources between 1979 and 1983 accounted for at least 50 per cent but generally more than two-thirds of total investment.[33]

Spatial Characteristics and Implications

The economic characteristics and objectives of the SEZs have been well documented, even though disagreement as to whether some of the economic objectives can be achieved may still exist.[34] However, the spatial and socio-political characteristics and implications of the SEZs do not seem to have been adequately explored. So far as the actual establishment of the SEZs (first known as special export zones) is concerned, some have demonstrated that the first proposal came from Wu Nansheng, who visited Fujian after the Third Plenary Session of the Eleventh Central Committee of the Chinese Communist Party and who proposed setting up a special export zone at Shantou modelled on the export-processing zones (EPZs) of Taiwan.[35] Others have argued that the whole idea originated from Ye Fei, then Minister of Transport, who, after returning from an overseas tour, encouraged China Merchants' Steam Navigation Co. to expand its scope of business to develop export-processing activities at Shekou, and that therefore the setting up of the SEZs was a local and sectoral (that is, foreign trade) policy issue that was very much transient in nature.[36] These views seem to suggest that the establishment of the SEZs in China has been accidental and local, and that the central government has been rather passive.

The spatial framework and the Chinese desire for modernization discussed in this chapter seem to suggest otherwise. Not only have the two factors combined readily identified the coast as the most promising area of rapid development, but also recognition of the possible emergence of a Pacific economic centre accompanying the so-called 'third wave' (industrial and technological revolution) has made a reorientation towards the Pacific coast most attractive to China.[37] Geographically, Hong Kong, Taiwan and Macau will be the most accessible and convenient stepping-stones. On the other hand, the widening disparity in economic, technological, and socio-political development between these territories and mainland China has been most acutely felt in the adjacent areas, as manifested in the perpetual problems of emigration, smuggling, and other centrifugal forces. It should also be recalled that the central government considered transforming Bao'an county into an integrated city with export commodity production, tourism and frontier functions in 1978 before all sectoral and local attempts, and that but for the visit of Wu Nansheng, Shantou might not have been included as one of the first four SEZs.[38] Moreover, 'the location of the Chinese SEZs paid particular attention to the proximity of international industrial and commercial cities and financial centres'.[39] In other words, Shenzhen, Zhuhai and Xiamen have been carefully chosen by the central government to take advantage, as well as to meet the challenge, of Hong Kong, Macau and Taiwan.

It is also possible that the Chinese design was first prompted by the economic boom in Hong Kong and the latter's increasing concern, since 1977, over the 1997 issue. In any case, there is ample evidence that China further developed her policy on the SEZs when formal negotiations between China and Britain started in 1982, with increasing freedom being granted to the SEZs in preparation for the ultimate return of Hong Kong and eventually other territories. The SEZs, first seen as a mainly economic component of the open-door policy, have since become a factor in the issue of political reunification.

Spatially, the Chinese SEZs are formally defined as 'a small area demarcated within a country's territory and suitably insulated for adopting special and flexible policies in external economic activities to attract and encourage foreign investments . . .', or 'a special economic area open externally and insulated domestically', where 'the market economy becomes the dominant law of value . . . foreign investors own the means of production, employ capital to exploit the workers, and take possession of part or the bulk of the fruit of labour without compensation'.[40] This is the first and foremost spatial distinction of the Chinese SEZs, for it means they are different not only from EPZs in other countries but also from all other major constructions in the past in that they are separated from the rest of the adjacent territories by what is known as the 'second line', a quasi-political boundary. It was also originally intended that once the 'second line' was ready, the 'international' boundary between, for example, Shenzhen and Hong Kong or Zhuhai and Macau, could be relaxed, turning the SEZs into a truly intermediary or economic 'buffer' zone. However, due to the high cost of enforcement and other pressures internally, none of the 'second lines' (that of Shenzhen was completed in 1984) has come into operation.[41]

Another spatial implication of the SEZs lies in the size of the country. Some Chinese geographers have long pointed out the inapplicability of EPZs or SEZs in solving problems such as employment, foreign trade, and so on, in a country the size of China.[42] What has been overlooked is the fundamental difference in the ultimate market objective of foreign investors. Whereas investors attracted to EPZs in small countries are producing for markets outside the host countries, those investing in China's SEZs are essentially attracted by the potentially vast domestic market. In other words, the pull of the Chinese market is so great that a situation has developed whereby not only do foreign investors clamour for greater domestic sales of their products, but also SEZs cadres, who are given incentives to promote foreign investments, vigorously compete on behalf of their 'clients' for higher and higher proportions of domestic sales. What is worse is that even local managers of collective enterprises in the SEZs try to exploit loopholes to expand the domestic market in spite of official stipulations to the contrary, and as a result production for export may be heavily subsidized by profits from internal sales.[43]

Since the SEZs enjoy unprecedented privileges and almost unlimited opportunities, there is no doubt tremendous pressure from other parts of China for the granting of the same or similar status; yet failure to recognize their spatial characteristics and implications seems to have led to the belief that the SEZs can be freely multiplied in number and form through the creation of quasi-SEZs. Nevertheless the continued extension of SEZ status from the first 4 SEZs to 14 other cityports and Hainan Island, and more recently to even small townships and satellites on the Zhu Jiang delta, will surely either reduce the 'special' character and therefore the attractiveness of the SEZs, rendering investment in infrastructure even more wasteful,[44] or, more seriously, defeat the original purpose of the insulation of the socialist economy.

The Purpose and Structure of the Book

This book, however, does not pretend to adopt a spatial framework or indeed any specific theoretical or conceptual theme. Instead, it aims at a more comprehensive, and at times varied, analysis and interpretation of the development of SEZs in China so far. Being adjacent to Shenzhen, the largest SEZ in China, Hong Kong is well placed both to observe and participate in this development and to share and facilitate interest in the SEZs. In spite of their relatively short history, the SEZs have aroused world-wide interest, and a number of scholars and research teams from Hong Kong and elsewhere have carried out in-depth studies on their geography, planning, environmental protection, economics, political structure, management, law, history, and so on. It is the co-editors' hope, therefore, that through a joint project such as this publication the invaluable experience and research results of these experts will be made readily available to the general reader as well as to other specialists. Apart from the extensive field-work that each of the contributors to this book has conducted for his own research purposes, a week-long visit to Shenzhen and Zhuhai was organized for the project in June 1984. Seminars conducted during this visit with local officials and scholars and specialists from the Guangdong Academy of Social Sciences, Zhongshan University, Shenzhen University, Jinan University, the Guangdong Economic Society and the Guangdong Financial Society provided valuable insights into the subject.

This book is organized into three parts, with three chapters each in Parts I and II, and five in Part III. Part I looks at the physical environment of the SEZs in general and the Shenzhen SEZ in particular in three different but related ways. Thus D.K.Y. Chu, in Chapter 2, focusing on the number, size, and location of the SEZs and problems of territorial containment in China, traces the origin and nature of the Chinese SEZs first by contrasting them against similar creations such as the EPZs in other parts of the world, and then by documenting the chronology of their establishment. The author also touches on the opening of another 14 coastal cities and Hainan Island, and, writing in the autumn of 1984, is quick to point out that 'though these cityports will not be called SEZs, few would contend that there are sharp contrasts between the "proper" SEZs and the "quasi" SEZs', and to predict that, 'if the current trend is allowed to persist, one may anticipate that further expansion of the zones in terms of number and size, and in terms of function, is not impossible. The most likely areas for territorial expansion include the various nodes of the inland transport system . . . whilst functional expansion is likely to occur in the multi-provincial and foreign trade sectors of the economy'. Chu concludes that in spite of the contradictory nature of the 'state capitalist' economy of the SEZs and attempts to restrict its influence on the masses, China finds the SEZs necessary and desirable in its drive for modernization. Hence, though 'introduced only five years ago as a mere territorial entity termed a special export zone, the concept of the special economic zone has developed into a functional and territorial construct of local and regional concern'.

In Chapter 3, R.Y.W. Kwok examines the structure and policies of planning in the SEZs. With special reference to the Shenzhen SEZ, Kwok finds that as a result of 'foreign investment-led' development with its inherent uncertainty in investment and in the demand and structure of the labour force, not only is planning extremely difficult, but it also tends to oversupply social overhead capital, that is, infrastructure. Because of the overwhelming concern to attract foreign investment, planning agencies are in a weak position with regard to policy-making. So far as the physical planning of the city is concerned, the diversity of spatial decision-making and the dispersal of production, commercial and administrative activities necessitate extensive infrastructure, resulting, in planning terms, in a lack of efficiency and a low utilization rate. In summing up, Kwok points out that the normal planning approach in a planned economy follows a 'permissive sequence', whereby social overhead capital is supplied in anticipation of directly productive activities, whereas in a market economy, where planning typically takes a reactive and remedial role, it follows a 'compulsive sequence', in that directly productive activities determine the demand for social overhead capital. He concludes that in a mixed economy such as that of the Shenzhen SEZ, the market economy element, which is the engine of growth, becomes the dominant initiator and controller of planning.

K.C. Lam, in Chapter 4, makes a detailed critique of the type of environmental problems facing the SEZs, which essentially aim at modern industry and high technology, and, taking the case of Shenzhen as an example, assesses the environmental strategies adopted. What is interesting is that, unlike other Chinese cities, which tend to rely on the traditional system of recycling industrial wastes, Shenzhen's environmental strategy is heavily reliant on modern technology guided by comprehensive environmental planning. Moreover, as a state project, Shenzhen is apparently endowed with sufficient funds for all essential if expensive works. Since Shenzhen is only a tiny part of the modernization programme which is based on modern technology, and since elsewhere in China environmental deterioration is not a consequence of affluence but of industrial inefficiency, a central question raised by Lam's study concerns the source of capital for the massive investment in environmental protection for the whole of China, if Shenzhen is a microcosm of what a modern China should be.

Part II of the book focuses on the political and legal framework of the SEZs, also from three different but related perspectives. Chapter 5, by Thomas Chan, E.K.Y. Chen and Steve Chin, examines the ideology and policy behind the experiment, tracing its origin to the special export zone and its ideological support, if only partially, primarily to Lenin's writings on concessions and state capitalism. The central theme of Lenin's ideas during the period of the New Economic Policy (NEP) was to offer concessions to foreign capitalists in order to organize and improve production in the Soviet Union in the early 1920s. In short, Chan *et al.* argue that originally the setting up of the SEZs was a local, sectoral policy that was very much transient in nature, and that after 1982 under central and local pressure the SEZs emerged as part of a national and global policy issue connected with China's national economic reform. At the same time, there was also a shift in the ideological basis of legitimacy for the SEZs from Lenin's NEP and concession policy to an open-ended 'Chinese-style socialism' advocated by Deng Xiaoping.

According to C.Y. Chang in Chapter 6, the SEZs have been devised to strengthen the enforcement of reform policies for modernization and thus illustrate the issue of the politicization of the bureaucracy and its possible effects on attempts at modernization in China. Having carefully analysed the process of functional and structural politicization in the SEZs, Chang believes that the practice of politicization of the bureaucracy remains unchanged and has not been diluted despite the tremendous forces of depoliticization, such as the presence of foreign investment, the emphasis on consumer goods, material incentives, and so on, for the SEZs are not special in the context of the state apparatus despite their more open economic policy. Chang concludes that, whilst it has been demonstrated that a politicized bureaucracy has not hindered modernization in East European states (if by modernization one refers only to industrialization and not democratization), in China it is clear that a politicized bureaucracy has hindered modernization.

Karl Herbst in Chapter 7 concentrates on the regulatory framework for foreign investment in the SEZs and surveys the development of the legislative framework governing the SEZs in Guangdong. He also discusses some specialized legislation and concludes that there has been a remarkable development of the legal structure in the SEZs, particularly in Shenzhen. Although the process is far from complete, some SEZ legislation may well provide the model for future national legislation.

There are five chapters in Part III. The purpose of Chapter 8 by C.H. Chai is to pinpoint some of the systemic differences between China's SEZs and other Asian countries' EPZs, and to assess their implications for foreign investors. Chai concentrates on two major aspects, namely, property rights and the allocation of resources. On the first he concludes that in the SEZs not only private property rights but also domestic private ownership and foreign ownership (of enterprises and the means of production) tend to be more restricted. Yet he believes that this results in a safer investment environment, for the Chinese government is prepared to subsidize the SEZs heavily and to guarantee the profit of foreign investors. In terms of the allocation of resources, China's SEZs originally differed from the EPZs in other Asian countries in that supplies of certain materials initially came through planned channels and the rest of the domestic economy had to be insulated. This is now changing and a process of marketization and liberalization of the SEZ economy is underway, but the advantages and disadvantages of these changes to foreign investors have yet to be assessed. In conclusion, Chai states that as long as the arrangement concerning property rights and the goals and values upheld by the Chinese government remain unchanged, the differences between China's SEZs and other EPZs will remain, and that this has mixed implications for foreign investors.

In Chapter 9, Y.C. Jao reviews and evaluates the banking and monetary system in the SEZs, and discusses the innovations and reforms that are necessary in order that the full potential of the SEZs may be realized. Since the present banking structure in the SEZs does not differ significantly from that in other parts of China, Jao feels that progress in the banking system of the SEZs falls far short of its role of encouraging the import of advanced technology and innovations, in the sense that there is a paucity of varied and sophisticated banking services, and an obvious lack of well-organized modern banking operations in a competitive environment. The currency issue in the SEZs presents both a dilemma and a challenge to the Chinese government, for multiple-currency circulation means not only multiple pricing and inefficient transaction costs but more seriously the loss of the monopolistic status of the legal tender. The explanation, according to Jao, lies in the nature of the currency, that is, the inconvertibility of the *renminbi*. In short, there are serious deficiencies and lacunae in the financial system which, if not rectified, will impede the further development of the SEZs. Jao therefore concludes that China suffers from 'financial repression' that results in stagnation or even atrophy of the financial sector. In a postscript, Jao incorporates developments that have occurred since the chapter was first written, including the operation of branches of foreign banks and the gradual devaluation of the *renminbi*, but the general situation described in his chapter remains little changed.

T.W.C. Lo, in Chapter 10, examines foreign investment in the SEZs from a management perspective. He begins by outlining the trends and development of industrial co-operation in Shenzhen and then discusses problems encountered by both Chinese and foreign partners. To minimize these problems, Lo offers advice on the steps towards establishing industrial co-operation, namely the choice of the form of industrial co-operation and the Chinese partner, negotiations and the planning, organization and control of joint enterprises. In summing up, Lo claims that industrial co-operation in Shenzhen presents many problems, some of which are caused by a difference in culture between the Chinese and the foreign partners or by a communication gap.

In sharp contrast, K.K. Shum and L.T. Sigel, by focusing on several specific joint ventures in Chapter 11, provide an in-depth examination of managerial reform in the SEZs, especially in Shenzhen and Zhuhai, for they rightly point out that as the most open areas of a more open China the SEZs have become China's vanguard in restructuring economic policies and methods. Specific joint ventures studied include a mattress and furniture factory, a printing company, a soft drinks factory, and a tourist complex. Most of these are found to have been successful, while the managerial difficulties that have been experienced are linked to the lack of autonomy in decision-making in some key areas of operation, such as the recruitment and dismissal of staff, and the wage and bonus systems. Yet although the SEZs are regarded as living laboratories of economic change in China, their results cannot necessarily be reproduced under normal circumstances in other parts of China. Thus the applicability of their experience and results remains doubtful. The authors conclude that, despite the fact that the SEZs have become the 'show-pieces' of modernization, China can succeed in its commitment to socialist modernization only if it can overcome its inability to generate intensive growth rather than continue to depend on increased accumulation of capital and expansion of the labour force.

The last chapter, by Victor F.S. Sit, deals with industrial development in Shenzhen as an example of China's attempt at industrialization through an open-door policy. After outlining the characteristics of the SEZs and the rationale behind their foundation, he traces the industrial development in Shenzhen from that of a small border town to a sizeable SEZ in 1983, and discusses the extent and forms of foreign participation in industrial projects as well as the level of technology involved. In conclusion, he argues that despite the fact that the SEZs were in some respects modelled on EPZs in other parts of the world, they are markedly different in their multi-sector development approach, in the limited access to the domestic market which foreign investors are allowed, and in their role as an agent for technological transfer. The author feels that being adjacent to Hong Kong, Shenzhen enjoys advantages not available to other open cities in China, and its role as a pioneer in the modernization drive will continue.

Finally, it should be noted that these chapters were completed between the latter part of 1984 and the early part of 1985, though the research on which they are based dates back to the beginning of the SEZs in many cases. As the general cut-off date for writing was the end of 1984, developments since then have not been incorporated. Nonetheless, it is hoped that this volume will provide a relatively comprehensive, albeit initial, analytical framework for understanding and evaluating China's SEZs.

Notes

1. For example, Huang Guoxian, 'Shenzhen jingji tequ liyong waizi diaocha', *Gangao jingji* (*Hong Kong and Macau Economic Digest*), No. 1, November 1980; *Jingji tequ dili wenji* (*Collections of Essays on the Geography of the Shenzhen SEZ*), Vol. 1, October 1981; Cai Renqun, 'Woguo jingji tequ xuanzhi yu heli guimo wenti ti tantao' ('On the Problems of the Rational Location and Size of Our Country's SEZ's'), and Xu Zice, 'Lun Zhuhai jingji tequ ti xuanzhi wenti' ('The Problem of the Location of the Zhuhai SEZ'), *Redai dili* (*Tropical Geography*), January 1981; *Jingjixue luncong* (*Collected Papers on Economics*) (Guangzhou, Zhongshan University, Department of Economics, 1983); Zhong Gongfu and Xu Zice (eds.), *Zhongguo jingji tequ dili yanjiu* (*The Geography of China's Special Economic Zones*) (Guangzhou, Guangdong People's Press, 1983); *Dili lunwen xuan* (*Selected Papers on Geography*) (Guangzhou, Zhongshan University, Department of Geography, 1984); and Gu Shutang, *et al.*, *Shenzhen jingji tequ diaocha he jingji kaifaqu yanjiu* (*A Study of the Shenzhen SEZ and Economic Development Zones*) (Tianjin, Nankai University Press, 1984).

2. See *Wen wei po* (Hong Kong), 7 July 1985; and *Xin bao* (*Hong Kong Economic Journal*), 17 and 26 July 1985.

3. D.K.Y. Chu, 'The Special Economic Zones of China: an Economic Geographic Appraisal', *Chinese University of Hong Kong, Department of Geography, Occasional Paper,* No. 30, 1982; M.K.L. Fong, 'Enhancing Shenzhen's Environment for Tourism', *Chinese University of Hong Kong, Department of Geography, Occasional Paper,* No. 32, 1982; T.X. Zheng, 'On Agricultural Landuse Patterns and the Export Potential of Shenzhen Municipality', *Chinese University of Hong Kong, Department of Geography, Occasional Paper,* No. 36, 1982; K.Y. Wong (ed.), *Shenzhen Special Economic Zone: China's Experiment in Modernization* (Hong Kong, Hong Kong Geographical Association, 1982); D.K.Y. Chu (ed.), *Zhongguo zuida di jingji tequ — Shenzhen* (*The Largest Special Economic Zone of China — Shenzhen*) (Hong Kong, Wide Angle Press, 1983); B.T.M. Che, 'A Study of the Economic Infrastructure and Organization of the SEZ (Shenzhen) of the PRC from an Investor's Point of View' (unpublished MBA thesis, University of Hong Kong, 1984); J.C.F. Ki, 'Hong Kong Investments in China's SEZs (Shenzhen and Shekou)' (unpublished MBA thesis, University of Hong Kong, 1984); and M.H. Chan, 'Financing Shenzhen's Economic Development: A Preliminary Analysis of Sources of Capital Construction in Shenzhen, 1979–1984', *University of Hong Kong, Department of Economics, Discussion Paper,* No. 54.

4. For example, Steven N.S. Cheung, *Will China Go 'Capitalist'?* (London, The Institute of Economic Affairs, 1982), Hobart Paper No. 94; and Gordon White, 'Introduction: The New Course in Chinese Development Strategy: Context, Problems and Prospects', in J. Gray and G. White (eds.), *China's New Development Strategy* (London, Academic Press, 1982).

5. See Sartai Aziz, *Rural Development, Learning from China* (London, Macmillan, 1978); Curtis Ullerich, *Rural Employment and Manpower Problems in China* (New York, M.E. Sharpe, 1979); Chung-tong Wu and David Ip, 'China: Rural Development — Alternating Combinations of Top-down and Bottom-up Strategies', in W.B. Stohr and D.R.W. Taylor (eds.), *Development Planning from Above or Below? A Radical Reappraisal of Spatial Planning* (New York, John Wiley, 1980); and C.K. Leung, *China: Railway Patterns and National Goals* (Chicago, University of Chicago, Department of Geography, 1980).

6. C.K. Leung and J.C.H. Chai, 'The Economic and Spatial Dimensions of Development in China', in C.K. Leung and J.C.H. Chai (eds.), *Development and Distribution in China* (Hong Kong, University of Hong Kong, Centre of Asian Studies, 1985), pp. 3–17. See also Mao Zedong, 'Lun shida guanxi' ('On Ten Major Relationships'), in Mao Zedong, *Mao Zedong sixiang wansui* (*Long Live Mao Zedong Thought*) (n.p., 1969), pp. 40–59; and David Ip and Chung-tong Wu, 'Structural Transformation and Spatial Equality', in C.K. Leung and Norton Ginsburg (eds.), *China: Urbanization and National Development* (Chicago, University of Chicago, Department of Geography, 1980).

7. Liu Guoguang, *Zhongguo jingji fazhan zhanlue wenti yanjiu* (*A Study of the Problems of China's Strategies for Economic Development*) (Shanghai, People's Press, 1984), p. 265; and Victor C. Falkenheim, 'Spatial Inequalities in China's Modernization Program: Some Political-Administrative Determinants', in Leung and Chai (1985), pp. 149–72.

8. Liu Zaixing, *Zhongguo gongye buju xue* (*A Study of Industrial Locations in China*) (Beijing, People's University of China, 1981), p. 64; and Suen Jingzhi, *et al.*, *Zhongguo jingji dili gailun* (*Introduction to the Economic Geography of China*) (Beijing, Commercial Press, 1983), pp. 93–8. See also K.M. Buchanan, *The Transformation of the Chinese Earth* (London, G. Bell & Sons, 1970); and Liu Junde, 'Yingxiang gongye quwei de yinshu he woguo gongye quwei de yanbian' ('Factors of Industrial Location and the Evolution of Industrial Location in Our Country'), *Dili jiaoxue* (*Geographical Education*), No. 1, 1981, p. 3.

9. Liu Guoguang (1984), pp. 14 and 265; and Ma Hong, *et al.*, *Zhongguo jingji jiegou wenti yanjiu* (*A Study of Chinese Economic Structure*) (Beijing, People's Press, 1981), p. 656.

10. Leung (1980), p. 155.
11. Leung (1980), p. 155; and Liu Guoguang (1984), pp. 14–15.
12. *Renmin ribao* (*People's Daily*), 10 June 1985.
13. Liu Guoguang (1984), pp. 265–6; Ma Hong, *et al.* (1981), pp. 657–8; and Liu Zaixing (1981), p. 104.
14. World Bank, *China, Socialist Economic Development* (Washington, DC, World Bank, 1983), Vol. II, pp. 145–6.
15. C.K. Leung, 'Transportation and Spatial Integration', in N. Lee and C.K. Leung (eds.), *China: Development and Challenge, Volume II, Political Economy, and Spatial Pattern and Process* (Hong Kong, University of Hong Kong, Centre of Asian Studies, 1979), pp. 323–42.
16. Leung (1980), p. 158.
17. C.K. Leung, 'Modernization of Railways: Emphasis and Directions', in S.S.K. Chin (ed.), *Modernization in China* (Hong Kong, University of Hong Kong, Centre of Asian Studies, 1979), pp. 129–48; and S.D. Chang, 'Urbanization and Economic Readjustment in China', in C.K. Leung and S.S.K. Chin (eds.), *China in Readjustment* (Hong Kong, University of Hong Kong, Centre of Asian Studies, 1983), pp. 193–215.
18. Liu Guoguang (1984), pp. 268–71; and Ma Hong, *et al.* (1981), pp. 663–5.
19. Hu Zhaoliang, 'Guanyu woguo gongye buju di zige wenti' ('On Some Problems of Industrial Location in Our Country'), *Gongye buju cankao ziliao* (*Reference Materials on Industrial Location*) (Beijing, People's University of China, 1984), pp. 60–71.
20. Liu Guoguang (1984), p. 270.
21. Liu Guoguang (1984), pp. 17 and 266; and Suen, *et al.* (1983), p. 100.
22. Leung, 'China in Readjustment: An Introduction', in Leung and Chin (eds.) (1983), pp. 3–9.
23. Mao (1969), pp. 43–5.
24. Leung, 'Modernization of Railways: Emphasis and Directions' (1979), pp. 129–48.
25. Zhou Enlai, 'Report on Government Work at the Third National People's Congress', 21–24 December 1964, and 'Report on Government Work at the Fourth National People's Congress', 13 January 1975.
26. Constitution of the Chinese Communist Party, passed at the Eleventh National Party Congress on 18 August 1977; and Constitution of the People's Republic of China (1978). See also Ye Jianying, 'Report on the Revision of the Constitution', speech delivered on 1 March 1978 at the Fifth National People's Congress.
27. Communiqué of the Third Plenary Session of the Eleventh Central Committee of the Chinese Communist Party, adopted on 22 December 1978, and *Hongqi* (*Red Flag*), No. 1, 1 January 1979, pp. 14–21; and *Renmin ribao,* 24 March 1979.
28. Zhao Ziyang's report on government work, 'The Present Situation and the Principles for Future Economic Construction', see *Renmin ribao* and *Xinhua* (New China News Agency, Beijing), both 14 December 1981, and *Peking Review*, No. 51, 21 December 1981, pp. 6–36; and Hu Yaobang's report to the Twelfth Party Congress, 'Quanmian kaichuang shehuizhuyi xiandaihua jianshe di xin jumian' ('Completely Develop the Situation of Socialist Modernization Construction'), September 1982.
29. Liu Guoguang (1984), pp. 23–7.
30. State Statistical Bureau, *Zhongguo tongji nianjian, 1981* (*Statistical Yearbook of China, 1981*) (Hong Kong, Economic and Information Agency, 1982), p. 310: and *Zhongguo tongji nianjian, 1984* (*Statistical Yearbook of China, 1984*) (Hong Kong, Economic and Information Agency, 1984), p. 316.
31. *Wen hui bao*, 9 October 1985.
32. Zhong and Xu (eds.) (1983), p. 22.
33. Gu, *et al.* (1984), p. 38, Table.
34. See *Jingjixue luncong* (1983), and particularly Wang Chengxian, 'Jingji tequ yu woguo jingji fazhan zhanlue', pp. 232–43.
35. See Chapter 2.

36. See Chapter 5.

37. *Wen hui bao*, 11, 17 and 26 February 1985; and *Ming pao*, 13 August 1985.

38. See the well-known document No. 38 issued by the central government in early 1978 as quoted by Chu in Chapter 2.

39. *Renwen dili xue* (*Human Geography*), an offprint of the *Chinese Encyclopaedia* (Beijing, Chinese Encyclopaedic Press, 1984), pp. 68–9.

40. *Renwen dili xue*, p. 68.

41. *Ta kung po*, 8 February 1984. See also figures in Chapter 2.

42. From the very beginning, it has been pointed out by some Chinese scholars that the expected functions of the EPZs, on which the SEZs are modelled, of creating employment and of promoting external trade would be more significant and effective in small countries than in China because her population and territory are many times those of other developing countries. Even the much-cherished function of technology transfer has to be seriously qualified in terms of China's industrial development and potential. See *Jingjixue luncong* (1983), and Zhong and Xu (eds.) (1983).

43. Field-work in Shenzhen and Zhuhai, June 1984.

44. *Wen wei po* (Hong Kong), 14 October 1985.

Part I: The Physical Environment

2. The Special Economic Zones and the Problem of Territorial Containment

D.K.Y. CHU

Introduction[1]

Well before China launched the programme of special economic zones (SEZs), many countries were already operating 'special zones'. Apart from the free ports, which can be dated back to ancient Roman times,[2] the first pioneer of the modern 'special zones' with export processing as its major economic activity was that established in Ireland at the Shannon International Airport in 1956. Many developing countries, for example, Puerto Rico, India, Taiwan, the Philippines, the Dominican Republic, Mexico, Panama, and Brazil, then followed suit.[3] Although their 'special zones' may be referred to by different terms, such as 'free trade zone', 'free export zone', 'export-processing zone' and so on, they can generally be defined as areas involved in the 'establishment of modern manufacturing plants inside an industrial estate, by offering a suitable package of investment incentives to both foreign and domestic entrepreneurs'.[4] Indeed, as defined by the United Nations Industrial Development Organization (Unido), they bear many similar features: first, they operate in a market economy; second, they are basically territorial constructs, their function being confined to export processing within a well-defined territorial limit; third, their special nature derives from the fact that they are 'enclaves' specializing in exporting their manufactured products to international markets under a package of incentives offered by the host country; fourth, their major objectives are primarily to attract foreign investment, to earn foreign exchange and to generate employment; and, fifth, technological transfer, development linkages and regional development are generally secondary to their major objectives. Consequently, it is easy to define their number, size and locational attributes.[5].

It is against this background that the Chinese decision-makers started contemplating their own 'special zones'. As early as 1978, the Chinese central government issued a document (No. 38) putting forward the idea of developing what was then Bao'an county into an integrated export commodity production complex, an attractive resort for Hong Kong and Macau tourists and a modern frontier town within a certain (unspecified) number of years.[6] In December 1978, the Third Plenary Session of the Eleventh Central Committee of the Chinese Communist Party (CCP) was held and the strategic decision to open up to the world on the one hand, and to activate the domestic economy on the other, was finalized in order to shift the focus of the work of the CCP on to socialist modernization. After the session, Wu Nansheng, later head of the Administrative Committee for the Special Economic Zones of Guangdong Province (ADCOM), went to Shantou to explain and pass on the message of the Third Plenary Session. He found that Shantou faced numerous problems left over from the extreme leftist period, including a large number of cases of injustice, especially towards those with overseas relatives, still unresolved. He thus proposed in January 1979 that Guangdong should set up a zone similar to the export-processing zones of Taiwan in Shantou. For Shantou, a seaport, had a long history of export trading, and yet was sufficiently remote geographically to restrict any 'bad' influence from infecting the Chinese hinterland if the experiment did not succeed. Wu did not favour the idea of starting with Shenzhen for he thought that there was not enough labour there. However, his proposal for Shantou was rejected by the provincial Party which favoured the idea of turning the entire province into a special zone.[7] In March 1979, Bao'an county and Zhuhai county were granted municipality status at the semi-prefectural level, although they were to be co-governed by the prefectural government and provincial government. This undoubtedly was the first move towards the development of special zones in both counties. A month later, Xi Zhongxun, then governor of Guangdong, reported on the progress of the special zones to the leaders of the central government in Beijing. The Fujian authorities at the same time also expressed a wish to set up their own special zones. Their proposals were endorsed by Deng Xiaoping in April, although he indicated that the central government did not have enough resources to finance such development and that the special zones had therefore to be self-financing and innovative.[8] Immediately after the meeting, a working party under the leadership of Gu Mu went to Guangdong and Fujian to examine the various proposals. On 5 July 1979, the central government announced in another statement that the provinces of Guangdong and Fujian would be allowed to practise special foreign economic policies and to experiment with 'special export zones' at Shenzhen, Zhuhai, Shantou and Xiamen. Between 15 July 1979 and the end of August 1980, the most important progress made on the issue was the drafting of the Regulations on the Special Economic Zones in Guangdong Province. Only two further signs of progress in this period are worth mentioning. First, Shenzhen was upgraded to the level of a municipality under the direct governorship of the provincial government in November 1979; and, second, in May 1980 the term 'special export zone' was replaced with that of 'special economic zone' for two reasons. The change in term made it clear that the zones were politically similar to other parts of China and were therefore not 'special political zones', and it took into account the comprehensive nature of Shenzhen, for the zone was to be involved in industry, commerce, agriculture, housing and tourism, and not merely export processing. The use of the term 'special economic zone' was confirmed with the promulgation of the Regulations on the Special Economic Zones in Guangdong Province in August 1980 by the Fifth National People's Congress.[9]

Three additional statements of significance were made by the central government in 1981 and 1982. First, Shenzhen was further promoted to the semi-provincial level, on a par with Guangzhou. Second, Bao'an county in the north of the Shenzhen SEZ was re-established. Third, it was made clear that both the Shenzhen SEZ and the Zhuhai SEZ would be comprehensive in nature whilst the Shantou and Xiamen SEZs would be restricted to export processing. At the same time more power was given to the SEZ authorities concerned. In early 1984, Deng Xiaoping visited the zones of Shenzhen, Zhuhai and Xiamen. After returning to Beijing, he broke new ground by proposing that, in addition to the existing SEZs, more cityports be opened to the world. He also commented on the inappropriate size of the Xiamen SEZ. Deng further suggested that the new cityports should not be called SEZs but that some SEZ measures and policies should be equally applicable to these cityports. Between 26 March and 6 April 1984, a major conference was held in Beijing to review the issue. Apart from the delegations from the four SEZs, representatives from eight other cities and Hainan Island also attended the meeting. Two resolutions were reached. First, 14 cityports, namely, Dalian, Qinhuangdao, Tianjin, Yantai, Qingdao, Lianyungang, Nantong, Shanghai, Ningbo, Wenzhou, Fuzhou, Guangzhou, Zhanjiang and Beihai, were to be opened to the world. Second, it was proposed that Xiamen, Shantou and Zhuhai be enlarged, the area around each zone being given a status similar to the 14 cityports.[10] The whole of Hainan Island was to become the Hainan Administrative Area, with quasi-provincial ranking higher than that of Guangzhou but lower than that of Guangdong province, where most, if not all, SEZ measures would be applicable.[11]

From the above chronological account of the development of the SEZs, it is evident that the Chinese concept of the 'special economic zone' has undergone many changes. It started as almost a replica of the export-processing zones of Taiwan and other developing countries under the title 'special export zone'. The term was later changed to 'special economic zone' to emphasize the zones' socialist nature and comprehensive development. From 1982 onwards, two types of special economic zone have been identified — the comprehensive zone and the export-processing zone. Since April 1984, not only has the concept of the 'proper' special economic zone existed, but also that of the 'quasi' special economic zone in which many measures and policies but not the term 'special economic zone' are applied. In other words, one has to recognize that territories with the formal title of 'special economic zone' and those with only SEZ policies and measures belong to two different categories. A closer investigation of Shenzhen, Zhuhai, Shantou and Xiamen in the ensuing sections will support the argument that the two concepts are not identical. As such, the number, size and location of the SEZs and their spatial organization are less easily accountable than they at first appear, especially if the functional definition is adopted.

The Shenzhen SEZ

The success and progress of the Shenzhen SEZ have been reported and discussed elsewhere; hence in this section only those issues related to the problem of territorial containment will be discussed. It will be of interest to note that well before Wu Nansheng's proposal to develop Shantou into an export-processing zone and before Bao'an county became the municipality of Shenzhen in March 1979, China's first export-processing zone was inaugurated on the peninsula of Shekou in what was then Bao'an county on 1 January 1979, some 20 months before the promulgation of the Regulations on the Special Economic Zones of Guangdong Province in August 1980.

Perhaps inspired by the document (No. 38) issued in 1978, China Merchants' Steam Navigation Co. Ltd. of Hong Kong (a branch of the China Merchants' Steam Navigation Co. (CMSN), established in 1872 and one of the oldest state-owned enterprises in China under the auspices of the Transport Bureau of the central government at Beijing), proposed to develop the peninsula of Shekou into an industrial zone for export production using its own investment and funds. This proposal was subsequently approved by the State Council and CMSN was given an area of 2 sq km, 50 million *yuan* from retained profits of its Hong Kong branch, and the authority to approve foreign investment projects under US$5 million at its own discretion.[12]

Indeed, at the very beginning, CMSN did not intend to develop an export-processing industrial estate as witnessed in the Shekou Industrial Zone of today. The company in fact began with the idea of searching for a coastal site outside Hong Kong where it could dispose of its aged and obsolete shipping, for land in Hong Kong was, and still is, too expensive for the company to start its own ship-breaking business. Since the clients of used steel plates and frames from obsolete vessels were mainly construction firms in Hong Kong, an electric blast-furnace to smelt the used iron and steel was necessary. To undertake ship-breaking and iron and steel smelting on a coastal site near the Hong Kong market would have been uneconomical, for CMSN would have had to have developed berthing facilities, an electricity plant and perhaps reservoirs — all for a relatively small industrial undertaking. The Hong Kong branch of CMSN was thus inclined to develop an industrial estate so that other types of industry could be established near the blast-furnace and the ship-breaking industry to share the developmental costs of the original proposal. The idea was endorsed by the State Council, and an area of 2 sq km (1.03 sq km as the first phase) on the Shekou peninsula opposite Hong Kong was assigned to the Hong Kong branch of CMSN on 1 January 1979.[13]

As mentioned in the preceding section, it was not until April 1979 that the idea of establishing four 'special export zones' at Shenzhen, Zhuhai, Shantou and Xiamen received the consent of the central decision-makers. Even with their agreement, official approval was not given until July 1979. In other words, before July 1979, none of these special export zones could proceed beyond the drawing board. Site selection and preliminary planning only started in September 1979.

The earliest form of the Shenzhen SEZ was pretty small, with a target of 200,000–300,000 residents by the end of this century and an area of several thousand hectares (with built-up areas amounting to 1,065 ha).[14] The SEZ was located to the west of the town of Shenzhen. In other words, there were to be two 'special zones' in the municipality of Shenzhen — that of Shenzhen and that of Shekou. This now outdated information is contained in many Chinese publications, for example, Wang and Chen's book on China's foreign economic relations.[15] The deliberate exclusion of the old town of

Shenzhen was based on a rationale similar to that of planning in other zones. First, such a distinction is common in export-processing zones outside China. Second, it was thought that the inclusion of the existing township would create further problems of management. Third, it was believed that the total absorption of the existing population would prevent the special zone authorities from selecting 'socialist' workers able to resist Western influences from outside the special zone.[16] However, this fragmented approach denied the special zone an existing urban core and attractive sites for tourist and commercial development, for example, the district of Luohu. It was thus counter-productive to the idea of developing Shenzhen into a comprehensive special zone, an integrated export commodity production complex and a modern frontier town as stated in document No. 38 of 1978. In addition, the Shenzhen SEZ was likely to encounter severe financial problems if it did not obtain the quick returns available on housing development and hotel sites at Luohu, for the area initially demarcated as the Shenzhen SEZ was far less promising than the present area and did not attract sufficient investment for a short pay-back period. The final solution, as witnessed in the area demarcated (327.5 sq km) after the announcement of the Regulations on the Special Economic Zones of Guangdong Province on 26 August 1980, indicated a victory for those who had advocated a larger size for the SEZ. The inclusion of the town of Shenzhen in the SEZ marked the defeat of those who took a cautious position on the necessity of confining 'capitalist influence' to an uninhabited area. The 'unified' approach also allowed the Shenzhen SEZ to exist as a territorial entity, of which the Shekou Industrial Zone was only a part, not a separate unit. This unification was not without problems at the time. The corporate tax rate levied on foreign enterprises at Shekou before unification was only 10 per cent, but the standard rate for the SEZ was set at 15 per cent. Shekou had to honour those contracts signed before August 1980 or change them by persuasion and by other subsidies from its own resources. Although by jurisdiction Shekou has been part of the Shenzhen SEZ since August 1980, administratively it has not been assimilated. Investment negotiations in the Shekou Industrial Zone are conducted in Hong Kong by the branch of CMSN and are beyond the control of the Shenzhen SEZ government. Similarly, the district of Shahe comes under the management of the provincial Overseas Chinese Affairs Commission which, besides Shahe, also runs the Guangming Farm in Bao'an county. Neither the land-use planning nor investment negotiations concerning the above two areas are under the full control of the Shenzhen SEZ government, although all preferential treatment and other rights of the SEZ are applicable to these two areas.[17]

Apart from the Guangming Farm in Bao'an county, there are also a few projects outside the zone's boundary which have been approved by the Shenzhen SEZ authorities and which are eligible for the special terms of the SEZ. These include the NMK Dyeing Factory at Kuichong, the Buji Industrial Estate and the Pepsi Cola Factory nearby, the Yulu Hot Spring Holiday Resort and perhaps the nuclear power plant at Dapeng (Fig. 2.1). In other words, the influence of the Shenzhen SEZ is not confined to the zone itself. Besides joint ventures with foreign investors, the Shenzhen SEZ authorities

Fig. 2.1 The Shenzhen SEZ

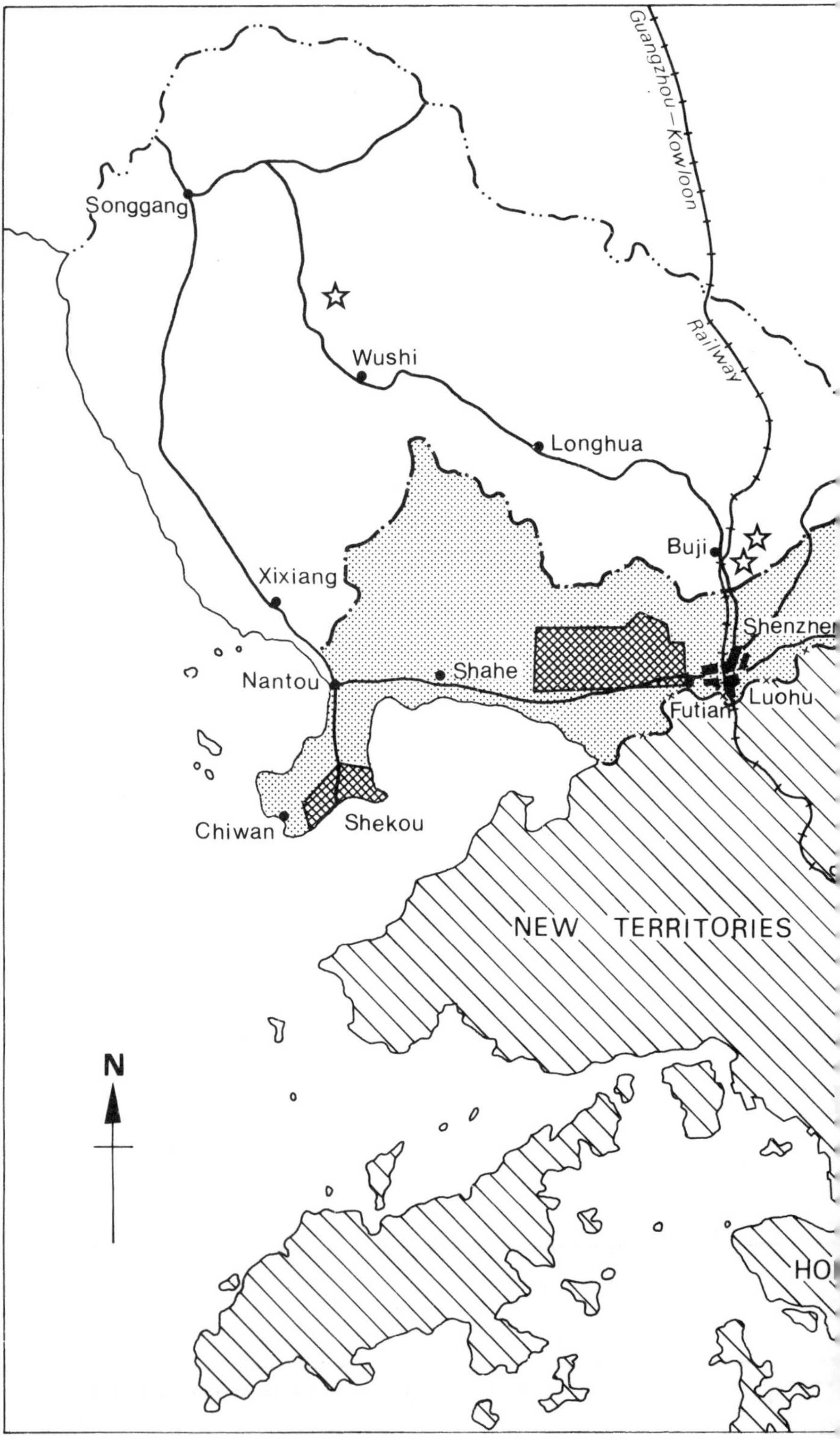

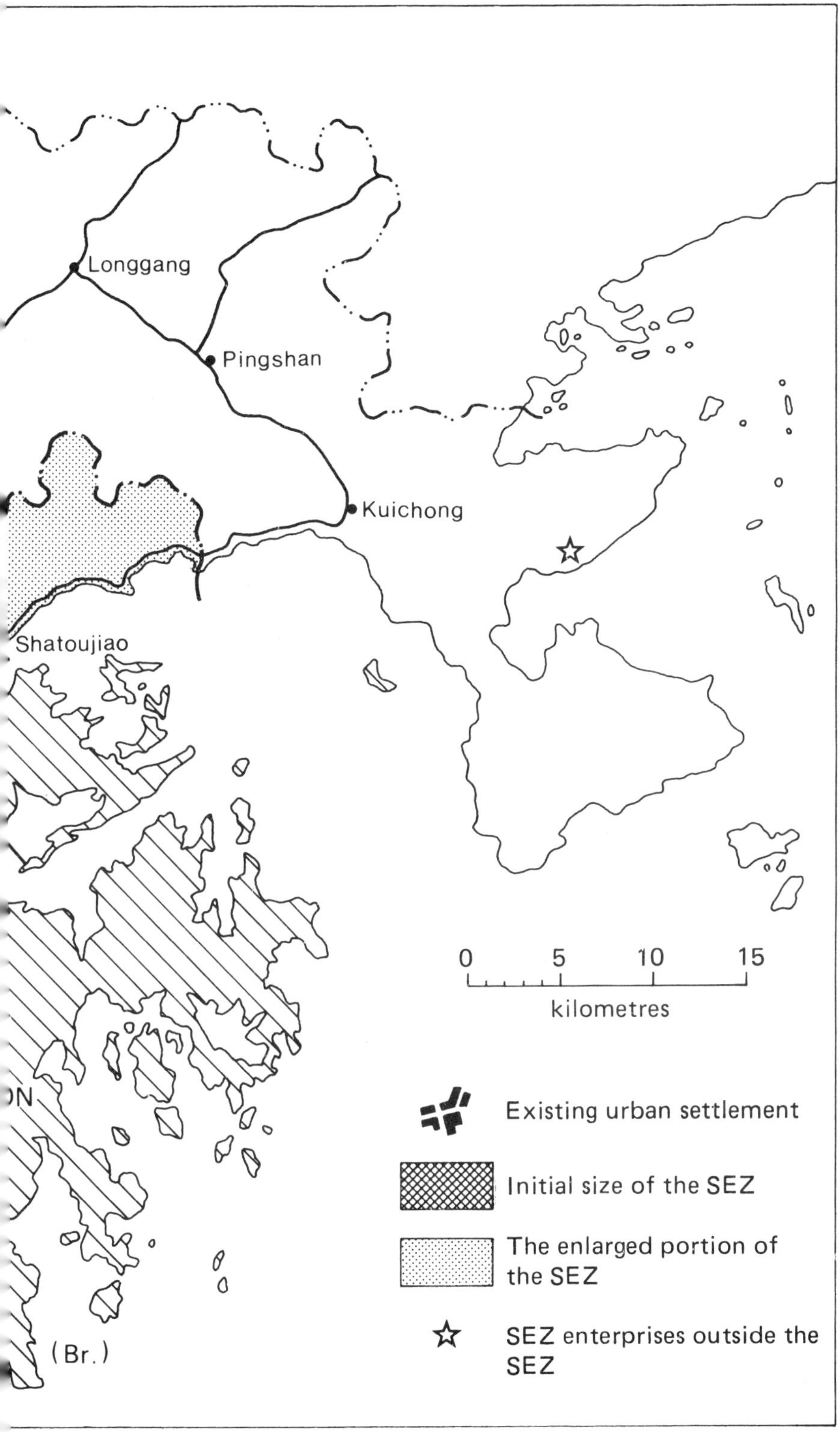
Longgang
Pingshan
Kuichong
Shatoujiao
)N
(Br.)
0 5 10 15
kilometres
Existing urban settlement
Initial size of the SEZ
The enlarged portion of the SEZ
SEZ enterprises outside the SEZ

have also jointly developed many trading and industrial enterprises with other Chinese provincial governments and companies, in order to fulfil their responsibility to activate the domestic economy of China. This can also be witnessed by the number of representative offices of various parts of China set up in the Shenzhen SEZ.

However, the sheer size of the Shenzhen SEZ and its belt-shaped configuration have created great difficulties in the control and management of the zone. In order to separate the Shenzhen SEZ from the rest of China, its 84.6 km border has had to be fenced and will be patrolled by the People's Liberation Army and customs officers. Along the fence, there are six customs stations where freight and passengers are examined to see whether they have complied with Chinese laws and regulations. The completion of the border fence now forms a 'second line' of customs regulation so that controls on the 'first line', that separating Hong Kong from the Shenzhen SEZ, can be relaxed. There is speculation that when the second line is complete, necessary imported raw materials, manufactured items and most daily necessities in the zone will be duty-free. Thus price levels on these items will almost match those in Hong Kong. It has also been announced that an SEZ currency will be issued for Shenzhen in 1985 and will be freely convertible to other foreign currencies. Bearing in mind all these arrangements, it is possible that the Shenzhen SEZ may become a genuine free trade zone with a well-developed industrial economy and a relatively strong tertiary sector instead of simply an export-processing zone as was initially conceived in 1979.

The Zhuhai SEZ

Almost at the same time as Bao'an county was upgraded to become the municipality of Shenzhen, Zhuhai county attained the same municipal status (March 1979). However, the development of the Zhuhai SEZ has received far less support from the provincial and central governments than has Shenzhen. Although Zhuhai was designated as an SEZ for comprehensive development, including export processing, agriculture, tourism and housing, the zone has not risen above its municipal status as has Shenzhen.

In 1980, the Zhuhai SEZ was established on 6.8 sq km of sparsely populated, low-yield paddy fields to the south of Xiangzhou. Geographically, it was divided into three major portions: the eastern portion, the central portion and the western portion (Fig. 2.2a). The eastern portion was separated from the central portion by the Gongbei–Macau immigration and customs check-point and the road passing through it. The western portion was separated from the central portion by the Qianshan Channel.[18] The rationale for the exclusion of Xiangzhou and the customs check-point was similar to that discussed in the case of the Shenzhen SEZ, that is, mainly for control and management.

Territorially, the central and western portions were planned for industrial and tourist development respectively, whilst the eastern portion was planned for real estate, hotel and commercial development. The Jiuzhou Harbour,

Fig. 2.2a The Initial Size of the Zhuhai SEZ

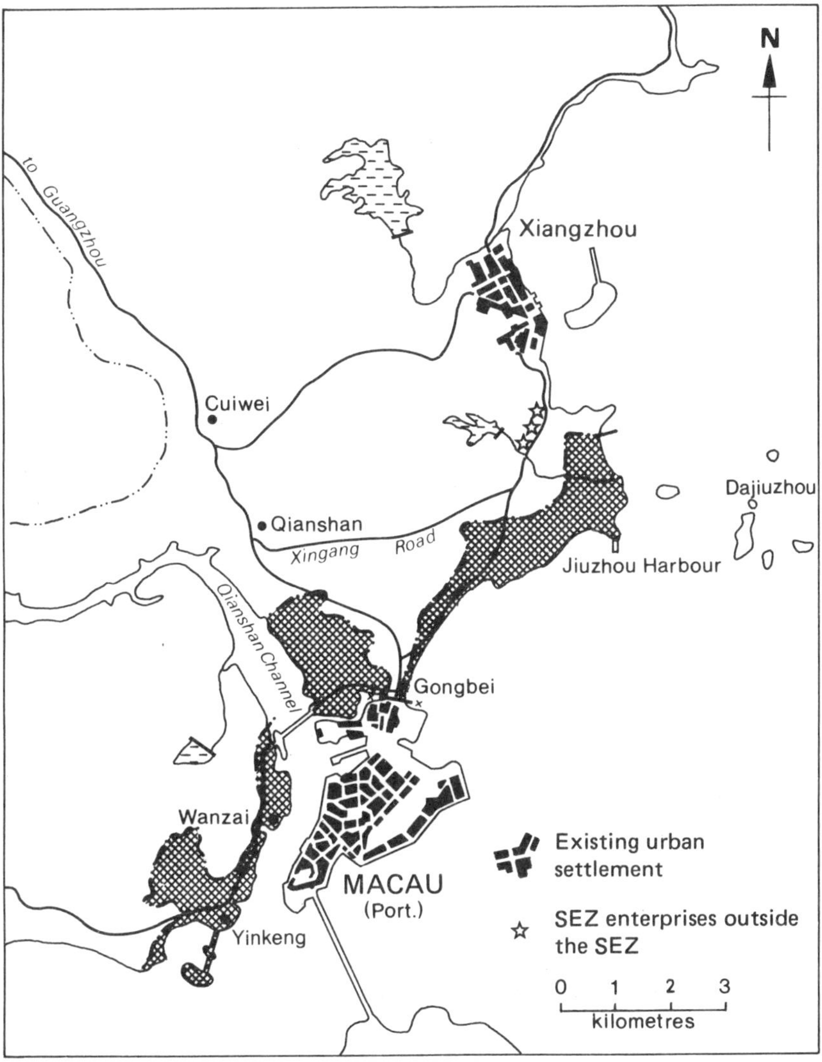

which connects Zhuhai and Hong Kong, was also built at the northern end of the eastern portion. Unfortunately, four years after the establishment of the zone, the central and western portions had had little success in attracting foreign investments and remained almost as undeveloped as they had been at the very beginning. The eastern portion, with its better transport linkages with the Gongbei customs check-point and the Jiuzhou Harbour, had attracted one hotel, one holiday resort and two housing estates[19] and was thus somewhat more successful.

However, the most publicized projects connected with the Zhuhai SEZ and those involving substantial investment were all outside its 6.8 sq km designated area. These included the Zhuhai Resort, the Shijingshan Tourist Centre and the Xiangzhou Woollen and Weaving Factory — all joint ven-

Fig. 2.2b The Enlarged Zhuhai SEZ

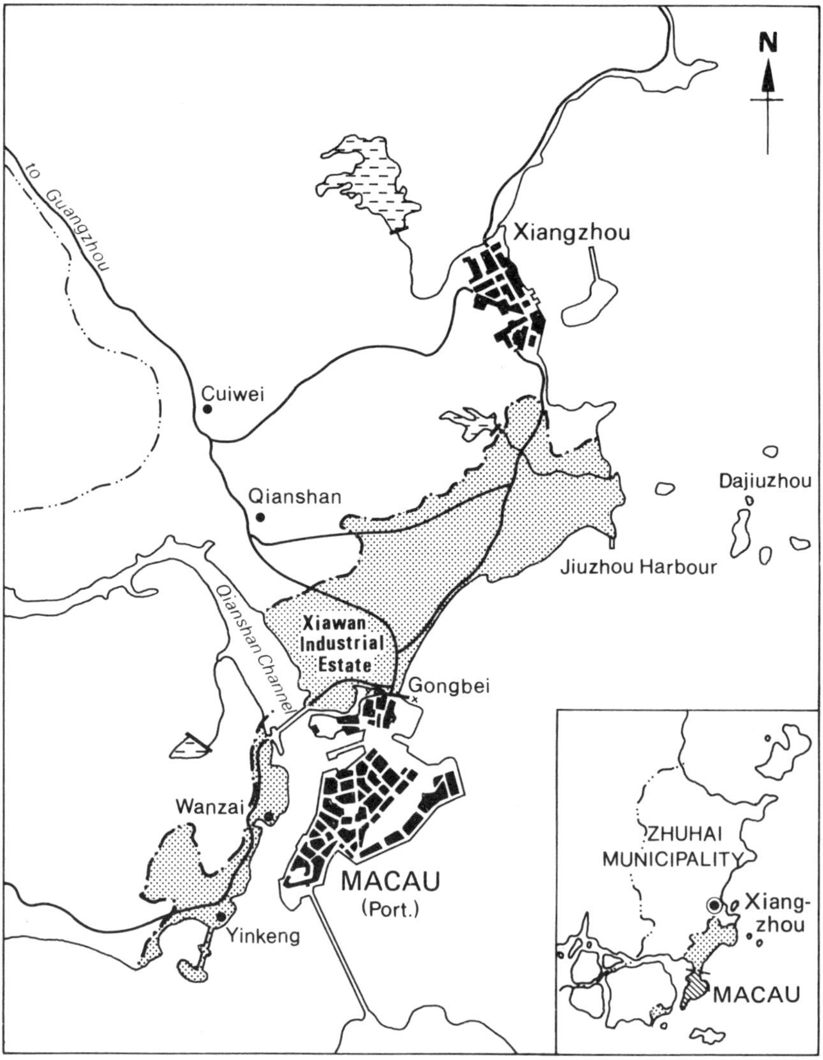

tures with sizeable foreign investment. They were approved by the Zhuhai Special Economic Zone Management Committee and were eligible for all the terms and preferential treatment available inside the Zhuhai SEZ. Such heavy foreign investment outside the territorial boundary of the Zhuhai SEZ, the relatively smaller investment in the eastern portion and the negligible investment in the central and western portions thus gave the impression that the Zhuhai SEZ had been turned inside out. This serious imbalance between the functional and territorial organization of the Zhuhai SEZ pointed to its inappropriate size, the poor location of two of the portions and difficulties in its physical location. It was these problems and difficulties that apparently led to the expansion of the Zhuhai SEZ from its original 6.8 sq km to 14.1 sq km in mid-1983. The 14.1 sq km cover the entire area of the eastern and central portions plus the interstitial corridor, which originally separated these two portions, and the vast stretches of land to their north where the Zhuhai Resort, the Shijingshan Tourist Centre and the Xiangzhou Woollen and Weaving Factory are located. On the other hand, the size of the western portion was reduced: the area of Wanzai reverted to a non-special status and only the area of Yinkeng, where the Yinkeng Holiday Resort is to be located, retained its status, becoming an 'exclave' of the Zhuhai SEZ. However, these changes were subsequently considered to be unrealistic and the western portion later resumed its original shape and size. All in all, the Zhuhai SEZ now totals 15.16 sq km (Fig. 2.2b). Territorially it is better organized than before and the Xiawan Industrial Estate seems less isolated from the rest of the SEZ.[20] Moreover, there is now no incongruity between the functional and territorial organization of the zone.

Overall, in the territorial adjustment of the Zhuhai SEZ, the deliberate avoidance of the town of Xiangzhou and its population (of about 10,000) is still evident. The rationale behind the unsuccessful attempt to demote Wanzai to a non-special area also reflects the same notion of keeping the influence of the SEZ away from local inhabitants as far as possible. This is an obvious difference between the Shenzhen and Zhuhai SEZs even though both are designated for comprehensive development.

Following the territorial readjustment, it is also intended that a 'second line' of immigration and customs control be set up along the zone's new boundary so that in future the Zhuhai SEZ may move towards the concept of a comprehensive free trade zone possessing a certain amount of manufacturing industry. This will speed up its economic growth.

The Shantou SEZ

Although Wu Nansheng, the chairman of ADCOM, advocated that the programme of SEZs should begin with Shantou, the Shantou SEZ was in fact the last to start its 'five linkages and one levelling'. The area designated for the Shantou SEZ was also the smallest — only 1.6 sq km,[21] as against 327.5 sq km in Shenzhen, 6.8 sq km in Zhuhai and 2.5 sq km in Xiamen. Its first phase of development was even smaller — 0.2 sq km at Longhu. The area so designated was for export processing alone. Functionally, the Shantou SEZ was also given the authority to approve foreign investment participation in the technological transformation of ageing industrial enterprises outside the Longhu Industrial Zone. It has, in addition, been vested with the responsibility of developing tourism, transport facilities and agriculture. Up to mid-1984, five industrial and commercial enterprises outside the Longhu Industrial Zone had been approved by the zone's Management Committee as eligible for the special terms applicable in the zones. A hotel has been constructed and is run by the Shantou SEZ authorities, while a fleet of taxis and public light buses serve the city of Shantou. The SEZ has also acquired a cargo vessel plying between Hong Kong and Shantou, with three more on order, including a passenger liner. A large stretch of agricultural land to the

Fig. 2.3 The Shantou SEZ

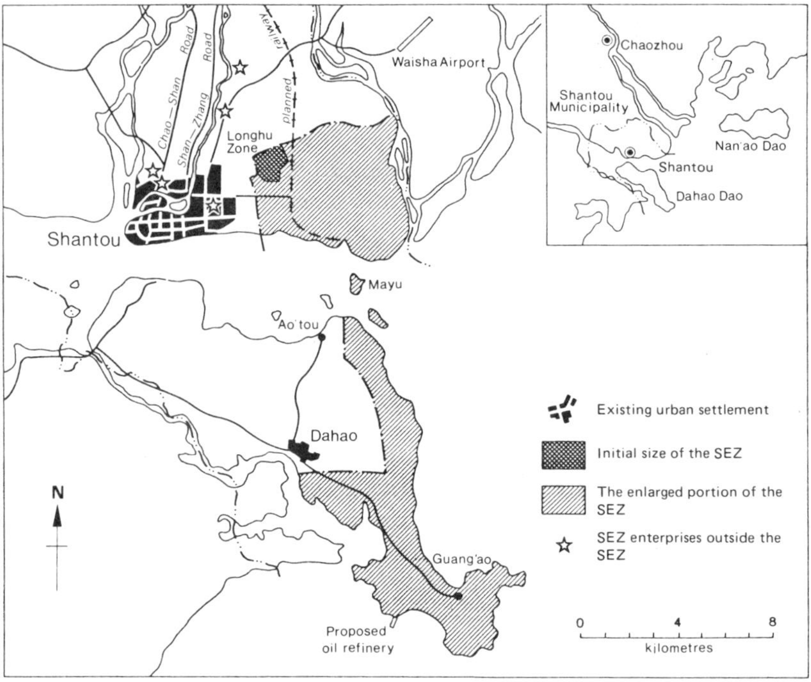

east and south-east totalling 19.3 sq km is run by the Agricultural Development Co. under the auspices of the Shantou Special Economic Zone Management Committee to experiment with new agricultural techniques and to export agricultural products to overseas markets.[22] To sum up, although the area officially designated as the Shantou SEZ is a mere 1.6 sq km in area, in reality the territory under its management is at least 14 times the size of the area designated. And this estimate excludes the activity area of its shipping fleet, taxis, public light buses and the five factories qualifying for SEZ terms.

Recently, the central government in Beijing has approved the setting up of an oil refinery at Guang'ao, the southern part of an island opposite the city of Shantou and the SEZ. This will also qualify for SEZ terms.[23]

The resultant incongruity between the functional organization of the Shantou SEZ and its officially designated territory highlights the problems inherent in the zone's size and location. It has been proposed and provisionally agreed that the new Shantou SEZ will comprise two portions (Fig. 2.3): a northern portion of 22.6 sq km including the Longhu Industrial Zone, the port zone and the agricultural area, and a southern portion of about 30 sq km mainly for the oil refinery plant and related petrochemical industries. The intervening island of Mayu will probably be included for the development of tourism.[24] The readjusted size and location of the Shantou SEZ will perhaps better reflect the real territorial coverage of the zone but again the city of Shantou has been deliberately left out for the same reason that Xiangzhou was excluded from the Zhuhai SEZ.[25]

The Xiamen SEZ

Like Shantou, the Xiamen SEZ was also assigned a small area of 2.5 sq km for export processing in October 1980.[26] However, the Xiamen SEZ authorities and many other Fujian SEZ supporters have never been satisfied with such a small territory for their operation. As early as 1981 when the 'five linkages and one levelling' was to start, Chen and Chen summarized the different conceptions of the appropriate size for the Xiamen SEZ that had been proposed.[27] These were 2.5 sq km, 123 sq km, 500 sq km and 1,500 sq km. The smallest was the Huli Industrial Zone, which was the area officially assigned by the central government to the Management Committee of the Xiamen SEZ, to the north of the city of Xiamen, for the development of export-processing industries. The second referred to the whole of Xiamen Island, including the city of Xiamen, the Huli Industrial Zone and their environs. The third covered Xiamen Island and the Xinglin industrial area and Jimei area. The largest was to include the entire municipality of Xiamen including its incorporated county, Tongan. Indeed, as stated in Tong's paper,[28] advocates of the SEZ in Fujian believed that the Xiamen SEZ should ultimately become an international trading centre. It would thus serve as Fujian's gateway to the outside world. Hence its status as an export-processing zone, a comprehensive SEZ, and a free port would be but interim stages in its transformation.

Whilst until 1984 the Xiamen SEZ was restricted territorially to 2.5 sq km, the Management Committee of the zone, with the support of the Fujian provincial government, has utilized the functional organization allowed by the central government to its fullest extent from the very beginning. The Xiamen SEZ authorities have been very active, with heavy investment in the seaport of Dongdu and the Xiamen International Airport, and in the technological transformation of ageing industrial enterprises on Xiamen Island and in the Xinglin industrial area. The authorities have purchased a fleet of taxis, coaches and buses, and intend to obtain aeroplanes for chartering. While undertaking the 'five linkages and one levelling' in the Huli Industrial Zone, they also continued to press for the enlargement of the SEZ to the entire island of Xiamen (Fig. 2.4). When their request was adopted by the central government in April 1984, it was planned that the Xiamen SEZ should become a free port like Hong Kong.[29] The inclusion of the city of Xiamen and its surrounding area on the island has given the zone the distinctive characteristic of having an urban core. Its population will increase to about 300,000, almost the same size as the Shenzhen SEZ, and it now possesses excellent port facilities, a modern international airport, hundreds of factories and also the University of Xiamen. Thus, the problem of spatial incongruity between the zone's functional organization and its restricted area in the Huli Industrial Zone has to some extent been solved. However,

Fig. 2.4 The Xiamen SEZ

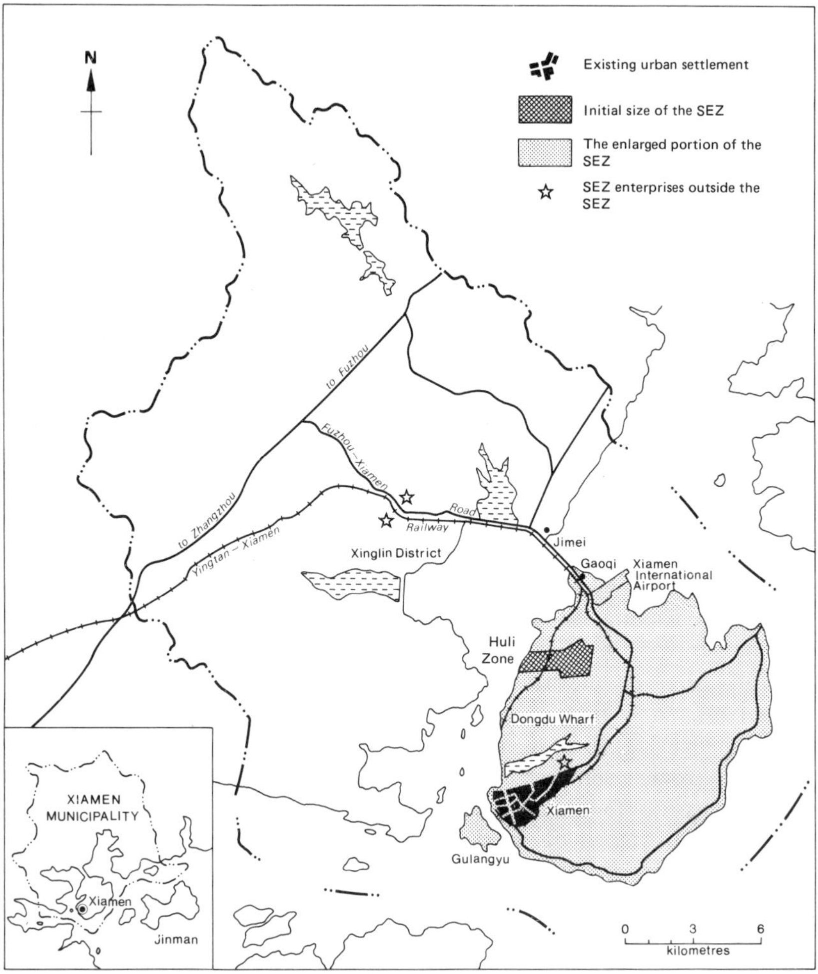

with the assimilation of the population of the city of Xiamen, an increasing need for infrastructural construction and administrative restructuring between the Xiamen SEZ and the rest of the municipality of Xiamen will become evident.[30] A period of consolidation seems inevitable.

Nevertheless, the Xiamen SEZ has continued to expand its sphere of influence. On 8 July 1984, the Xiamen Special Economic Zone Sanjiang Trading Co. was established in Zhangzhou, Fujian, as a regional economic entity with four specific purposes: first, to speed up the development of the hinterland of the Xiamen SEZ; second, to help reform the conventional economic structure of southern Fujian; third, to cater for the needs of overseas Chinese; and, fourth, to increase the economic well-being of the people of the region. With these as its objectives, the company will engage in developing the external and domestic linkages of agriculture and industrial enterprises in the region.[31] As such, the Xiamen SEZ will become a regional concern rather than a local economic entity. Thus the problem of territorial and functional incongruity will become even more acute than before.

The Fourteen Coastal Cities and Hainan Island

As mentioned in the introductory section of this chapter, 14 coastal cities have been allowed to adopt more liberal economic policies than inland China and are able to award concessionary terms and carry out various types of reforms akin to those of the SEZs. Hainan Island has also been granted quasi-SEZ status. Since this innovation has only occurred very recently, details on the way in which the 14 cityports and Hainan Island will open to foreign investors are not available. Based on the patchy information released so far, their 'special zone' treatment includes the following. First, they will have the authority to approve joint-venture projects involving investment of between US$5 and US$10 million (Shanghai and Tianjin will have a limit of US$30 million). This is somewhat less than the SEZs whose limits are US$30 million for light industrial joint-venture projects and US$50 million for heavy industrial concerns.[32] Second, some of the preferential terms available to investors in the SEZs, such as the tax-free import of all necessary raw materials and machinery, exemption from export duties, a tax holiday of 3–5 years, a 15 per cent profit tax after the tax holiday, and so on, will be awarded to all new approved joint-venture industrial undertakings and all technological innovations in old industrial enterprises.[33] Third, economic and technological development zones will be set up in a demarcated area, usually outside the existing urban core, for the concentrated development of new joint-venture-type industrial and research and development projects.[34] Finally, the development of tourist facilities and holiday resorts will be speeded up.[35]

In order to improve their economic foundations, the central government will lend 1.5 billion *yuan* to these cityports and areas for the construction of infrastructure.[36] State-owned companies in Hong Kong, including China Resources Co., the Bank of China and its sister banks, and other institutions, are being mobilized to give their support. Structural reforms, such as contract labour, floating wages, tendering for construction projects, and so on, pioneered by the SEZs, will be promoted in these cityports and areas.[37] In sum, though these cityports will not be called SEZs, few would contend that there are sharp contrasts between the 'proper' SEZs and the 'quasi' SEZs.

Conclusion

According to Xu Dixin, a leading Chinese economist, China's SEZs represent state capitalism, not socialism, because enterprises run by foreign or overseas Chinese capital constitute a type of capitalist economy. In a socialist economy like that of China, SEZs, by nature and by function, have a dual relationship which is both contradictory, and complementary, to the state.[38] In the SEZs, the state-owned and collective sectors are, by design, smaller than the capitalist sector, which is characterized by joint ventures between the Chinese government and foreign investors, and by enterprises set up solely with foreign funds, which are capitalist in nature. From this angle, the relationship between the socialist economy of the mainland and the 'state-capitalist' economy of the SEZs is contradictory. However, after almost two decades of isolation and extreme self-reliance, China has found itself some twenty years behind the developed capitalist countries in science and technology, and in industry, and some forty or fifty years behind them in agriculture.[39] The fastest way to modernize the backward sectors is to learn from the experience of the developed capitalist countries. It has been repeatedly stressed that the role of the SEZs is to experiment with and to digest Western technology and management techniques so that the inland socialist enterprises can benefit from their experience.[40] As such, the relationship between the SEZs and other parts of mainland China is a complementary one, because the former serve as laboratories for the latter.

It is because of the dualistic relationship between the SEZs and the rest of the country that China on the one hand finds the zones, both 'proper' and 'quasi', necessary and desirable for its current drive towards modernization, and on the other tries as far as possible to restrict their influence on the masses. It is this mixed feeling that led to the initial idea of setting up SEZs in remote frontier townships in the south-eastern provinces of Guangdong and Fujian. For the same reason, the initial sizes of the four SEZs were fairly small and they were located in relatively uninhabited areas away from existing urban settlements. Practical considerations and financial problems noted in the previous sections have, however, proved that the territorial containment of the four SEZs is unrealistic, especially when they are allowed to expand functionally beyond their territorial limit in order to acquire the essential ingredients of success, for instance, transport linkages, foreign investment and technology, rapid growth in earnings, and so on. Readjustment of their size and location seems inevitable, leading to the subsequent expansion of their territorial coverage and the setting up of other 'quasi' SEZs along the coast of China. If the current trend is allowed to persist, one may anticipate that further expansion of the zones in terms of number and size, and in terms of function, is not impossible. The most likely areas for territorial expansion include the various nodes of the inland transport system such as Chongqing and Wuhan, whilst functional expansion is likely to occur in the multi-provincial and foreign trade sectors of the economy. Geographically, the cityports will have their greatest impact on the coastal provinces. Owing to the friction of distance, the valuable experience gained in the introduction of foreign technology and management techniques will not be easily and quickly passed on to the inland provinces. In order to speed up the process, a few 'quasi' SEZs set up in inland provinces will not only be desirable but also necessary in order to diffuse newly gained experience quickly and adequately. The Shenzhen and Xiamen SEZs have overseen joint ventures between foreign investors and the Chinese on the one hand and between the inland provinces, the central ministries, departments or companies and the SEZs themselves on the other. These attempts could be further strengthened. Both methods of co-operation are beneficial to the Chinese economy. The SEZs are functional entities with their own territorial bases and, in activating the domestic economy and in fostering inter-regional and inter-sectoral co-operation, are an exciting new phenomenon in the Chinese economic structure. Introduced only five years ago as a mere territorial entity termed a special export zone, the concept of the special economic zone has developed into a functional and territorial construct of local and regional concern. The direction and form in which China's SEZs will further develop remain open.

Notes

1. The Board of Trustees of Lingnan University provided financial support for the research in this chapter which formed part of a research project on China's special economic zones by the Geography Department of the Chinese University of Hong Kong.
2. L.E. Kreider, 'Free Port', *Encyclopaedia Americana* (1975), pp. 43–4.
3. J. Currie, *Investment: The Growing Role of Export Processing Zones* (London, The Economist, 1979), EIU Special Report No. 64.
4. As quoted by Vittal from Unido, see N. Vittal, *Export Processing Zones in Asia: Some Dimensions* (Tokyo, Asian Productivity Organization, 1977), p. 1.
5. K.Y. Wong and D.K.Y. Chu, 'Export Processing Zones and Special Economic Zones as Generators of Economic Development: The Asian Experience', *Geografiska Annaler*, Vol. 66B, 1984, pp. 1–16.
6. Li Huajie, 'Guangyu jingji tequ jianshe di jige wenti' ('On a Few Problems in Building up the Special Economic Zones'), unpublished lecture notes, 1983, p. 2.
7. Unpublished speech by Wu Nansheng delivered at Shantou, January 1984 (in Chinese).
8. Ceng Jianhei, 'Yixiang chongyao juece di dansheng' ('The Birth of an Important Decision'), *Liaowang* (*Look*), No. 24, 11 June 1984, reprinted in *Wen wei po* (Hong Kong), 12 June 1984.
9. Ceng (1984); Wu (1984); and Li (1983).
10. Ceng (1984).
11. Field-work, 1984.
12. Ceng (1984).
13. K.Y. Wong, 'Shekou–Chiwan Development Model', in D.K.Y. Chu (ed.), *The Largest Special Economic Zone of China — Shenzhen* (Hong Kong, Wide Angle Press, 1983), pp. 125–33 (in Chinese).
14. Xu Zice and Cai Renqun, 'Guangyu woguo jingji tequ guihua dijidian yijian' ('A Few Points on the Planning of the Special Economic Zones of China'), in Zhong Gongfu and Xu Zice (eds.), *Zhongguo jingji tequ dili yanjiu* (*The Geography of China's Special Economic Zones*) (Guangdong, Guangdong People's Publishing House, 1983), pp. 6–34.
15. Wang Linsheng and Chen Yujie, *Zhongguo di dui wai jingji guanxi* (*China's Foreign Economic Relations*) (Beijing, People's Publishing House, 1982), p. 28.
16. Field-work.
17. K.Y. Wong and D.K.Y. Chu, 'The Investment Environment', in K.Y. Wong and D.K.Y. Chu (eds.), *Modernization in China: The Case of the Shenzhen Special Economic Zone* (Hong Kong, Oxford University Press, 1985), pp. 176–207.

18. Zhu Jianru and Wu Rende, 'Cong jingji dili jiaodu pingjia zhongguodi, jingji tequ' ('An Economic-Geographic Appraisal of the Chinese Special Economic Zones'), *Acta Geographica Sinica*, Vol. 38, 1983, pp. 262–72 (in Chinese).

19. *Zhongguo jingji tequ nianjian* (*Yearbook of China's Special Economic Zones*) (Hong Kong, Yearbook of China's Special Economic Zones Publishing Co., 1983), pp. 235–64.

20. *Zhongguo jingji tequ nianjian* (1983).

21. Zhu and Wu (1983).

22. Field-work.

23. Field-work.

24. Field-work.

25. Field-work.

26. Zhu and Wu (1983).

27. Chen Zhaobin and Chen Mingge, 'Xiamen jingji tequ di xingban he zhanwang' ('The Setting Up of the Xiamen Special Economic Zone and Its Outlook'), *Gangao jingji* (*Hong Kong and Macau Economic Digest*), No. 6, 1981, pp. 49–53.

28. Tong Guoru, 'Guangyu Xiamen jingji tequ jianshe di sanbu shexiang' ('On the Three Stages of Development of the Xiamen Special Economic Zone'), *Jingji tequ wenti tansuo* (Fujian, Fujian People's Publishing House, 1982), pp. 116–21.

29. Field-work.

30. Field-work.

31. *Xiamen ribao* (*Xiamen Daily*), 10 July 1984.

32. Field-work and China News Agency, Beijing, 19 June 1984.

33. Special issues on the opening of the 14 cityports to the world in *Wen wei po* (Hong Kong), July 1984 (various dates).

34. See note 33.

35. See note 33.

36. *Wen wei po* (Hong Kong), 11 July 1984.

37. Field-work.

38. Xu Dixin, 'Salient Feature: State Capitalism', *Beijing Review*, No. 4, 23 January 1984, p. 29.

39. Xue Muqiao, *China's Socialist Economy* (Beijing, Foreign Languages Press, 1981), p. 235.

40. Ceng (1984).

3. Structure and Policies in Industrial Planning in the Shenzhen Special Economic Zone

R.Y.W. Kwok*

Introduction

The experimental nature of the first and largest special economic zone (SEZ), that of Shenzhen, poses many unexpected and perplexing planning problems. An attempt is made here to review the SEZ in the light of a few key planning propositions. In addition, as the Shenzhen SEZ's special functions provide the framework for planning, this chapter discusses its planning tasks and problems within the context of five macro-planning issues selected with regard to its specific characteristics. Finally, as the SEZ's primary goals consist of economic growth, foreign investment and technology adaptation, planning is interpreted broadly as development planning rather than purely physical planning in the traditional sense.

Let us now turn to the five macro-planning issues. First, as a planning system responds to the dictates of the economic system, a review of the latter in Shenzhen is necessary. The Shenzhen SEZ has adopted a mixed economic system that combines the features of both the market economy and the centralized economy. The characteristics of this system determine the nature of planning. More specifically, foreign-capital-induced development has its special effects on the function of planning in the SEZ.

Second, the adoption of planning policies is a function of the balance between economic and political decisions. Shenzhen's economic goals are explicitly stated but its political concerns are unstated and implicit. China's political decisions are still primarily made at the state level and are then transmitted downward. As the administrative and management system provides the mechanism within which political decisions are made, an analysis of this system as a decision-making process will illustrate how planning operates within the political arena.

Third, in planning, the dual criteria of economic growth and social equity are universally accepted. However, they are constantly in conflict. It is assumed that planning under a centralized system can co-ordinate these goals and achieve a better 'optimal' solution and possibly avoid unnecessary conflicts. The extent to which these goals have been met in Shenzhen can be estimated from an examination of the supply of social overhead capital (for economic growth) and the provision of social services (for social equity).

---

*This chapter has been prepared in association with Kin-kwan Au. Errors and misinterpretations should be attributed only to the author.

Fourth, the planning problems presented by changes in human capital and population are especially severe in new urban development. Shenzhen is, *de facto*, a 'new town'. As in other new town development, one of the major planning problems in Shenzhen lies in its labour force. The experience in new towns elsewhere (most notably Brazilia) shows how drastic changes in the structure of labour can be during development. This is the major planning problem which plagues these cities and it has a long-term effect on their development. The labour force in Shenzhen is therefore examined to illuminate the issue.

Finally, the regional setting of development is another major planning issue, as no development takes place independently. Shenzhen, in particular, is a planned agglomeration whose specific aim is to develop external economic relations. Geographically, it is contiguous to Hong Kong, an international metropolis, and adjacent to the Zhu Jiang Delta, a major agricultural production basin in China. Existing and future regional economic relations which have a significant impact on planning will be discussed briefly.

Foreign Investment and Social Overhead Capital

Wu Nansheng, the ex-mayor of the Shenzhen SEZ, stated in 1981 that the functions of Shenzhen are: first, to understand capitalist society, especially those aspects related to modern economic development; second, to experiment with different policies; and, third, to study foreign advanced technology and management.[1] These functions were later modified by the present mayor, Liang Xiang, who stated that the advantages of the SEZ are as follows:

1. Through preferential policies these zones can use large amounts of foreign investment in a better way, import advanced technology, and acquire scientific techniques and management — all of which will enable the country as a whole to develop economically at a quicker pace.
2. By dealing regularly with foreign capital, we can further observe and understand the development of and exchanges in the modern capitalist world, and keep abreast of changes on the international market and in science and technology.
3. Through co-operation, we can learn modern construction and management methods and train professionals.[2]

The Shenzhen SEZ explicitly accepts the market economy as the primary economic system. And, because of the unavoidable mix of international capitalism and China's socialist economy, it also accepts their co-existence and the necessity to co-ordinate the two systems since Shenzhen's main economic function is to provide an environment for investment.

The special favour shown towards overseas investment derives from the fact that the growth of the Shenzhen SEZ is primarily generated by productive activities set up mainly with foreign capital. The development model adopted is based on the belief that infrastructure and the provision of land and labour are essential preconditions for overseas investment. Therefore the state has to supply them. Most of Shenzhen's income comes from wages. Labour is recruited from all parts of China and is trained with suitable skills for the various enterprises in the SEZ. Thus employment and the structure of labour are directly determined by foreign enterprises. In order to accommodate the labour force, housing and social services have, in the main, to be provided by the state.

Hence, in principle, there is a clear division between the roles played by the state and foreign investors. While the state supplies social overhead capital, basic infrastructure, land and labour in order to provide favourable conditions for overseas investment, direct production, the initiating force of development, is controlled and guided by foreign investors, and is mainly for the export market. Therefore production depends entirely on the international market network. As the SEZ opens up to overseas investment, modern technology, information and professional personnel will flow into Shenzhen. In anticipation of this, China has drawn up regulations and has prepared an environment designed to provide conditions conducive to foreign investment.

As development is dependent on the inflow of capital from foreign countries, planning of the region is in turn confined to the provision of basic infrastructure, land for development, a labour pool and other, supporting services. Under this model of development, Shenzhen's planning is therefore directly determined by the scale and speed of foreign investment. Foreign capital, which responds to the international capital market, thus becomes the overall framework for, and raises a number of issues in, planning. Amongst these issues, the most crucial is the conflict between the profit-maximizing objective of foreign enterprises and the rationalization objective of planning. Foreign enterprises desire cost-minimizing advantages, while planning attempts to realize economic efficiency in state investment. Since planning responds to foreign investment, a broad review of foreign investment in the Shenzhen SEZ is necessary in order to understand how planning there works.

Shenzhen's regulations on foreign enterprises stress preferential treatment and safeguards for overseas investment. Indeed, the relaxation of economic controls on overseas investment is the main characteristic of the SEZ's 'special nature'.[3] The three main provisions of the Regulations on the Special Economic Zones in Guangdong Province can be summarized as follows. First, goods produced in the SEZ by foreign enterprises are primarily for export, and these enterprises can operate free of state intervention. Second, foreign investors are guaranteed a reasonable rate of return on their invested capital through preferential treatment in the form of low income tax and exemption from duty on productive capital, and they are encouraged to reinvest in the SEZs. Third, the enterprises are free to manage their labour as they would in a free market economy.[4] These provisions essentially assure profit retention and the reduction of costs.

What then are the nature and extent of foreign investment in Shenzhen at present? Tables 3.1 and 3.2 show the value of foreign investment in Shenzhen and the number of foreign investment contracts in the period 1979–83. Although the value and number of these increased over the period, their rates of increase decreased. This decrease may indicate a waning in enthusiasm for investment over the period. The wide discrepancy between actual and contracted investment value was to a certain extent due to the complex bureaucratic procedures which had to be followed when firms were set up. In addition, many foreign entrepreneurs, after agreeing to invest, took time to assess the investment climate and production conditions before placing actual investment.

In 1982, there was an increase in the proportion of actual to contracted investment value, and in the amount of actual investment placed in the year.

Table 3.1 Foreign Investment in the Shenzhen SEZ (million *yuan*)

	1979	1980	1981	1982	1983
Contracted investment:					
Total contracted value	73.50	714.24	2,785.88	3,296.10	3,594.94
Annual increase in contracted value	73.50	640.74	2,071.64	510.22	298.84
Annual rate of increase (%)	—	871.76	290.05	18.31	9.07
Actual investment:					
Total actual value	37.53	111.48	291.63	572.69	807.39
Annual increase in actual value	37.53	73.95	180.15	281.06	234.70
Annual rate of increase (%)	—	197.04	161.60	96.38	40.98
Total actual value as a percentage of total contracted value (%)	51.06	15.61	10.47	17.37	22.46

Note: Documentary figures are given in Hong Kong dollars and the conversion of currency for each year is based on the exchange rate as at the end of that year. The exchange rates of *yuan* to Hong Kong dollars were 1:3.1971 (for 1979), 1:3.3190 (for 1980), 1:3.2918 (for 1981), 1:3.2129 (for 1982), and 1:3.6785 (for 1983). *Hong Kong Monthly Digest of Statistics* (Hong Kong, Census and Statistics Department, various issues).

Source: Renmin ribao (*People's Daily*), 29 March 1984.

Table 3.2 Foreign Investment Contracts in the Shenzhen SEZ

	1979	1980	1981	1982	1983
Total number of contracts	170	473	1,051	1,634	2,512
Annual increase in number of contracts	170	303	578	583	878
Annual rate of increase (%)	—	178.24	122.20	55.47	53.73

Source: Renmin ribao (*People's Daily*), 29 March 1984.

There were two reasons for this. First, Hong Kong was at the time undergoing an economic recession, particularly in the real estate sector. Hong Kong investors were thus looking for alternative outlets for a considerable amount of idle capital.[5] Much of this consequently found its way into Shenzhen. Second, within Shenzhen, the major obstacles to foreign investment in the early stages of development — the complicated administrative structure and the inadequacy of legislation regulating business — were largely removed at this time.[6] From early 1982, for example, various overlapping administrative departments were removed or amalgamated; the number of vice-mayors was cut from 17 to 3; the number of other middle-level leading cadres fell from 300 to around 100;[7] and several sets of draft regulations were drawn up in order to provide assurance to foreign entrepreneurs that their interests would be protected.[8]

Foreign-investment-led development, which is by nature volatile, makes the planning of social overhead capital extremely difficult, as the inflow of investment cannot be predicted or controlled by the state. In view of the uncertainty of demand, the planning of, and projections for, infrastructure and social services tend to be inaccurate. Moreover, as these state investments are 'lumpy', supply may not match demand, thus hindering development. Alternatively, demand may not match supply, resulting in economic inefficiency and waste.

From Table 3.3, which presents the relative amounts of foreign investment contracted in Shenzhen as at the end of February 1982, it is clear that a small number of large projects (of over HK$0.5 billion, or approximately 152

Table 3.3 The Relative Amounts of Foreign Investment Contracted in the Shenzhen SEZ as at the End of February 1982

Investment Amount	No. of Contracts	% of Total Contracts	% of Total Investment
Over 303.79 million *yuan* (HK$1 billion)	12	1.0	69.2
151.89–303.79 million *yuan* (HK$0.5–1 billion)	9	0.8	6.6
3.04–151.89 million *yuan* (HK$10–50 million)	35	3.0	13.1
Less than 3.04 million *yuan* (HK$10 million)	1,112	95.2	11.1
Total	1,168	100.0	100.0

Note: Documentary figures are given in Hong Kong dollars and the conversion of currency is based on the exchange rate at the end of 1981. The exchange rate of *yuan* to Hong Kong dollars was 1:3.2918. *Hong Kong Monthly Digest of Statistics* (Hong Kong, Census and Statistics Department, 1982).

Source: *Zhongguo jingji tequ nianjian* (*Yearbook of China's Special Economic Zones*) (Hong Kong, Yearbook of China's Special Economic Zones Publishing Co., 1983), p. 671.

million *yuan* each) formed over 75 per cent of the total investment value. In addition, small contracts constituted an overwhelmingly large percentage of the total number of contracts. So far, Shenzhen has been able to attract small foreign investors, but has been unable to persuade major overseas investors and large firms to commit themselves. The large number of small foreign investments may imply that these were experimental in nature. It may be that investors were testing the SEZ system and assessing results before making a further major commitment.[9]

The present skewed industrial structure has characteristics similar to those of an oligopolistic city, where the key entrepreneurs can and do exert much pressure and demand on social overhead capital services. If any of these enterprises decide to leave or not to renew their contracts, the growth of Shenzhen may be severely affected. In order to retain these major developments, the provision of appropriate social overhead capital and skilled labour must be adequate and efficient and Shenzhen must therefore plan the necessary production requirements and physical facilities.

At the other end of the industrial structure, a large number of small firms require the extension of infrastructure services. These branches will diminish the efficiency of scale economies. Since the present industrial structure is likely to remain for some time, planning cannot ignore this large group of consumers and will have to allocate a major part of the infrastructure to them.

Under this particular industrial structure, the planning tendency is to oversupply social overhead capital, in particular infrastructure, in order to provide an environment conducive to foreign investment, which is attracted by reductions in costs. However, this undermines the economic efficiency of state investment.

The Role of the Planning Agencies

Shenzhen's development has been planned by two local government planning units — the Shenzhen SEZ Development Co. and the Shenzhen SEZ Construction Co. Given the general goals of development, what are the functions of these units? In what economic and political contexts do they make planning decisions? What authority and power do they exercise? Before discussing these questions, a brief review of the administrative history of the SEZs is in order.

In January 1979, under the Ministry of Communication, the Shekou Industrial Zone, situated at the western end of what is now the Shenzhen SEZ, was set up by China Merchants' Steam Navigation Co.[10] In December 1979, the Shenzhen SEZ was established,[11] followed by the Administrative Committee for the Special Economic Zones of Guangdong Province (ADCOM) in August 1980.[12] Finally, the State Council Office of SEZ Affairs was set up to control all SEZs in Guangdong and Fujian in June 1982.[13] This sequence of events shows a reversal in the administrative establishment, as in a planned economy administrative units are usually set up from the top down. It also demonstrates the experimental nature of the SEZs as they developed from a local to a state concern with the concomitant transfer of control. Moreover, it reveals the increasing attention that the central government has paid and the significance it attaches to the role and functions of the SEZs. The gradual administrative upgrading of the SEZs has been in response to practical experience and their increasing economic importance, thus resulting in the necessity of bringing them more closely under state supervision.

The present administrative system is characterized by its complexity and diversity. Part of the SEZ administration is controlled at the state level and part at the provincial level, whilst still another part possesses local autonomy. In terms of enterprise administration, various ministries at the state level have set up profit-making units, sometimes with overseas investment, within Shenzhen. Foreign investors, in co-operation with other overseas or domestic enterprises, have also formed consortia to work on specific projects. While all these development units have been allocated sites, each has some autonomy in its operation. The SEZ's Planning Department has, on the one hand, to provide specific services to these individual developments and, on the other, to co-ordinate all development within the zone. It has also to provide facilities for inter-regional trade as well as the transfer of goods and personnel. Fig. 3.1 shows the administrative structure of government in Shenzhen. Fig. 3.2 shows those bodies that administer enterprises in the SEZ. The five large-scale foreign consortia projects in Fig. 3.2 have been contracted with, and are co-ordinated by, the Shenzhen SEZ Development Co.,[14] a government body. However, the planning services which allocate infrastructure are provided through another, parallel government body, the Shenzhen SEZ Construction Co.

This latter company is, in reality, the physical planning unit. Its position and role can be seen in Fig. 3.2. Once contracts are signed, and a location has been selected through the Development Co., the Construction Co. supplies land and infrastructure wherever they are needed. Within the SEZ administration, these two units respond to directives from the local, provincial and state levels, since large-scale developments are often negotiated at various higher levels. As a result, these units have little say in policy or land allocation for industrial development. They cannot guide spatial development, but respond to industrial demand by distributing industrial and social services to predetermined development areas.

Because of their unique functions, these planning units are frequently unable to follow the normal planning criteria of economic efficiency and social equity. The overwhelming concern to attract investment inevitably weakens their policy-making role. As local state units, their role and responsibility are reduced solely to supplying social overhead capital to facilitate development projects. Foreign investors, as the chief initiators of development, have, through their contracting units, much more political power to determine their requirements on spatial conditions and production facilities. Overseas investors often enter into joint ventures with domestic enterprises or units which are administered by bodies above the local level. The local planning units have little authority to countermand or amend orders from

Fig. 3.1 The Organization of the Shenzhen Municipal People's Government

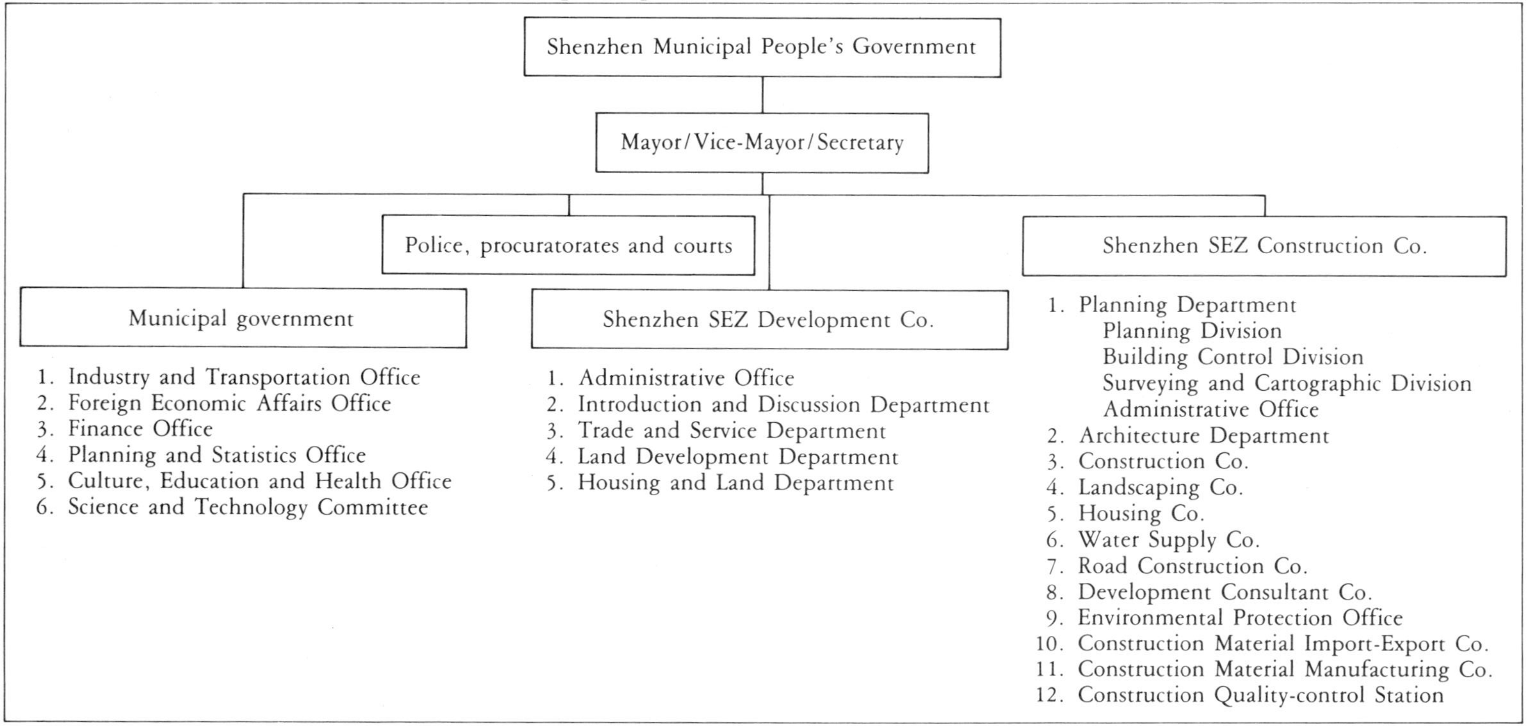

Sources: *China Building Development 1982/1983* (Hong Kong, Trend Publishing (HK) Ltd., 1983), p.38; and *Zhongguo zuida di jingji tequ — Shenzhen (The Largest Special Economic Zone of China — Shenzhen)* (Hong Kong, Wide Angle Press, 1983), p. 6.

Fig. 3.2 The Administrative Structure of the Shenzhen SEZ

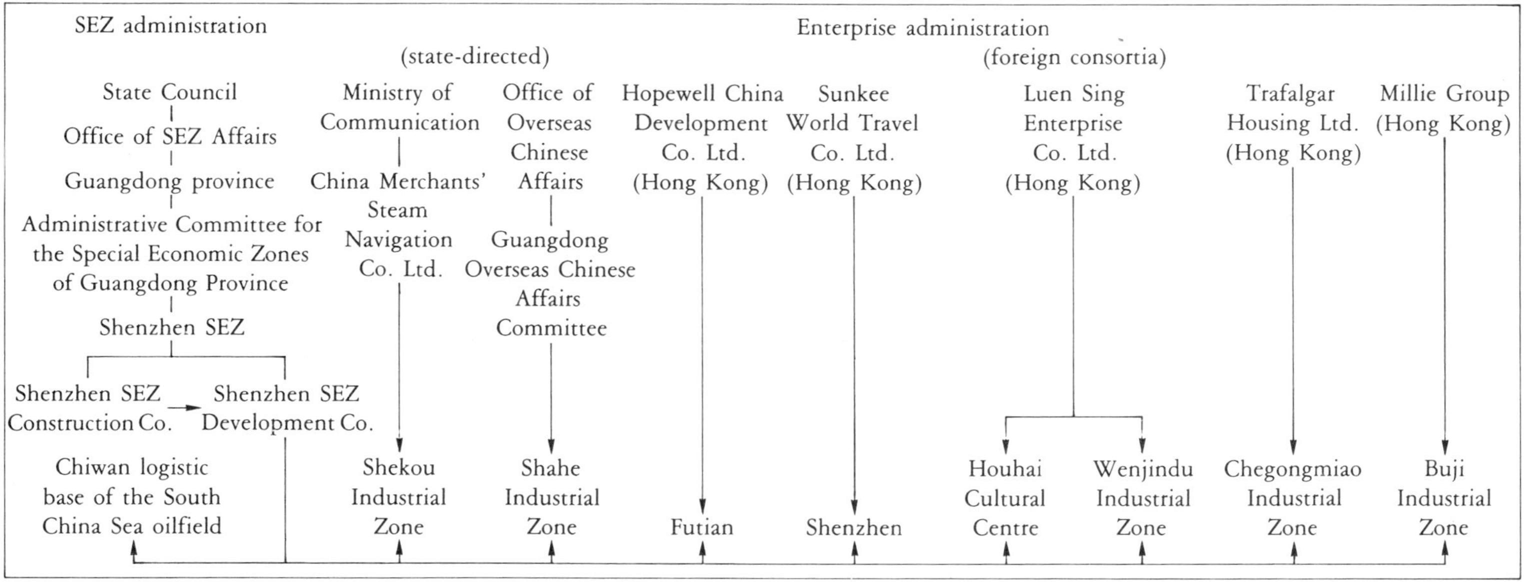

Note: The Chiwan logistic base of the South China Sea oilfield is being developed by Nanshan Development Holdings, and is jointly owned by Guangdong South Sea Oil (East) Co., China South Sea Oil United Service Co., China Near-sea Oil Service (HK) Co. Ltd., Shenzhen Development Co., the Bank of China (Hong Kong Branch), the China Resources Group, China Merchants' Steam Navigation Co. Ltd. (Hong Kong) and C.F. Wong Investment Co. Ltd. See *Jingji daobao (Economic Reporter)*, 14 November 1983, p. 17. All these companies, with the exception of C.F. Wong Investment Co. Ltd., are based in the People's Republic of China.

Sources: *Renmin ribao (People's Daily)*, 31 January 1979; *Ta kung pao*, 13 November 1981; *Wen wei po*, 10 December 1981; *Jingji daobao (Economic Reporter)*, 14 November 1984; and *Zhongguo tuozi zhinan (Investment Guide to China)* (Hong Kong, Economic Reporter Press, 1982).

above. Moreover, as control has been systematically transferred from the local to the state level, local agencies have increasingly limited power in directing or controlling development. Because policies and projects are frequently decided elsewhere, local planning units have relatively little say in 'planning', and must generally comply with investors' demands.

Infrastructure and Social Services

How does planning in Shenzhen generate economic growth and achieve social equity? This issue can be examined through examples of the supply of infrastructure for the former and the provision of social services for the latter by the state.

As infrastructure is spatially linked to land development and is constructed along transport routes, it is necessary first to review the location and distribution of development before assessing the economic efficiency of its provision. From Fig. 3.3 it can be seen that the major industrial development areas of Chiwan, Shekou, Houhai, Shahe, Chegongmiao, Futian, Buji, Shenzhen and Wenjindu and the government's own developments in Shangbu and Luohu are spread all over the western half of the SEZ. Tourism, fisheries, agriculture, commerce and housing are planned in the eastern part.[15] Thus the infrastructure network, which has to service all these areas, must at the very least cover most of the western half of the SEZ.

Fig. 3.3 also shows, together with Table 3.4, the main functions and locations of the development projects. Although each area has some specific functions there is much duplication between areas and no obvious policy of industrial agglomeration based on an industrial system, economic links or on their infrastructure requirements. In order to facilitate and service the various scattered developments in Shenzhen, the infrastructure network has to be extensive both in financial and spatial terms.

The planning slogan, *Qitong yiping* ('seven linkages and one levelling'), which calls for the provision of land, gas, electricity, water, sewerage, storm drainage, and communications (the seven linkages), as well as land formation (the one levelling),[16] summarizes the function of planning which is primarily to provide infrastructure in support of industrial development. As all these physical systems are to be provided by the Shenzhen planning units, they represent a substantial amount of state investment (see Table 3.5).

The supply of infrastructure requires an immense amount of state investment and labour. For example, in order to supply water from the Dong Jiang, several reservoirs have had to be constructed or expanded.[17] In order to supply electricity, generating plants are being planned and built at Dongguan and Daya Wan outside Shenzhen.[18] Apart from the local transport network, port facilities for international freight have had to be extensively developed, as Shenzhen's industries are export-oriented and much of their raw material comes from abroad. International passenger transport has also to be provided for those overseas workers and personnel who work in foreign-financed firms in the SEZ. For these reasons, the state has already committed

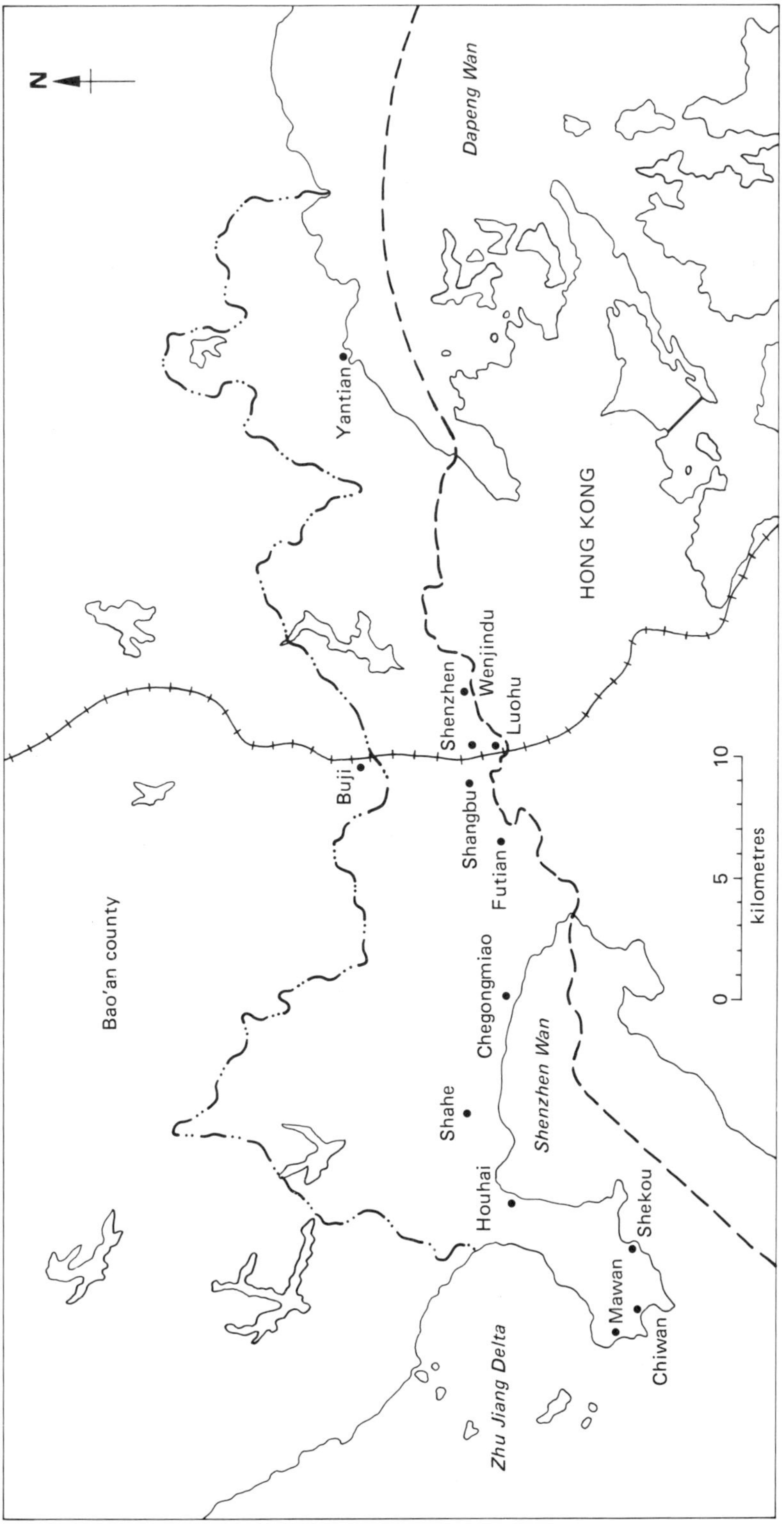

Fig. 3.3 The Districts of the Shenzhen SEZ

Table 3.4 The Major Functions of Selected Planning Zones in the Shenzhen SEZ

Planning Zones	Major Functions	Usable Land (ha)
Luohu	commerce, housing, industry	120,000
Shenzhen	commerce, housing, industry	40,000
Futian	comprehensive development	400,000
Shangbu	industry, housing, warehousing	100,000
Chegongmiao	comprehensive development	20,000
Shekou Industrial Zone	mainly industry	50,000
Shahe	mainly industry	50,000
Houhai	comprehensive development, education	30,000
Chiwan	industry, port	50,000
Buji Industrial Zone	mainly industry	—
Wenjindu Industrial Zone	mainly industry	—

Source: China Building Development 1982/1983 (Hong Kong, Trend Publishing (HK) Ltd., 1983), p. 36; and Hong Kong Federation of Students (ed.), *Jing-ji tequ mianmianguan* (*Aspects of the Special Economic Zones*) (Hong Kong, Wide Angle Press, 1983), pp. 95–6.

Table 3.5 Investment in Infrastructure in the Shenzhen SEZ (million *yuan*)

	1979	1980	1981	1982	1983
Total investment in infrastructure	49.88	174.75	445.14	1,077.79	1,963.72
Annual investment in infrastructure	49.88	124.87	270.39	632.65	885.93
Annual rate of increase (%)	—	250.34	154.73	142.12	82.20

Source: Renmin ribao (*People's Daily*), 29 March 1984.

itself to building a new international airport as well as extending the container port at Shekou.

By 1982, 43 domestic manufacturing enterprises had been jointly established with various ministries and other provinces or municipalities (such as Shanghai, Tianjin, Guangzhou, Nanjing, Xi'an, Liaoling and Jiling). These enterprises are called 'inward linkage enterprises'.[19] They are intended, amongst other things, to transfer technology from the SEZ inland, to obtain the latest market information for export production, and to produce intermediate products for foreign production in the SEZ. Because of their necessary links with the national industrial network, they create a substantial demand for inter-regional freight and labour transport.

Planning of the internal transport pattern, which runs primarily in an east–west direction, is further complicated by inter-regional passenger and freight traffic which runs north–south, as exemplified by the Guangzhou–Kowloon Railway. A highway link between Hong Kong and Guangzhou through the Zhu Jiang Delta will also cut across internal traffic. This crossing of the two types of transport will continue to have a great impact on all land development. As the designation of land use is based on agreement with foreign consortia, the potential for conflict between the state's plans on transport routes and the location of industrial zones, which should be co-ordinated with the transport routes, could become a major planning problem.

Table 3.5 shows the amount invested in infrastructure between 1979 and 1983. From 1980, investment increased at a decreasing rate. This pattern seems to have reflected that of actual foreign investment. In 1983, the rate of increase dropped markedly. Similarly, as shown in Table 3.6, the construction of floor space over the same period increased at a decreasing rate. Both trends indicate signs of stabilization in infrastructure and construction. If these trends continue, the demand for construction labour in Shenzhen will fall and the massive labour force employed to construct infrastructure will have to be repatriated to the hinterland or reallocated to other sectors. In either situation, the social and economic structure of Shenzhen will have to adjust.

The development of an international port in the SEZ represents another aspect of infrastructure that should be considered. In 1981 the first phase of a cargo port was built in Shekou to service the area's own imports and exports. As Shenzhen developed, Shekou also began to serve the entire SEZ's export industries as it was the only port in the region. Subsequently the port of Chiwan was developed by Nanshan Development Holdings,[20] and was originally designed to service oil exploration in the South China Sea. A recent visit shows that to the north of Chiwan, a large container port is being constructed at Mawan by the Shenzhen municipal government. All these port facilities are linked at the western end of the SEZ. This location, bordering on the Zhu Jiang Delta, has the advantage of possessing an inland freight transport link. Another deep-water seaport, however, is planned at Yantian at the eastern end of the SEZ.[21] The inland transport links with Yantian will have to pass through difficult and hilly terrain, and its inland link with Shekou–Chiwan–Mawan and the other industrial areas will have to cover the entire east–west width of the SEZ. Thus, the SEZ's two ports will require large amounts of social overhead capital. It is not clear whether such planned investment will be justified by the anticipated demand.

Transportation, as part of infrastructure, is closely related to land use; often it decides the land's nature and the functions for which it can be utilized. One of the major planning problems in Shenzhen is that whilst land functions are already broadly defined spatially, the land transport systems have yet to be determined. In fact, the planning process should be reversed. Moreover, the complexity and counteraction of the inter-regional, regional, and local transport networks, their movement and direction, and their attendant land requirements, environmental effects, and safety aspects, also have

Table 3.6 Floor Areas in the Shenzhen SEZ (sq m)

	1979	1980	1981	1982	1983
Total floor area	130,113	476,416	1,022,360	1,949,022	3,413,022
Annual increase in total floor area	130,113	346,303	545,944	926,662	1,464,000
Annual rate of increase (%)	—	266.16	114.59	90.64	75.11
Total housing floor area	52,617	231,163	465,230	920,917	1,544,917
Annual increase in total housing floor area	52,617	178,546	234,067	455,687	624,000
Annual rate of increase (%)	—	339.33	101.26	97.95	67.76
Total housing floor area as a percentage of total floor area	40.44	48.52	45.51	47.25	45.27

Source: Renmin ribao (*People's Daily*), 29 March 1984.

many planning implications. These physical planning problems must be unravelled in order to achieve a workable spatial pattern and land-use efficiency.

Inefficiency is also caused by the SEZ's specific spatial arrangement. The diversity of spatial decision-making, the dispersal of production locations and the extreme centrifugal siting of the seaports necessitate an extensive regional infrastructure network. The decentralization of industrial, commercial and administrative activities means that the advantages of scale economies in infrastructure are lost. In planning terms, therefore, the infrastructure is likely, in the short run, to be both inefficient and underutilized, and hence uneconomical and probably wasteful. The returns on this capital investment will take a long time to recover once all the industrial areas in the SEZ are occupied. In the long run, only sustained and continuous production will justify this initial 'big push' approach. The present policy of dispersal development reflects the diverse political influences discussed earlier. A planning policy of initial spatial concentration of development which allows for rational and flexible expansion would attain short-term efficiency without long-term diseconomies. This alternative policy, which seems to be more rational, however, implies a significant centralization of authority and power over the local planning units.

Let us now examine the goal of social equity. For the purpose of analysis social services are disaggregated into income-generating services and facilities for local residents in order to identify their 'real' contribution to equity. The adequacy and distribution of selected services are also analysed and assessed.

As Table 3.7 shows, state-employed workers in the commercial and social services sector comprised 21.5 per cent of the total labour force in 1980. This percentage seems reasonable, but the employment base excluded the large number of temporary workers in the SEZ. In that same year, actual personnel employed in this sector numbered around 2,000[22] which was considered insufficient. It has been recognized that the labour force for all services has fallen far short of demand.

Social services are used not only by 'permanent' residents, but also by temporary workers. There is, in addition, daily movement in and out of the SEZ. In 1983 each day an average of 20,000 people travelled between Hong Kong and Shenzhen and over 10,000 people travelled between Shenzhen and other parts of China.[23] Apart from tourists, this group consisted of businessmen, managers and technical advisers. The already sizeable transit

Table 3.7 The Structure of State Employment in the Shenzhen SEZ, 1980

Industry	Industry and Related Infrastructure	Commercial and Social Services	Finance, Research and Institutions	Agriculture and Related Sectors
Percentage employed by the state	35.5	21.5	20.4	22.6

Source: Jingji tequ dili wenti (*Collections of Essays on the Geography of the Shenzhen SEZ*), Vol. 1, October 1981, p. 21.

population is expected to increase. For tourism, which is part of Shenzhen's export economy, is developing rapidly, and business negotiations are expected to expand if Shenzhen's growth is maintained. This population will continue to demand higher quality and quantity in the provision of social, commercial and entertainment services. Furthermore, the daily movement of the transit population will continue to impose an immense burden on state investment in transport and will continue to necessitate special training for the service industries.

Restaurants are an example. In 1979, there were only four with a total of 1,500 seats in Shenzhen. At the end of March 1984, their number had increased to 174 with 23,475 seats. However, most of these restaurants are located in areas where visitors and tourists concentrate, and there is evidence that they are primarily provided for visitors. Local people complain that prices are too high and that restaurants and food outlets are scarce in new residential areas such as Shangbu.[24] The result of provision being made primarily for visitors is that the local population suffers from limited services at a high cost.

Because of development priorities far less importance is attached to services, unless they generate export income, such as tourism, than to industrial social overhead capital. As a social services sector is by nature labour-intensive, its large labour force represents a major consumer group which will demand more imported goods and additional social services. Moreover, this labour force does not contribute to foreign currency earnings.

The one essential social service provided by the state in the zone is workers' accommodation. Originally a floor area standard of 6 sq m per person was proposed for housing. According to this proposal, new housing and its necessary urban infrastructure require a per capita investment of 1,700 *yuan* for new construction or 700 *yuan* for redevelopment. As much as 3,420,000 sq m of floor area will be required by 1990 at a cost of approximately 1 billion *yuan*. By the year 2000, 1.65 billion *yuan* will be needed for new development. As existing urban housing will have to be renewed by that time, a further 21 million *yuan* will be required.[25]

Housing construction and floor area standards in Shenzhen between 1979 and 1982 are listed in Table 3.8. By 1982, the per capita housing floor area had exceeded the recommended standard, but this figure is misleading. A large amount of housing was developed by foreign consortia for sale and rent to overseas residents. These units are not for the use of local workers. Real

Table 3.8 Housing Construction in the Shenzhen SEZ (sq m)

	1979	1980	1981	1982
Total housing floor area	52,617	231,163	465,230	920,917
Annual increase	52,617	178,546	234,067	455,687
Per capita housing floor area	0.72	2.86	4.73	7.16

Source: *Renmin ribao* (*People's Daily*), 29 March 1984; and *Renkou yanjiu* (*Population Studies*), Vol. 2, 1984, p. 29.

estate development is encouraged as an income-generating activity, but it consists mainly of housing for overseas Chinese. Since this housing is built to a higher standard, it distorts the average per capita housing floor area upwards.

From the information available for 1982, a rough estimate indicates that local workers' housing formed approximately 22 per cent of the total area of housing built in that year,[26] and that it accommodated 2,000 families (approximately 10,000 people).[27] As the marginal increase in population in 1982 was 30,279, new construction in that year only satisfied one-third of the marginal demand.

In 1978, the average per capita housing floor area was 2.7 sq m; it increased to 9.0 sq m in 1983. Shenzhen's floor area standard was comparatively higher than that of most other Chinese cities. Most of the local workers' housing in the zone is built by the Housing Co., a division of the Shenzhen SEZ Construction Co. The units are distributed directly to the local population and different state departments — to the former by rent and to the latter by sale. In the latter case departments then allocate units to their staff according to the number of persons per household and their status.

The usual allocation for a three-person household is a flat of around 25–30 sq m, while a household with more than five persons occupies a 50–60 sq m flat. As in other parts of China, a higher status means a larger living area. The high floor area standard in the zone implies that housing units are allocated mainly to higher-level cadres. Recently, measures have been taken to reform the allocation system, based on the ability to pay rent. In the Shekou Industrial Zone, the monthly rent per square metre has been raised from 0.5–0.7 *yuan* to 0.9–1.0 *yuan*, and those who can afford to pay this rent have priority. Workers are also allowed to buy houses on a mortgage.[28] This system superficially removes the system of allocation by rank, but favours those who receive higher wages. As higher-status workers receive higher wages, they are in a better position to obtain housing units. Those with low wages and low status are at a considerable disadvantage under this system.

The costs of accommodating the work-force in the Shenzhen SEZ are high. Apart from those workers who are productive in the long term, there are a large number of temporary workers who will leave the SEZ when their productive work is no longer required. Housing units are not allocated to temporary workers, thereby minimizing investment in housing.

A recent visit to Shenzhen revealed evidence of efforts to develop new local workers' housing. However, there were also large tracts of temporary, but well-built, rush-mat housing alongside construction sites which provide shelter for temporary workers. This form of accommodation effectively fills the gap between the demand for housing and the supply. The quality of this form of accommodation is, of course, inferior. The shortage of accommodation in the zone will require a sustained commitment and considerable financial outlay on housing for the local labour force in the future. In 1982, the number of households without fixed housing units was around 2,000. This figure included only the permanent local population, most of whom were newly recruited from other parts of China.[29]

Information on other social services in the Shenzhen SEZ is scanty. However, there were five hospitals in Shenzhen with a total of only 200 beds in 1982. This is clearly insufficient; in that year, over 8 million *yuan* was allocated for the expansion of hospitals.[30]

Although the information on workers' housing and social services is not comprehensive, the available evidence indicates an immense gap between supply and demand. It implies that planning and the provision of housing and social services for the local population still have a long way to go to catch up with present development and population growth. It is quite clear that the supply of social services is at present determined by their economic viability. In this sector, economic efficiency and returns determine development priorities. As a result, there is evidence that social equity is often neglected and that those who have the least financial means tend to be left out, particularly temporary workers.

In general, there are many difficulties in planning for economic efficiency and social equity. The overriding concern of, and commitment to, economic goals tends to diminish consideration of these essential planning criteria. Instead of balancing them and reducing their conflict, Shenzhen seems to overlook them.

The Structure of Labour

Shenzhen faces a potential labour problem. When the initial phase of construction subsides in a new town development, the large construction labour force is displaced and left unemployed. However, population is not only a production problem, but also affects planned investment. In this section, labour conditions and the quality of labour in Shenzhen are reviewed in relation to production needs. Some of the measures taken to deal with the employment question are also examined.

Shenzhen's development strategy is to supply two of the three factors of production — labour and land (including social overhead capital) — to combine with the third factor, capital, which comes from overseas. In this developmental approach, the state plans and constructs social overhead capital in proportion to the expected foreign capital investment. Labour, whether deriving from migration or specific training, is supplied under the same conditions.

Tables 3.9 and 3.10 show that over 80 per cent of all contracts in Shenzhen during the period were, on average, for intermediate processing and compensation trade. Under intermediate processing, the state provides the plant, labour, water, electricity and other basic facilities, while the foreign investor pays salaries and supplies machinery, materials, designs and marketing. The foreign investor also pays the state for the production services received. Compensation trade is similar to intermediate processing, except that the costs of the plant, equipment and raw materials, instead of being repaid in cash, are compensated for in end-products of equal value.[31] As these forms of contract, especially intermediate processing, dominate the in-

Table 3.9 The Types of Foreign Investment Contracts in the Shenzhen SEZ (no. of contracts)

	End of Year				
Type of Contract	1979	1980	1981	1982	1983
Sole proprietorship	—	5	23	31	44
		(1.06)	(2.19)	(1.90)	(1.75)
Co-operative production and joint ventures	37	65	117	175	416
	(21.77)	(13.74)	(11.13)	(10.71)	(16.56)
Intermediate processing and compensation trade	133	403	911	1,428	2,052
	(78.23)	(85.20)	(86.88)	(87.39)	(81.69)
Total	170	473	1,051	1,634	2,512

Note: Figures in brackets give the percentage that the category forms of the total number of contracts for that year.

Source: *Renmin ribao* (*People's Daily*), 29 March 1984.

dustrial structure, Shenzhen earns a high proportion of its income from wages through the supply of labour.

Table 3.11 illustrates the population changes in Shenzhen between 1978 and 1982. From 1978, the population increased at an increasing rate, in contrast to the inflow of foreign capital which increased at a decreasing rate. The prime contributor to the increase in population has been migrating labour. The original agricultural population has rapidly changed to become predominantly non-agricultural. Since migrants are allowed to enter the zone on condition that they have obtained employment, the inverse relationship between the growth rate of foreign capital and the growth rate of the population indicates that industry has become increasingly labour-intensive.

Table 3.12 compares the educational level of the population — a useful measure of the quality of the labour force — in 1964 and 1982. It is clear that during the period concerned there was a significant improvement in the educational level of the population. However, only approximately 18 per cent of the population in 1982 had completed secondary school, and only slightly more than 2 per cent had completed tertiary education. From the 1982 educational structure, it is clear that Shenzhen has only a small technically trained labour force. The relatively low quality of human capital revealed in the statistics does not appear to be compatible with advanced technology production, or high-level services.

Table 3.13 shows the proportion of actual foreign investment in various sectors in 1983. The largest investment sector was manufacturing followed by real estate, which is normally labour-intensive and utilizes low-level skills. Projected from above, the manufacturing sector absorbed a large amount of labour. Because of the low level of human capital, foreign investment concentrated on low technology and labour-intensive types of enterprise in order effectively to utilize the labour force. The attraction of Shenzhen's labour

Table 3.10 Foreign Investment by Type of Contract in the Shenzhen SEZ (as at the end of February 1982)

Type of Contract	Total No. of Contracts	Total Contracted Investment (million *yuan*)	Average Investment per Project (million *yuan*)	% of Total Investment
Sole proprietorship	28	397.96	14.21	16
Co-operative production and joint ventures	130	2,071.24	15.93	82
Intermediate processing and compensation trade	1,010	65.83	4.10	2
Total	1,168	2,535.03	—	100

Note: Documentary figures are given in Hong Kong dollars and the conversion of currency is based on the exchange rate as at the end of 1981. The exchange rate of *yuan* to Hong Kong dollars was 1:3.2918. *Hong Kong Monthly Digest of Statistics* (Hong Kong, Census and Statistics Department, various issues).

Source: *Zhongguo jingji tequ nianjian* (*Yearbook of China's Special Economic Zones*) (Hong Kong, Yearbook of China's Special Economic Zones Publishing Co., 1983), p. 671.

Table 3.11 Population Growth in the Shenzhen SEZ

Year	Population	Annual Increase	% of Migration in Annual Increase	Non-rural Population (%)
1978	69,645	—	—	40
1979	72,785	3,140 (4.5%)	56.89	—
1980	80,809	8,024 (11.0%)	88.20	57.4
1981	98,337	17,528 (21.7%)	86.57	60
1982	128,616	30,279 (30.8%)	88.81	69

Note: Figures in brackets give the annual rate of increase for that year. The figure for the non-rural population in 1979 is not available.

Source: *Renkou yanjiu* (*Population Studies*), Vol. 2, 1984, p. 29.

Table 3.12 The Educational Level of the Labour Force in the Shenzhen SEZ (percentage)

	1964	1982
Primary or above	48.31	77.51
Primary	37.06	31.60
Junior secondary	7.51	25.93
Senior secondary	3.11	17.99
Tertiary	0.54	2.03
Illiterate (aged 12 or above)	23.34	9.05

Note: The 1964 figures given are for the same territorial area as the Shenzhen SEZ.

Source: *Renkou yanjiu* (*Population Studies*), Vol. 2, 1984, p. 29.

Table 3.13 The Structure of Foreign Investment in the Shenzhen SEZ as at the End of 1983 (million *yuan*)

	Actual Value of Investment	% of Total Actual Investment
Manufacturing	353.14	43.58
Agriculture (including livestock farming and fisheries)	12.18	1.50
Commerce	61.07	7.54
Transportation	10.07	1.24
Real estate and housing	214.59	26.48
Tourism	41.00	5.06
Others	118.30	14.60
Total	810.33	100.00

Note: Documentary figures are given in Hong Kong dollars and the conversion of currency is based on the exchange rate for that year. The exchange rate of *yuan* to Hong Kong dollars was 1:3.6785. *Hong Kong Monthly Digest of Statistics* (Hong Kong, Census and Statistics Department, various issues).

Source: *Renmin ribao* (*People's Daily*), 29 March 1984.

force, therefore, lies not in its skill but in its quantity of unskilled and semi-skilled cheap labour.

In order to avoid future employment problems, temporary workers have been introduced to provide a flexible labour structure that can respond to changes in demand. There are two categories of temporary worker. First, workers with certain specialized skills which are lacking in the existing population have been imported from other regions. For example, some construction workers of the Construction Co. have come from surrounding counties such as Dongguan and Huizhou. Second, because of economic incentives, local workers are leaving the rural sector for more desirable industrial jobs, thus creating a void in agricultural production. Temporary workers have had to be imported to fill this gap. From 1979 onwards, approximately 40,500 vegetable growers were imported to replace local peasants who had moved into other sectors.[32]

In 1980 the temporary population was estimated to be 50,000. By 1982 this figure had increased to 80,000.[33] The demand for labour in urban infrastructure development absorbs approximately 40 to 50 per cent of the temporary population.[34]

The dynamics of the labour force make migrant workers necessary and require an effective training programme. As Shenzhen's goal is to absorb advanced technology and modern management techniques, it must supply skilled labour to complement this development. The state must make a major commitment and investment in education and training. Human capital development to strengthen the labour force is unavoidably a key area of planning.

In planning, particularly for new towns, the size of the population is based on labour requirements. Shenzhen has adopted a population target of 800,000 by the year 2000.[35] However, as can be seen from the above, the demand for labour is mainly met by migration and temporary workers. As a function of foreign investment the demand for labour, as explained in the previous section, is unpredictable. Consequently it is impossible to project temporal changes in the population. Since the temporary population has been introduced as a flexible mechanism to cater for unpredictable demand and to reduce unemployment, it seems contradictory to determine a population size or assume a growth rate as a guide for planning.

The Regional Role of the Shenzhen SEZ

Shenzhen is located between the Zhu Jiang Delta and Hong Kong. Together, they form its immediate environment. Shenzhen has already established regional ties with its neighbours. In reviewing its regional role, the present relationship will be broadly examined, and future development will then be projected.

The Zhu Jiang Delta, one of the richest agricultural regions in China, is densely populated. Traditionally, its agricultural products and labour have been exported to Hong Kong and abroad. It is now also Shenzhen's agricultural hinterland and, as stated earlier, supplies Shenzhen with the necessary rural and low-skilled labour. As Shenzhen develops and its national significance increases, its role as a regional centre of the delta will grow, broadening and deepening its economic and political influence over the surrounding areas. The delta's development, both agricultural and industrial, and its commerce and trade, communications and administration, will be focused on and tied to the SEZ.

In reviewing the sources of foreign investment in Shenzhen, approximately 91 per cent of all investment has come from Hong Kong.[36] Shenzhen has so far not been able to attract a significant amount of overseas capital from elsewhere. If this pattern continues, Shenzhen's development will reflect the investment pattern of Hong Kong's entrepreneurs and the SEZ will become the location for subsidiaries of Hong Kong firms. Therefore its development will depend entirely on Hong Kong's economic growth and capital market. Unless Shenzhen is able to attract other overseas investment, it will become the industrialized hinterland of Hong Kong.

In 1982, 53 per cent of all investment in Shenzhen lay in the real estate sector.[37] In fact over half of actual real estate investment was in three large projects, all of which are being developed by Hong Kong firms. For example, Hopewell China Development Co. Ltd. is to invest 608 million *yuan* (HK$2,000 million) in developing 30 sq km of land in Futian as a 'new town in town'. Luen Sing Enterprise Co. Ltd. plans to invest 729 million *yuan* (HK$2,400 million) in the development of 6 sq km of land by Shenzhen Wan into a cultural and educational centre. The company also plans to establish a 260,000 sq m industrial district in Wenjindu for electronics and other industries.[38]

Given the importance of foreign capital in Shenzhen's development, it is evident that the present dominance of Hong Kong capital influences and directs the zone's economic and physical growth. Already almost all tourists visiting Shenzhen come from Hong Kong, and managers and technicians of production firms in the zone frequently travel to and from the city. Large amounts of production inputs and outputs are imported from or exported to Hong Kong and technology and management are transferred through the international city. If this investment pattern continues, Shenzhen will become economically dependent on Hong Kong, which will direct its economic development and management. As Hong Kong's economy is export- and world market-oriented, Shenzhen is likely to follow suit. The present tendency is recognized in Shenzhen, and apparently this future direction is acceptable.

Hong Kong's production, commercial and international facilities, such as its container port which is one of the busiest in the world, are abundant and their quality is high. They can and should be taken into account in Shenzhen's plans. Given their close proximity, Shenzhen can make use of some of these services and personnel, thus reducing its own investment burden. However, economic co-operation which will be mutually beneficial has yet to be planned and developed. If and when it takes place, the Hong Kong–Shenzhen agglomeration is likely to dominate the whole of the Zhu Jiang Delta, and will have a major economic impact on South China and probably South-east Asia as well.

Conclusion

In a planned economy, the state normally assumes the leading and guiding role in planning and plans for balanced and comprehensive development in order to satisfy social needs. It uses a 'permissive sequence' whereby social overhead capital is supplied prior to, and in anticipation of, directly productive activities. Planning, by locating social overhead capital, determines the size, location and economic interrelationship of directly productive activities. Under this system, the state has a great deal of control over planning investment, spatial expansion, timing and the scale of development.

In contrast, planning in a market economy is expected to take a reactive and remedial role. Private entrepreneurs set up directly productive activities to make a profit. Therefore economic growth is often unbalanced and sectoral. The sequence of development is 'compulsive', in that directly productive activities determine the demand for social overhead capital which, to a greater or lesser extent, is provided by the state. Under this system, private entrepreneurs decide on the type, scale and location of development, while planning supports, facilitates and supplements development.

The economic system of the Shenzhen SEZ, as officially proclaimed, is not entirely a planned economy, but a mixture of a planned economy and a market economy. In the above review, it is clear that the market economy 'leg', which is the engine of growth, has become the dominant initiator and controls planning. The mixed system tends to reflect the characteristics of a market economy rather than those of a planned economy. The provision of social overhead capital, which includes infrastructure, land and social services, is generally made in response to the demand of the capitalist entrepreneurs.

However, there is one difference in Shenzhen. Under a market system, entrepreneurs, when they set up firms for production, tend to make use of and take advantage of existing social overhead capital. Spatially this tendency creates agglomeration. Firms are set up close to each other where social overhead capital already exists. The agglomeration leads to the centralization of development which extends outwards contiguously. The reverse, however, is true in Shenzhen.

In its desire to capture overseas development, Shenzhen has explicitly agreed to provide advantageous conditions so that production costs can be reduced. The strong position of investors is further enforced by the limited power of the local planning units which cannot be effective in spatial control because they are primarily responsible for the provision of infrastructure. This condition relieves entrepreneurs from having to consider the availability of infrastructure when choosing a location. They are thus free to select a location of their own choosing. As a result, development projects are dispersed all over the SEZ. The local planning units, in anticipation of unpredictable future development, have to assume maximum demand and therefore tend to over-provide, thus creating short-term inefficiency.

Population growth in Shenzhen is also 'economy'-led. The population is seen as labour — a factor of production. Most of the present productive demand is for a young and moderately skilled labour force. A flexible and spatially mobile labour system — temporary labour — has been introduced, as foreign production demand for human capital is uncertain. This temporary labour force can be repatriated once it is no longer needed, thereby avoiding unemployment. The use of temporary workers also reduces the demand for housing and social services, as housing is given only to those workers employed in long-term productive work. The SEZ's solution to potential changes in the structure of labour and unemployment causes significant inequity in the distribution of housing and social services between the 'permanent' and the 'temporary' population.

Shenzhen is emerging as a transitional zone between Hong Kong and the Zhu Jiang Delta. The present inter-regional relationship indicates that Shenzhen's economy may well become integrated with that of Hong Kong and that together they may form an international regional complex. As economic control will come from Hong Kong, its market system will exert dominance over the development of Shenzhen. With the planned economy system already playing an auxiliary role, Shenzhen, in becoming an international industrial agglomeration, may become increasingly market-oriented.

In this chapter, the role of planning in Shenzhen has been analysed within its specific political and economic system, as planning is one part of the state apparatus. The purpose of planning is to perform those public functions to which it is designated. Its tasks, its effectiveness, and the manner in which they are discharged, have to be seen within this context. The political and economic system delineates the limits of, and presents opportunities for, planning. In a wider context, Shenzhen's experience provides some comprehension of how a planning system is formed and how it works, as well as its ability or inability to achieve goals and facilitate development in a mixed economy.

One of the functions of the Shenzhen SEZ is experimentation. Its specific nature has raised some unique planning issues, problems and contradictions. Thus it provides a case study for similar SEZs in other parts of China and overseas. In addition, the lessons learned in Shenzhen may also guide future development elsewhere in China, particularly in the 14 coastal cities and Hainan Island which are now being opened up to foreign investment.

Notes

1. Hong Kong Federation of Students (ed.), *Jingji tequ mianmianguan* (*Aspects of the Special Economic Zones*) (Hong Kong, Wide Angle Press, 1983), p. 92.
2. *Beijing Review*, Vol. 27, No. 4, 23 January 1984, p. 25.
3. *Beijing Review*, Vol. 27, No. 4, 23 January 1984, p. 31.
4. *Zhongguo jingji tequ nianjian* (*Yearbook of China's Special Economic Zones*) (Hong Kong, Yearbook of China's Special Economic Zones Publishing Co., 1983), pp. 46–8.
5. *Jingji daobao* (*Economic Reporter*), Vol. 1772, 7 June 1982, p. 13, and 5 July 1982, p. 8; and *Gangao jingji* (*Hong Kong and Macau Economic Digest*), Vols. 3–4, 1984, pp. 34–42.
6. Kwan-yiu Wong, 'Factors of Development in the Shenzhen SEZ: An Evalua-

tion', *Chinese University of Hong Kong, Department of Geography, Occasional Paper*, No. 28, 1982, pp. 22–3.

7. Hong Kong Federation of Students (1983), p. 33.

8. *Beijing Review*, Vol. 27, No. 4, 23 January 1984, p. 27.

9. Sun Ru (ed.), *Zhongguo jingji tequ zaiqianjin* (*China's Special Economic Zones in Progress*) (Beijing, Chinese Financial Economic Press, 1983), p. 85.

10. Hong Kong Federation of Students (1983), p. 89.

11. Hong Kong Federation of Students (1983), p. 90.

12. Hong Kong Federation of Students (1983), p. 90.

13. *Wen wei po*, 24 June 1982.

14. The functions of the Shenzhen SEZ Development Co. are land development and negotiations on development; those of the Shenzhen SEZ Construction Co. are the provision of environmental protection, building materials, gas, water, storm drainage and sewerage systems, roads, housing, and so on. See David K.Y. Chu (ed.), *Zhongguo zuida di jingji tequ — Shenzhen* (*The Largest Special Economic Zone of China — Shenzhen*) (Hong Kong, Wide Angle Press, 1983), p. 6.

15. *Jingji daobao*, Vols. 1838–9, 1 October 1983, p. 36.

16. *Ta kung pao*, 24 November 1981.

17. *Jingji daobao*, Vols. 1838–9, 1 October 1983, p. 37.

18. *Jingji daobao*, Vols. 1838–9, 1 October 1983, p. 37.

19. *Jingji daobao*, Vol. 1812, 28 March 1983, p. 26.

20. *Jingji daobao*, Vol. 1845, 14 November 1983, p. 17.

21. *Jingji dili* (*Economic Geography*), Vol. 1, 1983, p. 46.

22. *Jingji tequ dili wenji* (*Collections of Essays on the Geography of the Shenzhen SEZ*), Vol. 1, October 1981, pp. 21–2.

23. *Renkou yanjiu* (*Population Studies*), Vol. 2, 1984, pp. 21–2.

24. *Gangao jingji*, Vol. 26, June 1984, pp. 53–4.

25. *Redai dili* (*Tropical Geography*), Vol. 1, No. 1, 1981, pp. 54–9.

26. This figure is obtained by estimating that the standard per capita floor area is 10 sq m (another estimate of this standard gives 6 sq m, see note 25), since workers' housing built in 1982 could only accommodate approximately 10,000 people (see note 27) and the estimated total housing area for workers was 100,000 sq m.

27. *Shenzhen tequbao* (*Shenzhen Special Economic Zone Post*), 20 December 1982.

28. *Nanfang ribao* (*Southern Daily*), 16 July 1984.

29. *Gangao jingji*, Vol. 22, February 1984, p. 3.

30. *Ta kung pao*, 26 February 1982.

31. *Jingji tequ dili wenji*, Vol. 1, October 1981, p. 22.

32. *Jingji tequ dili wenji*, Vol. 1, October 1981, p. 23.

33. *Jingji tequ dili wenji*, Vol. 1, October 1981, p. 23; and *Renkou yanjiu*, Vol. 2, 1984, p. 29. In China, 'temporary population' usually refers to those people who are not registered and have no permanent residential status in the place where they settle.

34. *Jingji tequ dili wenji*, Vol. 1, October 1981, p. 23.

35. *Jingji tequ mianmianguan* (1983), p. 4.

36. *Jingji daobao*, Vol. 1745, 11 November 1981, p. 8.

37. *Zhongguo jingji tequ nianjian* (1983), p. 671.

38. *Ta kung pao*, 13 November 1981.

4. Environmental Protection in the Shenzhen Special Economic Zone: Achievements, Problems and Implications

K.C. LAM

Introduction*

By the end of this century, Shenzhen will have been developed into a large and modern industrial, residential and commercial complex with accommodation and job opportunities for 800,000 people. China expects, through the experience of Shenzhen and the other special economic zones (SEZs), to gain the modern advanced technology and management techniques which will speed up the nation's modernization programme. In the development of the SEZs, China provides land and labour, while foreign investors contribute capital and technology which are in limited supply domestically. This development has created all the complexities of a free-market economy in a socialist framework, and has posed a new challenge to the national environmental protection strategy which has proved to be fairly successful in other parts of China.[1]

Learning to manage the environmental problems arising from rapid development in an institutional framework that is so different from that in other parts of China will test the ingenuity of Shenzhen's environmental managers and planners. The meagre information available to date suggests that the present environmental quality has fallen short of earlier expectations,[2] and that some of those environmental problems which typify other Western industrial cities are now gradually emerging in Shenzhen.

The Shenzhen authorities are not unaware of the need to protect the environment. An Environmental Protection Office (EPO) was in fact established in Shenzhen as early as 1980. There have also been repeated calls since then to turn Shenzhen into a 'garden city'.[3] The Outline Master Development Plan of Shenzhen (Fig. 4.1) and the town plans of various districts all point to a conscientious effort on the part of the local authorities to protect the environment.

As in other socialist countries, China's environmental policy is formulated at the top level by the central government. Thus the basic approach to environmental management in Shenzhen is borrowed largely from China. Before the 1970s, China did not have any explicit environmental policy; environmental management was merely part of her economic and political

*This research was supported by the Board of Trustees of Lingnan University, New York.

Fig. 4.1 The Shenzhen Outline Master Development Plan

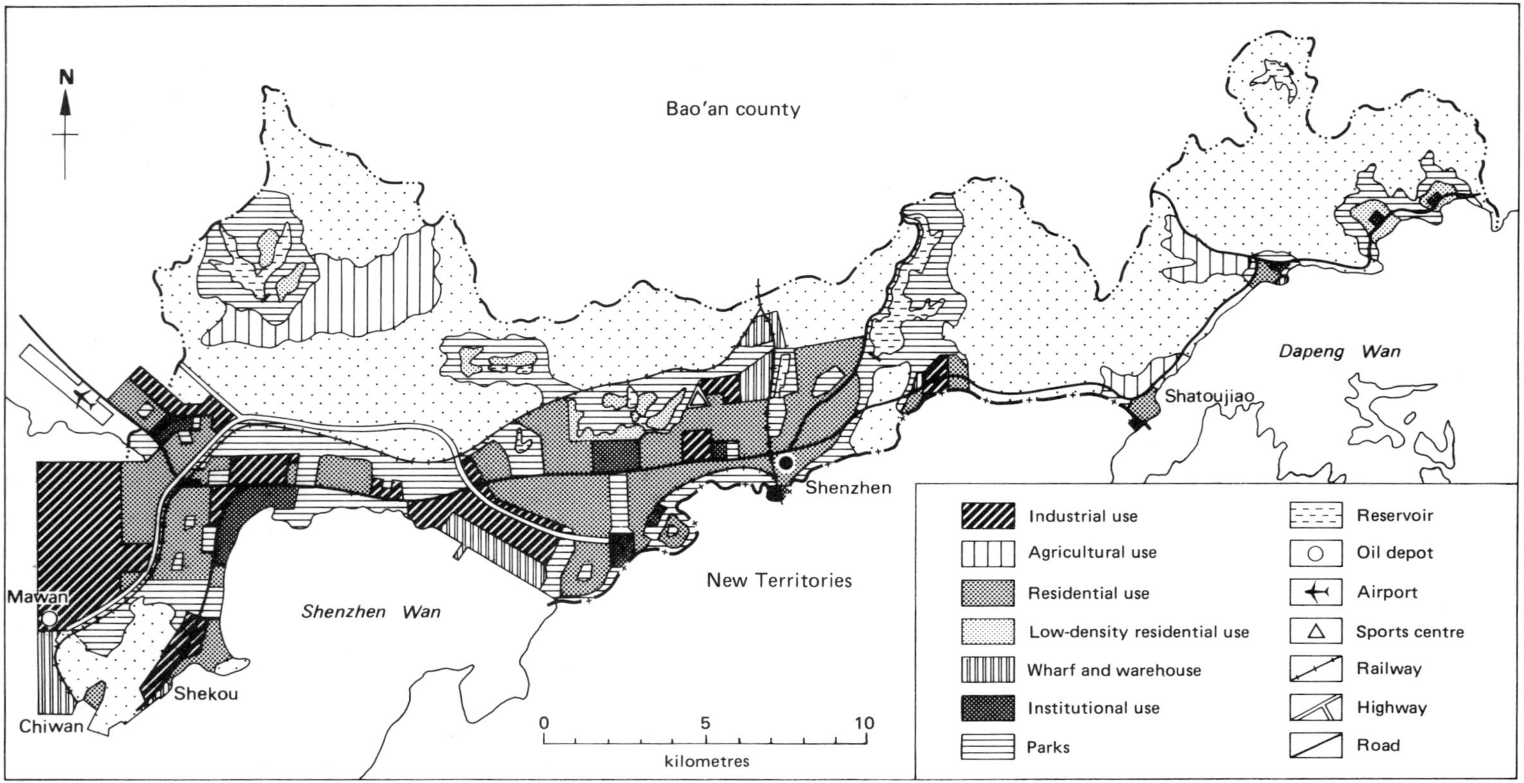

policies. In the last decade, a more formal environmental policy has begun to take shape. In practical terms, the principal guidelines are comprehensive planning, rational land-use allocation, integrated resource utilization and environmental impact assessment. It is evident that this strategy is focused mainly on productivity and resource conservation rather than on pollution control. Policy statements in national publications constantly reiterate the need to eliminate the 'three wastes' (air, water and solid wastes) and to recycle whatever is recyclable. Multiple utilization of resources is seen as a way to promote production, without which the quality of life and the environment cannot be enhanced.

Whilst this approach has achieved no mean results in other parts of China, its appropriateness to Shenzhen merits close scrutiny because of the unique economic and institutional setting of the SEZ. Although Shenzhen is supposed to follow the national environmental policy, it has departed from the nation's approach in that it relies heavily on modern capital-intensive waste treatment technology. This is a reflection of the Shenzhen authorities' desire to acquire modern technology. Again, in spite of the enormous capital expenditure which such programmes may incur, the cost-effectiveness of these programmes seems not to have been adequately evaluated.

The fundamental issues facing Shenzhen's environmental managers and planners are thus both complex and varied. Is the national environmental strategy appropriate for Shenzhen? How adequate is the approach adopted in Shenzhen, which largely depends on technical, architectural and engineering solutions embodied in a master outline plan? How cost-effective is the modern waste treatment programme? And, above all, what can be learnt from the Shenzhen experience so that any mistakes made may be avoided in other SEZs or in the nation's modernization programme?

These are some of the issues which this chapter attempts to address. In tackling them, the current environmental situation in Shenzhen, likely future trends in light of the development programme and the work of the EPO are outlined. The opportunities and constraints of environmental management in a rapidly developing urban complex with a unique economic and institutional setting are then discussed.

The Environment

Prior to the establishment of the SEZ, Shenzhen was a small township with a population of less than 20,000, engaged mainly in agricultural activities. The current scheduled increase in population and in agricultural and industrial activities will bring significant environmental changes. The following sections attempt to describe the present situation and assess the environmental impact of various projects.

The Quality of Stream Water

Most of the 160 streams in Shenzhen are short and gentle in gradient in the lower stretches. They flow either into Dapeng Wan in the east or Shenzhen

Wan in the west (Fig. 4.1). The longest is the Shenzhen He which drains an area of 312 sq km and flows into Shenzhen Wan. Velocities in these streams are very low for most of the year. A study undertaken in the early 1980s indicated that the water quality of the upper courses of these streams is good.[4] However, when these streams flow through small settlements in the lower courses, the water quality deteriorates. The most severe water pollution is found in the lower stretch of the Shenzhen He, particularly in the section between Wenjindu and Yumincun where the flow is sluggish and the water black. During the dry season, organic muds are exposed on the river banks, producing an offensive smell.

The three principal determinants of the quality of stream water in Shenzhen are the amounts of industrial effluent, animal manure and domestic sewage that are discharged into the streams. Of these three, the latter two are likely to increase substantially in the future, thereby causing the quality of the stream water to deteriorate.

Before the establishment of the SEZ in 1979, there were very few industries in Shenzhen. Although industrial development is emphasized in the SEZ programme, the Shenzhen authorities only welcome industries using advanced techniques and equipment and those that are not pollution risks.[5] Existing and projected industrial development is thus not likely to produce heavy pollution loads.[6]

important

On the other hand, it is anticipated that flourishing poultry and pig farming will aggravate stream pollution. The agricultural statistics show that the chicken population increased sixteen times during the first four years of the development of the SEZ.[7] Although no data is available for pigs, it is highly probable that the pig population has also increased by a similar order of magnitude. Unlike in other parts of China, chickens and pigs in the zone are no longer kept by ordinary farmers as a sideline business, but are bred in hundreds in large feedlots. This trend of specialization and greater sophistication is undesirable environmentally for two reasons. First, agriculture is gradually losing its valuable traditional role of waste assimilation. Second, large-scale pig and poultry farming can become an environmental nuisance, as the experience of Hong Kong has shown.[8]

The greatest increase in pollution load is likely to come from domestic sewage. Before 1979, only a small portion of the zone was sewered and domestic sewage was discharged into the watercourses without prior treatment. As a result of the rapid increase in population, the amount of domestic sewage is also expected to increase, from 1.9 million cu m in 1982 to 20 million cu m in the year 2000.[9] Like chicken and pig manure, domestic sewage is not only a source of organic matter which may cause oxygen depletion, but is also a rich source of nitrogen and phosphorus, which enhances eutrophication. There are now plans to sewer these watercourses to divert the sewage and storm-water out of the built-up area. Since the bulk of the sewage would finally converge on the Shenzhen He, pollution of the river is likely to be further exacerbated. The Shenzhen and Hong Kong governments have placed a very high priority on the mitigation of this pollution, and the matter is now being taken up by a joint expert working group.

Another matter of increasing concern is the pollution of water-supply reservoirs caused by recreational activities. In 1982, there were six large dams and over a hundred small dams in the zone.[10] Apart from being water-supply reservoirs, some of these dams have also been developed as holiday resorts,[11] where the foreshores are used for picnicking, horse-riding and other forms of passive recreation; while the water body is used for activities such as fishing, boating and paddle-skiing. Recreational activity on and around water-supply reservoirs is a widely accepted practice in some countries (for example, the United States and Australia) where no apparent public health hazard has been reported. However, it should be noted that in those countries where the recreational use of water-supply reservoirs is encouraged, most of the visitors are car-owners who seldom stay or camp overnight. Furthermore, unlike the SEZ, very few holiday resorts in these countries are actually built on the reservoir foreshore. It can thus be foreseen that unless strenuous efforts are taken to prevent pollution, domestic sewage and even stable manure may impair the use of these reservoirs. This would lead to serious problems because, according to recent estimates, the demand for water in Shenzhen will outstrip the potential supply before the year 2000.[12]

The Quality of Marine Water

The Shenzhen SEZ is bounded in the south-east by Dapeng Wan, in the south-west by Shenzhen Wan and in the west by the Zhu Jiang Kou (Pearl River Estuary).

In spite of the slow exchange of water in Dapeng Wan with the adjoining ocean, the quality of the water there is generally good. Since the bulk of urban and industrial development will be concentrated in the central and western parts of the zone, the water in Dapeng Wan is likely to remain clean. This is essential to the operation of Dameisha and Xiaomeisha as tourist resorts and Yantian as a fishing and agricultural settlement.

The quality of the water in Shenzhen Wan is a major cause of concern because it is already poor in certain parts, containing elevated levels of biochemical oxygen demand, phosphates and nitrates. The bay receives waste water carried by the Shenzhen He as well as a few grossly polluted streams on the Hong Kong side. Dispersion of pollutants in the bay is poor because the water which flows westward during the ebb tide is returned during the flood. There have been recent reports of periodic kills of fish and marine invertebrates and of sporadic algal blooms. All these indicate that the water in the bay is becoming unacceptably eutrophic, and any increase in the pollution load as a result of urban development may further aggravate the problem.

The coastal flats on the eastern bank of the Zhu Jiang Kou from Shekou to Shajiao (Fig. 4.2) are used predominantly for oyster cultivation. A total of 11,000 people from six communes are engaged in this activity. The oyster business is going to be affected by three projects related to the SEZ: a coal-fired power station at Shajiao, a petrochemical industrial complex at Mawan and a proposed sewage outfall off the coast at Mawan. At present, the power required by the zone is provided by the Guangdong province electricity network. This will have to be augmented by three local power utilities as the

Fig. 4.2 The Location of the Shenzhen SEZ

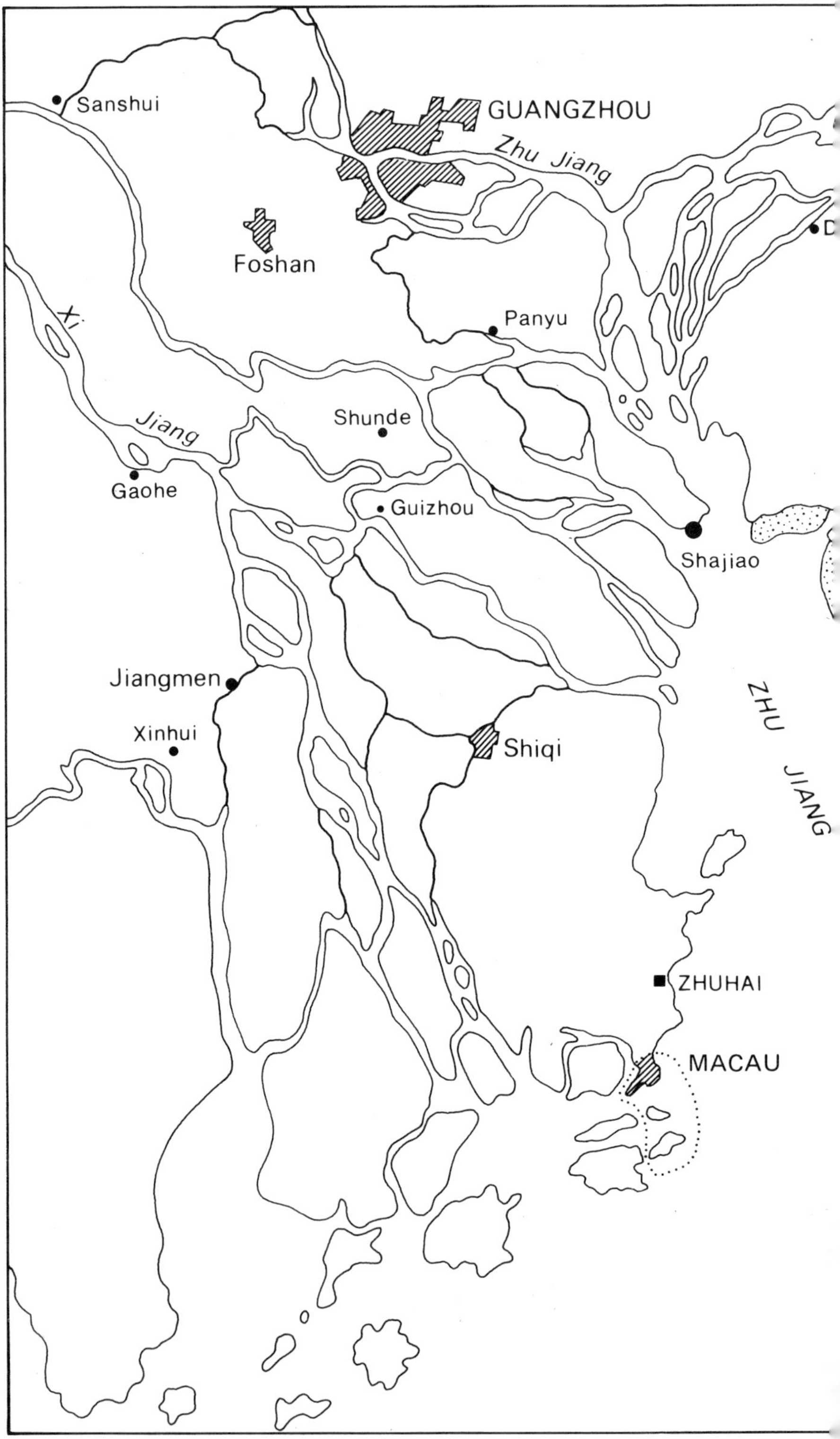

Boluo
Dong Jiang
Huizhou
Shima He
Huidong
Zhangmutou
Danshui
Daya Wan
SHENZHEN
NEW TERRITORIES
KOWLOON
HONG KONG ISLAND
N
Proposed nuclear plant
Proposed coal-fired power plant
Proposed oil-fired power plant
Oyster beds
Shenzhen SEZ

zone continues to develop. In addition to the 1,800 MW nuclear power station at Daya Wan,[13] there will also be a 250 MW oil-fired power station at Mawan and a 1,200 MW coal-fired power station at Shajiao. The potential impact of these power utilities on the surrounding environment is reported to be minimal.[14] However, the development of the petrochemical complex at Mawan is likely to have detrimental effects on fishing and mariculture activities in the Zhu Jiang Kou because, even at the moment, levels of oil and phenol in the water already exceed the country's surface water quality criteria.[15] The effects of a recent proposal to construct a sewage outfall off the coast at Mawan, as an alternative to the apparently more expensive sewage treatment programme put forth in the master plan, may be even more detrimental. Should this plan be implemented, the sewage collected in the zone would only undergo primary treatment before its discharge into the Zhu Jiang Kou via a long submarine outfall. This has recently been criticized[16] as an attempt to court environmental disaster because the water of the Zhu Jiang Kou is already eutrophic, as indicated by the increasing incidence of red tides. Any further increase in the sewage load will be beyond the assimilative capacity of the river estuary.

The Quality of the Air

The meteorological and topographical conditions in Shenzhen are such that there is potential for serious air pollution.[17] The major part of the zone is enclosed by a ring of hills rising to about 500 m in the north and north-east which forms a basin in which air pollutants may be trapped when the south-west wind prevails.

Early reports based on an environmental baseline study conducted in 1981 indicated that the air quality in the zone was well within the Chinese standard for residential areas.[18] This is in stark contrast to other large Chinese cities where the air quality is considered to be the poorest in the world, with particulate levels up to 10 times those of major US cities.[19] The high levels of particulates and sulphur dioxide in Chinese cities can be attributed to the consumption of coal as a primary residential cooking and heating fuel and as the major source of industrial energy. Fortunately, Shenzhen is free from this particulate and sulphur dioxide type of pollution because coal constitutes only 18.9 per cent of energy consumption,[20] as opposed to the national average of 70 per cent.[21]

However, a different type of pollution is gradually emerging in Shenzhen. More recent air-quality data[22] indicate that levels of nitrogen oxides and ozone, both major constituents of photochemical smog, have been rising gradually since 1981 and are now approaching the national ambient air-quality criteria. This trend is probably going to continue for three reasons. First, the number of vehicles in the zone has been escalating. A recent estimate put the vehicle population in the year 2000 at 53,000, a fivefold increase since 1982. By the end of this century, the total automobile emission volume could reach the following levels: carbon monoxide, 36.6 tonnes; hydrocarbons, 3.1 tonnes; and nitrogen oxides, 1.74 tonnes.[23] Second, the urban form and layout of buildings in Shenzhen are very different from those of other Chinese cities. Instead of dense, low-rise urban development, the Shenzhen urban landscape is now characterized by street canyons and high-rise buildings. This urban form is not particularly conducive to the dispersion of air pollutants. Because of the high level of solar radiation in Shenzhen, vehicle exhaust gases trapped in the street canyons are likely to form photochemical smog. Third, it can be anticipated that the petrochemical complex at Mawan will give off a substantial amount of hydrocarbon, an important catalyst in photochemical smog formation. The hydrocarbon emitted by or evaporated from the petrochemical complex may be carried by the westerly winds in the summer along east–west oriented street canyons to the city core to react with vehicle exhaust gases.

However, the improvement in air-flow conditions resulting from the construction of dual carriageways in the zone may partly mitigate the above effects. It should also be noted that a substantial proportion of vehicles in the zone are imported: the pollutant emission levels from such cars are significantly lower than from those of Chinese manufacture.[24]

The Disposal of Municipal Waste

The proper disposal of municipal waste is an aspect which has not been given much consideration by the Shenzhen authorities. In 1982, per capita waste generation in the zone amounted to 1.3 kg per day, more than that of Hong Kong or any other Chinese city. It is estimated that by the year 2000, the waste generated will amount to 0.33 million tonnes a year.

At present, this waste is not incinerated or used for reclamation, as is the case in Hong Kong; nor is it salvaged and reutilized, as in other Chinese cities. Most of it is dumped openly on the hill slopes to the north of the city.[25] This is environmentally most undesirable, because the leachates from these open dumps could migrate southward, polluting not only nearby surface water bodies and streams, but also the underground water aquifers which make up about one quarter of the total water resources of Shenzhen.

The disposal of municipal waste is admittedly not an easy task. Escalating fuel costs will probably make incineration less and less attractive in the future. Coastal tipping sites are not easy to find because the coastline in the eastern portion of the zone is designated mainly for recreational purposes, whereas in the west the coastal flats are either oyster beds or mangroves which have to be preserved. Thus it appears that tipping sites on land will have to be used. In fact, controlled tipping could be integrated with land reclamation to alleviate flood problems that have been aggravated by the urbanization process.

Noise and Other Nuisances

In addition to causing water and air pollution, development in Shenzhen may also cause nuisances such as noise, odours and the loss of amenity.

Noise is a serious environmental problem in other major Chinese cities,[26] caused mainly by the lack of buffer zones between roads and dwellings and also by ineffective traffic management. Information on noise levels in the zone is very sketchy. A study undertaken by the Shenzhen EPO in the early

1980s indicated that except in the city core, where levels in excess of 80 dB(A) were recorded, noise levels in Shenzhen were within acceptable limits. The effects of the projected increase in vehicles on the acoustic environment are difficult to assess at the moment. Yet positive measures appear to have been incorporated into the master plan to ensure that noise sources are separated from sensitive users. Trees are also to be planted along the major carriageways as local amenities as well as noise barriers. The high proportion of imported vehicles with much lower noise levels also helps to keep the general noise level down.

Nonetheless, an important aspect which the Outline Master Development Plan seems to have overlooked is traffic planning and management, particularly the provision of cycleways. As in other major Chinese cities, cycling is still the most important means of transportation. This mode of transport should be encouraged, not only to take advantage of the flat terrain in the built-up area of Shenzhen, but also to reduce air and noise pollution. Segregated cycleways should be planned to reduce the likely conflict between cyclists, pedestrians and vehicles, so that the use of horns, a major source of excessive traffic noise in China, can be minimized.

The Environmental Control Programme

Responsibility for pollution control in Shenzhen is vested mainly in the EPO. However, the work of a few other government departments also has significant bearing on the environment. Among these are the Introduction and Discussion Department, the Planning Department and the Environmental Hygiene Unit.

The Introduction and Discussion Department is a division of the Shenzhen SEZ Development Co., which handles all enquiries and applications related to the setting up of factories or other undertakings in the zone. Investment proposals are carefully studied and screened by this department, and environmental pollution is one of the key factors considered in determining whether or not a proposal is accepted. This procedure has enabled the Shenzhen authorities to accept only industries which do not produce excessive pollutants.

The Planning Department is chiefly responsible for formulating the Outline Master Development Plan and the Outline Social and Economic Development Plan. Experts were brought in from various parts of China and Hong Kong to evaluate these plans before they were finalized in 1982. Communication between the environmental specialists and other professionals — engineers, planners, architects and geographers — has allowed environmental considerations to be put at the forefront of decision-making. This is borne out by the Outline Master Development Plan, which has sensibly put the major emission sources far away from the zone (Fig. 4.2) and which has also provided adequate segregation between residential and industrial land uses. Moreover, a substantial portion of the land available, equivalent to 16 cu m per person, has been set aside as a green belt to improve the quality of the environment.

When it was first established in 1980, the Shenzhen EPO had a staff of about 20 professionals and 80 technicians. Its main duties are to monitor the environment, evaluate development projects, enforce environmental regulations and specify conditions or control measures with which investors must comply.

In collaboration with Zhongshan University in Guangzhou, the EPO undertook a comprehensive environmental baseline study of the air, water, noise, soil and vegetation, and health conditions of residents in the zone between 1980 and 1982. This study not only provides the reference against which future monitoring results can be compared, but also depicts those problem areas which warrant immediate attention. For example, the baseline study has called for a detailed analysis of the waste assimilative capacity of the Shenzhen He, a study scheduled to be completed in 1985.

As in most Western nations, environmental impact assessment (EIA) has gained acceptance in China as a major environmental planning tool and as a positive means of preventing environmental problems that would otherwise be expensive or difficult to control. In Shenzhen, EIA has largely been undertaken by consultants, mostly academics from various tertiary institutions in China, and has already been applied to a number of major development projects, including the nuclear power plant at Daya Wan and the coal-fired power station at Shajiao.[27] These studies have explicitly identified the potential environmental impact of these projects and have indicated mitigation measures that are needed to alleviate the problem.

At present, the Shenzhen EPO follows closely the regulations, decrees and environmental standards promulgated by the central government.[28] These environmental measures are meant to be applicable nation-wide. Such an assumption has, in fact, overlooked the possible variations in the environmental assimilative capacity in different parts of the country. This uniform and very rigid approach was rectified in 1983 through the enactment of the Shenzhen Environmental Protection Regulations which bestow on the local authorities more flexibility and freedom in formulating their own environmental standards and administrative procedures.

In enforcing the Chinese Environmental Protection Law, the Shenzhen EPO has censured a number of industrial undertakings which were found to have caused significant damage to the surrounding environment. These have included a laundry at Shahe, a toy factory and an iron and steel factory at Shekou and a large bleaching and dyeing factory at Kuichong.[29] Action will soon be taken against 15 Hong Kong-based tanneries which, because of stiffer environmental legislation in Hong Kong, took refuge in Shenzhen in the mid-1970s. The closing down of the bleaching and dyeing factory at Kuichong has caused some concern among prospective investors. This factory was introduced in early 1980 when the present stringent industrial policy had not yet developed. Despite the fact that the factory had a package wastewater treatment plant of its own, the effluent from the factory did not meet the national emission standards, and the quality of a nearby stream and sea inlet was seriously impaired. The closing down of this moderately large and modern factory indicates that the Shenzhen government has become rather firm in warding off polluting industries in the zone.

A Critique of the Shenzhen Environmental Strategy

From the above description, it is apparent that the Shenzhen authorities are determined to make the SEZ a clean and pleasant place in which to live and work. There is good reason to believe that such efforts will bring promising results.

First, Shenzhen is a newly developed area free from those pollution problems that have been troubling other Chinese cities. As a totally new project, the speed and comprehensive nature of development provide enormous scope and potential for incorporating environmental considerations into the planning process. In few places in the world has there been such an opportunity for the benefits of environmental planning to be realized so quickly and with such dramatic effect.

Moreover, the need to protect the environment was recognized at a very early stage in the development of the zone when considerable overseas experience in urban environmental management had been accumulated and the tools and methods of environmental control were already well understood. Indeed, this experience and knowledge are the greatest assets of environmental planning in Shenzhen, and they have allowed the Shenzhen authorities to infuse environmental ingredients into the economic and industrial policies at the planning stage of the SEZ.

Environmental protection in most countries is often hampered by a lack of sufficient resources. This does not appear to be true in Shenzhen. As a state project, the SEZ is apparently endowed with sufficient funds for all essential works and projects. This has perhaps enabled the Shenzhen authorities to embark on an ambitious sewerage and waste-water treatment programme (Fig. 4.3). To date, two secondary sewage treatment plants, costing more than 30 million *yuan*, have been put into operation at Shekou and Shangbu. Eight more similar plants have been planned to treat all sewage generated within the zone, at about seven to eight times the cost. This is in stark contrast to other Chinese cities where, on average, only 15 per cent of the sewage is treated, mostly only to the primary level.[30] When completed, such a comprehensive programme of sewage treatment will doubtless attract the envy of municipal engineers all over the world.

Unlike other Chinese cities, most of the industries in the zone are new and use imported modern technology. This is a sharp departure from the country's long-standing adherence to maximum self-reliance based on indigenous efforts or on technology borrowed from the Soviet Union in the 1950s. Greater use of energy and raw materials with older technology naturally results in higher pollution levels, and as the waste control technology on older processes is either missing or inadequate, serious air and water quality degradation follow. The environmental benefits of rejecting in-

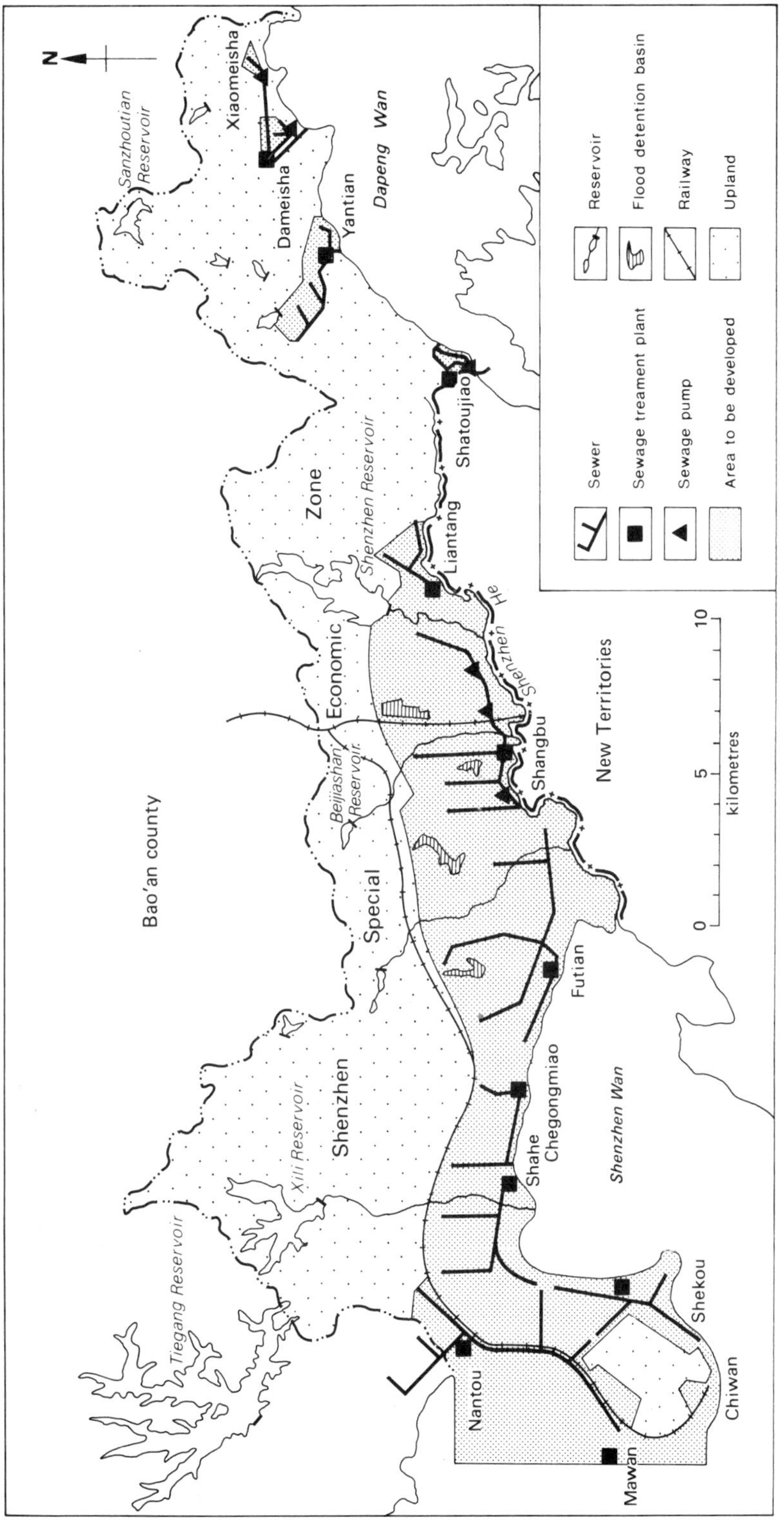

Fig. 4.3 The Sewage Treatment Programme

efficient and outdated technology in favour of the latest technology and managerial skills are obvious.[31] For example, particulate and sulphur dioxide emissions are much lower in Shenzhen than in other Chinese cities. Even in the realm of transportation, slow-moving and noisy tow-trucks which characterize the street scene of many Chinese cities are rarely seen in Shenzhen.

The environmental strategy of Shenzhen is, in a nutshell, heavily reliant on modern technology guided by comprehensive environmental planning. Pollution is controlled through heavy investment in waste treatment programmes. This strategy has many obvious merits. Yet is there room for complacency? There is no guarantee that Shenzhen will be free from all environmental ills; pollution problems different in nature from those in other Chinese cities are gradually emerging in Shenzhen. The lack of rural-urban integration, the financial burden of massive waste treatment programmes, the absence of a setting conducive to resource recycling, the seemingly unquenchable quest for rapid development, and the inflexible administrative set-up may all prove to be stumbling blocks in the battle against pollution.

What has been overlooked in the strategic planning of Shenzhen, and this is perhaps also true of other SEZs, is the integration of the city with the countryside. Unfortunately, the SEZs are so planned that they are separated administratively, and to a lesser extent also functionally, from the countryside. This is a departure from the socialist planning paradigm of maximum rural-urban integration.[32] The result, in the case of Shenzhen, is that the city has lost its valuable rural base to assimilate its waste. Sewage and municipal waste are thus dumped irresponsibly or have to be disposed of by very expensive technical means. The integration of the rural and urban sectors is in fact not only philosophically palatable and economically desirable, but also ecologically viable.

A heavy commitment of capital in the provision of infrastructure and massive waste treatment facilities also poses problems, although the capital required can be provided by the state. If industrial production does not keep up with capital investment, there will be a great deal of unused capacity, thereby creating a tremendous opportunity cost to the state. On the other hand, if the waste treatment programmes are held up, the sporadic development scattered over the zone would entail unabated pollution in many localities. This is the dilemma which one suspects the Shenzhen authorities are facing and is probably the reason why the massive sewage treatment programme has been slowed down pending the results of an investigation into less expensive alternatives.

The policy of attracting foreign capital and advanced technology to expedite economic development has disadvantages as well as advantages. In Shenzhen, as in other SEZs, the type, scale and technology of the industries introduced are primarily determined by the investors.[33] Apart from screening out polluting industries, the state has little influence on the industrial mix. This is very unfortunate because integrated resource utilization and recycling is dependent upon a suitable socio-economic structure and the right industrial mix. But neither of these conditions exists in Shenzhen. Furthermore, since the industries are privately owned rather than state-owned, there is very little co-operation and integration between different industrial undertakings which could have enabled the waste from one to be used in another. In other words, unlike other parts of China, Shenzhen lacks the kind of economic and social organization that is conducive to the elimination of waste through multiple utilization. On the contrary, Shenzhen possesses an industrial structure of very little diversity resulting in contending interests amongst investors. This is again a sharp departure from the Chinese strategy of relying on integrated resource utilization and recycling to take care of industrial waste.

The acquisition of advanced technology has also brought environmental repercussions, some of which Chinese environmental specialists have as yet little practical experience in tackling. For example, motor vehicles have produced pollutants that may form photochemical smog and industries have generated inorganic waste that is difficult to recycle. In addition, before long, Shenzhen's environmental managers will have to seek ways in which to get rid of hazardous nuclear waste.

The quest for modernization in Shenzhen has also created a rectilinear, dull and harsh urban landscape. In the drive to expedite the development process, a substantial portion of the picturesque landscape in Shenzhen has been 'levelled and aligned' to give way to high-rise buildings and street canyons. Even the tranquil water-storage reservoirs have been turned into hustling holiday resorts. Very few of the once treasured historic relics, luxuriant *fung-shui* woodlands and enchanting bird sanctuaries have been spared the tyranny of urban encroachment.[34] In fact, there can be no excuse for such thoughtless transformation. Development should not just mean industrialization and urbanization, but should also provide a humanistic milieu that facilitates the development of latent human capabilities, and that addresses basic human needs, including the human inclination to relate to the past and occasionally to retreat to nature.

In Shenzhen, one is also struck by the lack of flexibility in the implementation of the national environmental policy. This is a reflection of the 'top down' environmental decision-making system in China which allows very little feedback from those who are concerned with environmental control at the local level to the central decision-makers. The 'blanket' approach also fails to meet the special needs of Shenzhen's unique economic and institutional structure. For example, air pollution control is still very much reliant on the 'high stack' approach. Whilst this is a simple method of pollution control in densely developed low-rise cities, it is not equally effective in a high-rise city such as Shenzhen. Implementation of any policy should involve the judicious selection of different environmental instruments, such as prohibition, standards, charges, tax schemes, land-use controls, subsidies and court action, all tailored to suit the local situation. Appropriate controls, rather than mere tough censure, should be used to provide the optimum mix of 'carrots and sticks', and incentives and disincentives to guide investors in the choice of inputs, processes, and outputs of activities that affect the environment. Supportive measures should also be offered, wherever possible, to ease the hardship which foreign investors may face in a new environment. These may take the form of technical advice on waste treatment, or seminars to inform investors where they stand as regards environmental legislation, and how they can conform in the most cost-effective manner.

Lastly, although environmental assessment is an effective measure, the procedure has to be given more thought and has to be formalized. At present, environmental assessment is only undertaken for large projects. However, the pace of development in Shenzhen has been so rapid that the 'go-ahead' for a certain project often precedes the completion of environmental assessment (for example, the nuclear power plant and the petrochemical complex). Environmental assessment has thus become a justification vehicle rather than an effective environmental control measure. Furthermore, environmental assessment should not be a 'once and for all' exercise. To be effective, it has to be a continuous process that provides constant feedback for project implementation, adjustment and amendment. This constant feedback is needed to identify and correct minor planning errors to prevent them from getting out of control. In Shenzhen, the exclusion of small projects from environmental assessment has also proved to be unsatisfactory. An environmental consultant to the local authorities has recently succinctly pointed out the problems created by the hundreds of small quarries in Shenzhen: dust, visual blight and disruption and contamination of watercourses.[35]

Conclusion

It has been one of the objectives of this chapter to crystallize, from the experience in Shenzhen, the ingredients of environmental management which might benefit China. The Shenzhen experience is valuable in that it is probably a microcosm of what a modernized China may become.

Outsiders' impressions of the Chinese environment have changed significantly since the latter half of the 1970s. In the first half of the decade, it was widely believed that the Chinese environment was a Maoist miracle: the country was clean and green; soil erosion was checked by massive afforestation; pests were effectively controlled by biological methods; and waste was thoroughly recycled.[36] This view ceased to be held after the downfall of the 'Gang of Four' as more and more information concerning the environmental situation in China was gradually revealed. It is now known that environmental pollution in China is at least as serious as in any large modernized nation.[37] Environmental deterioration in China is not a consequence of affluence, as in some Western nations, but rather of industrial inefficiency.[38] Fortunately, Chinese society is so structured that waste is efficiently recycled and reutilized. At the end of the 1970s, China embarked on a very ambitious modernization programme which would not only improve her industrial efficiency but would also change her economic and social structure. These goals have a considerable bearing on the pattern of waste generation and reutilization. It would be interesting to research the effects of these changes on the quality of the environment in China.

Since the Chinese modernization programme is based largely on high-level foreign technology, a central problem has been the source of capital for massive investment. Owing to a lack of sufficient foreign exchange, the Chinese government has scaled down its modernization programme. Modernization has taken a new turn in that a number of SEZs have been established. These enable the country to acquire modern advanced technology and management skills without draining the limited public revenue. Instead of relying solely on state capital resources, the development of the SEZs is partly financed by foreign investors. This has created a uniquely 'mixed' economic system — the co-existence of the market economy and the centrally planned economy.

The development strategy of the Shenzhen SEZ in fact comes very close to the spirit of China's modernization programme. The problems that have occurred in the zone may well occur elsewhere in China in the process of modernization. This chapter has pinpointed some of the environmental problems. They include the inefficient recycling of waste, the emergence of new types of pollution, and the very low utility of massive capital-intensive waste treatment programmes. Some of these shortcomings can be attributed to the rigid application of the national environmental policy in an SEZ where the economic structure and the institutional framework are so very different. These problems are not insurmountable. Yet they do require that environmental managers give more consideration to rural-urban integration and a type of urban development which conserves resources. They also suggest that an approach that adopts technical, architectural and engineering solutions within the context of a master plan may not necessarily guarantee success in environmental management.

Notes

1. K.C. Lam, 'Environmental Management in Developing Countries: Some Lessons from China and Hong Kong', *Asian Geographer*, Vol. 2, 1982, pp. 67–79; and F. Sandbach, *Principles of Pollution Control* (New York, Longman, 1982).
2. Hou Jianqiu, 'Fazhan jingji yao zhu yi huanjing baohu' ('Emphasizing Environmental Protection in Economic Development'), paper presented at the Urban Ecology Conference, November 1984, Shenzhen; and Tang Yongluan, 'Shenzhen shi chengshi shengtai xitong de fenxi' ('An Analysis of the Shenzhen City Ecosystem'), paper presented at the Urban Ecology Conference, November 1984, Shenzhen.
3. Liu Kuanhua, 'Tequ jiangshe zhong de huanjing baohu' ('Environmental Protection in the Development of the Special Economic Zone'), *Huanjing* (*Environment*), No. 9, 1983, pp. 2–3.
4. *Shenzhen tequbao* (*Shenzhen Special Economic Zone Post*), 27 June 1983.
5. Shenzhen SEZ Development Co., *Investment Guide for the Shenzhen Special Economic Zone, Guangdong Province, People's Republic of China* (Hong Kong, Wen wei po, 1982).
6. K.C. Lam and S.I. Hsu, 'Environmental Considerations', in K.Y. Wong and David K.Y. Chu (eds.), *Modernization in China: The Case of the Shenzhen Special Economic Zone* (Hong Kong, Oxford University Press, 1985).
7. Zhang Changcai, 'Shenzhen jingji tequ nongye fazhan zhanlue jige wenti' ('Some Questions Concerning the Strategic Development of Agricultural Production in the Shenzhen Special Economic Zone'), *Nongye jingji wenti* (*Problems of Agricultural Economics*), No. 7, 1984, pp. 17–22.

8. K.C. Lam, 'Environmental Pollution and Conservation', in T.N. Chiu and C.L. So (eds.), *A Geography of Hong Kong* (Hong Kong, Oxford University Press, 1983).

9. Tang, 'Shenzhen shi chengshi shengtai xitong de fenxi' (1984).

10. Dong Zhaoying, 'Shenzhen jingji tequ gongshui shuiyuan wenti de yanjiu' ('A Study of the Problems of Water Resources and Water Supply in the Shenzhen Special Economic Zone'), in Zhong Gongfu and Xu Zice (eds.), *Zhongguo jingji tequ dili yanjiu* (*A Geographical Study of the Special Economic Zones in China*) (Guangzhou, Guangdong People's Press, 1984).

11. Yang Anquan and Lin Xingqing, 'Shenzhen shi luyou ziyuan jiqi kaifa liyong de chubu yanjiu' ('A Preliminary Study of the Development and Use of Recreational Resources in the City of Shenzhen'), in Zhong and Xu (1984).

12. Shen Canshen, 'Cong chengshi shengtai xue guandian dui Shenzhen tequ shiu ziyuan yanjiu chutan' ('A Preliminary Assessment of the Water Resources in the Shenzhen Special Economic Zone from the Urban Ecosystem Perspective'), paper presented at the Urban Ecology Conference, November 1984, Shenzhen.

13. Shang Mu, 'Zhongguo diyi zuo daxing hedian zhan' ('The First Large Nuclear Power Plant in China'), *Gangao jingji* (*Hong Kong and Macau Economic Digest*), No. 21, 1984, pp. 30–2.

14. Wang Jinsan, 'Shajiao dianchang fujin shuiyu wuranwu fenbu he kuosan guilu de yanjiu' ('A Study of the Distribution and Dispersion of Pollutants in the Water Bodies around the Shajiao Power Plant'), *Zhongshan daxue xuebao ziran kexue ben* (*Journal of Zhongshan University, Natural Sciences Division*), Vol. 4, 1984, pp. 118–30; and Tang Yongluan, 'Guangdong hedian zhan daqi huanliu yingxiang wenti taolun' ('A Study of the Sea-land Boundary Effect on the Dispersion of Radionuclides of the Guangdong Nuclear Power Plant'), *Zhongshan daxue xuebo ziran kexue ben*, Vol. 4, 1984, pp. 161–3.

15. Wang (1984).

16. Tang, 'Shenzhen shi chengshi shengtai xitong de fenxi' (1984); and Hou (1984).

17. S.I. Hsu, 'Environmental Problems in the Development of the Shenzhen Special Economic Zone', *Asian Geographer*, Vol. 2, 1982, pp. 23–34.

18. Tang Yongluan, S.I. Hsu and K.C. Lam, 'Dispersion of Vehicle Exhaust Gases and Oxidants around Buildings in the Shenzhen Special Economic Zone', *Chinese University of Hong Kong, Department of Geography, Occasional Paper*, No. 76, 1985.

19. L.A. Orleans, 'China's Environomics: Backing into Ecological Leadership', *Environmental Policy and Law*, Vol. 1, 1975, pp. 189–93.

20. Tang, 'Shenzhen shi chengshi shengtai xitong de fenxi' (1984).

21. Qu Geping, 'Zhongguo huanjing wenti de jiben tedian he zhu yao jiaoxun' ('The Characteristics and Lessons of the Chinese Environmental Problems'), *Huanjing baohu* (*Environmental Protection*), No. 10, 1983, pp. 2–5 and 10.

22. Tang, Hsu and Lam (1985).

23. Xiang Kezong, 'Shenzhen daqi huanliu yu chengshi jianshe' ('Urban Development and Atmospheric Circulation in Shenzhen'), paper presented at the Urban Ecology Conference, November 1984, Shenzhen.

24. Zhang Lin, 'Chengshi jiaotong yu chengshi wuran' ('Urban Transport and Urban Pollution'), *Huanjing baohu*, No. 3, 1982, pp. 14–17.

25. Hou (1984).

26. Cheng Mingkun, 'Woguo chengshi zaosheng xianzhuang qi kongzhi jianyi' ('Noise Levels in Chinese Cities and their Control'), in *Huanjing kexue yanjiu yu jinzhan* (*Research and Progress in Environmental Sciences*) (Beijing, Science Press, 1980), pp. 228–42.

27. Wang (1984); and Tang, 'Guangdong hedian zhan daqi huanliu yingxiang wenti taolun' (1984).

28. Guangdong geming weiyuan hui (Guangdong Revolutionary Committee), *Guangdong huanjing baohu shouce* (*Handbook of Environmental Protection in Guangdong*) (Guangzhou, Guangdong Provincial Government, 1981).

29. Hou (1984); Mo Dalun, 'Kuichong pandi huanjing bendi xianzhuang pingjia' ('An Evaluation of the Environmental Background in the Kuichong Basin'), *Zhongshan daxue xuebao ziran kexue ben*, Vol. 4, 1984, pp. 131–40; and Liu (1983).

30. Qu (1983).

31. V. Smil, 'The Technological Future of China', *Ambio*, Vol. 8, 1979, pp. 94–9.

32. Yu Qingkang and Gu Wenxuan, 'In Search of an Approach to Rural-Urban Integration', *Third World Planning Review*, Vol. 6, 1984, pp. 37–46.

33. R.Y.W. Kwok and P.K.W. Fong, 'The Economic and Social Impact of Shenzhen Special Economic Zone Development: A Planning Analysis', in V.F.S. Sit (ed.), *Resources and Development of the Pearl River Delta* (Hong Kong, Wide Angle Press, 1984).

34. Hou (1984).

35. Hou (1984).

36. D. Burhans, 'Ecology and Development, China-Style', *Journal of East-West Centre Impulse Magazine*, Vol. 6, 1979, pp. 75–7.

37. V. Smil, 'Environmental Degradation in China', *Asian Survey*, Vol. 20, 1980, pp. 777–88.

38. K.C. Lam, 'Environmental Implications of the Industrial and Agricultural Modernization Programme in China', *Chinese University of Hong Kong, Department of Geography, Occasional Paper*, No. 83, 1985.

Part II: The Political and Legal Framework

5. China's Special Economic Zones: Ideology, Policy and Practice

THOMAS CHAN, E.K.Y. CHEN AND STEVE CHIN

Introduction

As in almost all Communist countries, the Chinese Communist Party (CCP) and the political regime under it are highly ideological. Furthermore, this ideology is basically teleological in nature and provides the Party with a means of legitimizing and sustaining its continued hegemony. On the practical side, given the diversity of conflicting interests in a vast country like China, ideology is important for the pursuit of a centralized single-party rule. The official ideology of the Party is inseparable from policies advocated by the bureaucracies and later adopted by the Party. Thus, ideology is an integral part of a policy package. It is not really important which comes first, ideology or policy. Sometimes, it is actually ideology which gives rise to policies. But very often circumstantial factors lead to certain policies for the simple reason of expediency. Such policies will later be given *ex post facto* ideological justifications.

This relationship between Party ideology and policy is described lucidly by Konrad and Szelenyi:[1]

> That is why the Party is essential, a political organization distinct from the individual bureaucracies yet interlocking with all of them. The Party stands guard over socialism's highest achievements, the political coordination of the economy and the consequent integration of individual bureaucracies. It makes certain that economic and technical decisions will always be primarily political decisions and that these politicized decisions will always be correlated with a unitary socialist ideology, even if that can only be done by pragmatically reinterpreting the ideology from time to time.

Policies are implemented through different instruments and in different forms. There are various practices for the achievement of the objectives that define a policy package and these are subject to greater flexibility in the hands of local authorities. Changes in practice do not, of course, always mean a departure from the original policy, and therefore do not always necessitate a reinterpretation of ideology. But it sometimes happens that changes in policy instruments and practice are so drastic that new policies are implied and ideological justification becomes necessary.

Chinese economic reform since late 1978 is both an interesting and an important case study in which we can explore the interaction of ideology, policy and practice in the process of policy formulation and implementation. It would, however, be too large a task to undertake a study with reference to Chinese economic reform as a whole. This chapter will focus on one aspect of economic reform, the establishment of China's special economic zones

(SEZs) and related policies. We shall examine the evolution of the SEZ policy from a new practice in the prevailing foreign trade policy to an entirely new policy integrated with national economic development, necessitating a new ideological interpretation.

Special Export Zones

The idea of putting aside a tract of land in China specifically for foreign investment was probably first brought up in a meeting of the then minister of transport, Ye Fei, with officials of China Merchants' Steam Navigation Co. (a direct subsidiary of the ministry, hereafter referred to as CMSN) in Hong Kong in the autumn of 1978 when Ye returned from a trip abroad. The idea was evidently borrowed from export-processing zones which Ye had seen or heard about on his recent trip. It is said that Ye recommended to CMSN a new strategy of extending its activities beyond the traditional area of shipping, taking advantage of its access to capital and other resources available in Hong Kong and Macau.[2]

After the meeting, CMSN officials discussed the idea with the Guangdong provincial authorities and a proposal was made to the central government on 30 January 1979. Yuan Geng, head of CMSN, in fact reported the proposal directly to Li Xiannian, then senior vice-premier in charge of economic matters.[3] On the following day, the Party Central Committee and the State Council announced a joint decision that an 'industrial zone' would be set up at Shekou, to be financed and managed by CMSN.[4]

In March 1979 the Guangdong Provincial Party Committee proposed to the central authorities that the province be given special treatment in the state's economic policies. The committee argued that if it were allowed to make certain modifications to state policies on foreign trade and economic management, given the advantageous location of the province, the local economy would be boosted.[5]

In April, while attending a central work conference in Beijing, Xi Zhongxun and Yang Shangkun, the first and second secretaries respectively of the Guangdong Provincial Party Committee, spoke to Deng Xiaoping about the March proposal. Deng suggested that Guangdong mark out an area in which to set up a 'special zone', similar to the Shan-Gan-Ning Border Region during the civil war. A central work team, headed by Gu Mu, a vice-premier of the State Council, was dispatched later to investigate the possibility of setting up special zones in Guangdong and Fujian. On the basis of the work team's findings, the Party Central Committee and the State Council jointly decided in July 1979 that both Guangdong and Fujian were to be authorized to carry out a special policy and adopt flexible measures in external economic activities.[6] As part of the special policy for the two provinces, four experimental 'special export zones' were to be set up in Shenzhen, Zhuhai, Shantou and Xiamen.[7] The central document stated that the decision was important for the speeding up of China's Four Modernizations. In August 1979 the Guangdong provincial government began the drafting of regulations for the special export zones.

It is obvious from the above account that the special export zones derived from export-processing zones that had developed outside China since the 1960s. The special export zone policy did not constitute a new policy in itself. Originally it was nothing more than a new and more flexible practice recommended to a sub-ministerial company that had long been operating outside China and therefore unavoidably followed some 'capitalist' elements in its operations. Although the setting up of the Shekou Industrial Zone had to go through a process of central approval, this was only because it involved the leasing of an area of territory under local administration. It did not represent an innovation at the national or local level in economic administration or government. It was just part of an emerging new policy in the area of foreign trade, the primary objective of which was the expansion of China's trade with the outside world. In 1978, the Party Central Committee had already endorsed the practice of using foreign capital in China's export trade by way of compensation trade, local processing for export orders, or subcontracting.[8] The Shekou Industrial Zone was merely a further logical step along this line of development.

Similar practices in the area of foreign trade in fact existed prior to the setting up of the Shekou Industrial Zone. Since 1973, the Ministry of Foreign Economic Relations and Trade had been setting up special production bases for export trade in some parts of China. The management of the production units in these bases was given much greater flexibility because of the orientation of the bases to a frequently fluctuating and highly competitive overseas market. Standard rules and regulations of the state planning system were also often waived.[9] In other words, within the central planning system, these bases for export trade already constituted some sort of special subsystem or zone. The Shekou Industrial Zone was but a further development of these bases in the new context of allowing foreign investment in China and was easily endorsed and approved by the central authorities, probably precisely because it did not represent a completely new policy in foreign trade.

The evolution of the Shekou Industrial Zone into the Shenzhen Special Export Zone and the extension of the policy on special export zones should also be seen in this context. The special status given to Guangdong and Fujian was intended to promote foreign trade in the two provinces, and the resultant special policy and flexible measures did not differ greatly from the practices that had already been carried out by the Ministry of Foreign Economic Relations and Trade. The only difference was that the special policy was now extended to local governments.[10] Thus there seemed to be no need to provide an ideological justification for the policy.

From Special Export Zones to Special Economic Zones

The evolution from a single industrial zone, that of Shekou, to four special export zones created new problems for the central and local authorities. The Shekou Industrial Zone was basically an export-oriented production base.

Since it was managed by CMSN, a state-owned company originally working outside the jurisdiction of the local administration, it was more like a production base on a lease. One might easily have associated it with, for example, production bases of Shanghai in Anhui. Since the company operated outside China and had not always followed established rules and regulations in China, the exceptions to established domestic practices in Shekou were quite excusable. In addition, dealings with foreign capital by CMSN on behalf of Shekou were mostly carried out in Hong Kong in the early period and the company was thus able to bypass many of the restrictions it would otherwise have encountered.

However, with the creation of four special export zones, each much larger than the Shekou Industrial Zone, direct conflict between the new practices and existing state policies on customs, import and export controls, taxation and the like, and with the local authorities was less easy to avoid than had been the case when just Shekou existed. Shenzhen and the other zones were more than just production bases for export trade. They were local governments, with a sizeable territory and population under their jurisdiction. In order to facilitate a large influx of foreign capital on a scale unprecedented in the history of socialist China, certain modifications to, and major changes in, the traditional principles of local government, especially in the economic arena, had to be made.

Originally it seems that the provincial authorities took foreign export-processing zones, or free trade zones, as the model for their special export zones. But once conflicts with existing state policies became apparent, they soon realized that there existed fundamental differences between China's politico-economic system and the mostly capitalist system of export-processing zones in other countries. The special export zones of China had therefore to be different.

In September 1979, Gu Mu announced in Tokyo that China would set up two 'special zones' in Shenzhen and Zhuhai and would welcome the investment of foreign capital in the two zones, either in the form of joint ventures or under sole ownership. He also said that economic measures far more liberal than those practised in the interior would be adopted there. In the same month, after Gu had made an important policy speech to officials from the governments of Guangdong, Shenzhen and Zhuhai, a report on 'Some Problems that Must Be Resolved for the Speeding Up of the Development of Shenzhen' was submitted to the Guangdong Provincial Party Committee.[11] In October, after a seminar on special export zones organized by the Provincial Party Committee, an 'Outline Report on Some Problems Concerning the Setting Up of SEZs' was submitted to the Party Central Committee and the State Council. This was the first document in which the term 'special economic zone' was used.

In November 1979, a meeting of officials from the Guangdong provincial government, the Shenzhen city government and CMSN was held. The meeting produced an internal agreement which gave the Shenzhen city government the authority to extend its jurisdiction over Shekou and to bring various measures adopted in Shekou back into line with those to be formulated for all the SEZs in Guangdong.

The main difference between a special export zone and an SEZ lies in the more comprehensive nature of the latter. The administrative body of an SEZ is both a local government and a management apparatus of a special economic organization. Its nature is partly determined by the more extensive territory of the SEZ and the larger population attached or attracted to the territory. Another explanation for the renaming of Shenzhen as an SEZ was the desire to develop both Shenzhen and Zhuhai into comprehensive special zones with the emphasis not only on industry but also on the development of agriculture, husbandry, tourism, commerce and services, real estate, and science and education. Thus the SEZs were not planned simply as production bases for export. On the other hand, Shantou was planned as an export-processing zone.[12]

On 27 December 1979, the Guangdong Provincial People's Congress approved in principle the Regulations on the Special Economic Zones in Guangdong Province. The term 'special export zone' was then formally changed to 'special economic zone'.

In March 1980, a meeting of the two provinces of Guangdong and Fujian was held in Guangzhou and chaired by Gu Mu. At the meeting, the territorial boundaries of the Shenzhen and Zhuhai SEZs were formally drawn and some of the major policy issues concerning the SEZs were examined. The term 'special economic zone' was officially confirmed and was used in the Regulations on the Special Economic Zones in Guangdong Province revised by the Guangdong Provincial People's Congress in April, and subsequently approved by the Standing Committee of the National People's Congress in August.[13] The SEZs had finally acquired their official legal status.

Lenin's New Economic Policy and the SEZs

From the above account, it can be seen that the initiative for setting up the SEZs came mainly from below, from the provincial authorities of Guangdong and Fujian and from the sub-ministerial CMSN. The proposal for the change in name from special export zone to SEZ was also made by Guangdong officials. Soon after the development of these special zones, a significant difference in attitude towards them became evident between the local and central authorities. The central authorities regarded the SEZ policy as part of the new or revised practices in foreign trade policy, bearing little direct relation to domestic economic policies. Even within the policy area of foreign trade, the various practices of compensation trade, joint ventures, processing and subcontracting were not confined exclusively to the SEZs. Nor were they an outcome of the SEZ policy. In fact, the SEZs could be seen instead as a continuation and further development at a different level of these practices that had begun in 1978 upon the recommendation of overseas Chinese businessmen.[14] Even in 1981, after the National People's Congress had granted legal status to the SEZs, they were still regarded as a local experiment with little national significance. The State Council's Office of SEZ Affairs was only set up in June 1982.[15] In November 1981, the Standing Committee of the National People's Congress delegated to the Guangdong and Fujian Provincial People's Congresses the authority to enact legislation for the SEZs.[16] Thus the SEZs were only given local status.

In contrast to the central authorities, the provincial authorities, especially in Guangdong, have taken the SEZs very seriously. It is probable that they view the SEZs as the generators of faster growth in the provincial economy. And from the very beginning they have regarded the SEZ policy as rather more than simply a new practice in the prevailing foreign trade policy. The local authorities conceived of the SEZs as marking a basic change in the policy of national economic development. As a first step, the zones had to be integrated fully into the provincial administrative system. Shenzhen, for example, originally a border town under the administration of a *xian* government, became a city directly under the rule of the provincial government. The Shekou Industrial Zone was included as part of the Shenzhen SEZ, which in turn came under the jurisdiction of the Shenzhen city government. Parallel to the local governments to which the three SEZs were subordinate, a provincial management committee (the Administrative Committee for the Special Economic Zones of Guangdong Province, hereafter cited as ADCOM) was also created to oversee the development of the SEZs and coordinate policy. ADCOM serves in addition as a means to strengthen the links between the provincial government and the SEZ administration, so that policies introduced there receive direct provincial backing as well as supervision. These institutional arrangements have helped to transform the SEZs from a temporary experiment serving only foreign trade into a more or less permanent institutional innovation.

Since the local authorities regarded the SEZs as reflecting a change in policy, and gradually found them to be incompatible with the prevailing socialist economic system in China, an explanation, especially an ideological one, became not only necessary but urgently needed. It is for this reason that the first attempts to provide an ideological explanation for the SEZ policy took place at the provincial level. At the central level, the SEZs implied no change in policy and therefore needed no new explanation.

It is not clear precisely when the provincial authorities began to search for an ideological justification for the SEZs. The first published material relating to this appeared in January 1980,[17] but it consisted of a discussion of all new foreign trade measures that involved foreign capital and did not focus specifically on the SEZs.

The first major discussion of the SEZs in terms of the official ideological orthodoxy was given by Sun Ru, director of the Economic Institute of the Guangdong Academy of Social Sciences, in that institution's official journal in July 1980.[18] Given his status, his discussion should reflect the state of thinking of provincial leaders, theoreticians and ideologues at the time. His arguments were aimed at justifying the use of foreign capital in China's export trade. Some later articles published in 1980 and early 1981 also adopted the same line of argument.[19] This suggests that by late 1980 and early 1981 the provincial authorities had put together a more or less coherent and consistent set of ideological explanations for the SEZs and the policies and practices that involved the use of foreign capital. Thus, these writings, and the formal enactment of local laws for the SEZs, provided a legal and ideological framework and a basis of legitimacy for the development of the SEZs.

The arguments presented in these writings were very simple and straightforward. They relied primarily on Lenin's ideas on concessions and state capitalism, developed during the period of the New Economic Policy (NEP). The central theme of Lenin's ideas was a policy of inviting foreign capitalists to obtain concessions, which was endorsed by the Soviet government in the early 1920s. In Lenin's own words, a concession is 'a contract between the government and a capitalist who undertakes to organize or improve production, and to pay the government a share of the product obtained, keeping the rest as his profit'.[20] The rationale for the concessions was explained as follows:[21]

> Is it right for the Soviet government to invite foreign capitalists after expelling the Russian landowners and capitalists? Yes, it is, because seeing that the workers' revolution in other countries is delayed, we have to make some sacrifices in order to achieve a rapid and even immediate improvement in the conditions of the workers and peasants. The sacrifice is that over a number of years we shall be giving away to the capitalists tens of millions of pounds of valuable products. The improvement in the conditions of the workers and peasants is that we shall immediately obtain additional quantities of petroleum, paraffin oil, salt, coal, farming implements, and so forth. We have no right to forego the opportunity of immediately improving the conditions of the workers and peasants for our impoverishment makes it essential and our sacrifices will not be fatal.

The emphasis on sacrifice so as to obtain immediate improvement in material conditions was the point of departure of the whole argument presented in the articles on the SEZs. One of the articles quoted directly from Lenin's report on concessions:[22]

> Our goal is: in the capitalist encirclement to make use of the greed of the capitalists for profit and the rivalry between the trusts, so as to create conditions for the existence of the socialist republic, which cannot exist without having ties with the rest of the world, and must, in the present circumstances, *adjust its existence to capitalist relations* [our italics].

It was further argued, using Lenin's words, that the granting of concessions is not dangerous.

First, concessions do 'imply a development of capitalism, but this is not dangerous, because power will still be in the hands of the workers and peasants, and the landowners and capitalists will not be getting back their property'.

'Second, the Soviet government will see to it that the capitalist lessee abides by the terms of the contract, that the contract is to our advantage, and that, as a result, the conditions of the workers and peasants is [*sic*] improved'.

Third, 'there is nothing terrible about giving the concessionaires a few factories and in retaining the bulk in our own hands'.

Fourth, 'it is with the motive of extra profit that we must attract the capitalist. He will get surplus profit — well, let him have that surplus profit; we shall obtain the fundamentals that will help strengthen us; we shall stand firmly on our own feet, and shall win in the economic field'.

All these assertions by Lenin arrived at one conclusion, that is, concessions to foreign capital do not constitute a threat to the socialist system. On the contrary, this flexibility and these compromises only help to realize socialism.

Following the classical tradition of Marxism, Lenin believed that 'socialism is inconceivable without large-scale capitalist engineering based on the latest discoveries of modern science'.[23] The Soviet Union was far from this stage in the early 1920s, and it was for this reason that Lenin remarked: 'state capitalism would be a step forward as compared with the present state of affairs in our Soviet Republic'. Concessions were one of the various forms of state capitalism that Lenin considered as more progressive than the backwardness of Russia in the early 1920s. More concretely, Lenin believed the following:[24]

> By 'implanting' state capitalism in the form of concessions the Soviet government strengthens large-scale production as against petty production, advanced production as against backward production. It also obtains a large quantity of the products of large-scale industry (its share of output) and strengthens state-regulated economic relations as against the anarchy of petty-bourgeois relations.

In short, Lenin believed that with the assistance of concessions the Soviet Union would move one step nearer socialism.

Lenin's conviction was shared by the authors of these provincial-level articles who were, in fact, even more confident and optimistic. They argued that in the early 1920s, when socialism had just been established in the Soviet Union, Lenin still believed that concessions would not disrupt the socialist regime. In the early 1980s, after 30 years of socialist construction, the Chinese socialist regime was much stronger and it was unlikely that state capitalism in the form of SEZs would lead China back to capitalism. Nevertheless the Chinese were aware of the possible negative aspects of the SEZ policy. For example, Sun Ru emphasized that the SEZs constitute a sacrifice on the part of Communists, and that this sacrifice should be limited and temporary.[25]

The reference to Lenin's NEP in general and his concession policy in particular was intended not only to provide a legitimizing ideological basis for the SEZs, but also to serve as a guideline for the cadres and workers employed in the SEZs. The deployment of Lenin's authority by the local ideologues was made on the one hand to prove to the central leaders that the SEZs are compatible with the Marxist orthodoxy and socialism, and on the other hand to overcome criticisms and scepticism coming from below. For instance, it was reported in September 1981 that a meeting of local cadres was held in Shenzhen. During the meeting, local cadres were asked to study Lenin's writings concerning the utilization of foreign capital in socialist construction.[26] Since the SEZs were considered to be different from export-processing zones or free trade zones, local officials had no relevant examples or experience upon which they could plan the SEZs. Lenin's ideas on concessions therefore offered the best and most authoritative guideline for operating Chinese SEZs.

In a 1921 report Lenin outlined the basic principles adopted in the Soviet decree on concessions, which were summarized in 10 points.[27] A comparison of these 10 points and the SEZ policy adopted almost 60 years later in China shows the obvious influence of the former on the latter.

The first two points in Lenin's report allowed workers of the concession enterprises to have an income higher than the domestic average. This was to be provided by the foreign capitalists. In return, workers of these enterprises were to be required to meet a demand for higher productivity. These are evidently the principles behind Articles 20 and 21 of the Regulations on the Special Economic Zones in Guangdong Province approved in 1980 (hereafter cited as the SEZ Regulations). Under pressure from foreign investors, more drastic reforms in the wage and labour systems were later introduced in Shenzhen, but still did not go much beyond the principles put forth by Lenin.

The fifth and sixth points in the Soviet decree subjected the concessionaires to Soviet laws. However, Lenin was quick to add that 'we are prepared to accept for ourselves and our trade unions a norm equal to the average American or West European labour norm'. He even went so far as to say: 'we guarantee that none of the terms, aspects or clauses of our concession agreement will go beyond the framework of capitalist legislation', and 'we must take capitalist relationships as a basis to show that the capitalists will find these terms acceptable and profitable'. This stance of Lenin probably provided both the motivation and the ideological justification for the drafting of the various regulations and laws for the SEZs and for joint enterprises and foreign investment in China.

Point eight in Lenin's outline stated: 'a special clause in each agreement shall regulate the question of payment to the workers employed at the concession enterprises of wages in foreign currency, special coupons, Soviet currency, etc.' Lenin added that 'we are prepared to accept payment in any currency, whether foreign or Soviet, or in coupons'. For Lenin the special coupons were those issued by foreign capitalists, not by the Soviet government, as a new form of local currency. Nevertheless it suggests that Lenin was not opposed to the issue and circulation of a local currency other than the official Soviet one in the concession territory. The introduction of foreign exchange certificates and the proposal for a convertible SEZ currency seem to have had their origin in this position of Lenin's.

The last two points, which allowed foreign capitalists to recruit their own staff and workers from within and without the host country, are also reflected in Articles 10 and 19 of the SEZ Regulations.

The 1982 Crisis

We have emphasized that, until the end of 1981, the SEZs were generally considered by the central authorities as part of a policy package for foreign trade, and were seen as a local experiment that would have few or no direct and immediate consequences for national economic policies. Thus the SEZs were not consciously linked with the reform of the national economic system undertaken since early 1979. Xu Dixian, then director of the Economics Institute of the Chinese Academy of Social Sciences, did suggest at one time that the SEZs might serve as a testing ground for economic reform, but he regarded this as a minor objective *vis-à-vis* the more important ones of facilitating foreign investment and the transfer of foreign technology and management skills to China.[28]

The elevation of the SEZs from a strictly local experiment to an issue of national concern came in the second half of 1981 and the beginning of 1982 in the form of a crisis in which the very existence of the SEZs was under threat.

In the second half of 1981, criticism of the SEZs began to emerge among central officials. Originally the criticism was not directed exclusively at the SEZs, but rather at the open-door policy of which the SEZs were seen to be a major component. The immediate cause of this criticism was the growing concern over widespread smuggling in the coastal provinces, mainly Guangdong, Fujian and Zhejiang. An anti-smuggling conference of these three provinces was called by the State Council in August 1981. It was after this conference that the central authorities began to take an active part in anti-smuggling activities and pay greater attention to the local administration of these provinces.[29]

This criticism gradually became focused on the SEZs and especially on Shenzhen, which had become a major smuggling centre. Goods from abroad were smuggled into Shenzhen across the border with Hong Kong, quite often with the help of local cadres and Hong Kong businessmen who worked in joint ventures. These goods were then shipped to other parts of China and sold on the black market at very high prices. The central leaders believed that the growth of smuggling in the SEZs not only disrupted the local economy and society but also contributed to the emergence of a national network of black markets. This was why some central leaders disliked, and were suspicious of, the setting up of SEZs in China. A report by economists of the State Council's Economic Research Centre indicated that some of the central cadres had two particular worries: first, that the SEZs might become foreign concessions like those established before 1949 under unequal treaties and, second, that the SEZs would become a breeding ground for economic crimes.[30]

In early 1982, it was said that Chen Yun, an economics expert and senior member of the Standing Committee of the CCP's Politburo, made a comment that the 'SEZs could be continued, but their experience must be summed up and reviewed continually'.[31]

In response to the doubts and concerns of the central leaders, the Shenzhen Party Committee held a meeting of all cadres at the level of *xian* and above in March 1982. At this meeting the Shenzhen Party Committee conducted a self-criticism session in which it admitted that outside bourgeois thoughts had affected the cadres and the social life of the local population, for example, in the form of corruption, smuggling and a capitalist lifestyle. As a result of the meeting it was decided to impose stricter discipline on the cadres and to take measures to combat bourgeois thoughts.[32]

Despite the self-criticism, opposition from central leaders has continued. Since 1982, central leaders have visited Shenzhen very frequently, with the evident purpose of keeping its development under constant and careful review. It has been through this process of criticism and review that the SEZ policy has gradually become an issue of national importance and has emerged as a national policy in its own right. It is no longer regarded simply as a new practice within the original framework. The escalation of the importance of the SEZ policy has also raised the question of whether the earlier ideological explanation built upon Lenin's ideas on concessions is adequate and acceptable from the point of view of the central authorities.

Since 1982, Lenin's ideas on concessions and the NEP have continued to play an important part in the ideological explanation of the SEZ policy.[33] Moreover, some economists in the central government have also turned to Lenin's ideas for theoretical guidance when discussing the SEZs.[34] But it is of interest to note that these ideological justifications on the basis of Leninism are largely confined to unofficial statements and academic discussions. Local officials and central leaders seldom explicitly refer to Lenin's ideas for the legitimization of the SEZ policy.

There are two reasons for this. First, Lenin's NEP has a specific policy meaning in national economic reform, which is closely linked with Chen Yun. Generally, Chen Yun's approach to economic reform differs from that endorsed by Deng Xiaoping. Hamrin states that the 'orthodox reformers' headed by Chen Yun have a 'limited' vision of reform.[35]

> They are willing to pursue 'regressive' NEP decollectivization when required to revive the economy and consolidate support for the regime, but only on a temporary basis. Their willingness to allow non-socialist elements to persist in the economy and society while a solid economic base is steadily laid down is premised on maintaining the Party's total monopoly on power... Thus, they smell a whiff of Maoist voluntarism when Deng's pragmatic reformers question Marx and Lenin, explore capitalist management theory and techniques, stress that reform of the superstructure is a prerequisite or even a 'guarantee' for economic development, and speak of 'individual responsibility systems' as a permanent feature of 'Chinese style socialism'.

The conflict between the approaches to economic reform of Chen and Deng is very obvious, and extends to the SEZ policy. In an internal speech given to a meeting of first Party secretaries of provinces, municipalities and autonomous regions on 22 December 1981, Chen argued against the establishment of more SEZs or the territorial expansion of the existing SEZs, and pinpointed some possible problems that the SEZs would create.[36]

Thus, the publicity given to Lenin's NEP and concession policy as the basis of legitimacy for the SEZs has not gained the support of the 'orthodox reformers' who tend to associate Lenin's NEP with a more 'limited' vision of reform. At the same time, too much emphasis on Lenin's NEP may run the risk of losing the support of the 'pragmatic reformers' for the NEP is also closely linked with Chen Yun's 'orthodox reformers'.

Second, Lenin's ideas on concessions and the NEP cannot provide a sound basis of legitimacy for the SEZs as a long-lasting, permanent policy in socialist China. Lenin repeatedly told his comrades:[37]

> It would be grossly mistaken to think that a peaceful agreement on concessions is a peaceful agreement with capitalists. It is an agreement concerning war, but an agreement that is less dangerous to us. . .we must therefore use all methods, and at the cost of economic concessions, develop our economic forces and facilitate our economic rehabilitation.

He also said:[38]

> concessions are also a form of struggle, and are a continuation of the class struggle in another form, and in no circumstances are they a substitution of class peace for class war.

The decision to implement the NEP was also clearly political. It was more an expedient measure than a policy formulated for the development of the national economy in a 'normal' period. As such the NEP and concession policy were meant to be temporary. Once the Soviet economy was restored and economic forces developed, these policies would be abandoned. The Chinese, including Deng himself, have argued that the time for the abandonment of NEP-like measures in China is a long way off. It has even been said that Lenin's NEP is an absolutely necessary path for eventual socialist construction, and that as such it should last for a long time and should not be treated just as a temporary retreat before aggression.[39] But this reasoning cannot be found in the words of Lenin. Soviet history also confirms that the NEP did not last long after Lenin's death. Bettelheim asserts that the NEP became limited in 1925 and that by 1928–9 it had finally ended.[40] To argue that the Soviet experience is inapplicable to China would cause additional problems in refuting Stalin and reinterpreting the policy struggles after the death of Lenin. This is certainly a formidable task, which very few would feel is worth the high political risk involved.

Thus both Lenin's original ideas and the Soviet experience indicate that concessions and the NEP are necessarily of an expedient and temporary nature. Unless the Chinese leaders intend to treat the SEZs similarly as an expedient and temporary policy, it would be politically more appropriate to find another source of ideological rationale to supplement, if not to replace, Lenin's NEP and concessions.

Events since 1983 have shown a shift from Lenin's NEP to Deng Xiaoping's 'Chinese-style socialism' in official discussions concerning the legitimacy of the SEZs.[41] By 1984, the SEZs had become an integral part of national economic reform and are now closely associated with the approach to economic reform represented by Deng and the 'pragmatic reformers'. This has been demonstrated by the personal affirmation of the SEZ policy by Deng in January–February 1984, and the extension of the SEZ policy to 14 coastal cities. Since April 1984, Shenzhen as the prototype of SEZs has become a national model. Some of the reform measures adopted in Shenzhen, for example the tender system in the construction industry, have also become demonstration models of reform for the rest of the nation.[42]

Thus the basis of legitimacy for the SEZs is now Deng's Chinese-style socialism, and the SEZ policy is now a part of national economic reform under China's new socialism. In the ensuing section, we shall discuss these developments in greater detail.

The SEZs and National Economic Reform

As early as 1981, a view emerged in Beijing which argued that the SEZs could serve as a testing ground for China's economic reform.[43] This view was shared by economists from the State Council's Economic Research Centre who visited Shenzhen. They argued that Shenzhen, basically an outward-looking economy exposed to outside market forces, should be allowed to have a more flexible system of economic management. In particular, enterprises in the SEZs should have autonomy in management and government should confine itself to general supervision of the economy by means of economic levers and economic legislation.[44] These proposals were in fact in line with the reform proposal for the national economy that had been discussed by the central authorities since late 1978.

In 1982, the open-door foreign trade policy with which the SEZ policy had been associated since its inception ran into difficulties. Widespread smuggling and economic crimes, as well as chaos caused by the sudden decentralization of foreign trade controls, were brought to the attention of the central leaders. To continue the close association of the SEZs with the foreign trade policy package would therefore only subject the SEZ policy to further unnecessary pressure from the central government. Moreover, the failure of Shenzhen and the other SEZs to attract a large influx of industrial investment from outside and the slowing down of real estate development in 1982 also created practical problems for the SEZ and provincial authorities.

All these developments led the local authorities and ideologues to reconsider the SEZs in relation to national economic reform. The opportunity came in September 1982 when the CCP held its Twelfth National Congress. The congress reaffirmed the need for economic reform, and placed it on a par with the policy of readjustment, thus ending the uncertainty that had beset the economic reform movement since the central work conference in December 1980. Under such circumstances, it was clear that an alliance between the SEZ policy and that of economic reform was not a political disadvantage, and was certainly more advisable than continuing the subordination of the SEZs to the foreign trade policy. In the first place, an association with a nation-wide policy package was more sensible than with a partial policy package since ideological justification of the national policy by the central authorities would automatically be carried over to the SEZ policy. Secondly, SEZ officials then considered it necessary to introduce economic reforms to solve some practical problems.

Thus, even before the Twelfth National Congress was adjourned, local officials in Shenzhen began to identify the SEZs with national economic reform.[45] At the First Shenzhen Party Congress in November 1982, Liang Xiang, the first Party secretary and mayor of Shenzhen, announced that Shenzhen had already begun some initial reforms in the economic management system.

Local officials' views on the importance of economic reform to the SEZs were followed by the argument of local ideologues that the SEZs could contribute greatly to national economic reform through the experiments in economic management being carried out there. In 1982 leading economists in Guangdong, such as Sun Ru, began to echo the view from Beijing that the SEZs could serve as a testing ground for China's economic reform.[46] Their arguments were supported by some of the experimental reforms carried out in the SEZs which proved to be successful.

Reform in the local economic system was in fact absolutely necessary to accompany the freedom of flexible policies given to the SEZs. For example, since the SEZs were originally set up as part of the foreign trade policy, no special modifications in the local planning system were made. SEZ projects, especially those involving foreign capital, were not included in the state's central or local plans. Thus materials required for projects could not be obtained from state planning channels. In 1982 it was said that a considerable amount of cement, steel, wood and glass needed in construction projects in Shenzhen was supplied by non-planning channels. Also, only 10 per cent of the total output of state industrial enterprises in Shenzhen was covered by state material allocation plans.[47]

The involvement of foreign capital in the SEZ economy through joint ventures also created a need for reform of some of the local economic institutions. The tender system and a new wage system are good examples. A decision was reached in July 1981 that a tender system would be adopted for a joint venture construction project in Shenzhen. Since then the tender system has become the rule in the construction industry in Shenzhen. In 1982 the local government announced that all construction projects would have to adopt an open tender system and a set of provisional regulations was promulgated in May 1983.[48] A system of job-specific, floating wage rates was first introduced in a joint venture, the Zhuyuan Hotel, in April 1982.[49] Although the new wage system is consistent with the provincial regulations on the management of labour and wages in SEZ enterprises approved in November 1981, its implementation still constitutes a drastic change in the rigid system of fixed salaries that has long been the norm even in the SEZs. This change in the enterprise wage system has been accompanied by a system of employment contracts, under which workers and staff are employed on a contract rather than permanent basis. This reform was originally confined to the 40-odd joint ventures and sole foreign ownership enterprises, but was later gradually extended to all state and collective enterprises in the SEZ.

The SEZs have thus become the forerunners of national economic reform in China. This is important not only because reforms are necessary to overcome many of the practical problems existing in the SEZs, but also because the association of the SEZs with national economic reform gives the SEZ policy package solid ideological and administrative support from the central authorities.

Conclusion

This chapter has attempted to analyse how the nature of, and ideological justification for, the SEZs in China has undergone significant changes since their establishment. Originally, the setting up of the SEZs was a local, sectoral policy that was very much transient in nature. But after 1982, as a result of central and local pressure, the SEZs emerged as part of a national and global policy issue connected with China's national economic reform. At the same time, there occurred a shift in the ideological basis of legitimacy for the SEZs, from Lenin's NEP and concession policy to an open-ended 'Chinese-style socialism' advocated by Deng Xiaoping.

The study of the evolution of China's SEZs in this chapter provides a useful illustration of the interaction of ideology, policy and practice in the context of reform and changes under a socialist regime. Inasmuch as current national economic reform in China is far from complete, we should expect that further interaction of ideology, policy and practice will continue to take place in the shaping of China's SEZs.

Notes

1. George Konrad and Ivan Szelenyi, *The Intellectuals on the Road to Class Power* (New York, Harcourt Brace Jovanovich, 1979), pp. 145–84.
2. Interview with Hu Zhiming, adviser to the Management Committee of the Shekou Industrial Zone, 11 June 1984.
3. See note 2.
4. *Zhongguo jingji tequ nianjian* (*Yearbook of China's Special Economic Zones*) (Hong Kong, Yearbook of China's Special Economic Zones Publishing Co., 1983), p. 365; Hong Kong Federation of Students (ed.), *Jingji tequ mianmianguan* (*Aspects of the Special Economic Zones*) (Hong Kong, Wide Angle Press, 1983), p. 89.
5. Quoted in Zhang Hanqing, 'Woguo shiban jingji tequ wenti chutan' ('A Preliminary Study of China's Experiment on Special Economic Zones'), *Xueshu yanjiu* (*Academic Research*), No. 4, 1982, p. 6.
6. The central document which granted special status to Guangdong and Fujian was issued on 15 July 1979. See *Nanfang ribao* (*Southern Daily*), 16 July 1982. For details about the special policy, see also *Nanfang ribao*, 8 June 1980.
7. Zhang (1982); *Zhongguo jingji tequ nianjian* (1983), p. 365; Sun Ru, 'Guanyu Guangdong shezhi jingji tequ de lilun yu shiji' ('The Theory and Practice of the Setting Up of Special Economic Zones in Guangdong'), *Xueshu yanjiu*, No. 4, 1980, p. 11; and Zeng Jianhui, 'Yixiang zhongyao juece de chansheng' ('The Birth of an Important Decision'), *Liaowang* (*Look*), No. 24, 1984, reprinted in *Wen wei po* (Hong Kong), 12 June 1984.
8. 'Tupo jinqu, wei sige xiandaihua dagan maoyi' ('Break Through the Restricted Area and Expand Trade for the Four Modernizations — A Report on the Meeting between Minister Li Qiang and Hong Kong Businessmen and Industrialists'), *Economic Reporter*, No. 1,600, 20 December 1978, p. 6.
9. See the following articles: Bureau for Production Bases in the former Ministry of Foreign Economic Relations and Trade, 'Chukou shangpin shengchan jidi' ('Production Bases for Export Commodities'); Zhang Chaoxuan, 'Guanyu jinyibu banhao chukou zonghe jidi de jidian yijian' ('On Improving the Comprehensive Bases for Export Commodities'); and Wu Enlin, 'Gaohao nongfu chanpin de chukou he shougou gongzuo' ('Improving the Production and Purchasing Work of Agricultural and Sideline Export Commodities'); all in *Zhongguo duiwai maoyi wenti yanjiu* (*Studies in China's Foreign Trade Problems*) (Beijing, Zhongguo duiwai jingji maoyi Press, 1983), pp. 170–96. For a list of the 24 production bases, see Feng Wanzhen, 'Woguo ershisige chukou shangpin jidi jianjie' ('A Brief Introduction to the 24 Production Bases for Export Commodities'), in Li Zhongfan, Xie Wensia and Song Tingming (eds.), *Chenshi he jingjiqu* (*Cities and Economic Zones*) (Fuzhou, Fujian

renmin Press, 1984), pp. 429–31. Even in 1979 the setting up of production bases for export commodities was still a major policy issue. See 'Zhongguo maoyi jixu fazhan' ('China's Foreign Trade Continues to Develop'), *Economic Reporter*, No. 1,618, 9 May 1979, p. 26. For the case of Hebei, see 'Hebeisheng waimao fazhan qianjing guangkuo' ('A Blueprint of the Development Prospects of Hebei's Foreign Trade'), *Economic Reporter*, No. 1,597, 29 November 1978, pp. 28–9.

10. The special policy for Guangdong and Fujian consists, apart from the SEZs, of the right to export local products directly, greater authority in carrying out barter trade, and the right to set up joint ventures with overseas capital and production bases for export commodities. All these do not go much further than the existing foreign trade policy. See Feng Xieyan, head of the Guangdong Bureau of Foreign Trade, 'Guangdong duiwai maoyi jiangyou dafazhan' ('There Will Be a Great Development of Guangdong's Foreign Trade'), *Economic Reporter*, No. 1,634, 29 August 1979, pp. 4–5.

11. *Zhongguo jingji tequ nianjian* (1983), pp. 365–6.

12. Zhang (1982), p. 7; also Zeng Muye, 'Zhuliu, wenti, jianyi' ('Mainstreams, Problems and Suggestions'), *Xueshu yanjiu*, No. 4, 1982, p. 30.

13. Zhang (1982), p. 8; and *Zhongguo jingji tequ nianjian* (1983), p. 367.

14. Cao Guangbiao of Hong Kong claimed that he was the first to propose barter trade to the Chinese authorities. *Economic Reporter*, Nos. 1,601 and 1,602, 1 January 1979, p. 23. The influence of overseas Chinese capitalists on China's open-door policy in general is also discussed in Terry Cannon, 'Foreign Investment and Trade: Origins of the Modernization Policy', in S. Feuchtwang and A. Hussain (eds.), *The Chinese Economic Reform* (London, Croom Helm, 1983), pp. 288–345.

15. Hong Kong Federation of Students (1983), p. 98.

16. *Zhongguo jingji tequ nianjian* (1983), p. 370.

17. Huang Zhongyi, 'Yinjin waiguo ziben, jishu he jingyan, fazhan shehuizhuyi jingji' ('Import Foreign Capital, Technology and Experience, Develop Socialist Economy'), *Xueshu yanjiu*, No. 1, 1980, pp. 54–8.

18. Sun Ru (1980), pp. 11–17. This was written in May.

19. Song Zihe and Lin Hao, 'Shilun duiwai jingji huodong zhong de guojia zibenzhuyi xingshi' ('A Preliminary Discussion of the State Capitalist Forms in External Economic Activities'), *Xueshu yanjiu*, No. 1, 1981, pp. 15–19; and Li Yanshi's two articles on the SEZs in *Nanfang ribao*, 4 and 18 October 1980.

20. V.I. Lenin, 'Recorded Speeches: 2. Concessions and the Development of Capitalism' (25 April 1921), in *Collected Works* (Moscow, Progress Press, 1965), Vol. 32, p. 368.

21. Lenin, 'Concessions', p. 365.

22. V.I. Lenin, 'Report on Concessions at a Meeting of the Communist Group of the All-Russia Central Council of Trade Unions' (11 April 1921), in *Collected Works*, Vol. 32, pp. 300–15; quotation from pp. 313–14. The article that carries this quotation is Huang (1980), pp. 54–5.

23. V.I. Lenin, 'The Tax in Kind (The significance of the New Policy and its Conditions)' (21 April 1921), *Collected Works*, Vol. 32, p. 334.

24. Lenin, 'The Tax in Kind', p. 346.

25. Sun Ru (1980), p. 16.

26. *Nanfang ribao*, 1 September 1981.

27. Lenin, 'Report on Concessions', pp. 300–15.

28. Xu Dixin, 'Guanyu jingi tequ de renshi' ('On Understanding the Special Economic Zones'), *Shijie jingji daobao* (*World Economic Herald*), 15 June 1981. See also his 'Jingji tequ de wenti', in *Zhongguo shehuizhuyi jingji fazhan zhong de wenti* (*Problems in China's Socialist Economic Development*) (Beijing, Zhongguo shehui kexue Press, 1982), pp. 117–25.

29. 'Guowuyuan zhaokai sansheng daji zousi gongjuo huiyi' ('The State Council Calls Three-province Anti-smuggling Conference'), *Renmin ribao* (*People's Daily*), 29 August 1981, p. 1. See also the editorial of the same date.

30. Xu Xuehan, Mao Rongfang and Wu Jian, 'Guanyu jingji tequ jianshe zhong

de jige wenti' ('Some Problems in the Construction of the SEZs'), *Renmin ribao*, 13 September 1982, p. 5; reprinted in *Shenzhen tequbao* (*Shenzhen Special Zone Post*), 20 September 1982, p. 7.

31. Zeng (1984); *Shenzhen tequbao*, 22 November 1982, p. 1; and *Nanfang ribao*, 19 December 1982. Chen's comments were first raised in a meeting with first Party secretaries of provinces, municipalities and autonomous regions on 22 December 1981. They were repeated in a meeting with officials of the State Planning Commission on 25 January 1982. See *Zhonggong nianbao, 1983–4* (*Yearbook of Chinese Communism, 1983–4*) (Taibei, Institute for the Study of Chinese Communist Problems, 1984), Section 8, pp. 72–4.

32. *Nanfang ribao*, 20 March 1982, pp. 1 and 3. For reference see Guangdong provincial leaders' comments in *Shijie jingji daobao*, 31 May 1982, p. 1.

33. See, for example, the discussion in a seminar on the economic theory of the Shenzhen SEZ held in April 1984 in Shenzhen, in Qian Jiaju and Lu Zufa (eds.), *Tequ jingji lilun wenti lunwenji* (*Collected Essays on Questions of Economic Theory Concerning the SEZs*) (Beijing, Renmin Press, 1984).

34. Lu Zufa and Ou Xuante, 'Lun Shenzhen jingji tequ de jingji xingzhi' ('On the Economic Nature of the Shenzhen SEZ'), *Xueshu yanjiu*, No. 4, 1984, pp. 5–11; Jin Zhiguo, 'Jianshu Liening guanyu fazhan duiwai jingji guanxi ji zurangzhi de lilun yu woguo jingji tequ de shijian' ('A Brief Account of Lenin's Theories of the Development of Foreign Economic Relations and the Concessions System and the Practice of SEZs in China'), *Jingji wenti tansuo* (*Inquiry into Economic Questions*), No. 5, 1984, pp. 19–22; Zhao Texu, 'Shehuizhuyi tiaojian xia shezi jingji tequ de lilun yiju' ('The Theoretical Basis for Setting Up SEZs under Socialist Conditions'), *Beifang luncong* (*Northern Commentaries*), No. 1, 1984, pp. 15–21; Guo Zhemin, 'Lun shezhi jingji tequ de yiju' ('On the Basis of Setting Up SEZs'), *Zhongguo jingji wenti* (*China's Economic Problems*), No. 5, 1984, pp. 1–7; and Qian Jiaju, 'Guanyu jingji tequ de jige wenti' ('On Some Questions about SEZs'), *Zhongguo jingji wenti*, No. 4, pp. 1–6.

35. Carol Lee Hamrin, 'Competing "Policy Packages" in Post-Mao China', *Asian Survey*, Vol. 24, No. 5, May 1984, p. 516.

36. Chen Yun, 'Dui jingji gongjuo de jidian yijian' ('Some Comments on Economic Work, 22 December 1981'), quoted in *Zhongguo nianbao* (1983–4), Section 8, pp. 72–3.

37. V.I. Lenin, 'Report on Concessions Delivered to the RCP(B) Group at the Eighth Congress of Soviets' (21 December 1920), *Collected Works*, Vol. 31, p. 484.

38. Lenin, 'The Tax in Kind', p. 346.

39. See *Renmin ribao*, 12 October 1984.

40. Charles Bettelheim, *Class Struggles in the USSR, Second Period: 1923–30* (Sussex, The Harvester Press, 1978).

41. It is best exemplified by Deng's own definition of Chinese-style socialism. See *Liaowang*, No. 34, 1984, reprinted in *Wen wei po*, 20 August 1984.

42. For the case of Shenzhen's impact on reform in the construction industry, see *Guangming ribao* (*Guangming Daily*), 16 April 1984, p. 2.

43. Two articles in the central magazine, *Liaowang*, had shared this view. See Ruan Ming, 'Jiakuai Xiamen tequ jianshe shi zhanlue de xuyao' ('Speeding up the Construction of the Xiamen SEZ is Strategically Necessary'), No. 6, September 1981, pp. 10–12; and Zhang Hongbin and Lei Lizing, 'Shenzhen jingji tequ de jueqi' ('The Emergence of the Shenzhen SEZ'), No. 2, April 1981, pp. 11–13.

44. Xu Xuehan *et al.* (1982).

45. *Nanfang ribao*, 4 September 1982.

46. Sun Ru, 'Gong zhanlue yiyi tan jingji tequ de zuoyong he jianshe' ('The Role and Development of SEZs from a Strategic Perspective'), *Xueshu yanjiu*, No. 4, 1982, pp. 19–27. This was written in June 1982 before the Twelfth National Congress.

47. Chen Zhaobin, 'Lin jingji tequ de jiage yundong tedian he shichang tiaojie zuoyong' ('On the Characteristics of the Price Movement in the SEZs and the Role of the Market Mechanism'), in *Zhongguo jingji tequ nianjian* (1983), pp. 675–82.

48. *Nanfang ribao*, 5 June 1983.

49. *Shenzhen tequbao*, 6 October 1983, p. 2; and *Zhongguo jingji tequ nianjian* (1983), pp. 180–1. See also *Nanfang ribao*, 4 October 1983, pp. 1–3. Similar examples of wage reform can be found in the Shenzhen Galo Furniture Factory. See *Shenzhen tequbao*, 1 November 1982, p. 6.

6. Bureaucracy and Modernization: A Case Study of the Special Economic Zones in China

C.Y. Chang

Introduction

In observing the modernization process in Communist states, socio-political scientists generally agree that bureaucracy is an important modernizer within the context of achieving rapid industrialization. But if modernization is understood within the meaning of democratization, then a dispute is likely to arise.

Merle Fainsod, for example, in his study of bureaucracy and modernization in the Soviet Union, argues that 'democratizing and industrializing tendencies do not necessarily go hand in hand'. As he firmly states:

> Political modernization, as the Communists conceive it, has nothing to do with competitive party politics and a system of regularized institutional restraints on the exercise of political power. It involves using all of the powerful instruments which modern science and technology make available to enforce political unanimity and to mobilize the energies of the nation to carry out the leadership's plans. Communists and Western democrats share a vision of modern industrial society, but their views of the requirements of political modernization are at opposite poles.[1]

The Soviet case has convinced Fainsod that industrial élites are unable to dominate in such a context even though their decision-making tends to be more rational under successful industrialization.

But others tend to believe that industrialization itself naturally breeds an industrial élite which becomes increasingly rational in its decision-making. This development is likely to bring about a situation where the industrial élite finally occupies a responsible position with sufficient authority and knowledge to comment on the subjective plans of the political leadership. Unlike Fainsod, Carl Beck believes that in all circumstances, 'industrialization places a premium on technology and science, not on charisma. Industrialization requires routinized economic and political processes, not inspiration. In short, industrialization demands the establishment of a legal-rational authority structure'.[2] Beck does not believe that an exception should be made for Communist states. The political structure in Communist states

> would become increasingly rationalized; career channels would become increasingly routinized, with a major emphasis placed upon expertise; and decision strategies would be based more upon computation and bargaining than on inspiration. These changes would not necessarily be incremented in nature, but the political systems of totalitarianism would move in this direction. Such a movement would mean the

eventual erosion of the ideology and revolutionary character of Communist regimes.[3]

Even though holding this position, Beck is cautious in his findings. As regards the 'new managerial class being created in the East European countries', he points out that 'this new managerial class is beginning to be represented in the leading administrative and political councils'.[4] But Beck reminds us that it cannot be taken for granted that this development will start a revolution where the 'logic of political Communism will become dissipated under the impetus of the rational interests of this new group'. It cannot be assumed that 'this new group *per se* holds different political perspectives from those now in control and that these perspectives are in opposition to the less reactional characteristics of the system'.[5] To assume that 'industrial man will come even further into the forefront in the future' is equally unrealistic. As Beck puts it, 'it can be demonstrated that industrial man has become more important in Eastern Europe. It cannot be demonstrated that industrial man has achieved, or will automatically achieve in the future, a dominant position. Further, there is little support for the view that industrial man must be a different type of political man than those now in power'.[6]

In viewing these disputes, one can sum up two fundamental points. First, the Communists can achieve modernization by mobilizing and setting on course the modernizer, that is, the bureaucrat; second, the industrial élite has become increasingly more influential in the overall decision-making process in Communist states, but it has yet to be seen whether it can achieve a dominant position politically. Due to this uncertainty, modernization in the Communist states cannot be considered as complementary to the development of democracy.

In following this line of argument it is evident that the function of politics and bureaucracy in China is very similar to that in the Soviet Union and East European countries. Like them, the Chinese Communist regime has, since its establishment in Beijing in 1949, pledged to modernize the country. But unlike them, Communist China has been far less fortunate in its attempts at modernization, whether within the context of industrialization or of democratization. In addition, most of the studies dealing with the issue of bureaucracy and modernization in China have not stressed the extent to which the bureaucrat has contributed towards modernization, as in Soviet and East European studies. Instead, most have tried to find out why the function of the bureaucrat does not favour economic and technical advances. Vogel, for example, suggests that bureaucracy is far more politicized in China than in other Communist states. By politicization in bureaucracy, Vogel means that:[7]

(a) bureaucrats are under pressure to demonstrate a high degree of political commitment;
(b) bureaucrats are expected to conform in their political thinking;
(c) cadres do not possess the skills and time required to undertake special tasks;
(d) disciplinary measures to insure political reliability are applied far too

negatively to bureaucrats and undermine their enthusiasm and initiative;

(e) outbursts of political activity and the pressures generated within the bureaucracy disrupt ordinary routine procedures;

(f) changes in political policy cause more disruption to bureaucratic organization than they do in Western countries; and

(g) many problems which are viewed in the West as problems of work morale, accident proneness and waste, are treated in Communist China as political problems, causing a large number of dismissals.

Heady, in his comparative study of public administration in Communist totalitarian systems, agrees with Vogel's observation. He points out that there are two consistent themes which have persisted since 1949. The first is 'a determination to politicize the bureaucracy and make it responsive to party direction, using various devices. The fundamental is the practice of putting party members in most of the important government positions. Another is to recognize a party fraction in each organizational unit, consisting of the leading party members in the unit, as the vehicle for making sure that party policies are being carried out'.[8] The second is 'decentralization by the transfer of administrative powers to the lowest feasible level. This diffusion strategy is designed to prevent the build-up of a non-productive administrative superstructure and at the same time strengthen local initiative and responsibility. Carried to an extreme during the Great Leap Forward, the central ministries essentially lost control over lower administrative levels, and local party committees became the effective decision-makers. A by-product of this involvement turned out to be a bureaucratization of politics as the CCP organs themselves became identified with administrative specifics, leading later during the Cultural Revolution to the charge that the CCP itself had become over-bureaucratized'.[9] Based on this observation, both Vogel and Heady have concluded that Chinese politics are bureaucratized, while the regime tries to politicize the bureaucracy. This two-way function between politics and bureaucracy has finally crippled the functions of both politics and bureaucracy. Therefore, as most social scientists believe, modernization is only slowly coming about in China.

Apparently, Chinese leaders, both past and present, seem to dispute the positive value of an independent rational-bureaucratic organization as far as efficient modernization is concerned. In this sense, their thinking on the correlation between bureaucracy and modernization is still close to the Soviet view, as Fainsod has observed. Until recently, Party members still played a dominant role in all organizations. A large number of political campaigns have been launched to criticize the common attitude of 'red' but not 'expert' Party cadres. But when one examines the organizational structures in the four areas designated as special economic zones (SEZs), Shenzhen, Zhuhai, Shantou and Xiamen, the politicization of the bureaucracy, as Vogel observed earlier, has not died out. The two 'consistent themes' noted by Heady still persist, despite official promises that the industrial élite would be given a free hand to lead in the SEZs. This latest development has proved that, as social scientists believe, it is difficult to get rid of a politicized bureaucracy.

This chapter uses the SEZs to illustrate the issue of the politicization of the bureaucracy, and its possible effects on attempts at modernization in China.

The Politicization of the Bureaucracy in the SEZs

In his government report of 15 May 1984, Zhao Ziyang proposed a state recruitment policy for economic cadres and stressed that all economic cadres must learn economic management and modern technology and know-how. Their knowledge would be tested and promotion based on the test. Heads of factories and managers would also have to sit for an examination set by the state and would be unable to secure a post if they failed.[10]

In fact, the state policy had first been discussed earlier by some top leaders such as Deng Xiaoping. In August 1980, Deng gave a very important speech in a specially enlarged meeting of the Politburo,[11] in which he pointed out that two undesirable practices of government existed in the state and Party apparatus. First, too much power was concentrated in too few hands. Second, too many Party leaders had responsibility for too many state posts. Such practices had damaged the Party leadership and had eroded the efficiency of the state bureaucracy ever since the Cultural Revolution. To ensure the survival of the state and Party, and to remedy this damage, Deng suggested some reforms which would draw a line between the state apparatus and the Party organization, since the Party cannot replace the state. As a result, some leaders in the Party Central Committee are no longer allowed to take up posts in the state apparatus, and are obliged to concentrate their efforts on Party work and policy-making in order to maintain consistency in policy and administrative leadership. Deng's speech was actually a review of the state and Party reform undertaken earlier. As a result of this additional reform, many top leaders, such as Hua Guofeng, Chen Yun, Xu Xiangqian, Wang Zhen and Deng himself, dropped their positions in the state apparatus. In fact, some of them have even faded away from their top posts in the Party. Deng claimed that this reform was necessary for the success and realization of modernization.[12]

The SEZs were established against the background of this campaign for state and Party reforms. They are intended to strengthen the enforcement of reform policies and, no doubt, to support the 'open policy' (*kaifang zhengce*) initiated by the leadership in Beijing. But the 'open policy' only provides the principle of acceptance of foreign investment, modern management and advanced technology in a limited area to a limited extent. It does not provide guidance in the setting up of a government structure and government functions in the zones. Thus the four zones are only 'special' in the economic sense since these places allow outsiders to invest financially, introduce new techniques in management, and bring in new technology. As far as the Party organization and state apparatus are concerned, the principle of governing is no more 'special' than elsewhere in China for the SEZs are not special 'administrative' zones.[13] Party discipline, the state constitution and laws, and state administration all remain the same. The four fundamental principles of socialism, the democratic dictatorship of the people, the leadership of the Communist Party, and the rule of Marxism-Leninism and the Thought of Mao Zedong, apply as much in the SEZs as elsewhere. Some Communist leaders in Guangdong have attempted to define the SEZs in political terms. Zhang Kelang, an official from the College for Cadres of Foreign Trades, has pointed out that, 'It is an economic special zone, not a political special zone. Therefore, when one tries to construct materialistic civilization, one is obliged to construct socialist spiritualistic civilization'.[14] Liang Musheng, a Party leader from the Guangdong Provincial Party College, has also commented in an article that the 'two civilizations, material and spiritual, ought to be complementary to each other, to help each other, at no cost to each other'.[15] Zhang Hanqing, a Party leader from the Policy Research Office of the Guangdong Party Committee, has expressed the view that if material prosperity is achieved at the cost of socialist spiritual civilization, then the SEZs will be considered a total failure.[16] Sun Ru, a scholar from the Academy of Social Sciences, has also pointed out that the fundamental difference between socialist SEZs and capitalist SEZs lies in their spiritual civilization.[17]

Based on the principle that 'special' does not refer to the political setting of the SEZs, the state apparatus and Party organization are still very much interwoven. There have been calls for the extension of the campaign to separate the state apparatus and Party organization raised by the central Party leadership to the SEZs. But as far as the politicization of the bureaucracy is concerned, the practice remains unchanged in principle although a lesser degree of politicization may occur in some instances.

The Structural Politicization of the Bureaucracy

First, the bureaucracy in the SEZs is, in terms of structure, politicized. For example, in Shenzhen the top government positions are occupied by the top Party leaders of the city. Liang Xiang is the mayor as well as the first Party secretary in the city. He is also the deputy governor of Guangdong province. Four vice-mayors, Zhou Ding, Zhou Xuwu, Luo Chang Ren and Zhe Xipai, are all leading figures in the Party organization of Shenzhen. The rest of the government posts are occupied by leading Party members in the city. Non-Party members have never been known to be posted to leading jobs in government offices.[18] This pattern of posting Party leaders to all leading positions in government also occurs in the Zhuhai, Shantou and Xiamen SEZs. Furthermore, the hierarchy of the state administration is comparable to a similar-ranking hierarchy of Party committees, thereby ensuring the proper checking of state operations and the correct implementation of Party policies by bureaucrats. It is surprising to find that the Party organization and state apparatus are still very closely interwoven since this practice has been condemned during the state-wide political campaign for urgent reforms.[19]

From researchers' comments on the problem of the politicized state apparatus in the SEZs, one can sum up the critical points raised by some scholars in China as follows:

(a) Due to their lack of administrative power in their own jurisdiction, many SEZ state officials are helpless when asked to consider or reject requests from other state firms which would like to set up in the SEZs. This is because most of these firms are state-owned and are led by Party leaders who are unlikely to be overruled by the zone's officials. It is also the policy of the central Party authority to pledge the support of other provincial or city authorities to develop the SEZs. Officials in the SEZs are naturally reluctant to take action against those unwelcome elements with Party status.[20]

(b) As one internal source has indicated, despite the separation of the state and Party authorities, each having its own jurisdiction, very often Party members intervene in state affairs in Zhuhai. Senior officers from the two respective sides often ignore each other, at times confronting each other. The source has suggested that it would be better to integrate the two, and put all Party cadres under the leadership of the state authority. This arrangement, the source believes, would produce better cohesiveness and efficiency.[21]

(c) Two scholars from the Economics Department of Zhongshan University have pointed out that the government structure's two-level system in Shantou creates too many heads and complicates procedures. To eliminate the inefficiency caused by this system, they have suggested that authority be centralized under the management of the Shantou government.[22]

(d) After learning of the defects created by the politicization of the bureaucracy, some academic staff from Huanan Normal University have proposed that the best way to set up a governing body to run the SEZs would be to learn from Shekou where China Merchants' Steam Navigation Co. Ltd. is managing the area without political intervention. As a result, growth in business and industry in Shekou has surpassed that in the SEZs. Further, Zheng Deliang, a member of the Economics Department of Zhongshan University, has suggested that the best way to improve the administration in the SEZs would be to enlarge its decision-making base and define clearly its terms of reference and responsibility.[23]

Other than the above comments, attempts have been made by economic cadres to secure a system free from Party intervention. The following are some of the tactics used which sometimes seem effective:

(a) Instead of receiving the manager directly nominated from the Party, some production units of state-owned enterprises have started to hire or secure their managers by an elective system. This system provides a chance for workers inside the enterprise to elect or select their manager and enables a manager to mobilize support and to secure his post free from intervention by the Party man.[24]

(b) An effective way to prevent political intervention is to express grievances to a visiting VIP leader from Beijing or to go to Beijing to complain. Though traditional, this tactic works. It is reported that after Deng

Xiaoping's visit to Shenzhen, reform of the personnel system was accelerated to reduce the degree of politicization in the bureaucracy.[25]

(c) The drawing up of guidelines and rules to define the extent of a manager's responsibility and authority allows for the elimination of a non-professional or political appointee and protects a manager from removal for political reasons. Within the rules, an indicator to show good or bad performance is established, taking economic, rather than political, considerations into account. In this context some production units have required that their leader set production targets. If he fails to achieve these targets, he has to report to workers in the unit in order that they may take disciplinary measures against him.[26]

(d) The use of the media to combat political interruption from Party cadres is also an effective channel. In this matter, Shenzhen seems to be more fortunate than the rest. It has its own newspaper, the *Shenzhen Special Zone Daily*, which publishes a lot of reports to help activate the reform of separating the Party organization and the state administration. Stories are published occasionally to disclose undesirable Party intervention that causes great loss to state-owned property.[27] This kind of report cannot be ignored by Party officials as the zone is easily accessible to the outside world. How much effect this kind of reporting has in checking 'square-head' Party cadres is hard to evaluate. However, it has been reported that there have been at least a few cases which have resulted in some cadres being dismissed.[28]

Nevertheless, attempts to prevent a politicized bureaucracy as such have frequently been made in the SEZs. Some have resulted in the dismissal of the Party cadres involved. But one cannot conclude from this that structurally the bureaucracy is safe from the threat of politicization, especially when the bureaucrats involved are high-level Party cadres who are, at the same time, state officials. In the circumstances, an individual may actually contradict himself in his dual capacity as Party and state official respectively. Whilst if he is in a high post, he is likely to be in a better position to defend himself under the four fundamental principles which provide a good ideological escape-hatch for those unwilling to go too far lest they be persecuted later. In fact, one can easily pick on ideological issues to counter depoliticization in the state apparatus, especially in the SEZs where Party loyalists are likely to feel that the 'open policy' endangers socialism. Some issues raised in the SEZs are thus potential weapons in the argument against the depoliticization of the state apparatus.

First, the issue of economic crimes committed by managerial officers can cast a shadow over state administrators in the economic field. Due to a lack of administrative laws, political manoeuvring to judge the misconduct of an officer can be resorted to. Worse, there is no 'administrative court' to conduct a proper trial of an officer charged with misconduct. The present practice is that a state administrator's misconduct will first be investigated by a Party cadre. Normally he will lose his Party membership as a result of the 'crime'. Subsequently, the Party committee will seek from the state authority his dismissal from any administrative post he is holding. Further, the committee will suggest that the court proceed with the trial to establish his legal responsibility.[29] In the West, the practice is first to take the case to the court concerned, or to an independent body such as a public service commission, for a hearing. Only after the crime is established legally will the offender be removed from his public post. This procedure is a device to rule out the possibility of any pressure from the political authority. But the procedure established in China is exactly the reverse: a political trial first, followed by a court trial. Obviously, with judicial independence still weak in China, a court decision cannot be reached without considering the earlier judgement made by the Party.[30] The refutation of a Party judgement in an open trial is unknown. A report shows that economic crimes in the SEZs are far too prevalent for provincial and national Party leaders to tolerate.[31] The issue has been raised continually in the Guangdong Provincial People's Congress, the National People's Congress, and the Party Congress at both the provincial and national levels.[32] The discussions in these meetings show that the crimes involved are caused mainly by a lack of well-defined economic laws. But many Party cadres are inclined to regard these crimes as political symptoms that will lead to the ideological decay of Communism. It is natural for these Party cadres to adopt this mentality simply to protect the Party and safeguard Communist ideology. This in itself has undoubtedly generated their attempts to safeguard their position in favour of a continuing politicized bureaucracy.

Second, inflation in food prices, which is occurring all over China, but which is worst in the SEZs, is causing Party cadres to ask for further political caution over the open policy in the SEZs. Inflation is considered a very serious problem precisely because the Communist regime has always prided itself on its success in eliminating such inflation while other countries have failed. However, following the removal of restrictions on free trading in some secondary agricultural products, prices for items such as meat and vegetables have gone up significantly all over China. Guangdong has been especially hard hit, with inflation rising to 18.9 per cent in 1982.[33] Shenzhen has been even more seriously affected. The prices of some food items there have gone up two to three times.[34] This trend has undoubtedly fuelled the discontent of some Party cadres. To combat inflation, the State Council has issued 10 emergency rules to regulate the prices of major daily necessities.[35] A law to regulate the sale of secondary food items has also been imposed.[36] These legal impositions are likely to give Party cadres an opportunity to manipulate politics further to tighten Party control. State administrators responsible for the daily management of public services will be the first to be affected.

Third, poor planning in some major projects has created another political problem for Party cadres who have to take into account the conflict of interest between socialism and capitalism. It has been reported that at least a few projects depending on Hong Kong investment have not been successful.[37] All problematic projects involve the Chinese in heavy financial losses and give higher authorities the chance to intervene. Such intervention is at times resisted. Some observers believe the problem has emerged not simply because of a conflict between the socialist and capitalist approach in handling business but because compromise between the two approaches is not possible.[38]

Again, poor planning, or a failure to anticipate market fluctuations, has weakened the position of state administrators and economic cadres. These is evidence to show that some have volunteered to correct themselves and their production units and that others have even volunteered to work overtime without pay to gain social respect.[39]

Fourth, the Chinese leadership has made it clear that the twin goals of the SEZs are to achieve material progress and socialist spiritual civilization; failure to achieve either one is tantamount to complete failure. It would appear from the evidence that the authorities are more concerned with 'socialist spiritual civilization' in the SEZs,[40] for they know they cannot justify material prosperity without the development of the necessary spiritual civilization that distinguishes them from capitalists. So far, efforts to promote material development seem to have been far more successful than efforts to promote spiritual development. This is because most material projects have been financed by outside investors. There are no comparable proportional funds available within China to promote the growth of spiritual civilization. A report has stated that various forms of spiritual pollution in the SEZs, such as the preference given to Hong Kong currency in the market and, worse, the changing of money on the black market, have already annoyed the SEZ authorities. These are considered to represent serious spiritual misconduct and to pose a threat to Communist ideology. Other offences, such as smuggling, the receipt of gifts in return for services, entertainment, gambling, and so on, are also considered to be polluting elements.[41] Some measures have been taken to counter these problems. For instance, regulations have been drawn up in Shenzhen prohibiting Party cadres from accepting gifts, as this undesirable practice is widespread in Shenzhen. It is not unusual for cadres who are found guilty of this practice to be dismissed.[42]

To overcome the problem, a new principle in the selection of cadres was adopted in March 1984. This is that, first and foremost, the candidate must adhere to the four fundamental principles and to the political line laid down by the Third Plenary Session of the Eleventh Central Committee of the Chinese Communist Party and must have a good and clean record.[43]

However, after reviewing the differences in opinion between the two forces, one for and the other against depoliticization, one gets the impression that whilst the recruitment of professional state administrators is thought to be desirable, they are not intended to be politically independent but rather should be directly under the leadership of the Party, working under political instructions. A significant number of the industrial élite have been recruited to the SEZs from all over China.[44] But these élites still work in a very politicized state structure, the only difference now being that professional administrators are thought to be desirable. This does not mean that the political element is completely ignored and that the state apparatus is completely free from Party control. In this sense, Fainsod's observation of the Soviet case applies to China: 'The Communist response to industrialization has been to recognize its rational imperatives where productivity considerations are involved, but to permeate and control the new social groupings which it creates in order to preserve the party's monopoly of power'.[45] This statement accurately describes the situation in the SEZs. It is still too early to conclude that politicization in the government apparatus is being diluted.

The Functional Politicization of the Bureaucracy

As shown in the previous section, the state apparatus is closely linked to the Party organization, using structural devices to appoint Party members to most of the top government positions, and creating a host of Party committees at each level of the state administrative hierarchy to ensure that the government apparatus is controlled by the Party. Thus, in this context, the bureaucracy is mainly structurally politicized. However, the bureaucracy is also politicized functionally and it is this aspect which we will now examine.

In the West, in the modern period, the belief that the best government is the least government has predominated. Thus, increasingly, bureaucrats have not been allowed to intervene in affairs in which they were formerly entitled to do so, for example in the sale of land and food, both traditionally monopolized by the monarch. Feudalism has been replaced by capitalism. The Chinese Communists believe that the best way to eliminate capitalism is to place all major living resources under tight control again. Hence, bureaucrats in China possess the power to intervene in a wide range of human affairs considered conducive to capitalism.

In his speech to the Third Session of the Fifth National People's Congress, Hua Guofeng, premier of the People's Republic of China, pointed out that the fundamental factor in the rise of bureaucratism in Communist China has been the socialist system, under which the state apparatus has been given the power to intervene in almost all aspects of human affairs. Never before in Chinese history has the state shouldered such a responsibility. As a government leader, Hua called for reform.[46]

However, an examination of the bureaucracy in the SEZs four years after Hua's speech reveals that the state apparatus is still omnipotent. The extent of the state administration's intervention inevitably means that its functions are politicized. The following are examples.

First, in developed countries, banks are not responsible for monitoring the manner in which business is conducted in the market. They will assess the credibility of an individual or a firm for business purposes only. They will not consider such political matters as whether a firm has made money morally or not, whether it has unethically or illegally monopolized a business, or whether it has manipulated the market to maximize its profit. These are matters for the politicians. Bankers generally remain neutral politically. In certain Western nations, laws exist that provide them with legal protection in not disclosing any financial information about their clients. In most developed countries, a bank will not under any circumstances report suspected misconduct to the government, unless a court order has been obtained for a specific investigation. It is definitely not the bank's job to report a suspect to the government authorities voluntarily. This principle of political neutrality is considered to be part of its professional code of conduct.

In China the practice of banking is different. Ideologically the Communists believe that the control of banking activities helps to counter capitalism. Therefore, the banking system does not recognize the principle of political neutrality. Instead, it is an important political tool with which to monitor misconduct. For this purpose, banks in China are (regularly or irregularly) required to help the government in countering undesirable economic activities. Other than their professional function as banks, they also have to perform a non-professional political function. For instance, in trying to cope with inflation in food prices, especially in the SEZs, the State Council has told banks in China to tighten up their management of loan credits and to supervise trading activities to ensure proper business conduct. Again, when food prices increase illegally, banks have to try to restrict this trend.[47] In the SEZs, despite the open policy and the use of Hong Kong currency, management of the banks is still a major function of the bureaucracy.[48] The banks also contribute another device in the control of economic crimes, such as corruption and smuggling, which frequently occur in the SEZs. To avoid incurring the suspicion of the banks in the SEZs, some corrupt money is reportedly being deposited in foreign banks in Hong Kong.

Second, land use is another politically controversial problem for the bureaucracy. Throughout Chinese history, land use has always presented a problem. Under the present Communist regime, the private ownership of land is banned. During the Cultural Revolution, even the free use of land became an issue which involved the state administration: bureaucrats busily engaged themselves in banning cash crops, an unpleasant job for state administrators. After the Cultural Revolution, around 1978, Beijing decided to lift the ban. Limited cash crops were allowed to be grown: nevertheless, land management, collective land-use sharing, taxation, and the operation of production teams are still controversial issues confronting state administrators.

In the SEZs, this problem of land use is even more acute. The open policy of inviting foreign investors to develop property jointly in the SEZs has triggered off political problems for state administrators. The Hong Kong media has indicated that in joint property development projects, officials in the SEZs have often undervalued the lease price, thereby giving away to foreign investors profits of thousands of millions of dollars and reducing the profits of the SEZs.[49] This creates a sensitive political problem since it makes officials look stupid and is humiliating. It could also easily bring about the downfall of the state administrator if a radical campaign erupts again.

In fact, the land-use policy in the SEZs, especially in Shenzhen and Zhuhai, has already put the bureaucrat in a difficult position.[50] Land is used as a resource to attract capital for development expenses which could not be obtained from the central government. In carrying out this policy, officials have to invite land developers, especially from Hong Kong, to provide easy money in a short time. As a result, some Party officials from the Central College for Cadres have pointed out that many land development projects have ended up being monopolized by a few capitalists.[51] Most of the land contracts, which cover large tracts of land, will restrict China's position in the future determination of land use. Poorly defined land-use terms in contracts have also jeopardized the interests of China. Such cases have demonstrated that a highly politicized land-use policy poses problems for the state administrator. As a result, bureaucrats are placed in a vulnerable position which may ruin their political neutrality and the stability of the state apparatus.

Third, the Chinese Communists believe capitalist exploitation is possible only if a wage system works in favour of the employer. They believe, too, that replacing the individual employer with the state as the employer will stop exploitation. All in principle are to be paid equally. To do this, the Chinese Communists have transferred the problem of wages from the individual employer to the state, thereby presenting the bureaucrat with a further highly politicized function. This move has created many problems, the worst of which is the lack of incentive and discipline amongst workers, as many observers have pointed out.

In the SEZs, this problem could be even more explosive politically. Although the SEZs have only existed for a short time, the political problem created by the wage and labour system is complicated. Studies conducted by scholars and Party men in China reveal the following problems:[52]

(a) As a result of the use of incentives to boost worker morale and thereby raise output, some wholly and partly owned foreign enterprises are allowed to fix their own wage rates and are not obliged to follow the unified wage-rate system in use in the rest of China.
(b) Consequently wage rates are very inconsistent in the SEZs. Generally, workers in wholly and partly owned foreign enterprises receive much higher wages than workers in state-owned enterprises and state administrators. Even among enterprises owned by outsiders, the pay is not uniform.
(c) The consequence of these two factors has been that the highest wages are paid by wholly owned foreign enterprises, followed by joint-venture enterprises, and, last of all, state-owned enterprises and the state administration.

As a whole, wages in the SEZs are much higher than elsewhere in China. This fact raises a political problem. How long will state workers tolerate this situation? Can the regime impose the national wage system on the SEZs, or will the wage system in the SEZs be imposed in non-SEZ areas? Which system is more conducive to a socialist state? The higher wages in the SEZs have already affected the standard of living of state workers and officials whose incomes cannot keep up with inflation there. A social scientist from Guangdong has suggested that this situation cannot be tolerated further. Since it would be irrational to sacrifice those who receive higher pay, and also irrational to see state workers suffer further from the effects of inflation in the SEZs, he has suggested the establishment of a cost of living index to adjust wage increments for state workers, especially administrators. For unless this is done the process of modernization will not be smooth.[53]

China's employment system is also being challenged in the SEZs. A national employment system was established and glorified during the Cultural Revolution. Under this system, the private operation of business in China practically ceased. All workers were legally employed only by the state, and the state was the only employer. In the recent campaign against ultra-leftists, this system was criticized. There are now some self-employed workers but the state is still the biggest employer. However, in the SEZs, this is no longer the case. The national hiring system is considered inappropriate in the SEZs,[54] where the aim is to attract foreign investment. It has been replaced with a contract system whereby a worker is hired on specific terms of employment. The worker can be fired if he does not meet these terms. The principle centres around the point that the job cannot be considered as permanently secure during the lifetime of the worker. The latter is widely known as 'the iron rice bowl'. The new hiring system in the SEZs, however, follows the principle of 'the more you work, the more you earn', and the company reserves the right to fire a worker it considers unworthy. Under this principle, political complications are bound to arise. Some have suggested establishing a form of unemployment insurance, a social welfare system and a manpower service to cope with this new situation.[55]

A large number of articles and reports have appeared in China's media in support of the contract system of hiring labour in the SEZs.[56] Although the state apparatus appears to have been freed from the pressure of being an overall employer, an even worse new political headache is developing for administrators in the contradiction between socialism and capitalism that the new employment system presents.

However, other than the three issues — banking, land-use control and the employment system — that have politicized the functions of the bureaucracy, further matters, such as the operation of the media, the development of technology, currency and foreign exchange control, and the control of food prices, have also placed a heavy burden on bureaucrats. For all these issues are prone to controversial political debate. It is for precisely this reason that some nations leave the operation of these businesses in private or semi-private hands so that their administrative apparatus does not become embroiled in politics.

In the SEZs, as elsewhere in China, the media is run as a state enterprise and is used as a political tool of the regime.[57] Historically, in the PRC, the control of the media has always formed part of the political struggle. In the SEZs, the operation of the media is particularly complex since it covers a wider socio-political spectrum.

One of the main goals of the SEZs is the attraction of high technology to promote modernization. This aim therefore constitutes one of the major tasks of administrators in the SEZs.[58] The task is not an easy one since most advanced technology or machinery is produced by private firms in developed nations, where government restrictions on the leaking of information apply. These private firms are therefore usually more inclined to deal with a private representative rather than a government official. The theft of technological skills commonly practised by developed countries could cause particular embarrassment to a country where a state official was involved.[59]

Currency and foreign exchange controls constitute another difficult area for the state administrator. China is one of the very few nations in the world which maintains tight control on currency export and exchange. In most areas in China this control may not pose a particular problem since these areas have very limited trading contacts with the outside world. But in the

SEZs, this policy causes great inconvenience,[60] and has encouraged people to give preference to foreign currency in their trading, simply because the use of foreign currency is more convenient and profitable in trade with foreign companies.[61]

Finally, the massive operation required to control food prices presents further problems for bureaucrats in the SEZs. No doubt, a limited and controlled food-price ceiling is conducive to social and political order. But the overzealous exercise of control is unhealthy both economically and politically. The implementation of a new economic policy of free trading in secondary food items has resulted in massive exports of these items to Hong Kong in order to obtain better prices. As a result, food prices have soared, especially in Shenzhen which has easy access to Hong Kong.[62] Consequently, the traditional extensive control exercised over food prices is that much more difficult to achieve in the SEZs. Politically the exercise of this control has already provoked a constant battle between the political and economic sectors, the authority of local bureaucrats being undermined in the eyes of economic operators each time they are exposed by the powerful state apparatus as having committed an economic crime. Economic crime is more prevalent in the SEZs than elsewhere, and serves to underline the point that the operation of a price-control system by the bureaucracy is unsound.

To conclude this section, it has been found that state administrators have been forced to shoulder the responsibility for a variety of highly controversial issues which have unavoidably involved them in politics. This constant involvement in political matters has damaged the state apparatus, resulting in inefficiency, corruption, controversy, incompetence and indecisiveness. Since the SEZs have adopted a more open policy, areas such as banking, land, employment, the operation of the media, and the control of currency and food prices have become rather more controversial politically. As a result, the state apparatus is facing greater problems in the SEZs than elsewhere, and thus its reform is being discussed more actively in the SEZs. Yet nothing concrete has been done to relieve the political burden borne by the state apparatus. Its functions are still being politicized. To put it another way, the state apparatus is still functionally responsible for some controversial matters that cannot be insulated from political involvement.

Conclusion

Throughout the above discussion, it has been quite clear that the SEZs in China are not special in the context of the state apparatus despite their more open policy in economic matters. The administration remains politicized both in structure and function. Structurally, Party leaders are still assigned to government posts and occupy a dominant position. A few thousand Party cadres from all over China have been posted to various leading jobs in the economic field. Also, the traditional Party control of the state administration remains in the SEZs. 'A hierarchy of party committees at each level of the state administrative hierarchy, with oversight functions designed to assure the supremacy of politics', as Heady has observed, persists in the SEZs.[63] Functionally, the administration is still responsible for too many jobs which are politically controversial. Its handling of these will continue to damage its competency, efficiency, credibility, neutrality and incorruptibility. In short, although a campaign for reform is being publicized, little change has taken place. Heady and Vogel's observations still apply even in the SEZs.

What are the advantages or disadvantages of this politicized state apparatus for the promotion of modernization in China? On this issue scholars are undecided. Certainly, when one examines the East European states, as Fainsod and Beck have done, it is clear that a politicized bureaucracy has not hindered modernization if by modernization one refers only to industrialization and not democratization.[64] Yet in China it is clear that a politicized bureaucracy has hindered modernization, a fact which might well be used in a comparative study to demonstrate the differences in terms of scope and degree between the two systems. Vogel has provided a fair assessment of the advantages and disadvantages of a politicized bureaucracy for modernization in Communist China and has pointed out that the high degree of politicization has given an immeasurable effectiveness to the modernization of bureaucratic organizations. 'Because functionaries do engage in continuous political study and because those in responsible positions are highly politicized, the bureaucracy can be mobilized in a way that officials in Western representative democracies cannot'.[65] On the negative side, Vogel has also pointed out that because of politicization, bureaucratic organizations are 'subject to attack and modification in the event of mobilization. With the massive mobilization, routine administrative tasks were neglected. In the end this proved the undoing of mobilization efforts'.[66] Vogel has claimed that this was precisely the problem with the Great Leap Forward. Heady has also made a comparable comment on the disadvantages of a politicized bureaucracy, finding that politicization has actually pushed Party cadres into becoming involved in the massive job of state administration, resulting in what he has called the 'bureaucratization of politics'. When this tendency goes to extremes, that is, when Party organs became heavily engaged in administrative work, crises such as the Cultural Revolution are hard to avoid.[67]

The present leadership is well aware of the damage done to national development by the Great Leap Forward and the Cultural Revolution. Hua's government report of 1981 cited above clearly demonstrates this.[68] But this is not the first time in the PRC's history that the leadership has made cautious noises about the problem of bureaucracy. Both Mao and Deng have in the past warned of bureaucratism. However, since power politics dominate institutional politics, Chinese leaders seem to have had little opportunity to put into practice a non-politicized bureaucracy. Some Communist scholars have claimed this is a traditional problem. For instance, Wang Yanan, a former rector of Xiamen University, has observed that prolonged feudalism and backwardness in China was in large part due to the cohesion between productive forces and the bureaucracy.[69] Wang explains that the main reason for the lack of progress in modernizing China's traditional productive forces was the strenuous efforts made by the feudalistic bureaucracy to preserve the status quo in order to protect their vested interests. Wang claims that its removal was necessary for the improvement of conditions for modernization, but that this could not be accomplished without revolution or war. Even so, its removal will not guarantee the success of modernization unless a new bureaucratic organization and productive forces are formed to replace the feudalistic system. But this process takes an immense amount of time and effort.

Wang is regarded as an expert on the issue of modernization and bureaucracy in Chinese history, and his research seems to have inspired the present leadership in Beijing. His earlier work on *The Study of China's Politics of Bureaucracy* has now been reprinted in China. The damage done to modernization by the politicized bureaucracy has also been discussed in China since the downfall of the Gang of Four.[70] It is, however, still too early to judge whether calls for the reform of the politicized bureaucracy are merely lip-service. The continued existence of politicization in the state apparatus in the SEZs cannot be taken as proof of the insincerity of present calls for reform. Rather, it may be interpreted as a natural outcome of a traditional and deep-rooted politicized system.

In fact, some favourable factors for depoliticization in the SEZs do exist. First, the fact that a large number of investors have been invited to invest in the SEZs could be regarded as being favourable to the depoliticization of the state apparatus. So far, it has been reported that over 90 per cent of all factories and enterprises in the SEZs are solely or jointly owned by foreign investors.[71] The management board of a solely owned foreign company is completely filled with foreign directors. In jointly owned companies, local and foreign directors sit on the board, the former being in the majority. So far there are fewer solely owned foreign companies than jointly owned companies. However, there are no strict rules against the setting up of a solely owned foreign company, except that it has to be technologically advanced. All these enterprises and factories are set up by contract and have the right to make their own business decisions. It is still premature to judge how well foreign investments are protected. But given the fact that contracted projects are generally honoured, it is reasonable to believe that foreign investments are likely to be free from political interference. The present leadership in Beijing, when referring to foreign investments in the SEZs, has given its assurance that foreign investments will be protected according to the contract.[72] Since so many foreign investors have been invited to play a role in the modernization attempt in the SEZs, which have been much publicized, the chances of a political purge occurring are less likely. In the circumstances, the attempt at modernization may be able to take firm root in the SEZs under the guise of protecting foreign investments. In the past, it was impossible to find an area that was safe from political purge. However, once successful modernization has been achieved in one city, the Beijing leadership believes that this can easily be copied in another city. Once modernization in one area has been achieved, the tactics and strategy for modernization will also be more effective. Hence the attraction of foreign investments to the SEZs can be considered a factor in preventing political intervention in economic activities.

Second, the current trend of emphasizing consumer goods, housing, agriculture, and non-military technology in the SEZs may also favour de-politicization. The key to the success of this development pattern lies in foreign markets. To secure foreign markets the authorities have to obtain the co-operation of foreign political entities. To secure foreign co-operation requires better international relations which occasional revolutionary campaigns, conducted to purge either individuals or foreign capitalists, would damage. Therefore, the current development pattern of the SEZs tends to act as a moderating influence on Chinese leaders in their policies because of the need to secure markets abroad. The same influence helped Japan after the Second World War when that country's industrial development pattern relied heavily on consumer goods, housing, agriculture, and non-military technology. However, the reverse has been the case in the USSR, where the emphasis has been on military-oriented industrialization, especially under the leadership of Stalin. This has meant building up military strength and constructing a heavy industry base conducive to fast industrial growth and the production of advanced armaments, military hardware and factory machinery. This strategy has led the Soviets into a pattern where consumer goods, housing, and agriculture are neglected.[73] If the present trend in the SEZs continues, significant success will be assured. Moreover, if the model is widely copied, a market-oriented industrialization programme will be developed. This will involve building up the elements of market strength and constructing a light industrial base conducive to a high rate of industrial growth and the production of advanced machinery and factory plants for consumer market needs. If this is the case, a more rational and professional bureaucracy may be able to develop. However, this is only an assumption given that the SEZs are still young.

Third, the policy of involving ethnic Chinese from Hong Kong, South-east Asia and elsewhere is another factor favourable to depoliticization. Chinese businessmen from these areas generally have no desire to become involved in politics when they do business with Communist China. This is because most South-east Asian nations are anti-Communist or non-Communist. Since these countries worry about Communist penetration, they may not allow their citizens to do business with Beijing unless they are apolitical. For this reason, it is natural for those who intend to invest in the SEZs to show their disinterest in politics. Also, Beijing's present overseas Chinese policy sets great store on the economic contribution that overseas Chinese can make to China. The past policy of emphasizing the revolutionary potential of the Chinese community in the South-east Asian region proved to be counter-productive, for the policy caused damage not only to the Chinese community abroad, but also to those returned overseas Chinese at home. During the Cultural Revolution, the returned overseas Chinese were severely persecuted and the regime is now trying to heal the wound.[74] As often indicated in Beijing, the current open policy in the SEZs is part of a campaign to offer economic opportunities to Chinese abroad.[75] By doing this, the regime believes that Chinese abroad will have greater faith in Beijing. As Taiwan under the Guomindang remains a competitor, Beijing cannot ignore the fact that rapid economic growth in Taiwan offers better business opportunities. Better economic ties mean better relations. If the Guomindang develops increasing support abroad, the likelihood of peaceful reunification between Taiwan and mainland China will be slimmer. It is sensible, therefore, to offer economic benefits to those who are only interested in economic matters and who might otherwise be attracted to Taiwan.

Notes

1. Joseph LaPalombara (ed.), *Bureaucracy and Political Development* (Princeton, NJ, Princeton University Press, 1971), p. 234.
2. LaPalombara (1971), p. 270.
3. LaPalombara (1971), p. 272.
4. LaPalombara (1971), p. 296.
5. LaPalombara (1971), p. 296.
6. LaPalombara (1971), p. 296.
7. Fred W. Riggs (ed.), *Frontiers of Development Administration* (Durham, NC, Duke University Press, 1970), pp. 562–5.
8. Ferrel Heady, *Public Administration: A Comparative Perspective* (New Mexico, University of New Mexico Press, 1979), p. 375.
9. Heady (1979), p. 376.
10. Zhao Ziyang, *Zhengfu gongzuo baogao* (*Working Report of the Government*) (Hong Kong, Joint Publishing Co., 1984), p. 17.
11. Deng Xiaoping, *Deng Xiaoping wenxuan* (*The Collected Works of Deng Xiaoping*) (Hong Kong, Joint Publishing Co., 1983), pp. 280–302.
12. Deng (1983), p. 280.
13. This is widely indicated in various policy announcements concerning the SEZs. For instance, see *Zhongguo jingji tequ nianjian* (*Yearbook of China's Special Economic Zones*) (Hong Kong, Yearbook of China's Special Economic Zones Publishing Co., 1983), p. 92.
14. *Zhongguo jingji tequ nianjian* (1983), p. 630.
15. *Zhongguo jingji tequ nianjian* (1983), p. 630.
16. *Zhongguo jingji tequ nianjian* (1983), p. 630.
17. *Zhongguo jingji tequ nianjian* (1983), p. 630.
18. This information was obtained from sources closed to officials in the SEZs.
19. See *The Seventies*, Vol. 146, March 1982, pp. 24–5.
20. See Sun Ru, 'Cong zhanlue yiyi tan jingji tequ de zuoyong he jianshe' ('The Strategic Significance of the SEZs') in *Xueshu yanjiu* (*Academic Research*), Vol. 4, 1982.
21. See *Zhongguo jingji tequ nianjian* (1983), p. 595.
22. *Zhongguo jingji tequ nianjian* (1983), p. 595.
23. *Zhongguo jingji tequ nianjian* (1983), p. 595.
24. *Shenzhen Special Zone Daily*, 17 April 1984, p. 1; and 22 June 1984, p. 1.
25. *Shenzhen Special Zone Daily*, 18 March 1984.
26. *Shenzhen Special Zone Daily*, 22 June 1984, p. 1; and 24 April 1984, p. 1.
27. *Shenzhen Special Zone Daily*, 6 April 1984, p. 1.
28. *The Seventies*, Vol. 146, March 1982, p. 22.
29. The trial procedure can be seen from some cases reported in the Chinese media. See *Ta kung pao*, 25 February 1982, p. 3.
30. *Ming pao Monthly*, Vol. 215, November 1983, pp. 9–12.
31. *The Seventies*, Vol. 146, March 1982, pp. 20–3.
32. *Ta kung pao*, 4 March 1982, p. 4.
33. *Ta kung pao*, 15 June 1982, p. 3.
34. This has been reported quite frequently in the Hong Kong media.

35. *Ta kung pao*, 9 January 1982, p. 2.
36. *Shenzhen Special Zone Daily*, 10 March 1984, p. 2.
37. *The Seventies*, Vol. 146, March 1982, pp. 18–23.
38. *The Seventies*, Vol. 146, March 1982, p. 23.
39. For a typical example, see *Shenzhen Special Zone Daily*, 6 April 1984, p. 1.
40. *Zhongguo jingji tequ nianjian* (1983), pp. 630–3.
41. *The Seventies*, Vol. 146, March 1982, pp. 20–3.
42. *Ta kung pao*, 25 May 1982, p. 3; and 23 January 1982, p. 2.
43. *Shenzhen Special Zone Daily*, 9 March 1984, p. 1.
44. It has been reported that over one thousand cadres had been recruited to Shenzhen alone up to January 1984. See *Shenzhen Special Zone Daily*, 20 January 1984, p. 1.
45. LaPalombara (1971), p. 234.
46. *Renmin ribao* (*People's Daily*), 15 September 1980, p. 2.
47. *Ta kung pao*, 9 January 1982, p. 2.
48. Xinhua News Agency and New Evening Post, *Zhongguo jingji tequ shouce* (*Handbook for China's Special Economic Zones*) (Hong Kong, New Evening Post, 1984), p. 40.
49. *The Seventies*, Vol. 146, March 1982, pp. 16–23.
50. Xu Xuehan, Wu Jian and Mao Rongfang, 'Dui Guangdong jingji tequ jianshe de diaocha he jianyi ('Some Suggestions for SEZs in Guangdong'), in *Internal Distributed Articles* (*Neibu wengao*), Vol. 103.
51. Xu *et al.*
52. See *Zhongguo jingji tequ nianjian* (1983), pp. 624–7.
53. *Zhongguo jingji tequ nianjian* (1983), p. 625.
54. *Zhongguo jingji tequ nianjian* (1983), pp. 624–7.
55. *Zhongguo jingji tequ nianjian* (1983), pp. 624–7.
56. It has been reported that over two hundred enterprises have adopted this contract system of hiring labour in Shenzhen alone. See *Shenzhen Special Zone Daily*, 13 March 1984, p. 1.
57. See note 47.
58. See *Zhongguo jingji tequ nianjian* (1983), p. 659.
59. *Zhongguo jingji tequ nianjian* (1983), p. 659.
60. *Zhongguo jingji tequ nianjian* (1983), pp. 575–6 and p. 678.
61. *Zhongguo jingji tequ nianjian* (1983), pp. 675–82.
62. See *The Seventies*, Vol. 146, March 1982, pp. 20–2; and *Zhongguo jingji tequ nianjian* (1983), pp. 620–3.
63. Heady (1979), pp. 375–6.
64. LaPalombara (1971), Chapters 8 and 9.
65. Riggs (1970), p. 567.
66. Riggs (1970), p. 567.
67. Heady (1979), p. 376.
68. *Renmin ribao*, 15 September 1980, p. 2.
69. Wang Yanam, *Zhongguo guanliao zhengzhi yanjiu* (*The Study of China's Politics of Bureaucracy*) (Beijing, China's Social Sciences Academy Press, 1980), Chapter 13.
70. *Renmin ribao*, 30 October 1980, p. 5.
71. *Ta kung pao*, 18 March 1982, p. 1.
72. Some legal measures have been established to protect foreign investments.
73. LaPalombara (1971), Chapter 8.
74. See C.Y. Chang, 'Overseas Chinese in China's Policy', in *China Quarterly*, June 1980, pp. 281–303.
75. *Ta kung pao*, 5 December 1981, p. 1.

7. The Regulatory Framework for Foreign Investment in the Special Economic Zones

KARL HERBST

Introduction

Since 1979, China's four special economic zones (SEZs), located in Guangdong and Fujian, have been perhaps the most publicized aspect of China's opening to the West. Shenzhen, Zhuhai and Shantou in Guangdong province and Xiamen in Fujian province were targeted for a major experiment in economic development, as special zones offering special incentives to foreign investors, unavailable in other parts of China. The SEZs were conceived as export-oriented areas, able to obtain foreign exchange and advanced technology, and as laboratories in which to test new legislative initiatives and train Chinese officials in modern management techniques. Although Chinese perceptions of the success of the SEZs vary,[1] there is no doubt that they have been the prime beneficiary of foreign investment in China.

Actual foreign investment in all four zones at the end of 1984 amounted to US$840 million according to a report by State Councillor Gu Mu to the National People's Congress Standing Committee in January 1985.[2] In April 1985, He Chunlin, director of the State Council's Office of SEZ Affairs, said that contracts signed with foreign firms by the end of 1984 represented a potential additional investment of US$3.2 billion.[3]

Shenzhen, by far the most successful of the SEZs, had reportedly received US$580 million of actual investment by the end of 1984.[4] According to another report, up to June 1984, it had received 61.5 per cent of the total number of joint ventures in China and 36.3 per cent of the total number of co-operative projects.[5]

The SEZs have been allowed to develop a legislative framework which in many ways differs from the regulatory scheme for investment allowed in other parts of China. Until recently, the Guangdong SEZs and particularly Shenzhen were the primary area for legislative activity. However, in February 1985 the Standing Committee of the Fujian Provincial People's Congress promulgated five sets of regulations for the Xiamen SEZ.[6] Regulations have also begun to appear for the 14 newly opened coastal cities,[7] where many of the incentives, formerly an exclusive aspect of the SEZs, will be available. This chapter will summarize the important legislative initiatives developed in the Guangdong SEZs and analyse several of the most significant recent laws, comparing them with national laws where appropriate.

The Legislative Framework

The basic regulatory framework for the Guangdong SEZs was established on 26 August 1980, when the Fifteenth Session of the Standing Committee of the Fifth National People's Congress adopted the Regulations on the Special Economic Zones in Guangdong Province (hereafter cited as the SEZ Regulations). The SEZ Regulations made it clear that wholly owned foreign enterprises, as well as joint ventures, were welcome in the Guangdong SEZs.[8] Indeed, until the development of the 14 coastal cities, wholly owned foreign enterprises were only allowed in the SEZs and not elsewhere in China. Article 2 of the SEZ Regulations raised an issue of continuing uncertainty in viewing the legal structure of the SEZs, that is the relationship between national and local law. It indicated that national laws apply in the SEZs unless contradicted by a specific provision in the SEZ Regulations. This has been the standard interpretation of all SEZ legislation which has followed, confirming the point that the SEZs are not developing a totally autonomous regulatory structure.[9] However, this interpretation has led to the practical need to integrate national and SEZ legislation in order to understand fully the applicable legal framework.

The SEZ Regulations created a variety of preferential treatment in the areas of profit tax (a 15 per cent enterprise income tax and special preferences for investment of over US$5 million and high technology projects),[10] land-use fees[11] and the simplification of entry and exit procedures.[12] Also 'machinery and equipment, spare parts, raw and semi-processed materials, means of transportation and other capital goods required for production imported by enterprises in the special zones shall be exempted from import duties'.[13] However, this benefit presupposed that the production input would lead to the ultimate export of products. If approval is obtained under Article 9 for sale within China, the previous exemption from import duties and the consolidated industrial and commercial tax is lost and payment must be made. The SEZ Regulations further contained provisions relating to labour management which seem to provide a high level of autonomy to enterprises, including the power to dismiss workers.[14]

The SEZ Regulations also provided for the establishment of a provincial-level structure, the Administrative Committee for the Special Economic Zones of Guangdong Province (ADCOM) with wide overall powers of administration within the Guangdong SEZs. ADCOM was given the authority to formulate development plans for the zones and organize their implementation; to examine and approve the investment projects of investors; to handle industrial and commercial registration and land allotment; to co-ordinate working relations among the banking, insurance, taxation, customs, frontier inspection, postal and telecommunications and other SEZ organizations; to provide staff and workers needed by SEZ enterprises; to establish educational, cultural and health facilities and public welfare institutions in the SEZs; and to maintain public order.[15]

The SEZ Regulations further provided a framework for the development of a legal structure in the Guangdong SEZs. However, they were too general to provide more than a very basic outline and it soon became clear that supplementary legislation was needed. In November 1981, the Standing Committee of the National People's Congress adopted a resolution 'to authorize the Guangdong and Fujian Provincial People's Congresses and their Standing Committees to formulate various specific economic regulations for their Special Economic Zones according to the principles laid down in the related laws, decrees and policies. . . and to submit them to the Standing Committee of the National People's Congress for the record'.[16] Thus legislative competence had to a certain extent been delegated to the two provinces. However national legislation still applied unless expressly contradicted.

After this delegation of authority, four regulations were adopted by the Standing Committee of the Guangdong Provincial People's Congress further to amplify the provisions contained in the SEZ Regulations. These were the Entry and Exit Regulations,[17] the Labour and Wage Regulations,[18] the Business Registration Regulations,[19] and the Shenzhen Land Regulations.[20] These four regulations, along with the SEZ Regulations, created the original legal framework for the Guangdong SEZs.[21] Although views vary regarding the effectiveness of these regulations in providing attractive preferential treatment for investors, it is fair to stress that the promise of enterprise autonomy over the labour force contained within the SEZ Regulations has not been fulfilled.[22] In particular the SEZ labour bureaux have presented obstacles to the dismissal of workers by enterprises.[23] It is interesting to note that lack of control over the dismissal of workers by a joint venture is a problem throughout China and is by no means restricted to the SEZs.[24] Indeed recent national implementing regulations for labour management in equity joint ventures have attempted to increase enterprise autonomy in this matter.[25]

Another problem which has developed is uncertainty regarding which entity approves and supervises investment in the SEZs. The SEZ Regulations give that authority to ADCOM.[26] However, certain regulations promulgated by Guangdong province give such authority to individual municipal governments as well.[27] The Regulations of the Shenzhen Special Economic Zone on Foreign Economic Contracts, which will be discussed later, specifically delegate the authority to approve contracts to the Shenzhen Municipal People's Government.[28] Furthermore, there is uncertainty regarding when national-level approval is necessary and when municipal approval is sufficient.[29]

Recently, two more regulations were promulgated to supplement the 1981 Guangdong regulations, for application in Shenzhen. They are regulations relating to land-use fees in Shenzhen,[30] and detailed regulations for the registration of enterprises in Shenzhen.[31] The Land-use Fee Regulations of 1984 modify existing land-use fees and develop seven new categories for the reduction of, or exemption from, land-use fees. Interestingly, special provision is made for high technology projects[32] and for enterprises established with the aid of financial contributions from overseas Chinese or from Hong Kong, Macau and Taiwan compatriots.[33]

The Detailed Registration Regulations make it clear that the Shenzhen Municipal People's Government has the authority to approve the registration of foreign enterprises in Shenzhen and that the Shenzhen Municipal Administration for Industry and Commerce issues business licences and registration certificates.[34] Reportedly, this delegation of authority to allow local administrative bureaux of industry and commerce to handle and ratify independently the registration of foreign enterprises has been extended to all the SEZs and the 14 coastal cities.[35] The regulations lay down registration fee standards[36] based on the national registration fees defined in the Provisional Regulations on Standards for the Payment of Registration Fees by Joint Ventures Using Chinese and Foreign Investment. They also give the Shenzhen Municipal Administration for Industry and Commerce the power to impose fines on enterprises which violate registration rules.[37]

Specialized Legislation

The regulations which have been discussed above are essentially regulations defining preferences and administrative structure and authority in the SEZs. However Shenzhen, in particular, has been used as a test area for certain types of legislation which could ultimately be incorporated into national law.[38] This section will analyse several of these new Shenzhen regulations and in some cases compare them to newly drafted national laws.

Foreign Economic Contracts

Although a domestic Economic Contracts Law has existed in China since 1981,[39] the Shenzhen Contract Regulations constituted the first law to regulate contractual relations between Chinese and foreign business entities. Many observers believed that the Shenzhen Contract Regulations were expected to be a model for a forthcoming national law.[40] There are several provisions in these regulations, which contain 41 articles, which are worthy of note. The regulations appear to apply to both trade and investment contracts as long as performance is to occur in the Shenzhen SEZ.[41] Articles 15 to 19 define the contractual requirements for contracts involving joint ventures, co-operative ventures, compensation trade, assembly and processing and those entered into by wholly owned foreign enterprises. However, Article 20 refers to other specialized Shenzhen legislation for certain types of contracts such as technology transfer. Article 20 also refers to various national laws that govern contracts in defined areas, such as sale and purchase, insurance, the supply of electricity and the leasing of property. This provision (Article 20) apparently reduces the scope of the Shenzhen Contract Regulations. Furthermore, in areas such as equity joint ventures in which national legislation already exists, the specific Shenzhen requirements must be read in conjunction with the national regulations.

Article 9 provides that both sides must produce evidence of their legal capacity and identity and also a statement of short-term assets and liabilities and a credit certificate from a financial institution.[42] Most significantly, Article 12 requires that both parties provide guarantees. Reportedly in some negotiations, the Chinese have demanded that a subsidiary obtain the guarantee of its parent company for all contractual obligations.[43] This has been viewed as a particularly burdensome obligation by foreign investors.

Another especially onerous provision relates to the standard of liability for breach of contract. Article 21 includes a standard reference to the need for compensation for losses caused by late payment or late delivery. However, it goes further in requiring a penalty payment of 0.1 per cent of the total amount of the overdue portion for every day of late delivery or late payment. Western businessmen may find this rather startling although the concept of a statutory penalty payment is included in China's domestic Economic Contracts Law.[44]

In accordance with China's planned economy, contracts can only be altered or dissolved with the consent of the approval organ (Article 26), which is presumably the Shenzhen Municipal People's Government (Article 5). Also, contracts that violate laws and regulations of the People's Republic of China or damage China's sovereignty and the public interest are invalid.[45]

A particularly disturbing feature of the Shenzhen Contract Regulations relates to the power given to the Shenzhen Municipal Administration for Industry and Commerce, defined as the contract control organ.[46] Under Article 32, the contract control organ has the right to supervise the performance of the contract, mediate disputes arising from a breach of contract, stop and rectify illegal conduct by both parties, and, where the circumstances are serious, impose fines. These powers are both considerable and vaguely defined. It is unclear whether the contract control organ can independently determine whether a breach of contract has occurred. Also, the procedural basis and standards for assessing fines have not been revealed.

Article 40 of the Shenzhen Contract Regulations requires that if there are two language texts of the contract, the Chinese version is to prevail. Interestingly, under the Joint Venture Implementing Act, if there are contract texts in Chinese and a foreign language they are considered to be equally valid and binding.[47] A recent article stresses that it is surprising to find a more stringent requirement in Shenzhen than at the national level.[48] The Chinese language priority governs joint ventures in Shenzhen since particular SEZ legislation apparently takes precedence over conflicting national legislation. It has been alleged that, in practice, Shenzhen Chinese enterprises have at times been willing to sign contracts exclusively in English.[49] If that is so it will certainly please foreign investors who have been extremely disturbed by the Chinese language priority.

The Shenzhen Contract Regulations are ambiguous as to whether a foreign governing-law clause is acceptable. Article 35 mandates the use of Chinese law for 'contracts having a close bearing on the sovereignty of China' such as joint ventures, co-operative ventures and contracts for the co-operative development of natural resources to be performed in the Shenzhen SEZ. However, it is unclear whether other types of contract may be placed under foreign law. Similar ambiguity exists in the area of dispute settlement. Article 34 authorizes arbitration as a dispute settlement mechanism and does not appear to restrict the venue to China. However, Article 35, while discussing joint-venture, co-operative venture and natural resource development contracts, indicates that if arbitration is needed it should be conducted by the arbitration organization established in the SEZ. Indeed, under the auspices of the China Council for the Promotion of International Trade, an arbitration centre was opened in Shenzhen to deal with disputes involving foreign investors in the spring of 1984.[50] The language of Article 35 is quite ambiguous and it is uncertain whether the call for arbitration in Shenzhen is mandatory. The Joint Venture Implementing Act allows foreign arbitration for equity joint ventures,[51] if the parties contract to that effect. It would be surprising if the Shenzhen authorities proved to be more restrictive on this point. Although the issue remains unresolved it has been reported that Article 35 has not prevented the drafting of contracts calling for foreign arbitration.[52]

In March 1985 the long-awaited Foreign Economic Contracts Law was adopted.[53] Since the Shenzhen Contract Regulations had been viewed as a possible national model, it is useful to see whether the national law follows some of the more controversial aspects of the Shenzhen Contract Regulations.

The Foreign Economic Contracts Law allows the parties to the contract to choose a foreign governing law: if no choice is stipulated, the law of the country with the closest connection to the contract applies.[54] However, as in the Shenzhen Contract Regulations, equity joint-venture and contractual joint-venture contracts and contracts on the co-operative development of natural resources which are performed within China must be governed by Chinese law,[55] and are thus an exception to the general rule.

The Foreign Economic Contracts Law allows disputes to be settled by a foreign arbitral institution if the parties so agree.[56] Thus the national law is clearer and more beneficial to foreign interests than the Shenzhen law in the area of arbitration.

The national law further provides that a guarantee clause is optional.[57] There is no statutory penalty payment provision, although the contract can stipulate an amount of liquidated damages which is ultimately to be based on actual losses.[58] The national law further defines *force majeure* as an event which the parties cannot foresee at the time of the conclusion of the contract and whose occurrence or consequences the parties can neither avoid nor overcome. Interestingly, it allows the parties to the contract to specify the events which signify an excuse due to *force majeure*.[59] The Shenzhen Contract Regulations in Article 24(3) include a similar provision of contractual autonomy. However, in practice, Chinese entities are unlikely to define events of *force majeure* as broadly as in the West.

Finally, the Foreign Economic Contracts Law allows the parties to determine which language is to be the effective language of the contract.[60]

In general the national law appears, at least in theory, to give greater contractual autonomy to the parties and to be more attractive to foreign interests than are the Shenzhen Contract Regulations. Of course, in practice much will depend on the actual administration of the new law and the willingness of Chinese entities to choose, for example, a foreign governing law in a technology transfer deal. Nevertheless it seems that in drafting the Foreign Economic Contracts Law, Chinese officials were sensitive to complaints raised about the Shenzhen Contract Regulations.

Technology Transfer

The Shenzhen Provisional Technology Regulations[61] are another example of the use of Shenzhen as a potential model for future national legislation. As the first technology transfer regulations approved by the PRC, they have reportedly been extensively used by analogy by Chinese entities in other parts of China during negotiations on technology transfer,[62] although they are not mandatory outside Shenzhen.

The Shenzhen Provisional Technology Regulations contain certain provisions which are of serious concern to potential foreign investors. In particular, there is a very long list of documents, data and equipment that must be provided when transferring know-how.[63] The supplier is responsible for training the Chinese party and must ensure that the recipient masters the entire technology.[64] He must also guarantee the legal effectiveness and the anticipated technical results of the introduced technology.[65] Finally, the technology must be capable of producing products suitable for the international market: if losses are caused by the influence of the supplier on sales the supplier is liable for those losses.[66] Furthermore, in cases where the supplier has transferred the same technology to other persons, he must submit a duplicate of the original contract to the Chinese party.[67] The Shenzhen Provisional Technology Regulations also provide that technology transfer agreements, except for the use of technology as investment capital, should generally not exceed five years, although extensions are possible.[68] If the foreign party to a joint venture uses technology as investment capital the ratio of its technology capital is not to exceed 20 per cent of the registered capital of the joint venture.[69] In addition, the regulations require the maintenance of confidentiality although the standards for defining losses caused by the divulgence of secrets are unclear.[70] There are also tax advantages and preferential land-use rates for technology submitted that is of an advanced level or that has major economic results.[71]

It has recently been observed that although Shenzhen was to be a showpiece for the introduction of advanced Western technology it has in reality failed to obtain the desired level of technology.[72] Perhaps a reason for this comparative failure has been the burdensome requirements codified in the Shenzhen Provisional Technology Regulations. Foreign businessmen have been particularly concerned about the extremely short five-year duration period and the various guarantees, particularly that the Chinese master the technology.

Recently, the State Council promulgated national Technology Import Regulations.[73] These regulations are much shorter (only 13 articles) than the Shenzhen regulations (25 articles) and far less detailed. Significantly, the national Technology Import Regulations authorize a 10-year norm for the length of technology transfer contracts which can be extended.[74] The foreign supplier must guarantee the effectiveness of the technology, but in general the requirements appear to be less onerous than under the Shenzhen Provisional Technology Regulations, although the contract cannot forbid continued use by the recipient of the technology after its expiry.[75] However, in early 1985, both Xiamen[76] and Guangzhou[77] released new legislation governing the import of technology which is in many ways similar to the Shenzhen legislation.[78] Therefore it remains to be seen to what extent the Shenzhen Provisional Technology Regulations will be used as a model. It is possible that the new national Technology Import Regulations will serve as a more general statement of requirements and that local areas, particularly the new coastal cities, will enact more detailed legislation based on the Shenzhen model.

New Financial Legislation

Shenzhen has recently begun to produce legislation creating a financial market, the first such legislation in China since 1949. Two regulations were released in late 1984 which had been approved by the head office of the People's Bank of China. They are regulations covering the activities of non-banking financial institutions[79] and authorizing bank mortgage loans.[80] The Non-Banking Financial Institutions Regulations seek to encourage Chinese companies involved in finance, trusts, credit, investment, financial leasing, specialized insurance and stock exchanges to set up offices in the Shenzhen SEZ.[81] The regulations define the permissible scope of activities, including the possible creation of a stock exchange, and set the requirements for registered capital, as well as the registration requirements. The Shenzhen branch of the People's Bank of China authorizes approval of specialized business operations and registration is then necessary with the Shenzhen Municipal Administration for Industry and Commerce. The State General Administration of Exchange Control controls approvals of foreign exchange business.

The Bank Mortgage Loan Regulations authorize mortgage loans to industry and commerce as well as to tourist and transport concerns.[82] They allow banks to make loans against negotiable securities, defined mainly as stocks and bonds that can be marketed on the mainland and in Hong Kong and Macau.[83]

The most significant new financial legislation authorizes foreign banks to set up branches in the SEZs.[84] These regulations are an obvious use of the SEZs as an experimental area for potential national legislation allowing branch activities in other parts of China. Branch activities must be approved by the head office of the People's Bank of China and the SEZ branches of the People's Bank are to exercise control and supervision over foreign and joint-venture banks. The regulations cover the requirements for approval and define the range of business activities. These include: (a) the granting of loans in local and foreign currencies; (b) the handling of inward remittances; (c) the settling of export transactions and outward documentary bills; (d) the handling of local and foreign exchange investments and local and foreign currency guarantees; (e) the buying and selling of stocks and securities; (f) trust and consultancy services; (g) the handling of outward remittances by overseas Chinese enterprises, foreign enterprises, and joint-venture enterprises; and (h) the settlement of their import transactions and inward documentary bills.[85] Foreign bank branches can also accept local and foreign currency deposits and overdrafts by foreign, joint-venture and overseas Chinese enterprises. Ambiguously, the regulations add 'other business activities' to this list of potential operations.[86]

The branch office of a foreign bank in an SEZ must hold operating funds in foreign exchange equivalent to 40 million *yuan*. The foreign bank must register with the Administration for Industry and Commerce in order to obtain a business licence. Branches of the People's Bank of China can fine foreign banks in the SEZs for violation of the regulations and appeal can be made to the People's Bank of China, but apparently not to the courts.[87]

These new regulations have already been criticized by bankers in Hong Kong. The requirement that foreign banks opening branches in the SEZs have to register working capital equivalent to 40 million *yuan* has been found to be especially onerous.[88] Bankers have also been upset to learn that they must pay the industrial and commercial consolidated tax on their turnover even if they fail to make a profit. Another area of concern lies in the fact that foreign banks can deal with foreign enterprises and joint ventures but not with state-owned enterprises. Finally, although the regulations allow the banks to deal in local currency transactions subject to approval, it is unclear how they can obtain *renminbi* which is issued and controlled by the People's Bank of China.[89] It is of course too early to tell whether these new regulations will lead to much foreign bank activity in the SEZs. However, it will be possible to ascertain the reaction of foreign businessmen and make improvements in the SEZ banking regulations which might eventually lead to a national law.

It is safe to expect that there will be more legislation in Shenzhen dealing with the creation of a financial market. Such legislation can be expected in the areas of foreign exchange guarantees and the issue of shares and bonds.[90] The process of development is certainly likely to continue in this area, indicating the use of the SEZs in making significant changes to the old Maoist economic structure.

Tax Preferences

As discussed earlier, the 1980 SEZ Regulations defined the basic tax preferences for the Guangdong SEZs. Unpublished rules have led to various preferences in the area of tax holidays and to lower personal income tax.[91] However, due to the uncertain legal validity of these unpublished rules, there has often been doubt regarding the extent of certain preferences. In November 1984, the State Council attempted both to deal with this uncertainty and to establish a new tax and customs regime for the 14 coastal cities. The resulting Provisional Regulations of the People's Republic of China Concerning the Reduction and Exemption of Enterprise Income Tax and the Consolidated Industrial and Commercial Tax for the Special Economic Zones and Fourteen Coastal Cities (hereafter cited as the 1984 Tax Regulations) to a large extent resolve the tax scheme for the SEZs.[92] The 1984 Tax Regulations confirm the 15 per cent enterprise tax. In addition, the two-year tax holiday and subsequent three-year 50 per cent reduction for enterprises engaged in industry, communications and transport, agriculture, forestry and livestock breeding with a contract life of at least 10 years is maintained.[93] Enterprises engaged in the service trade get similar but somewhat reduced preferences.[94] The SEZ government can decide to reduce local income tax or grant exemption[95] and there is a reduction to 10 per cent on the withholding tax on passive income earned by foreign businesses which have not set up establishments in China.[96] The 1984 Tax Regulations confirm substantial reductions or exemptions in the consolidated industrial and commercial tax which may, however, be lost by shipping goods into the interior of China.[97] The 1980 SEZ Regulations had failed to indicate whether the foreign participants in an equity joint venture in the SEZs would have to pay the 10 per cent withholding tax on the remittance of after-tax profits assessed under the Joint Venture Income Tax Law.[98] Indeed SEZ officials themselves were apparently uncertain as to whether this tax would have to be assessed.[99] The 1984 Tax Regulations resolve this issue by exempting foreign participants in equity joint ventures in the SEZs from this tax.[100]

It remains to be seen whether or not the SEZ authorities can provide incentives greater than those codified in the 1984 Tax Regulations. However, some have argued that this is acceptable with the permission of the State Council's Office of SEZ Affairs.[101]

Conclusion

The last few years have witnessed a remarkable development in the legal structure in the SEZs. A basic framework has been developed in the Guangdong SEZs and is slowly beginning to develop in the Xiamen SEZ in Fujian province.[102] Some of the SEZ legislation has been used as a potential model for national legislation or as a basis for analogy in other parts of China. It is clear that this legislative development is far from complete. It is equally clear that a final assessment of the merits of the SEZ concept and of the effectiveness of its laws and role as a potential model is premature.

Notes

1. For criticism of the SEZs see R. Delfs, 'Changing the Pattern', *Far Eastern Economic Review*, 9 May 1985, pp. 70–1.
2. Delfs (1985), p. 70.
3. Delfs (1985), p. 70.
4. Delfs (1985), p. 70.
5. Tang Huozhao, 'Shenzhen Offers Diverse Investment Channels', *Intertrade*, February 1985, pp. 54–5.
6. They consist of regulations on the registration of enterprises, labour manage-

ment, land use, economic association with other parts of China, and imports of technology, promulgated on 24 February 1985.

7. They are Dalian, Qinhuangdao, Tianjin, Yantai, Qingdao, Lianyungang, Nantong, Shanghai, Ningbo, Wenzhou, Fuzhou, Guangzhou, Zhanjiang and Beihai.

8. SEZ Regulations, Art 1. An English translation can be found in *China's Foreign Economic Legislation* (Beijing, Foreign Languages Press, 1982), Vol. I, pp. 193–200.

9. T. Gelatt, 'China's Special Economic Zones', in J. Cohen (ed.), *Legal Aspects of Doing Business in China 1983* (New York, Practising Law Institute, 1983), pp. 158–9. See also M.J. Moser, 'Law and Investment in the Guangdong Special Economic Zones', in M.J. Moser (ed.), *Foreign Trade, Investment and the Law in the People's Republic of China* (Hong Kong, Oxford University Press, 1984), pp. 147–8.

10. SEZ Regulations, Art. 14.

11. SEZ Regulations, Art. 12.

12. SEZ Regulations, Art. 18.

13. SEZ Regulations, Art. 13.

14. SEZ Regulations, Art. 20.

15. SEZ Regulations, Art. 23.

16. The Resolution on the Authorization of the Guangdong and Fujian Provincial People's Congresses and their Standing Committees to Formulate Various Specific Economic Regulations for their Special Economic Zones, adopted on 26 November 1981 by the Twenty-first Session of the Standing Committee of the Fifth National People's Congress. An English translation can be found in *Laws and Regulations of the People's Republic of China* (Hong Kong, Kingsway, 1982), Vol. I, p. 72.

17. The Provisional Regulations of the Special Economic Zones in Guangdong Province Governing the Entry and Exit of Personnel (hereafter cited as the Entry and Exit Regulations), adopted by the Thirteenth Session of the Standing Committee of the Fifth Guangdong Provincial People's Congress on 17 November 1981. An English translation can be found in *China's Foreign Economic Legislation* (1982), Vol. I, pp. 207–11.

18. The Provisional Regulations of the Special Economic Zones in Guangdong Province Governing Labour and Wages for Business Enterprises (hereafter cited as the Labour and Wage Regulations), adopted by the Thirteenth Session of the Standing Committee of the Fifth Guangdong Provincial People's Congress on 17 November 1981. An English translation can be found in *China's Foreign Economic Legislation* (1982), Vol. I, pp. 223–8.

19. The Provisional Regulations of the Special Economic Zones in Guangdong Province Governing the Registration of Business Enterprises (hereafter cited as the Business Registration Regulations), adopted by the Thirteenth Session of the Standing Committee of the Fifth Guangdong Provincial People's Congress on 17 November 1981. An English translation can be found in *China's Foreign Economic Legislation* (1982), Vol. I, pp. 215–19.

20. The Provisional Regulations Governing Land in the Shenzhen Special Economic Zone (hereafter cited as the Shenzhen Land Regulations), adopted by the Thirteenth Session of the Standing Committee of the Fifth Guangdong Provincial People's Congress on 17 November 1981. An English translation can be found in *China's Foreign Economic Legislation* (1982), Vol. I, pp. 233–9.

21. For a detailed analysis of these regulations see Gelatt (1983), pp. 165–79; and Moser (1984), pp. 154–63.

22. Moser (1984), p. 159.

23. See Labour and Wage Regulations, Art. 17; and Moser (1984), p. 159.

24. See S. Hood, K. Herbst and G. Lau, *Equity Joint Ventures in the People's Republic of China* (Hong Kong, Longman Professional Intelligence Reports, 1985), p. 37.

25. Provisions for the Implementation of the Regulations on Labour Management in Joint Ventures Using Chinese and Foreign Investment, Art. 10. An English translation can be found in *China Economic News*, 12 March 1984, pp. 2–4.

26. SEZ Regulations, Art. 23.
27. Business Registration Regulations, Art. 3.
28. The Regulations of the Shenzhen Special Economic Zone on Foreign Economic Contracts (hereafter cited as the Shenzhen Contract Regulations), approved by the Standing Committee of the Sixth Guangdong Provincial People's Congress on 11 January 1984 and promulgated by the Guangdong Provincial People's Government on 7 February 1984, Art. 5.
29. Moser (1984), p. 149.
30. The Regulations Concerning the Adjustment, Exemption and Reduction in Land-use Fees in the Shenzhen Special Economic Zone (hereafter cited as the Land-use Fee Regulations), promulgated by the Shenzhen Municipal People's Government on 25 December 1984. They went into effect on 1 January 1985.
31. The Detailed Regulations for the Registration of Enterprises in the Shenzhen Special Economic Zone (hereafter cited as the Detailed Registration Regulations), approved by the Guangdong Provincial People's Government on 18 January 1984 and promulgated by the Shenzhen Municipal People's Government on 9 February 1984. An English translation can be found in *China Economic News*, 29 October 1984, pp. 1–4.
32. Land-use Fee Regulations, Art. 4(e).
33. Land-use Fee Regulations, Art. 4(f).
34. Detailed Registration Regulations, Arts. 5 and 2. Also see the discussion by Nee in his paper, 'China's Special Economic Zones and Fourteen Coastal Cities', delivered at a conference entitled 'Evaluating the New Business Opportunities in China's SEZs and Coastal Cities', organized by the Institute for International Research in Hong Kong on 14 June 1985, pp. C–32 and 33.
35. *China Economic News*, 19 November 1984, pp. 1–2; and Nee (1985), p. C–33.
36. Detailed Registration Regulations, Art. 11.
37. Detailed Registration Regulations, Arts. 13 and 14.
38. Nee (1985), p. C–14.
39. Economic Contracts Law of the People's Republic of China (hereafter cited as the Economic Contracts Law), approved by the Fourth Session of the Fifth National People's Congress on 13 December 1981. An English translation can be found in F. Chu, M. Moser and O. Nee (eds.), *Commercial, Business and Trade Laws: People's Republic of China* (Dobbs Ferry, Oceana Publications Inc., 1983), Pt. 5, pp. 5–36.
40. J. Cohen, 'Shenzhen's New Contract Law: A Model for China?', *China Business Review*, September – October 1984, p. 16.
41. Shenzhen Contract Regulations, Arts. 1 and 2.
42. Cohen (1984), p. 16.
43. Cohen (1984), p. 17.
44. Economic Contracts Law, Art. 35.
45. Shenzhen Contract Regulations, Art. 6.
46. Shenzhen Contract Regulations, Art. 31.
47. The Implementing Act for the Law of the People's Republic of China on Joint Ventures Using Chinese and Foreign Investment (hereafter cited as the Joint Venture Implementing Act), promulgated by the State Council on 20 September 1983, Art. 9. An English translation can be found in *China Economic News*, 3 October 1983, Supp. No. 4, p. 3.
48. Cohen (1984), p. 17.
49. Nee (1985), p. C–21.
50. 'Second Arbitration Centre in Shumchun', *South China Morning Post Business News*, 16 March 1984, p. 1.
51. Joint Venture Implementing Act, Art. 110.
52. Cohen (1984), p. 17.
53. The Foreign Economic Contracts Law of the People's Republic of China (hereafter cited as the Foreign Economic Contracts Law), adopted at the Tenth Session of the Standing Committee of the National People's Congress on 21 March

1985. An English translation can be found in *China Economic News*, 1 April 1985, pp. 1–4. The law went into effect on 1 July 1985.

54. Foreign Economic Contracts Law, Art. 5.
55. Foreign Economic Contracts Law, Art. 5.
56. Foreign Economic Contracts Law, Art. 37.
57. Foreign Economic Contracts Law, Art. 15.
58. Foreign Economic Contracts Law, Art. 20.
59. Foreign Economic Contracts Law, Art. 24.
60. Foreign Economic Contracts Law, Art. 12(10).
61. The Provisional Regulations of the Shenzhen Special Economic Zone on the Introduction of Technology (hereafter cited as the Shenzhen Provisional Technology Regulations), approved by the Standing Committee of the Sixth Guangdong Provincial People's Congress on 11 January 1984 and promulgated by the Guangdong Provincial People's Government on 8 February 1984.
62. Nee (1985), p. C–17.
63. Shenzhen Provisional Technology Regulations, Art. 9.
64. Shenzhen Provisional Technology Regulations, Art. 10.
65. Shenzhen Provisional Technology Regulations, Art. 12.
66. Shenzhen Provisional Technology Regulations, Art. 12.
67. Shenzhen Provisional Technology Regulations, Art. 11.
68. Shenzhen Provisional Technology Regulations, Art. 19.
69. Shenzhen Provisional Technology Regulations, Art. 23.
70. Shenzhen Provisional Technology Regulations, Art. 13.
71. Shenzhen Provisional Technology Regulations, Art. 6. Also see discussion by Nee (1985), p. C–16.
72. Nee (1985), p. C–17.
73. The Regulations of the People's Republic of China on Technology Import Contract Administration (hereafter cited as the Technology Import Regulations), promulgated by the State Council on 24 May 1985. An English translation can be found in *China Economic News*, 17 June 1985, pp. 1–2.
74. Technology Import Regulations, Art. 8.
75. Technology Import Regulations, Art. 6 and 9(8).
76. The Regulations on Technology Imports to the Xiamen Special Economic Zone (hereafter cited as the Xiamen Technology Regulations), approved at the Eighth Session of the Standing Committee of the Sixth Fujian Provincial People's Congress on 14 July 1984 and promulgated on 24 February 1985. An English translation can be found in *China Economic News*, 22 April 1985, pp. 3–4.
77. The Interim Regulations of the Guangzhou Economic and Technological Development Zone Concerning the Introduction of Technology (hereafter cited as the Guangzhou Technology Regulations), adopted at the Guangzhou Mayor's Work Meeting on 6 March 1985 and promulgated by the Guangzhou Municipal People's Government on 9 April 1985. An English translation can be found in *China Economic News*, 17 June 1985, pp. 2–6.
78. The Guangzhou legislation is more detailed than the comparable Xiamen Technology Regulations and includes guarantees of the technology and training requirements. See Guangzhou Technology Regulations, Art. 24. However, like the national Technology Import Regulations, a 10-year contract period is specified. Guangzhou Technology Regulations, Art. 16.
79. The Interim Procedures of the Shenzhen Special Economic Zone for Non-banking State-owned Financial Institutions (hereafter cited as the Non-banking Financial Institutions Regulations), promulgated on 5 December 1984. An English translation can be found in *China Economic News*, 21 January 1985, pp. 1–3.
80. The Interim Procedures for Bank Mortgage Loans (hereafter cited as the Bank Mortgage Loan Regulations), promulgated on 5 December 1984. An English translation can be found in *China Economic News*, 21 January 1985, pp. 3–4. For another recent Shenzhen law dealing with mortgages of real estate in the SEZ see the Rules of the Shenzhen Special Economic Zone on Property Management, adopted by the

Fourth Session of the Standing Committee of the Sixth Guangdong Provincial People's Congress on 15 November 1983 and promulgated by the Guangdong Provincial People's Government on 23 January 1984.

81. Non-Banking Financial Institutions Regulations, Art. 1. See also discussion by Nee (1985), p. C–22.

82. Bank Mortgage Loan Regulations, preamble to the regulations.

83. Bank Mortgage Loan Regulations, Art. 4. See also Nee (1985), p. C–21.

84. The Regulations Governing Foreign Banks and Joint Chinese-Foreign Banks in the Special Economic Zones of the People's Republic of China (hereafter cited as the Foreign Bank Regulations), promulgated by the State Council on 2 April 1985. An English translation can be found in *China Economic News*, 29 April 1985, pp. 2–4.

85. Foreign Bank Regulations, Art. 6.

86. Foreign Bank Regulations, Art. 6(12).

87. Foreign Bank Regulations, Art. 16.

88. 'Banks Get Cold Feet over Shenzhen Plans', *South China Morning Post Business News*, 18 June 1985, p. 1.

89. 'Banks Get Cold Feet' (1985), p. 1.

90. *China Economic News*, 21 January 1985, p. 1.

91. Moser (1984), p. 163.

92. An English translation of these regulations can be found in *China Economic News*, 3 December 1984, pp. 1–3. See also discussion in Nee (1985), p. C–25.

93. 1984 Tax Regulations, Art. I, 1(1).

94. 1984 Tax Regulations, Art. I, 1(2).

95. 1984 Tax Regulations, Art. I, 2.

96. 1984 Tax Regulations, Art. I, 4.

97. 1984 Tax Regulations, Art. I, 5–9.

98. The Income Tax Law of the People's Republic of China Concerning Joint Ventures Using Chinese and Foreign Investment (hereafter cited as the Joint Venture Income Tax Law), adopted by the Third Session of the Fifth National People's Congress and promulgated on 10 September 1980. An English translation can be found in *China's Foreign Economic Legislation* (1982), Vol. I, pp. 36–40, Art. 4.

99. Moser (1984), p. 153.

100. 1984 Tax Regulations, Art. I, 3.

101. Nee (1985), p. C–26.

102. For English translations of the five new laws in the Xiamen SEZ, see *China Economic News*, 25 March 1985, Registration Regulations and Labour Management Regulations; 15 April 1985, Land-use Regulations and Regulations on Economic Association Between the Xiamen Special Economic Zone and Inland Areas of China; and 22 April 1985, Regulations on Technology Imports.

Part III: Economic and Management Perspectives

8. The Economic System of a Special Economic Zone under Socialism

C.H. Chai

By establishing four special economic zones (SEZs) in the provinces of Guangdong and Fujian, China appears to have followed other Asian countries in opening up export-processing zones (EPZs), also known as duty-free zones, within her national boundaries to attract foreign investment. Despite superficial similarities in terms of various facilities and financial incentives offered to foreign investors, China's SEZs differ significantly from other Asian EPZs in many respects. First, workers in China's SEZs do not commute from the domestic zone (DZ) but live in the SEZs and are allowed to spend their wages there.[1] Second, economic activities in the SEZs are not confined to export-oriented manufacturing industry but also include agriculture and services as well as other non-industrial activities. Third, the SEZs have been set up not only to attract foreign capital and technology but also to serve the national political objective of the reunification of Hong Kong and Taiwan with China by providing a buffer zone between the two systems — socialism and capitalism under one country.[2] Last, but not least, the economic system of China's SEZs differs markedly from that of other Asian EPZs.

The purpose of this chapter is to pinpoint some of the systemic differences between China's SEZs and other Asian EPZs and to assess their implications for foreign investors. Due to constraints on space the chapter only focuses on two aspects of the system, namely the arrangement of property rights and the mechanism by which resources are allocated. In addition, because of a shortage of data, the chapter focuses almost exclusively on the system prevailing in the Shenzhen SEZ and leaves aside the other SEZs. Finally, the chapter concentrates mainly on the joint-venture form of foreign investment and does not discuss other forms. For the joint venture is considered by the Chinese government to be the preferred form of foreign investment in the zones. Hence, it is likely to become the predominant form in the near future.

Most of the data used here has been obtained either from Chinese publications or through briefings during the author's several visits to Shenzhen. The available data is far from being sufficient for serious research. Hence, conclusions arrived at in this chapter should be regarded as tentative and remain to be verified when more data becomes available in the future.

The Arrangement of Property Rights

In terms of the arrangement of property rights, China's SEZs differ from the EPZs in other Asian countries in that private property rights tend to be more restricted. This can be seen from the ownership pattern prevailing in Shenzhen. At present the pattern is mixed: four different forms can be found, namely state, collective, joint public-private, and private. The private form is subdivided into domestic and foreign ownership.

Domestic private ownership is very much restricted in Shenzhen. Though the number of domestic privately owned enterprises has soared in recent years,[3] their significance is still limited. They are confined mainly to individual pedlars, handicraftsmen, and so on. Both the area of their economic activity and the number of people they are allowed to employ are strictly controlled by the government.

Foreign ownership is also very restricted in Shenzhen and is limited in several ways. To begin with, there has been little 100 per cent foreign ownership in the form of wholly owned foreign enterprises in Shenzhen. Table 8.1 reviews the various forms of foreign investment agreements concluded between 1979 and 1983 in the zone. It shows that, although China tolerates wholly owned foreign enterprises in Shenzhen, their share in the total number of agreements has been relatively small, at a level of around 2 per cent over the five-year period.

As revealed by some Chinese economists,[4] there are two main reasons for this restriction. First, it is difficult for the Chinese authorities to control the activities of wholly owned foreign enterprises as they have only limited access to information on these enterprises. Second, owing to this limited access, it is also difficult for China to absorb and transfer the technology brought in by these foreign enterprises.

Most foreign ownership in China's SEZs is restricted to less than 100 per cent in the form of an enterprise jointly owned by a Chinese state-owned or collective body and a private foreign company. As shown in Table 8.1, the number of foreign investment agreements in Shenzhen involving both equity and contractual joint ventures is almost 10 times that of those involving wholly owned foreign enterprises.

Despite its increasing importance, the joint enterprise does not yet dominate the ownership pattern in the SEZs due to past policies. Thus, for example, in Shenzhen it was found that the prevailing form of ownership is

Table 8.1 Foreign Investment in Shenzhen, 1979–83 (concluded agreements)

Form of Investment	1979	1980	1981	1982	1983	1979–83
Equity joint ventures	7	4	13	11	92	127
Contractual joint ventures	30	24	39	47	149	289
100 per cent equity investments	—	5	18	8	13	44
Others[1]	133	270	508	517	624	2,052
Total	170	303	578	583	878	2,512

Note: 1. Subcontracting and compensation trade deals.

Source: Liang Xian, 'Jianshe jingji tequ de juece shi wanquen zhengque de' ('The Policy Decision to Establish SEZs is Absolutely Correct'), *Renmin ribao* (*People's Daily*), 29 March 1984.

still socialist in nature, namely state and collective ownership: out of 2,071 enterprises in Shenzhen as of the end of 1982,[5] at most 175, or less than 9 per cent, were joint enterprises (see Table 8.1). However, the joint enterprise is regarded as the optimal form of ownership to be promoted in the SEZs as it facilitates both government control of the foreign firm's activities and the transfer of technology to China.[6] Hence, as more and more domestic state-owned and collective enterprises in the SEZs enter into joint-venture deals with foreign firms the joint venture will eventually become the dominant form of ownership.

Theoretically, foreign firms may have more than 50 per cent ownership in a joint venture since there is only a restriction on the minimum but not on the maximum foreign share in the joint-venture legislation. In practice, however, foreign ownership is seldom allowed to occupy a majority position in most of the approved joint enterprises. Thus, according to Ji, out of 83 equity joint ventures approved in 1982 both in the SEZs and the DZ, only 15 per cent were majority-owned, 38 per cent co-owned, and 47 per cent minority-owned by foreigners.[7] Similarly, out of 81 equity joint ventures approved in Shenzhen between 1979 and 1983 listed in *Almanac of China's Foreign Economic Relations and Trade 1984*, the majority were either co-owned or minority-owned and only 11 per cent were majority-owned by foreigners (Table 8.2).

Table 8.2 Forms of Foreign Ownership of Selected Equity Joint Ventures Approved in Shenzhen between 1979 and 1983

Form of Foreign Ownership	No.
Majority-owned (51 to 99 per cent)	9
Co-owned (50 per cent)	33
Minority-owned (5 to 49 per cent)	32
Unknown	7
Total	81

Source: *Almanac of China's Foreign Economic Relations and Trade 1984* (Hong Kong, China Resources Trade Consultancy Co., Ltd., 1984), pp. 1103–43.

As in the DZ, most of the joint enterprises approved in the SEZs are cooperative enterprises or contractual joint ventures. As shown in Table 8.1, 70 per cent of the joint-venture agreements concluded during the period 1979–83 in Shenzhen were contractual joint ventures. Under this arrangement,[8] association between the Chinese firm and the foreign firm is entirely based on a contract in which the foreign firm agrees to supply funds, equipment and technology, while the Chinese firm supplies the site, labour and other facilities. No equity capital is involved. Risks and profits arising from the joint venture are shared between the partners, not in relation to their capital share, but according to a formula agreed upon in the contract, which usually takes the form of an allotted ratio of products, sales volume and profits. This type of joint enterprise is considered to be more flexible for the Chinese, for unlike the equity joint venture it does not require China to invest any cash and hence frees the Chinese from the difficulty of raising funds to match the foreign contribution.[9] Thus the contractual joint venture is promoted as China's preferred form of venture with foreign firms, as confirmed by the Guangdong Five-year Plan (1981–5).[10]

In contrast to the equity joint venture, foreign ownership is even more restricted under the contractual joint-venture agreement, for in this arrangement the foreign capital contribution takes the form of a deposit rather than an equity share. Hence, it does not provide the foreign partner with equity ownership to the assets created in the venture. On the expiry of the agreement, the assets of the venture will pass to China without compensation. Though a foreign partner enjoys no formal title to the assets of the venture, he does exercise rights of control over the venture jointly with the Chinese partner through participation in the mixed management board and through the appointment of key operational personnel to the venture. He also shares the income from the venture jointly with the Chinese partner. Usually the foreign partner is accorded a larger income share in relation to his capital contribution[11] to compensate for his lack of entitlement to equity ownership as well as to ensure that he recovers his initial investment plus interest by stages over the lifetime of the venture.

Regardless of the form of joint enterprise in which he is participating, the proprietary rights of the foreign partner in relation to his capital contribution tend to be more restricted when compared with those enjoyed by his Chinese counterpart.

First, a foreign partner apparently enjoys relatively less control than his Chinese counterpart over the joint enterprise. For while the composition of the mixed management board is normally based on the relative capital contribution of each side, Chinese joint-venture legislation requires that the board chairman be Chinese irrespective of the relative capital contribution of the foreign partner.[12] Though there is no restriction on foreigners occupying other key management positions, various disincentives and obstacles appear to be in force to phase out foreign management as soon as possible. One such disincentive confronting foreign managers is the principle of 'equal pay for equal work': the Chinese insist that Chinese managers be paid the same salaries as are received by their foreign counterparts despite the differences in their training, experience and living standards.[13] For several reasons, it is also difficult to attract sufficient numbers of able foreign managers. A particular stumbling block is foreign exchange controls. Until recently only 50 per cent of the after-tax salary of a foreign manager could be repatriated as a matter of right. Recently the restriction has been much relaxed and the remittance of up to 100 per cent of after-tax salary is now possible. However, foreign managers still need to apply to the Bank of China and are usually not allowed to remit all of their after-tax income as a deduction for their living expenses in China is usually made.[14] Another obstacle is that foreigners are not used to linguistic, cultural and physical conditions in the zones.[15] Hence, it is difficult to find able foreign managers who are willing to spend an extended period of time there.

Second, the income rights of the foreign partner in the joint enterprise are also limited. To begin with, profits from the joint venture tend to be restricted to a 'reasonable level'. In line with Marxist ideology, profit is regarded as 'surplus value' created by labour. Hence it accrues to its owner — labour, or the state in the case of a state-owned enterprise. However, in the case of joint ventures, a portion of the profits is paid out to the capitalist and hence labour is considered to be partially 'exploited'. To limit the extent of 'exploitation' and yet not scare away foreign investment, a joint enterprise in China is allowed to make only a 'reasonable profit'.[16]

The level of profits of the joint enterprise is manipulated mainly through the pricing of Chinese inputs sold to the joint enterprise and pricing of the latter's output destined for internal sale. Though China has not made public what it considers to be a reasonable profit level, policy guidelines stress the importance of allowing the foreign investor to reap a rate of return not lower than the prevailing interest rate on the international money market. Thus, it was revealed that the rate of profit for equity joint ventures in both the DZ and the SEZs in 1981 seldom approached 20 to 25 per cent.[17] The average rate of profit in Shenzhen in 1983 was 15.2, 16.1 and 18.3 per cent respectively for foreign, joint and other foreign-related enterprises in industry, commerce and transportation.[18] Foreign-related enterprises in the real-estate sector, however, were reported to have obtained a rate of return of 49 per cent in Shenzhen.

The profit of a joint enterprise is subject to various deductions before it can be distributed to the partners. These deductions include income tax, a contribution to the three enterprise funds and any obligatory reinvestment as agreed in the contract. The income-tax rate is 15 per cent, which is lower than that in the DZ (33 per cent). As in the DZ, provisions are also made for tax relief during the early years of the venture and for reinvested profits. The three enterprise funds are the reserve fund, the bonus and welfare fund for workers and staff, and the expansion fund. The establishment of these three funds is obligatory according to the Joint Venture Implementing Act.[19] The exact percentage to be deducted from the after-tax profit for these three funds is not known. However, according to Cohen, it ranges from less than 15 per cent to about 20 per cent.[20] Even after deductions for income tax and the three enterprise funds, not all the net profit is usually available for distribution, as the joint-venture contract normally provides for a certain percentage of net profit to be reinvested in the joint enterprise, especially in the initial years.

Through the above-mentioned restrictions and deductions, the share of the foreign partner in joint income from the venture in relation to his capital contribution tends to be substantially less than that of his Chinese counterpart, as has been publicly admitted by Ji.[21] This is because formally the Chinese government owns the Chinese partner. It derives income from the joint enterprise not only through its share of joint-venture profits but also through its various visible and invisible taxes on the joint venture. It also derives income from its sale of inputs to the joint venture. The visible taxes include the above-mentioned income tax, the consolidated industrial and commercial tax (whose rate is 3 per cent), as well as other unknown taxes, the total of which approaches 20 per cent of the profit from a joint venture, according to one source.[22] The much-publicized invisible tax is the retention by the government of 25 per cent of the total wage bill paid to the Chinese workers as a compulsory social security contribution and as compensation for state subsidies on food, housing, medical care and education for the workers.[23] Due to the lack of market-determined prices for many domestic inputs, China is also able to manipulate the prices of these inputs sold to the joint enterprise and reap a handsome profit therefrom. Thus, it was admitted by Ji that if the various sources of government income from the joint venture are properly accounted for, the income share of the Chinese partner tends to be at least one-third larger than that of his foreign counterpart even though the two partners are contributing an equal share to the joint-venture capital.[24]

Third, the transfer rights of the foreign partner in the joint enterprise are also limited. They are restricted during the term of the joint venture as the Joint Venture Implementing Act prohibits a reduction in the venture's registered capital during the venture's lifetime.[25] Upon termination of the contract or dissolution of the venture, his transfer rights are further limited by the requirement that the Chinese partner be given the first right of refusal, the right to veto any transfer and the pre-emptive right to purchase the equity interest on no less favourable terms than those offered to a third party.[26] The transfer rights of the foreign partner are also restricted by foreign exchange controls on the repatriation of capital, for he can only remit his share of capital abroad upon termination if the joint enterprise has sufficient foreign exchange available.[27]

The fact that private property rights are restricted in China's SEZs has important implications for foreign investors. First, it limits their choice of the form of investment in the zones. In a capitalist special zone where private property rights are less restricted, a foreign investor's choice is relatively unconstrained. Thus he may engage in 100 per cent direct foreign investment through the establishment of a wholly owned subsidiary, or participate in various forms of inter-firm co-operation such as subcontracting, compensation trade or a joint venture with the domestic firms of the host country. In China's SEZs, however, since private ownership is more restricted, the choice of the form of investment is generally limited to inter-firm co-operation. This is clearly evident from Table 8.1, which shows that 98 per cent of foreign investment agreements concluded during the period 1979–83 in Shenzhen were within the category of inter-firm co-operation.

Second, the restrictions on private property rights increase the risks, uncertainties and cost for foreign investors. Unlike inter-firm co-operation in a capitalist special zone, a foreign investor's choice of partner in China's SEZs is limited to a public firm. A public firm tends to represent the interest of the government which is more macro-oriented (hard currency earnings, growth, the transfer of technology), whereas the interest of the foreign investor tends to be micro-oriented (profit maximization).[28] Hence, conflict between the two partners tends to occur.[29] Though conflict can be resolved through negotiation and bargaining,[30] the organizational costs involved are likely to be substantial.

To reduce risks and uncertainties, foreign investors tend to limit the duration and scope of their commitments by engaging in lower forms of co-operation with Chinese firms. Thus, as can be seen from Table 8.1, 82 per cent of foreign investment agreements concluded so far in Shenzhen involve lower forms of inter-firm co-operation, namely subcontracting and compensation trade.

More recently, as China has decided to phase out lower forms of co-operation in the SEZs,[31] it has had to offer larger concessions in terms of tax relief, lower land-use fees and even the opening up of China's market to induce foreign investors to enter into higher forms of co-operation.[32] As can be seen from Table 8.1, upon the announcement of these concessions in 1983, the number of agreements involving higher forms of co-operation in Shenzhen shot up by 736 and 217 per cent respectively for equity and contractual joint ventures as compared with 1982.

Third, the restrictions on private property rights affect the kind of technology transferred by foreign investors to China. Recent developments in the theory of technology transfer suggest that the multinational corporation (MNC) makes use of different forms of foreign investment to transfer its different kinds of technological skills to a host country.[33] According to Brada, the technology that a firm deploys in support of its market position can be divided into two types, product technology and process technology. Product technology deals with the development of goods which have few substitutes. A firm's advantage in product technology derives from the exercise of its ownership rights over the technology embodied in the new product which yields monopoly profits for the innovating firm.[34] Process technology entails the firm's ability to produce and market a given product at less cost than its rivals. Brada suggests that both the costs of development and the price of process technology are more easily determined than are those of product technology. The price of process technology can be easily ascertained because it can always be compared to old technology. Hence process technology is more easily transferred on an inter-firm basis via trade, licensing or inter-firm co-operation. Product technology, on the other hand, is difficult to transfer through the market, for its price cannot be easily established because of its uniqueness. Furthermore, the innovating firm may also wish to protect its new product from being imitated. Hence, this kind of technology is usually transferred on an intra-firm basis through the setting-up of a wholly owned subsidiary in the host country.[35]

In a study of 57 US-based MNCs, Coughlin found strong empirical evidence to support Brada's theory.[36] This theory has important implications for China's SEZs. First, since the form of foreign investment in China's SEZs is confined mainly to inter-firm co-operation, the technology transferred to the zones will tend to be process technology rather than product technology. Second, since the foreign partner has to share his technology with a public firm and since his property rights in the joint enterprise are restricted, he is likely to be less prepared to transfer any new technology to the zones.

Detailed data about the type and age of technology transferred to China's SEZs is scanty. However, as confirmed by Chinese economists, relatively little advanced technology has been transferred so far.[37]

Though investing in an environment with restricted private property rights entails several disadvantages for foreign investors, it is worth remembering that there are also certain attractions: for instance, since the Chinese government is able to manipulate the profit of a joint enterprise, China's SEZs may be regarded as one of the safest places in which to invest. This is because the government, in pushing its political as well as its macro objectives, may well be prepared to subsidize foreign investors heavily by guaranteeing them a 'reasonable' profit. Thus, it was learned that in 1983, for example, most of the foreign-related firms in Shenzhen were able to make a profit, and only 16.5 per cent were reported to have suffered a loss.[38]

The Mechanism for the Allocation of Resources

The mechanism for the allocation of resources in China's SEZs differs from that in other Asian EPZs in that there is more government control of the economy in various areas and forms.

At present, the SEZs are still in their construction phase, and many legacies of the centrally planned period still operate there. Thus, in Shenzhen, for instance, as confirmed by a local official, the authorities continue to formulate an annual plan for the state enterprises under their ownership and control.[39] These enterprises continue to receive directive targets from the government which severely restrict their input and output decision-making powers. Supplies of certain important materials and machinery in Shenzhen are still available only through planned channels. Furthermore, the domestic sector of the economy is still largely separated from the foreign sector by various 'isolation layers'.

For example, domestic enterprises in general are not allowed to participate directly in foreign trade. All their import and export transactions, as well as their dealings with foreign and joint enterprises in Shenzhen, have to go through special foreign trade corporations, which control both the terms and the conditions of the transactions.[40]

Another isolation layer exists in the inconvertibility of the Chinese currency, the *renminbi* (RMB). Holders of RMB normally have no right to convert it into another currency. Neither have they the right to import or to purchase a wide range of commodities in Shenzhen.

The separation of domestic and foreign prices constitutes yet another isolation layer. This is to prevent domestic production and consumption from being completely dictated by foreign prices and is achieved mainly through the maintenance of an arbitrary exchange rate and the control of domestic prices. Normally, a country's domestic market price level is linked to its foreign counterpart through the introduction of an operational exchange rate for its currency. This operational exchange rate reflects the relative purchasing power of the currency in the light of domestic and foreign price levels. Hence, domestic prices of exports and imports tend to be equal to the relevant foreign prices translated at the operational exchange rate. The exchange rate of the RMB, however, is non-operational. Currently three different exchange rates can be found in Shenzhen: the official rate (approximately 2.3 *yuan* = US$1 as of 23 July 1984); the internal settlement rate for domestic enterprises (2.8 *yuan* = US$1); and the negotiated rate on the restricted internal foreign exchange market where domestic enterprises holding foreign exchange earned through the system of retention quotas are permitted to sell this foreign exchange to other domesic enterprises that have a quota for spending foreign exchange (3.8 *yuan* = US$1).[41] Both the official rate and the internal settlement rate are known to overvalue the RMB as domestic prices of exports and imports are in general higher than the relevant foreign prices translated at the arbitrary exchange rates. Thus, there is generally a loss in terms of RMB on the export side, while profits are realized on imports. A complex set of specific taxes and subsidies has, therefore, to be maintained for domestic enterprises to cover the difference between these two sets of prices.

While the artificial exchange rate prevents an alignment of the domestic price level with that of foreign prices, the control of domestic prices ensures that the domestic price structure is not dominated by that of foreign prices. Thus, as in the DZ, prices in Shenzhen are controlled to a varying degree by the government. There are three types of prices: fixed, negotiated or floating, and free prices. Free prices are determined by market forces. Floating prices imply some degree of flexibility within certain specified upper and lower limits set by the authorities. Fixed prices are set by the government.

According to the head of the Shenzhen Price Bureau,[42] basic production and consumer goods are currently subject to fixed prices in the zone. Ordinary commodities are subject to negotiated or floating prices where prices are allowed to float within a certain percentage of the government's fixed prices. For all other commodities, prices are allowed to be freely established by the market.

Due to the existence of the above isolation layers, foreign and joint enterprises are not fully integrated with the rest of the economy in the zone. They form a 'quasi-enclave' in the local economic system. Thus, unlike domestic enterprises, they are not subject to centralized planning and control. However, they are required to develop their own economic plans and file these with their respective chief administrative bureaux, which then incorporate them into the Shenzhen plan.[43]

The transactions of joint enterprises with domestic enterprises are subject to various restrictions. Thus, for instance, a joint enterprise's sales to a domestic enterprise are restricted. According to regulations, a joint enterprise, in general, is required to sell its products on the international market (that is, export them). Domestic sales are allowed only in exceptional cases, namely for products which incorporate either a large quantity of Chinese materials and parts or advanced technology badly needed on the domestic market. The domestic sales quota for the former group of products does not usually exceed 20 per cent, though for the latter group it may.[44]

Purchases from domestic enterprises are encouraged in theory but are limited in practice. According to both the Joint Venture Implementing Act and the SEZ foreign investment regulations, a joint enterprise is obliged to procure as many supplies from Chinese firms as is possible so long as the terms of purchase are the same as those for the alternative source of supply, namely imports.[45] In practice, however, due to the arbitrary domestic price system, the overvalued exchange rate and problems of supply and quality, joint enterprises often find it cheaper to import from abroad.[46]

Whereas in other Asian special zones, joint enterprises' purchases from, and sales to, domestic firms are normally calculated in domestic prices and currencies, in China's SEZs they are valued in two sets of prices and two kinds of currency. Thus, according to China's Joint Venture Implementing Act,[47] joint enterprises' purchases of six materials (gold, silver, platinum, oil, coal and timber) used directly in production for exports are to be priced according to foreign or world market prices and paid for in either foreign currency or RMB. Joint enterprises' purchases of materials normally imported and exported by China's foreign trade corporations are to be reckoned in terms of world market prices and paid for in foreign currency. Joint enterprises' purchases of all other materials, including coal used for fuel and oil for motor vehicles needed to produce goods destined for internal sale, as well as utilities and services, are to be reckoned in terms of domestic prices and paid for in RMB.

Domestic sales by joint enterprises are normally to be reckoned in terms of domestic prices and paid for in RMB. However, there are exceptions. Thus, for instance, if the product is one which a Chinese foreign trade corporation plans to import, domestic sales may be based on the world market price and the settlement may be made in foreign currency.[48]

These systemic differences which separate the joint enterprise from the local economic mechanism have important implications for foreign investors. First, they raise the organizational costs incurred in establishing, administering and monitoring a joint enterprise in the zone. Due to the separation of domestic and foreign prices, the inconvertibility of Chinese currency and the absence of an operational exchange rate, the cost of communication is high and negotiation is very often bogged down by disputes over the correct prices and exchange rates used.[49] The cost of accounting is also very high as accounts need to be maintained in two sets of currencies and transactions are valued and settled in two sets of prices and currencies. Conversion from one currency to the other needs to be performed frequently.

Second, these differences also cause unnecessary delays in the implementation of the investment programme in the SEZs. Thus, according to the mayor of Shenzhen, out of a total investment of about US$1.8 billion pledged by foreign investors during the period 1979–83, only US$0.4 billion, or less than one quarter, has been expended so far.[50] As revealed by Chinese economists, the delay in investment expenditure by foreign investors in Shenzhen is partly caused by currency restrictions and the arbitrary exchange rate. Foreign investors fear that they may not be able to repatriate their capital if they bring in hard cash because of foreign exchange controls.[51] This is evident from the fact that investors seldom bring in cash, but rather machinery and materials, as their capital contribution. Thus almost 80 per cent of actual investment by foreign investors in Shenzhen has in fact taken the form of imported machinery and materials.[52] Investors also fear that they may be disadvantaged by the overvalued RMB rate if they bring in hard currency.

Third, such differences reduce the attraction to foreign investors of access to the domestic market. As domestic sales are not only based on domestic prices but are also paid for in RMB, an investor can neither remit the resulting profits in RMB abroad nor use them to import materials.[53] To make domestic sales worthwhile, foreign investors have very often to employ sophisticated financial techniques and produce the right mix of exports and domestic sales to allow them to be paid back in foreign exchange while earning enough RMB to cover their domestic expenditure, which can be settled in RMB.[54]

Over the past few years, partly due to the government's conscious efforts to reform the system and partly due to the increased volume of foreign economic activity in Shenzhen, many of the legacies of the centrally planned period in Shenzhen have been eroded. Thus, the role of market forces has increased and that of central planning and administration has declined. According to one source, by 1983 only slightly more than 10 per cent of the supply of five major industrial materials and equipment in Shenzhen was still obtained through planned channels. The rest was obtained through either decontrolled or free-market channels.[55] Similarly, with the exception of basic necessities, an increasing proportion of consumer goods in Shenzhen are now also allocated through non-planned, or decontrolled, and free-market channels.[56]

Over the past few years some of the isolation layers which separate the domestic sector of the economy in Shenzhen from the foreign sector, and especially from the Hong Kong economy, have also been broken, and the domestic sector is gradually being integrated with the world, and particularly with the Hong Kong economy.

One of the isolation layers — currency inconvertibility — has been broken through with the increased circulation of more convertible currencies, such as foreign exchange certificates (FECs) and Hong Kong dollars, in the zone. The inconvertible RMB has been gradually driven out of circulation in Shenzhen by convertible FECs and Hong Kong dollars (see Table 9.4 on p. 171). The share of retail sales settled in terms of RMB declined from 69 per cent in 1981 to 66 per cent in 1983, whereas the share of those settled in terms of FECs and Hong Kong dollars rose steadily from 31 per cent to 34 per cent during the same period.

Another isolation layer — the separation of domestic from foreign prices — has also been partially removed through the introduction of two measures. One of these is the *de facto* devaluation of the RMB. This has been achieved by allowing three different prices to be set for the same commodity, one for each currency. The RMB price is in general higher than the FEC price which, in turn, is higher than the Hong Kong dollar price when compared at the official rate.[57] This implies that the cross rate of the RMB used in any transaction is much lower than its official rate. Hence the RMB is, *de facto*, devalued. This has enabled domestic prices in the zone to realign with foreign or Hong Kong prices without an official devaluation of the RMB.

Another measure introduced to realign domestic prices in Shenzhen with foreign prices has been the decontrol of the former. As mentioned earlier, three kinds of prices used to exist in the zone: fixed, negotiated or floating, and free prices. Over the past few years, an increasing number of commodities have been taken out of the fixed-price category and are allowed to be determined by firms themselves in response to market conditions either with or without government guidance. Hence, the significance of decontrolled prices has increased, as is evident from the increased amount of both consumer and producer goods allocated under negotiated prices in Shenzhen.

The realignment of domestic prices with foreign prices has led to the increasing divergence of Shenzhen prices from those of the DZ and the increasing convergence of Shenzhen prices with those of Hong Kong. Thus, as revealed in one study,[58] Shenzhen price levels have undergone a remarkable transformation over the past few years. Initially they were closely linked to those of the DZ. As in the DZ, Shenzhen's agricultural price levels used to be much lower and its industrial price levels much higher than those in Hong Kong. During the last few years, the price levels of agricultural goods have increased whereas those of industrial goods have declined in the zone. Price levels are now somewhere between those of the DZ and Hong Kong. Specifically, industrial prices are now lower than those of the DZ but are still higher than those of Hong Kong. Agricultural prices, on the other hand, are now higher than those prevailing in the DZ but are still lower than those in Hong Kong.

It appears that more reform measures aimed at eradicating the remaining legacies of the centrally planned period and reducing the systemic differences of Shenzhen are in the pipeline. Several of these reform measures mentioned below were originally proposed by a group of Chinese SEZ specialists.[59] They are known to have been agreed upon and, according to the mayor and other government officials of Shenzhen, some are now being implemented and others will follow in the near future.[60]

Thus it is envisaged that the role of market forces will increase and that of centralized planning and administration will be further reduced in Shenzhen. The emphasis of planning will shift from an annual and detailed central specification of production and supply (that is, short-term micro-planning) to medium- and long-term planning of investment for structural change (long-term macro-planning). The nature of the plan will also change from imperative to indicative. In other words, enterprises will no longer receive directive plan targets from the authorities. The time-honoured system of the planned allocation of important raw materials and intermediate goods will be largely dismantled and replaced by market allocation. With the abolition of directive targets and the planned material allocation system, enterprises will be allowed greater freedom to determine the level and composition of their outputs and inputs, and to obtain inputs and place outputs through direct 'horizontal' market relations with other firms. To control enterprise behaviour, the authorities will rely increasingly on adjusting general 'parameters', such as taxes, credits, prices, and so on, and less on issuing specific administrative orders.[61]

It is also envisaged that the Shenzhen economy will be made more open and hence more integrated with the world, and especially with Hong Kong, through the dismantling of the remaining isolation layers which separate the domestic economy from the foreign economy. Thus, the current monopoly on foreign trade exercised by the foreign trade corporations will be largely abandoned. Like their foreign counterparts and joint enterprises in Shenzhen, most domestic enterprises will be given the right to engage in foreign trade directly.[62] The currency will be made more convertible through the issue of a Shenzhen SEZ currency in 1985.[63] Upon its issue, the new currency will be the only legal tender in Shenzhen and the circulation of all other currencies, including Hong Kong dollars and RMB, will be banned.[64] With the backing of the central government gold and foreign exchange reserves, the new currency will be freely convertible with other currencies.[65]

The level of domestic prices in Shenzhen will be more closely linked to those of foreign and especially Hong Kong prices by the introduction of a realistic exchange rate reflecting the relative purchasing power of the new currency in the light of domestic and Hong Kong price levels. The rate of the new currency will be pegged to the Hong Kong dollar, with allowance for a certain degree of 'managed flexibility'.

The structure of domestic prices in Shenzhen will also be more closely linked to those of foreign and Hong Kong prices through further decontrol of domestic prices. It is envisaged that, with the exception of a few essential services such as water, gas, medical care, and so on, the prices of most commodities, including such basic necessities as rice and cooking oil, will be decontrolled.[66]

Upon the completion of the transformation of the Shenzhen economic system, it is anticipated that foreign and joint enterprises will be more closely integrated into the domestic economic system in that they will be treated in more or less the same way as any other domestic enterprise in the zone. Their accounts will be maintained in the Shenzhen SEZ currency and their transactions valued and settled essentially in terms of domestic prices and the new currency.

Despite the increased marketization, liberalization and opening up of the Shenzhen economy, it is worth remembering that its character is likely to remain socialist. Unlike the capitalist special zones in other Asian countries, government control of the economy in Shenzhen is very likely to continue to be maintained in many areas and in various forms. During a discussion on reform among Chinese SEZ specialists, it was clear that, although economic activities in Shenzhen will mainly be co-ordinated by the market, in the future some kind of planning is to be retained to guide economic activities.[67] Specifically, according to the reform proposals, medium-term, long-term, and even annual plans will continue to be formulated for Shenzhen. These plans will be approved by the central government and will be incorporated into the national plan. Though planning will be mainly indicative in nature to ensure stable supplies, directive planning will continue for certain basic necessities.[68]

The legitimacy of government control and planning in Shenzhen is based on the fact that the state is the co-owner of the assets of the enterprises in the zone. It is also based on the fact that Shenzhen is part of China's socialist economy even though a 'second line' will divide it off to some extent. Thus, planning is needed to ensure that the development of Shenzhen is not only in line with that of the DZ but also complements it in terms of the transfer of foreign capital and technology.

For the same reasons, it is also very unlikely that Shenzhen will be fully integrated with the Hong Kong economy even after the establishment of the 'second line'. It is anticipated that the SEZ economy will continue to be separated from the Hong Kong economy by certain isolation layers. Thus, though enterprises in the zone will be allowed to engage in foreign trade directly, the trading rights they enjoy are unlikely to remain unrestricted. For instance, their right to export is likely to be subject to some form of control, such as export licensing, so as to ensure that enterprises in the zone do not infringe upon China's quotas or engage in cut-throat competition with exporting firms in the DZ.

Similarly, the convertibility of the new Shenzhen SEZ currency is unlikely to be unrestricted. To prevent the loss of foreign exchange reserves and an outflow of capital, the government is unlikely to grant Chinese residents in the zone free access to convertible currencies for either foreign travel or the transfer of funds abroad. Neither is the government likely to permit Chinese enterprises in the zone to obtain convertible currencies to import or transfer capital abroad. Hence, the convertibility of the new currency is likely to be confined to foreign firms, joint enterprises, foreign residents and non-residents only.

Finally, domestic prices in Shenzhen are unlikely to be completely realigned with Hong Kong prices as some form of price control will probably continue to be maintained. During the recent price reform debate among Chinese SEZ specialists, it became obvious that the principle of price setting in Shenzhen would continue to differ from that in Hong Kong or any other capitalist special zone. As in the DZ, complete price flexibility or the free determination of prices by market forces is very unlikely to be tolerated in the zone. This is because the government will continue to pursue certain goals other than that of efficiency in the setting of prices. Thus it has been proposed that, as in the DZ, basic price stability should also be maintained in Shenzhen.[69] It has also been proposed that price regulation of monopolies should be introduced so as to prevent excessive use of market power by monopolistic firms. Last, but not least, it has been proposed that a certain link between Shenzhen prices and DZ prices should be maintained so as to minimize the disruption to DZ economic activity caused by development in Shenzhen.[70] Specifically, it is envisaged that Shenzhen agricultural prices will continue to be linked to those of the DZ and maintained at a level only somewhat higher than that in the DZ so as to prevent any disruption of the DZ market for agricultural products by Shenzhen. Similarly, Shenzhen industrial prices will continue to be linked to those in the DZ and maintained at a level only somewhat lower than that in the DZ so as to protect the DZ industries. These proposals imply that the price gap for both agricultural and industrial goods across the three zones (the DZ, Shenzhen and Hong Kong) mentioned earlier is likely to be maintained in the future even though the gap may be somewhat narrowed.[71]

With the retention of some form of price control, the three sets of prices which are currently found in Shenzhen would continue to exist even after the reform.[72] Specifically, according to the head of the Shenzhen Price Bureau, there would continue to be fixed prices for basic commodities, floating prices for ordinary commodities, and free prices for all other commodities.

Turning now to the question of how the new reform measures will affect the foreign investment environment in Shenzhen, it is anticipated that the reform will at least have the following two beneficial effects. First, as has been mentioned earlier, the systemic differences in Shenzhen have increased organizational costs for foreign investors. Through reform, the systemic differences would be reduced, and foreign and joint enterprises would be more integrated into the economic mechanism of the zone, thereby probably reducing organizational costs. Second, with increased currency convertibility, access to the domestic market is likely to become more attractive to foreign investors in the zone. This is because foreign investors will be paid in the convertible SEZ currency instead of in RMB for domestic sales of their joint-venture products in the zone.

However, it must be noted that such reforms may also be accompanied by certain undesirable side-effects. First, the proposed reforms attempt to establish a 'visible-hand' system in place of the centrally planned economy in the zone. The 'visible-hand' system will combine the use of both the plan and the market to direct economic activities. Thus, while enterprises will be allowed freedom in input and output decisions (micro-decisions) which are co-ordinated by a market mechanism, a government plan which determines the development strategy for the entire economy (macro-decisions) will be used to guide the micro-decisions. The experience of Eastern European countries suggests that it is difficult to combine plan and market successfully in a closed economy, and that this is even more the case in an open economy, where foreign economic disturbances such as inflation and unemployment can easily be imported. Thus, if co-ordination of planned macro-decisions with decentralized, market-co-ordinated micro-decisions fails, the 'visible hand' is likely to fail. In this case, it will be tempting either to move the system back to the traditional planned economy or to move it forward to the traditional market economy. This means that the system in the zone is likely to experience a certain degree of instability. An unstable system means that rules, regulations and policies are constantly subject to change. Such change increases risks and uncertainties for foreign firms investing in the zone and hence impairs the investment environment.

Second, with the levels of Shenzhen prices increasingly linked to and approaching those of Hong Kong, some of the cost advantages of investing in the zone are likely to diminish. Thus, for instance, as the price levels of agricultural, subsidiary and other consumer goods approach those of Hong Kong, the cost of living in the zone will increase. Hence the government will find it progressively more difficult to maintain labour costs in the zone at a level lower than in Hong Kong, unless it is prepared to subsidize heavily the labour employed by foreign and joint enterprises.

Third, with the issue of the new currency, the circulation of Hong Kong dollars will be banned. Foreign investors will have to keep at least a certain amount of new currency for transactional purposes. Payments hitherto made in Hong Kong dollars will in future have to be made in the new currency. Foreign and joint enterprises will be expected to accept the SEZ currency for domestic sales which hitherto have been settled in Hong Kong dollars. Since the new currency will be less convertible than the Hong Kong dollar, the financial convertibility of foreign investors is likely to be impaired.

To sum up, the beneficial effects of the new economic system as envisaged by Chinese planners for Shenzhen are not clear-cut. From the foreign investor's point of view such a system has both advantages and disadvantages. Thus one should not expect the investment environment in the zone to be greatly improved through the introduction of the new system alone.

Conclusion

From the above discussion, it is clear that the economic system of China's SEZs differs from that of other Asian EPZs both in terms of the arrangement of property rights and in the mechanism for allocating resources.

In terms of the arrangement of property rights, both private and foreign ownership tend to be more restricted in China's SEZs. The dominant form of ownership is limited to joint public-private ownership in the form of a joint enterprise. Though China does not formally limit foreign ownership to a minority position in a joint enterprise, the control, income and transfer rights of the foreign partner are very much restricted in comparison to those of his Chinese counterpart.

In terms of the mechanism for the allocation of resources, the existing system in the SEZs still bears elements of a centrally planned economy with directive planning, currency inconvertibility, and administrative pricing. The domestic sector in the zones is relatively closed to external influences. Foreign and joint enterprises in the zones are not fully integrated with the rest of the economy. They form a quasi-enclave in the local planning, currency and price system.

The proposed reforms aim to introduce more market forces, to open up the domestic sector, and to allow foreign and joint enterprises to be more fully integrated into the local economic mechanism. However, as long as the arrangement of property rights and the goals and values upheld by the Chinese government remain unchanged, the differences in economic mechanism between China's SEZs and other Asian EPZs are expected to remain: government control of the economy will very likely continue to be maintained in various areas and in various forms.

The implications of the systemic differences of China's SEZs for foreign investors are mixed. Such differences imply both disadvantages and advantages. On the one hand, the lack of strong foreign ownership and control increases the risks and uncertainties of investing in the zones. It also limits the forms of investment which foreign investors can choose from and affects the kind of technology they are willing to transfer to China via investment. The continued use of planning to guide the allocation of resources and the resultant internal market and price controls, as well as the separation of domestic and foreign prices, also increase foreign investors' organizational costs in establishing and operating ventures in the zones.

On the other hand, the systemic differences of China's SEZs also offer some special attractions for foreign investors. The Chinese government, as the co-owner of joint enterprises in pursuance of its macro-economic goals, may well be prepared to grant generous concessions to foreign partners to ensure them a reasonable return on their invested capital. Similarly, since the domestic market and prices are controlled by the government, prices of most inputs including labour, land and raw materials can be maintained at a relatively stable and low level for foreign investors.

In light of the above, any reform to reduce the systemic differences of the zones is likely to have both beneficial and undesirable side-effects for foreign investment. The pros and cons of the proposed reform measures should be carefully assessed and weighed up before they are implemented.

Notes

1. K. Hamada, 'An Economic Analysis of the Duty-free Zone', *Journal of International Economics*, Vol. 4, 1974, p. 226.
2. Sun Ru, 'Cong zhanlue yiyi tan jingji tequ de zuoyong huo jianshe' ('Discussing the Role and Construction of SEZs from the Strategic Point of View'), *Zhongguo jingji tequ nianjian* (*Yearbook of China's Special Economic Zones*) (Hong Kong, Yearbook of China's Special Economic Zones Publishing Co., 1983), p. 652.
3. The number of individually run enterprises amounted to 234 at the end of the third quarter of 1982. See Chen Zhaobin, 'Lun jingji tequ de jiage yundong huo tedian huo shichang diaojie zuoyong' ('On the Special Features and Movement of SEZ Prices and the Function of Market Regulation'), *Zhongguo jingji tequ nianjian* (1983), p. 682.
4. Chen Huiqin and Giu Jingji, 'Shekou gongye qu de jingyan yu wenti' ('Experiences and Problems of the Shekou Industrial Zone'), *Gongye jingji guanli congkan*, No. 1, 1983, p. 45.
5. Li Huajie and Li Qiying, 'Shenzhen tequ qiye shixing hetong yonggong zhidu'('Shenzhen SEZ Enterprises Experimenting with Contract Labour System'), *South China Economy*, No. 2, 1983, p. 58.
6. Guangdong Research Centre for Special Economic Zones, '1982 nian tequ lilun yangjiu chengguo zongshu' ('A Summary of Findings of 1982 SEZ Theoretical Research'), *Zhongguo jingji tequ nianjian* (1983), p. 606.
7. Ji Chongwei and Wu Chao, 'Guanyu zhongwai heji qiye de jige renshi wenti' ('Several Problems in Understanding the Nature of Joint Ventures Using Chinese and Foreign Capital'), *International Trade*, No. 7, 1983, p. 21.
8. J. Chai, 'Industrial Co-operation between China and Hong Kong', in A.J. Youngson (ed.), *China and Hong Kong: The Economic Nexus* (Hong Kong, Oxford University Press, 1983), p. 107.
9. O. Sin, 'Guangdong Seeks More Co-operative Projects', *South China Morning Post Business News*, 19 June 1984.
10. *Guangdong jingji tequ yaolan* (*A Compendium on the Guangdong Special Economic Zones*) (Guangzhou, Guangdong Research Centre for Special Economic Zones, 1982), p. 88.
11. *Guangdong jingji tequ yaolan* (1982), p. 92.
12. The Implementing Act for the Law of the People's Republic of China on Joint

Ventures Using Chinese and Foreign Investment, Art. 34 (hereafter cited as the Joint Venture Implementing Act)

13. J. Chiang, 'What Works and What Doesn't', *China Business Review*, September–October 1983, p. 27.

14. J.A. Cohen and J.P. Horsley, 'The New JV Regulations', *China Business Review*, November–December 1983, p. 45.

15. Li Yuyi 'Shekou jizhuang xian chang de zhong wai hezuo guanxi' ('The Co-operative Relations between Chinese and Foreigners in a Shekou Container Factory'), *Gangao jingji* (*Hong Kong and Macau Economic Digest*), No. 3, 1983, p. 48.

16. J.A. Cohen, 'Equity Joint Ventures: 20 Potential Pitfalls that Every Company Should Know About', *China Business Review*, November – December 1982, p. 27.

17. Cai Ninglin and Wang Yiping, 'Guanyu liyong waiji de guimo, touxiang huo fangshi wenti de tantao' ('Issues on the Scope, Direction of Application and Form of Foreign Capital Utilization'), *Gongye jingji guanli congkan*, No. 5, 1982, p. 13.

18. Briefing material.

19. Joint Venture Implementing Act, Art. 87.

20. Cohen (1982), p. 30.

21. Ji Chongwei and Wu Chao (1983), p. 21.

22. Chen Zhaobin, 'Ba jingji tequ de jianshe tigao dau xin de shuiping' ('Raising the Construction of SEZs to a Higher Level'), *Gangao jingji*, No. 4, 1983, p. 57.

23. Provisional Regulations of the Special Economic Zones in Guangdong Province Governing Labour and Wages for Business Enterprises, Art. 8 (hereafter cited as the Labour and Wage Regulations).

24. Ji Chongwei and Wu Chao (1983), p. 22.

25. Joint Venture Implementing Act, Art. 22.

26. Joint Venture Implementing Act, Art. 22.

27. Cohen (1982), p. 27.

28. J.C. Brada, 'Markets, Property Rights, and the Economics of Joint Ventures in Socialist Countries', *Journal of Comparative Economics*, Vol. 1, No. 2, 1977, p. 179.

29. Brada (1977).

30. J. Svejnar and S.C. Smith, 'The Economics of Joint Ventures in a Centrally Planned and Labour-managed Economy', *Journal of Comparative Economics*, Vol. 6. No. 2, 1982, pp. 148–72.

31. Xinhua News Agency and New Evening Post, *Zhongguo jingji tequ shouce* (*Handbook for China's Special Economic Zones*) (Hong Kong, New Evening Post, 1984), p. 136.

32. *Zhongguo jingji tequ shouce* (1984), pp. 125–6.

33. J.C. Brada, 'Technology Transfer by Means of Industrial Co-operation: A Theoretical Appraisal', in Paul Marer and E. Tabacznski (eds.), *Polish – U.S. Industrial Co-operation in the 1980s* (Bloomington, Indiana University Press, 1981), pp. 207–23.

34. Brada (1981), p. 209.

35. Brada (1981), p. 210.

36. C.C. Coughlin, 'The Relationship Between Foreign Ownership and Technology Transfer', *Journal of Comparative Economics*, Vol. 7, No. 4, 1983, pp. 400–14.

37. Briefing material.

38. Briefing material.

39. Briefing material.

40. Yang Zhihuo, 'Jingji tequ waimao guangli tizhi gaige wenti' ('Issues in the Reform of the Foreign Trade System in the SEZs'), *South China Economy*, No. 4, 1983, pp. 62–3.

41. The cited internal settlement rate and the negotiated rate were communicated to the author during a research trip to Shenzhen and Zhuhai between 9 and 13 June 1984.

42. Huang Zanqian, 'Shenzhen tequ shichang wujia jiben wending' ('Basic Price Stability in the Shenzhen Market'), *Gangao jingji*, No. 1, 1983, pp. 58–9; and

Huang Zanqian, 'Shilun Shentequ wujia gaige zhong guodu cuoshi' ('A Discussion of the Transitional Measures in the Shenzhen Price Reform'), *Gangao jingji*, No. 4, 1983, pp. 61–2.

43. Joint Venture Implementing Act, Arts. 54–6.

44. Yang Zhihuo, 'Baohu zhuyi huo tequ chang pin de neixiao' ('Protectionism and Domestic Sales of SEZ Products'), *Gangao jingji*, No. 1, 1984, p. 64.

45. Joint Venture Implementing Act, Art. 57.

46. Zhong Douxiang and Wang Hanyong, 'Guanyu Shenzhen jingji tequ tizhi gaige de jige wenti' ('Issues in Shenzhen SEZ Economic Reform'), *South China Economy*, 1983, No. 6, p. 45.

47. Joint Venture Implementing Act, Art. 65.

48. Cohen and Horsley (1983), p. 46.

49. Briefing material.

50. Liang Xiang, 'Jianshe jingji tequ de juece shi wanquen zhengque de' ('The Policy Decision to Establish SEZs is Absolutely Correct') *Renmin ribao* (*People's Daily*), 29 March 1984, p. 5.

51. Yuan Shibang, 'Jingji tequ de liutong wenti' ('The Circulation Problem in the Special Economic Zones'), *Gangao jingji*, No. 2, 1984, p. 59.

52. Yuan Shibang (1984), p. 59.

53. Zhong Douxiang and Wang Hanyong (1983), p. 45.

54. J. Chiang (1983), p. 28.

55. Briefing material.

56. Chen Zhaobin in *Zhongguo jingji tequ nianjian* (1983), p. 681.

57. Chen Zhaobin in *Zhongguo jingji tequ nianjian* (1983), p. 678.

58. Chen Zhaobin in *Zhongguo jingji tequ nianjian* (1983), pp. 667–8.

59. Guangdong Research Centre for Special Economic Zones (1983), pp. 584–633.

60. The author was informed of these reform measures during a research trip to Shenzhen and Zhuhai between 9 and 13 June 1984. Some of these reforms were subsequently announced in *Ta kung pao*, 5 August 1984, and in *Renmin ribao* (*People's Daily*), 3 November 1984.

61. Zhang Zhizheng, 'Zai quojia jihua zhidao xia zhuyao shixing shichang diaojie' ('Under the Guidance of the State Planning, Mainly Using Market Regulation'), *Jingji xue lun cong*, 1983, pp. 224–52.

62. Yang Zhihuo (1983), p. 62.

63. After the completion of this chapter it was reported that China might have second thoughts about issuing a special currency for the SEZs as the Bank of China was known to have strong objections (see *South China Morning Post*, 19 December 1984). However, on 28 March 1985, Vice-Premier Yao Yilin confirmed that the issue of such a currency would definitely go ahead although no date has yet been set (*South China Morning Post*, 28 March 1985).

64. Guangdong Research Centre for Special Economic Zones (1983), p. 615; and Zhang Yuanyuan, 'Tan tan Shenzhen tequ de huobi wenti' ('A Discussion of the Problems of the Shenzhen SEZ Currency'), *Zhongguo jingji tequ nianjian* (1983), p. 674.

65. Briefing material.

66. Briefing material.

67. Guangdong Research Centre for Special Economic Zones (1983), pp. 591–4.

68. Zhang Zhizheng (1983), pp. 249–51.

69. Guangdong Research Centre for Special Economic Zones (1983), p. 622.

70. Guangdong Research Centre for Special Economic Zones (1983), pp. 621–3.

71. Guang Jingwen, 'Jianli juyou zhongguo tese de jingji tequ jiage tixi' ('Establishing a Chinese-style SEZ Price System'), *South China Economy*, No. 2, 1983, p. 91.

72. Huang Zanqian, 'Qianyi Shenzhen tequ wujia gaige' ('A Brief Discussion of the Shenzhen SEZ Price Reform'), *South China Economy*, No. 5, 1983, p. 71.

9. Banking and Currency in the Special Economic Zones: Problems and Prospects

Y.C. JAO*

A special chapter on banking and currency in the special economic zones (SEZs) can be justified on two grounds. First, the establishment of SEZs represents an attempt to accelerate economic development in certain designated areas by attracting foreign investment and technology transfer through various incentives, importing new management practices, and initiating reforms in diverse fields. It is hoped that the SEZs will act as a catalyst in facilitating China's modernization through the diffusion of their experience to other regions. In principle, innovations in banking, currency and finance are just as important as those in other real sectors for the modernization of a socialist economy. Previous studies have, however, tended to confine themselves to the non-financial aspects of the SEZs. Second, in the past 15 years or so, there has been a resurgence of interest among economists in the role of financial institutions and policies in economic development. It is widely recognized that the prevailing condition of 'shallow finance' or 'financial repression' in most lagging economies constitutes a serious impediment to development, and that a sustained programme of financial liberalization and reform will promote 'financial deepening', which in turn will facilitate economic growth.[1] Seen in this light, problems of banking and currency in the SEZs take on a new dimension and significance not otherwise obvious at first sight.

This chapter accordingly reviews and evaluates the present banking and monetary system in the SEZs, and examines the innovations and reforms which are necessary in order that the full potential of the SEZs may be realized.

The Banking System

The present banking structure in the SEZs does not differ in any significant respect from that prevailing in other parts of China. The banking scene is dominated by state-owned banks and financial institutions. Thus, in Shenzhen, the largest and most developed of the SEZs, there are branches of the People's Bank of China, the Bank of China, the People's Construction Bank,

---

*The author is indebted to the late Professor Jozef Wilczynski for discussions and correspondence over a number of years on money and banking in centrally planned economies, and to Mr Walter Yao for research assistance.

the Agricultural Bank, the Industrial and Commercial Bank of China, and the People's Insurance Company. Between them they handle all banking and financial business in the zone. Foreign banks are at present only allowed to operate representative offices.

As shown in Table 9.1, in June 1984 there were 14 foreign (or more correctly, non-China-incorporated) banks in the SEZs, all but 2 having the status of representative office only. Most of them are, moreover, located in Shenzhen and its industrial zone, Shekou. Only four are represented in Xiamen and there are none in either Zhuhai or Shantou.

As the name implies, a representative office is not permitted to engage in the normal banking business of taking deposits, making loans, transferring funds, and so on. Its principal function is to represent its head office in assisting and advising bank customers who have business interests in the SEZs, and generally to undertake information-gathering and liaison work.

At the moment only two banks operate branches in the SEZs. The Overseas Chinese Banking Corporation, a bank owned and run by Singaporean Chinese, still retains a branch in Xiamen, which was established well before the Communist take-over in 1949. The branch office is therefore a historical relic rather than a new enterprise. Moreover, it is located in the city of Xiamen, rather than in the SEZ of the same name, or the Huli Industrial Zone. However, as the Xiamen SEZ is now being widened, the branch can be treated as being within an SEZ. The other case is much more substantive. The Nanyang Commercial Bank is, as is well-known, a Chinese state-controlled bank incorporated in Hong Kong, one of the 12 'sister banks' of the Bank of China. On 9 January 1982, the bank opened a branch in Shenzhen, the first non-China-incorporated bank ever permitted to do so. Barely one year later, on 8 January 1983, the bank opened another branch in Shekou, the industrial zone of Shenzhen.[2] The bank can therefore engage in the whole gamut of banking business. In this respect, it enjoys a head start over all other foreign banks.

Officially, China's policy is that foreign banks will be given full-service branch licences 'as soon as the situation permits'.[3] It is not clear what this phrase actually means. One obvious interpretation is that the lack of basic facilities, such as commercial premises and residential accommodation, has prevented the admission of full-service banks. It is well-known, for example, that most foreign banks in China have had to operate out of a hotel room.[4] But one suspects that a more important reason is China's desire to protect the domestic banking market, at least until China's own banks are sufficiently modernized to withstand the full force of foreign competition. Nanyang is given special treatment only because it is one of the 'sister banks'.

This protectionist and discriminatory stance towards foreign banks has understandably given rise to much unhappiness in the foreign banking community. One frequently heard complaint is that China is not observing the 'reciprocity' principle in international banking. Just across the border in Hong Kong, for example, there are no less than 13 licensed banks owned or controlled by China which can transact all conceivable banking business; each of these banks, moreover, has its own deposit-taking company.[5] In other words, they can compete with any other bank on equal terms. By con-

Table 9.1 Foreign Banks in the SEZs (as at 30 June 1984)

Bank	Country of Incorporation	Status	Location
Bank of Orient	USA	Representative office	Xiamen
Banque Indosuez	France	Representative office	Shenzhen
Banque Nationale de Paris	France	Representative office	Shenzhen
Chartered Bank	United Kingdom	Representative office	Shenzhen
Chiyu Banking Corporation	Hong Kong	Representative office	Xiamen
Citibank, NA	USA	Representative office	Shenzhen
Hongkong and Shanghai Banking Corporation	Hong Kong	Representative office	Shenzhen and Xiamen
Lloyds Bank International	United Kingdom	Representative office	Shenzhen
Mitsubishi Bank	Japan	Representative office	Shenzhen
Nanyang Commercial Bank	Hong Kong	Branch	Shenzhen and Shekou
Overseas Chinese Banking Corporation	Singapore	Branch	Xiamen
Sanwa Bank	Japan	Representative office	Shenzhen
Société Générale	France	Representative office	Shenzhen
Takugin International (Asia) Ltd. (wholly owned subsidiary of Hokkaidō Takushoku Bank Ltd.)	Japan	Representative office	Shenzhen

Source: Banking authorities in the SEZs and current press announcements.

trast, only four foreign banks now maintain branches in China. They are the Bank of East Asia (one branch in Shanghai), the Hongkong and Shanghai Banking Corporation (one branch in Shanghai), the Overseas Chinese Banking Corporation (one branch each in Shanghai and Xiamen), and the Chartered Bank (one branch in Shanghai).[6] However, these branches are left-overs from pre-Liberation days — the remnants of a substantial network of branches of foreign institutions steadily reduced to almost nothing since 1949. The fact is that since China proclaimed its open-door policy in 1978, no foreign bank or financial institution has been allowed to establish a full-service branch inside China. Most of the 55 foreign banks now in China have to be content for the time being with representative office status. Even the branches of the four banks can only transact limited banking business, primarily external trade financing.

In an interview with a left-wing Hong Kong newspaper, *Ta kung pao*, the vice-president and head of the China Office of Citibank, Hong Kong, Mr Luis A. Viada, complained that while the Bank of China has a branch in New York that can freely take deposits and make loans in US dollars, no US bank has so far been able to open a full-service branch in China. He therefore hoped that China's new banking law would provide for a more positive role for foreign banks by permitting them to engage in normal profit-making banking business.[7]

Perhaps as a result of such complaints and criticisms, the authorities in Shenzhen are reported to be studying the promulgation of a new banking law that could eventually pave the way for the upgrading of foreign banks' representative offices to full-service branch status. However, so far no progress has been reported. A recent gesture to mollify the foreign banking community was the appointment, in February 1984, of a leading Japanese bank as the financial consultant to the state-owned Shenzhen SEZ Development Co. Under a three-year agreement, a finance company, Takugin International (Asia) Ltd., and its parent bank, the Hokkaido Takushokü Bank of Japan, will provide the Development Co. with financial advice and possibly credit as well for a number of major projects in the area, ranging from tourism and housing to airport facilities and industry. The aim, according to the Chinese authorities, is to import sophisticated financial management techniques and high technology from Japan. The Japanese side presumably will benefit by securing a regular flow of income from consultancy fees and interest earnings.[8] But whether this special favour bestowed upon a Japanese bank signals a more liberal banking policy in general remains to be seen.

As already mentioned, a representative office is merely a liaison or public relations office expressly forbidden to engage in direct profit-making business. Even so, it is still required to observe stiff reporting requirements with China's central bank, the People's Bank of China, in respect of its activities. Since operating costs for foreign enterprises in China, especially office rents or hotel rates, are very high, a representative office is usually a loss-making undertaking. And yet the number of representative offices in the SEZs and other major cities, as well as that of prospective entrants, still keeps on rising. How can this apparent paradox be explained?

A short answer to this lies in the fact that, typically, a representative office in the SEZs, particularly Shenzhen, is merely an extension of a foreign bank's branch in Hong Kong. While a representative office inside the SEZs cannot grant loans directly, the Hong Kong branch is of course free to provide income-generating credit facilities and other financial services to Hong Kong firms that invest in or trade with the SEZs. In essence, therefore, the Hong Kong branch subsidizes the representative office, a practice followed by most international banks. But the representative office is not of course entirely useless. It maintains contacts with the relevant authorities, liaises with existing and prospective customers, undertakes on-the-spot economic surveys and research, and relays relevant information to the Hong Kong branch or head office. More fundamentally, an international bank that decides to establish representative offices in the SEZs or other Chinese cities typically takes a long view of the business potential in such a venture. The general strategy seems to be to establish a presence in China first, cultivate goodwill with the Chinese authorities, and then wait for business opportunities to develop. Currently, there are two large investment projects that excite the attention of international bankers. One is the nuclear power plant in Daya Wan, Guangdong province, a joint venture between the Guangdong provincial government, the Hong Kong government, and China Light & Power Co. of Hong Kong. The plant is designed to generate and transmit electricity, not only for the whole of Guangdong province (including the SEZs), but also for Hong Kong. The total cost of this project has been estimated at HK$24 billion (approximately US$3.1 billion). It is also reported that more than 30 foreign banks have approached the Bank of China and expressed interest in financing the project, and that some US$2 billion would initially be raised from a number of leading international banks, though no definite agreement has been signed so far with any bank.[9] Another large investment project is, of course, the South China Sea oil development programme. Western and Japanese sources estimate that, in the next decade, China's offshore oil exploration and development programme, when fully operational, could generate demand for financing totalling between US$35 billion and US$75 billion.[10] The South China Sea project will probably account for a large part, though not all, of the huge funding. Most foreign banks hope that, by maintaining a presence in the SEZs, other major Chinese cities, and Hong Kong, they will be able to claim a share in the potentially lucrative lending business, especially as the Chiwan port of Shenzhen has been officially designated as one of the logistic bases for the South China Sea oil exploration programme.[11] The 'herd instinct' is as compelling in international banking as it is in other areas: many banks feel that they simply cannot afford not to be in China if their competitors are already there. The lack of success so far in the drilling efforts in the South China Sea has apparently not dampened the long-term expectations of foreign bankers.[12] However, these two huge projects are only the most publicized ones; there are hundreds of other smaller, but equally viable, projects that require funding. It may safely be predicted that, given the country's size and poverty, China's total demand for external financing will be virtually insatiable if its ambitious modernization programme is to be realized. Moreover, the fact that

China's foreign exchange reserves have been steadily improving in recent years (see Appendix A) as a result of its prudent financial policy has enhanced China's credit standing among international bankers, disillusioned as they are by their traumatic experiences with debt-ridden Third World countries.[13] Although China prefers, and indeed has access to, preferential loans from international bodies such as the World Bank, the International Monetary Fund, and government export credit agencies of industrialized countries, foreign bankers feel that there is still considerable need for China to borrow from private financial institutions on commercial terms.

Be that as it may, as things now stand foreign banks in the SEZs are handicapped by their representative status. The Bank of China and its 'sister banks', by virtue of their full-service branches in the SEZs, enjoy a formidable competitive advantage. This has been admitted as being the case in a revealing article in a pro-Beijing economic journal in Hong Kong.[14] According to the article, the Bank of China Group (the Bank of China branch and 12 other sister banks in Hong Kong) plays a predominant role in promoting economic relations between Hong Kong and Macau on the one hand, and the Chinese mainland on the other. Among the advantages the group enjoys is the 'extensive network of branches and sub-branches' inside China. Because of this privilege, the group can accommodate clients' credit needs much more quickly and flexibly than can a rival bank that does not have a branch in the SEZs. The Bank of China Group also participates in direct equity investments, and provides advisory services to clients wishing to invest in or trade with the SEZs. These customer services are clearly facilitated by the presence of a branch network. For obvious reasons, the authorities in the SEZs also prefer to deal with the Bank of China Group. In 1983, for example, the Xiamen authorities formed a joint venture called the Xiamen Special Economic Zone United Development Corporation with the Bank of China and five of its 'sister banks' in Hong Kong and Macau.[15] By the end of 1983, the Bank of China Group was reported to have financed investment originating from Hong Kong and Macau totalling some HK$2,297 million for 457 projects. Relevant details are given in Table 9.2. It should be noted that since the Bank of China Group can take deposits in *renminbi* inside China, and in foreign currencies in Hong Kong, it is able to grant loans denominated in at least three currencies, a servicing capability that cannot be matched by foreign banks.

The Bank of China Group's preponderant role in financing investment and trade in the SEZs may also help to explain a recent statistical trend that has puzzled analysts for some time. Since 1979, statistics on the external liabilities and assets of Hong Kong's financial institutions have been regularly compiled by the Banking Commissioner's Office in Hong Kong at the request of the Bank of International Settlements in Basle. As shown in Appendix B, before 1982 Hong Kong was a net creditor against China, meaning that Hong Kong's licensed banks and deposit-taking companies on balance lent more to China than they borrowed. This net creditor status was consistent with Hong Kong's position as a financial centre and its role in financing China's modernization programme. However, after peaking in the first quarter of 1981, Hong Kong's net claims against China decreased rapidly

Table 9.2 Hong Kong and Macau Investments in China Financed by the Bank of China Group (cumulative total as at the end of 1983)

By Geographical Distribution

Area	No. of Projects	Amount (HK$ million)
Guangdong SEZs	347	1,050
Xiamen, Fujian	15	42
Beijing, Shanghai and others	91	1,190
Total	453	2,297

By Industrial Distribution

Industries	No. of Projects	Amount (HK$ million)
Textiles and clothing	120	841
Other light industries	230	487
Heavy industries	37	453
Total	453	2,297

Source: Fu Wen, 'Zhongyin jituan — cujin gangao yu neidi jingji guanxi de qiaoliang' ('The Bank of China Group — the Bridge for Promoting Economic Relations between Hong Kong, Macau and the Hinterland'), *Economic Reporter*, 2 April 1984.

through the rest of the year. Writing two years ago, I explained this decline in China's indebtedness in terms of its retrenchment in capital investment during the period 1979–81, and the exorbitantly high level of interest rates charged by commercial banks all over the world at that time.[16] Since 1982, however, China has reversed its status *vis-à-vis* Hong Kong. From being a net debtor it has now become a net creditor. Moreover, the net claims against Hong Kong rose spectacularly from HK$713 million in the first quarter of 1982 to HK$13,784 million in the third quarter of 1984, or by about 19 times in only two years. Several possible interpretations of this unusual phenomenon suggest themselves. One straightforward interpretation, from the perspective of contemporary banking, is that the Bank of China Group's branches and subsidiaries in Hong Kong have learned the trick of 'liability management', an innovation pioneered by US banks in the early 1960s. Among other things, this technique entails heavy borrowing by branches and or subsidiaries from their head offices and overseas offices to fund their local lending.[17] In the Hong Kong case, this might, for example, involve lending to Hong Kong businessmen investing in, or trading with, the SEZs. The fact that the period 1982–4 was one of rapid expansion of the SEZs, and particularly of Shenzhen, is consistent with this interpretation. A more 'political' interpretation would highlight the fact that the period was one of great nervousness in Hong Kong due to the 1997 issue,.and suggest that, in an effort to stabilize the situation, China had quietly injected funds, via the

Bank of China Group, into Hong Kong in the form of loans to companies directly or indirectly controlled by China, as well as to financial institutions, especially those banks and deposit-taking companies that had liquidity problems. There may be considerable validity in this view, since the period saw an enormous rise in China's investments in the territory, as well as serious strains in the financial sector. China's steadily improving foreign exchange situation in the same period (see Appendix A) would lend support to either of these interpretations. However, due to the traditional secretiveness of China's financial institutions, and the confidentiality rule of Hong Kong's Banking Commissioner's Office, the truth may not be known for some time. Whatever the final definitive explanation, however, it may be inferred that Hong Kong's heavy involvement in the SEZs, and the Bank of China Group's strong support of this involvement, constitute an important element in such an explanation.

Finally, no full discussion of banking and finance in the SEZs can be made without reference to banking reforms in China in the post-Mao period. Space does not permit any elaborate analysis, but certain salient features of post-1976 developments may be noted. Of fundamental importance is the shift from a philosophy of virtual autarky to a more outward-looking and pragmatic view of international banking and finance. This change in policy and outlook has resulted in China's willingness to use foreign credit and foreign capital for its modernization programme, and to observe standard international practices in banking and finance. It has also proved to be a boon for the Bank of China — the bank designated to specialize in international trade and finance — and its branches and subsidiaries in Hong Kong. In banking structure, the People's Bank of China, hitherto literally a 'monobank', was reorganized in September 1983 to become a conventional central bank, its commercial banking functions being hived off to a new bank, the Industrial and Commercial Bank of China.[18] The Bank of China was upgraded in 1979 as an independent bank directly responsible to the State Council. Its articles of association were amended and its capital was raised in the following year to enable it to function more effectively in international financial markets.[19] Banks suspended during the Cultural Revolution, such as the Agricultural Bank and the People's Construction Bank, were reinstituted.[20] As an integral part of the policy of *jinji tizhi gaige* ('reforming the economic system'), banking reforms aim to transform China's banks from being mere Treasury agents into real financial intermediaries, and to allow interest rates to perform their real function as 'levers' in the economic system.[21] In banking practices, the Bank of China has introduced some much-needed innovations, such as foreign currency loans, export credits for heavy industry, syndication, and so on.[22] Foreign firms operating in the SEZs can also apply to the Bank of China for foreign currency credits.[23] The Bank of China's sister bank, the Nanyang Commercial Bank, launched a pilot mortgage scheme in 1983 for buyers of industrial and residential properties in Shenzhen. This is considered a pioneering innovation, since private property ownership in China is still restricted, and private leasing of property is a rare phenomenon.[24]

Such reforms and innovations represent, of course, a great improvement on the chaotic and isolationist days of the Maoist period. In Shenzhen, for example, simply as a result of the normalization of organizational structure and business operations, and the establishment of the SEZ, the whole banking and finance sector is reported to have grown rapidly in terms of deposits, loans, employees, and offices, as may be seen in Table 9.3. Similar statistical information for the other SEZs is, unfortunately, not available.

But the progress depicted in Table 9.3 falls far short of the potential of a special zone that is supposed to encourage the import of advanced technology and innovations in all areas of economic activity. No serious student of China's financial system can fail to be struck by two sharp contrasts: first, between the variety and sophistication of banking and related financial services in Hong Kong, reputedly the third largest financial centre in the world, and the extreme paucity of such services in China;[25] and, second, between the high degree of modernization of the Bank of China Group in Hong Kong, operating as it were in a competitive environment, and the lack of it in China's domestic financial system.[26] Ideally, the SEZs should serve as a conduit through which modern banking and related financial management techniques and services can be imported from Hong Kong and abroad, and diffused to the whole country. But so far little headway has been made in this direction.

The Currency Question

Nothing illustrates the dilemmas and challenges facing the SEZs better, perhaps, than the currency question. The present monetary system is characterized by multiple-currency circulation, a state of affairs unusual even in a capitalist society. In most SEZs, and particularly Shenzhen, three different currencies are in circulation, namely, the official Chinese legal tender, the *renminbi* (RMB), foreign exchange certificates (FECs) issued by the Bank of China since April 1980, and the Hong Kong dollar. In Zhuhai, which is adjacent to Macau, it is said that the Portuguese patacas also circulates side by side with the above three currencies.

Under present Chinese law, only the RMB and FECs are allowed to circulate in China. The FECs are bought with foreign currency by foreigners, overseas Chinese, and Hong Kong and Macau residents from Bank of China branches and offices when they cross the border into China. These proxies for foreign currency can only be used by the same groups of people to pay for goods and services. Unused FECs may be redeemed for foreign currency when the same people leave China. In principle, the tolerance of the Hong Kong dollar may indicate that the Chinese government is prepared to adopt a more liberal attitude towards the use of foreign currency in the SEZs.

The circulation of different currencies has, however, some serious consequences for the Chinese monetary authorities. Prices are quoted in three different currencies. This multiple pricing is of course a source of confusion and inefficient costs in transactions. More embarrassingly, on the free market (or the black market, depending on one's view), the RMB invariably suffers a

Table 9.3 The Growth of Banking and Finance in Shenzhen

	End of 1979					End of 1982				
	PBOC	ABOC	BOC	PCBOC	PICOC	PBOC	ABOC	BOC	PCBOC	PICOC
Deposits (million *yuan*)	94		n/a	3.8	—	219	187	n/a	147	—
Loans:										
domestic currency (million *yuan*)	61		12	—	—	204	130	127	89.4	—
foreign currency (US$ million)	—		—	—	—	—	—	20	—	—
No. of branches/offices	1	1	1	1	1	18	1	4	5	1
No. of employees	104[1]	156[1]	179	19	4	326	256	431	68	33
Insurance premium (million *yuan*)	—	—	—	—	0	—	—	—	—	3.2

Notes: PBOC = People's Bank of China.
ABOC = Agricultural Bank of China.
BOC = Bank of China.
PCBOC = People's Construction Bank of China.
PICOC = People's Insurance Company of China.
n/a = not available.
1. Figures for 1980.

Source: Shen Shuigen, 'Jinrongye gaikuang' ('Survey of Banking and Finance'), in *Zhongguo jingji tequ nianjian* (*Yearbook of China's Special Economic Zones*) (Hong Kong, Yearbook of China's Special Economic Zones Publishing Co., 1983), pp. 189–91.

depreciation relative to both the FECs and the Hong Kong dollar. While the official Chinese media is silent on the subject, the *de facto* devaluation of the RMB is an open secret among the population of the SEZs, and residents of Hong Kong and Macau. Chinese academic economists have, however, been much more candid in discussing this phenomenon. For instance, Yuan Shibang wrote in 1981 that 'at present in Shenzhen and Zhuhai, and especially in Shenzhen, there exist three means of payment and three sets of prices. "Open" black-market rates exist among the three means of payment. According to the official Bank of China quotation on 11 May 1981, HK$100 equal 31.17 *yuan*. But the black-market rate is about 45–50 *yuan*. In exchanging for FECs, the RMB has to suffer a discount of 30–40 per cent'.[27] Another Chinese economist, Qian Jiaju, noted in early 1984 that 'the value of the RMB is approximately 30 per cent lower than that of the foreign exchange certificate. This is inappropriate. Recently I visited the SEZs and confirmed this discrepancy. For instance, a box of moon-cakes costs seven *yuan* in FECs but eleven *yuan* in RMB. Many kinds of goods are priced quite differently in RMB and in FECs. This has a profound adverse effect and discredits the RMB'.[28] Although the Hong Kong dollar itself has depreciated substantially since 1982, primarily because of the 1997 question, it continues to command a premium over the official rate on the black market. The Hong Kong press is full of specific details about the *de facto* depreciation of the RMB. For instance, during the crisis of the Hong Kong dollar in late September 1983, when the official rate dropped to an all-time low of HK$100 for 22.12 *yuan* (or 1 *yuan* = HK$4.5188), the black-market exchange rate in the SEZs and Guangzhou was about HK$100 for 36 *yuan* (or 1 *yuan* = HK$2.76).[29] Apparently, the Hong Kong dollar circulates freely in the SEZs, but illicitly in Guangzhou and other cities in Guangdong province. Because the restrictions on FECs are tighter outside the SEZs, these proxies for foreign exchange also command a higher price in the SEZs. Thus, one report has it that while FECs and the RMB have the same nominal value, on the black market one FEC equals 1.38 *yuan* in Guangzhou, and 1.5 *yuan* in the SEZs.[30]

Another notable trend, documented by the Chinese economists, is the rising proportion of retail sales in Shenzhen denominated in FECs and the Hong Kong dollar. As shown in Table 9.4, the proportions of retail sales denominated in FECs and the Hong Kong dollar have both increased in recent years. Taken together, retail sales denominated in FECs and Hong Kong dollars increased from 31 per cent in 1981 to 42.6 per cent in the first half of 1983.

The mere fact that a rising proportion of retail sales is denominated in FECs and Hong Kong dollars does not in itself imply anything sinister. While it may mean that retail outlets prefer to accept FECs and Hong Kong dollars, it may also simply mean that more foreigners and Hong Kong residents are now visiting the SEZs. What has alarmed the Chinese authorities is the persistent displacement of the RMB as a means of payment, and the *de facto* devaluation of the RMB *vis-à-vis* FECs and the Hong Kong dollar.

The dismay and frustration of the Chinese authorities are not difficult to understand. Politically and ideologically, it is preposterous that FECs and a

Table 9.4 The Currency Denomination of Retail Sales in Shenzhen (percentage of total)

	1981	1982	First Half of 1982	First Half of 1983
RMB	69.0	67.65	64.0	59.9
FEC	22.0	22.17	26.7	25.2
HK$	9.0	10.18	9.3	17.4

Source: Yuan Shibang, 'Jingji tequ de luitong wenti' ('The Circulation Problem in the Special Economic Zones'), *Gangao jingji* (*Hong Kong and Macau Economic Digest*), No. 2, 1984, p. 61.

colonial currency should usurp the place of the official legal tender in a socialist state. Particularly galling and ironic is the fact that before 1949 the wide circulation of the Hong Kong dollar in South China, then under Guomindang rule, was vehemently attacked by the Communists as a hallmark of China's 'semi-colonial status'. Now that the same thing is happening again, after three decades of Communist rule, party ideologues and bureaucrats are hard put to explain such an 'aberration' when China is supposed to be independent and strong. The *de facto* devaluation of the RMB is of course also extremely damaging to China's prestige.

On purely economic grounds, the displacement of the domestic currency by foreign currency implies the loss of what economists call 'seigniorage'. Originally the term (after the old French word for the lord of a manor) denoted the difference between a coin's value as money and its value as a commodity under a metallic monetary standard. Nowadays, however, it is generalized to mean the profits accruing to monetary authorities for issuing inconvertible paper currency, given that the costs of printing (especially marginal costs) are trivial relative to the real resources that the fiat money can command. When only a single currency circulates within a country, the whole seigniorage is of course appropriated by the home government; however, when a foreign currency also circulates as a means of payment, at least part of the seigniorage will be competed away by the foreign issuing authority. This is of course a well-known result of standard economic analysis.[31] Although the word 'seigniorage' is not actually used by Chinese economists in their discussions of the question, the same conclusion is nevertheless reached. For instance, an article in a Beijing-controlled newspaper in Hong Kong makes the following comment:

> A currency issued by a monetary authority is equivalent to a non-interest-bearing promissory note. If foreign currencies amounting to one billion *yuan* circulate in Shenzhen, then in effect Shenzhen is losing interest on deposits worth one billion *yuan*.[32]

The question then arises: what causes a domestic currency to lose its monopolistic legal tender status? To answer that monetary regulations are more flexible and lax in the SEZs is to explain the appearance, but not the substance, of the issue, for as already mentioned, the Hong Kong dollar also circulates, and the FECs are quoted (illegally) at a premium over the RMB outside the SEZs. Thus, one must seek an 'economic' explanation of the phenomenon.

It is tempting to draw a parallel with the late 1940s, when the Hong Kong dollar, and to lesser extent the US dollar, circulated widely in Guangdong because people had lost faith in the currency issued by the Nationalist government due to rampant inflation. The analogy is however false. Whatever the economic ills of Communist China, hyperinflation is not one of them. Over the period since the SEZs were formed, it can be argued that China's inflation is at least not worse, if not actually lower, than that of Hong Kong.[33]

The real explanation lies in the nature of the currencies concerned. The RMB is an inconvertible currency: private agents (individuals and firms) cannot freely convert the domestic currency into any other foreign currency, either as a financial asset or as a means of payment. Under the existing exchange-control system, all foreign exchange assets can only be held by the state-owned banks, and applications by private agents for foreign exchange must be approved by the exchange-control authorities in accordance with state economic plans. It follows that the RMB has only a limited access to goods and services because of its inconvertibility. The Hong Kong dollar, on the other hand, by virtue of the absence of exchange controls, can be freely converted by its holder into any foreign currency, or at least any major foreign currency, that is quoted on the exchange market. Accordingly, the Hong Kong dollar also has a much wider command over real resources. The same attribute applies to the FECs, which are proxies for foreign currencies. For instance, holders of the Hong Kong dollar and FECs can use them to buy both home-produced and imported goods; holders of the RMB, however, can buy only a very limited range of imported goods at highly inflated prices. The other side of the coin is of course that sellers of goods and services prefer to accept the Hong Kong dollar and FECs. The Hong Kong dollar and FECs are also widely perceived to be sound 'stores of value' or financial assets. A corollary of the inconvertibility of the RMB is that the official exchange rates can hardly be expected to coincide at all times with the 'true' rates determined by free-market forces. Invariably, the official rate overstates the value of the domestic currency and this, not surprisingly, also results in the *de facto* devaluation of the domestic currency on the black market. However, this phenomenon is by no means unique to China; indeed, it can be shown to be endemic in any Communist-ruled country and, more inclusively, in any country that prohibits the free convertibility of the domestic currency.[34]

Many Chinese economists in fact agree with this line of reasoning. For instance, Yuan writes:

> Why can the Hong Kong dollar squeeze into our country's sphere of circulation? From the monetary point of view, the Hong Kong dollar is a freely convertible currency, a kind of free foreign exchange. The Hong Kong dollar can be bought and sold for any major international currency at any time according to freely floating rates, and can consequently also be used to purchase any commodity on the world market at a freely determined price. At the same time, Hong Kong is a free port, and is in itself a comprehensive world commodity market. But the RMB can only buy a limited

range of commodities inside China depending on whether the supplies are planned, rationed, or freely available. Furthermore, the Hong Kong dollar can be exchanged for the RMB or FECs at any time according to official quotations, but the reverse is not true. Since the RMB is an inconvertible domestic currency, whereas the Hong Kong dollar is a convertible currency with wide acceptability, and even many state-run organizations in China are eager to demand foreign exchange as a means of settlement, it follows that the general public is also only too glad to accept the Hong Kong dollar. The result is that the Hong Kong dollar has become 'good money' in the SEZs and adjacent areas, while the RMB has become 'bad money' in its own country.[35]

Although all economists in China agree that monetary reform in the SEZs is urgently needed, there is still no consensus on how such reform should be carried out. In fact, a controversy has been raging since 1981 on whether an independent and convertible currency should be issued in the SEZs as the core of a financial reform programme. Because of constraints on space, only a summary of the debate can be attempted here.

The chief proponents of an independent and freely convertible currency for the SEZs are Yuan Shibang, Zhang Yuanyuan and Yan Xianyu of Jinan University, and Xie Guoxuan of the Shenzhen branch of the People's Bank of China.[36] Yuan in particular is a most outspoken and persuasive advocate. They propose that once a freely convertible currency is issued, the FECs should be abolished, and other currencies (including the RMB) should be banned from circulation in the SEZs. The principal advantages claimed for a convertible SEZ currency are that it could eliminate, once and for all, the chaotic state of multi-currency circulation, and restore the Chinese government's prestige and seigniorage. In addition, the new currency system could provide a powerful impetus to the further development of the SEZs. The proponents emphasize the fact that the SEZs have reached a stage of development where no further progress can be made without radical reforms of the currency system. Both Xie and Yuan liken the currency problem to a 'malfunctioning of the circulatory system', Yuan even warning of the danger of 'thrombosis'. Xie points out that in terms of total value, direct investment in real estate and tourism in the SEZs far exceeds that in manufacturing industries. One main reason for this is that residential units can easily be sold, or even pre-sold, in Hong Kong for Hong Kong dollars. Similarly, hotels and tourist resorts whose clients are mainly visitors from Hong Kong or abroad accept payment only in FECs or Hong Kong dollars. By contrast, industrial firms whose products are not wholly exported face the problem of accumulating inconvertible RMB balances realized from domestic sales.[37] Yuan notes that at the end of March 1983, of the pledged investment in Shenzhen totalling some HK$12 billion, only one-sixth, or about HK$2 billion, had actually been paid. While it is recognized that most investment plans are 'pledged' over a period of time, Yuan argues that the 'monetary obstacle' is nevertheless an important disincentive to investors. Many investors are also reluctant to set up permanent offices in the SEZs because of the lack of banking and other financial back-up services, preferring to keep their headquarters in Hong Kong to make full use of the superior facilities there. Yuan ingeniously uses Marx's formula for the circulation process of money capital, G — W . . . . . . W' — G', and quotes Marx's famous remark that 'commodities are in love with money, but "the course of true love never did run smooth" ' to underline the importance of a freely convertible currency for an open economy, of which the SEZs are a modified form.[38]

Opponents of the proposal are represented by Zhou Shengye of the People's University of China, Liu Guangdi of the Central College of Finance and Economics, and Tang Huai of the Hong Kong and Macau Research Centre.[39] Their main arguments are that, politically, a separate currency for the SEZs undermines the monetary unity of the nation and that, historically, there are no precedents in other export-processing zones or free trade zones. On purely economic grounds, they emphasize that the economic base of the SEZs is still too weak, that China's foreign reserve position is not strong enough to justify the risk of issuing a convertible currency and, last but not least, that the monetary authorities do not have the necessary experience and expertise for the management of a convertible currency.

Yuan makes a devastating critique of such arguments. He cites the example of the Isle of Man to deny the alleged damaging political effects and the lack of historical precedents. He also refers to the experiences of Hong Kong and Singapore to show how free convertibility can actually facilitate rapid economic development and a healthy balance of payments. As for the lack of experience and expertise, Yuan argues that this can gradually be overcome by a process of 'learning by doing'. Any innovation entails some risk, he says, but this should not be used as an excuse for opposing much-needed reforms. Finally, Yuan curtly dismisses 'compromise proposals' to issue new RMB notes or FECs for circulation in the SEZs only put forward by some officials and economists, arguing forcibly that such proposals can only exacerbate the current confusion.[40]

A group of economists and bank officials, while not in principle opposing the proposed new currency, nevertheless stress the importance of a transitional period before a new currency for the SEZs is formally issued.[41] During the transition, certain reforms and preparatory work in rationalizing the control of foreign exchange and the gradual build-up of foreign exchange reserves should be carried out. The completion of the so-called 'second border', that is, the official demarcation line between Shenzhen and the hinterland, is generally regarded as the right time to consider seriously the actual issue of the new currency.

After more than three years of controversy, opinions on the currency question appeared to be coalescing and converging towards a consensus at the time of writing (June 1984). The desirability of a new currency for the SEZs is no longer in dispute, according to an authoritative Guangdong source. Only timing and certain technical problems are still under discussion and consideration.[42]

Policy Implications

An analysis of the banking system and currency question clearly shows that there are serious deficiencies and lacunae in the financial system which, if not rectified, will impede the further development of the SEZs. As is usually the case, the academic economists are among the first to recognize these problems, and discuss possible reform measures. Recently, however, there have been signs that the authorities have also become more aware of the need for financial liberalization and reform.

In May 1984, the State Council was reported to have approved a 'trial scheme for the reform of Shenzhen's banking system'. These reform measures include five particular points. First, the Shenzhen branch of the People's Bank of China is to specialize in central banking functions as conventionally understood, such as the issue of currency, the regulation of money and credit, the custody and management of foreign exchange reserves and gold and silver, the supervision of other banks and financial institutions, and so on. This implies that the People's Bank in Shenzhen is to shed many of its previous functions as a 'monobank', leaving, for example, the commercial banking functions to the newly established Industrial and Commercial Bank of China. Second, in order to support the development of the SEZs, banks and insurance companies in the SEZs can keep their deposits and credit balances for their own use, without these being arbitrarily transferred by their 'superior offices'. Banks are also allowed to increase their borrowing from domestic and foreign banks. Third, banks can experiment with new operating procedures and methods as long as they are consistent with the needs of the SEZs. Fourth, banks in the SEZs can adopt interest-rate policies different from those in the hinterland on both deposits and loans. Specifically, both lending and deposit rates can be higher than those in the hinterland but lower than those in Hong Kong. Finally, to co-ordinate financial activities in Shenzhen, a system of joint conference is to be established, with the president of the municipal People's Bank acting as the convenor.[43]

As regards foreign banks, the same Guangdong source also indicates that a new law covering foreign banks (including overseas Chinese banks and private Chinese banks in Hong Kong) is under consideration and will be promulgated soon. It is possible that applications by individual foreign banks to upgrade their representative offices to branches will be granted on a case-by-case basis. The Bank of China is said to be bracing itself for an invasion of foreign banks, a trend which it regards as inevitable. However, even if foreign bank representative offices are upgraded eventually, their business is likely to be confined to foreign currency deposit-taking, lending, and trade financing only, that is, they will be given an 'offshore' status.[44]

On the currency question, the general secretary of the Chinese Communist Party, Hu Yaobang, is reported to have told a Tokyo daily, *Nihon Keizai Shimbun*, in an article published on 14 June 1984, that a new currency is to be issued in Shenzhen in 1985 on an experimental basis, and will be extended to other SEZs if it proves successful.[45] The Guangdong source mentioned earlier also indicates that past controversy on who should issue the new currency has been resolved: it has been agreed that the People's Bank, as the *de jure* central bank, will be the sole issuing authority. The new currency, being 100 per cent backed by foreign exchange and gold, will be fully convertible into the major foreign currencies, and will probably be pegged to the Hong Kong dollar, for economic and geographical reasons.

Two major technical problems that remain to be solved are the rate of exchange between the new currency and the *renminbi* (whether it should be fixed or flexible), and the desirability or otherwise of a transitional period during which the *renminbi* will still be allowed to circulate in Shenzhen.[46]

Another financial reform that is being considered is the re-establishment of a capital market. This idea, which used to be floated from time to time, has received renewed publicity after Jing Shuping, the executive director of the China International Trust and Investment Corporation, told the *Financial Times* of London in early June 1984 that the Chinese authorities were considering reopening stock exchanges in major cities, banned after 1949, in order to facilitate the raising of equity capital for infrastructure projects. In principle, the SEZs should provide a good experimental ground for such a proposal. However, my interviews with Shenzhen officials suggest that while proximity to Hong Kong is undoubtedly an advantage, the Chinese authorities also fear that a fledgling market in Shenzhen is likely to be easily manipulated by experienced speculators and syndicates operating just across the border. No early decision is therefore expected on this proposal.

Conclusion

Like many other developing countries, China also suffers from what economists call 'financial repression' that results in the stagnation or even atrophy of the financial sector, and deprives the economy of the invigorating effects emanating from the mutual stimulation of the financial and real sectors. Among the more salient features of financial repression are government monopoly of the financial sector that prohibits new entry and stifles competition, excessive administrative controls on interest rates that result in the misallocation of credit, and inept management of the exchange rate that overvalues the domestic currency and hence causes the emergence of a black market.

The establishment of the SEZs provides a golden opportunity for experimenting with financial innovations and reforms that hopefully can cure the economy of the deleterious effects of financial repression. This is widely recognized by the Chinese economists and perhaps the authorities also. Unfortunately, whether due to ideological rigidity, or bureaucratic inertia, or even intra-Party political opposition, the reform measures so far taken have been slow and timid.[47]

However, financial innovations and reforms cannot succeed in the absence of an institutionalized 'rule of law' which fully respects and protects private property rights.[48] The recent upsurge in 'economic legislation' shows that the Chinese authorities are aware of the importance of legalization. But scepticism among potential investors resulting from past experiences and memories is still too deep-rooted to be overcome within a short period of time.

In the long run, even if, given the best conditions, financial reforms are fully implemented in the SEZs, China may still fail to reap the benefits of financial deepening if such reforms are not diffused to the rest of the country. The SEZs would then remain at best enclaves of modernization, with no real impact on the whole economy. This can hardly be regarded as a fulfilment of the original aim of the SEZs. Thus it cannot be overemphasized that the SEZs, to be really effective, must act as the catalyst for a comprehensive reform of the nation's economic and financial system.

Postscript

My chapter was first completed in July 1984. This note summarizes subsequent developments in banking and currency up to 7 May 1985.

One important development on the banking side has been that foreign banks, joint-venture banks, and banks from Hong Kong and Macau have finally been permitted to establish full-service branches in the SEZs under new regulations announced by the State Council on 2 April 1985. Such banks, licensed by the People's Bank of China, may transact a wide range of banking business denominated in both *renminbi* and foreign currencies, including the taking of deposits from foreigners, overseas Chinese, and residents of Hong Kong and Macau. It is not clear, however, whether these licensed banks can take *renminbi* deposits directly from Chinese citizens. Nevertheless, the new regulations represent a step forward in the liberalization of the banking market in the SEZs. At the time of writing, some 12 foreign banks were reported to have applied for licences to operate in Shenzhen. It is also understood that those banks which have already set up representative offices will be given preferential treatment. The currency situation in the SEZs, however, has remained chaotic. From 1980 until very recently, China operated a *de facto* dual exchange rate system: an official rate posted by the Bank of China, and another 'internal settlement rate' for domestic enterprises engaged in external trade. According to *International Financial Statistics*, published by the International Monetary Fund (IMF), the average official rate between the *renminbi* and the US dolllar was 1.705 *yuan* = US$1 in 1981, 1.8887 = US$1 in 1982 and 1.9772 =US$1 in 1983. The 'internal settlement rate', however, was fixed at 2.8 *yuan* = US$1 when it was introduced in 1980. This system, which is a variant of the multiple exchange rate system long frowned upon by international organizations such as the IMF and the General Agreement on Tariffs and Trade (GATT), has drawn strong complaints from foreign countries, especially the United States. Partly to placate foreigners, and partly for domestic reasons (for example, to attract more foreign investment, and to discourage black-market activities in both the SEZs and the hinterland), China has since 1981 adopted a policy of gradually devaluing the *renminbi* in order to bring the official rate into line with the 'internal settlement rate'. In 1984, however, the speed of devaluation accelerated. By the end of the year, the official exchange rate of the US dollar had been brought into parity with the 'internal settlement rate'. In effect, the Chinese currency was devalued by 30 per cent within one year against the US dollar.

When Qian Jiaju, a senior Chinese economist and an adviser to the Chinese Academy of Social Sciences, gave a seminar to the Centre of Asian Studies at the University of Hong Kong in January 1985, I asked him whether the devaluation of the *renminbi* was a deliberate policy measure and part of the overall economic reform programme. He confirmed that it was. Embarrassingly for the Chinese government, the devaluation has failed to stamp out the black market. On the contrary, by all accounts the black market has continued to flourish, and the *renminbi* has continued to depreciate, in both the SEZs and the hinterland. Thus, the *Asian Wall Street Journal* reported on 24 December 1984 that the black-market rate was currently about 4 *yuan* = US$1, representing another 30 per cent devaluation from the already adjusted official rate. The *renminbi* has also depreciated sharply against the Hong Kong dollar in the past 18 months. When the Hong Kong dollar was pegged to the US dollar in mid-October 1983 at the height of Hong Kong's financial crisis, the official rate was 1 *yuan* = HK$4.0124. By 4 May 1985, the official rate had been devalued to 1 *yuan* =HK$2.7226, representing a cumulative devaluation of 32.3 per cent. However, on the black market, the rate had fallen to as low as 1 *yuan* = HK$1.00 (*Wen wei po*, 25 March 1985). Foreigners and Hong Kong residents visiting the SEZs and other major cities in China are openly accosted by touts offering black-market rates for foreign currencies and Hong Kong dollars, according to press reports. As a frequent visitor to the SEZs myself, I can testify to the accuracy of these reports. Moreover, apart from the black market, there is also a 'grey market' where Chinese state-owned enterprises also scramble for foreign exchange, reportedly at more than double the official rate, in order to import coveted supplies and equipment. There are also reports that people in China are hoarding foreign exchange, estimated at between US$1 billion and US$3 billion, as a hedge against inflation (*South China Morning Post*, 19 December 1984).

Perhaps because of these problems, China appears to have had second thoughts about issuing a convertible currency in the SEZs. There is considerable evidence that internal controversy on the suitability and feasibility of the new currency has remained unresolved. There are also signs that the SEZs and Beijing do not see eye to eye on the matter. For while top officials of Shenzhen, including its mayor and vice-mayor, have often touted the virtues of the new currency, and have hinted that its issue is imminent, they have been just as frequently contradicted by the higher authorities in Beijing, who insist that the matter is still under consideration, and no final decision has been taken.

The dilemma facing China is that a convertible currency for the SEZs by itself will be totally ineffective in solving the problems of multi-currency circulation and prices, black-market activities, and stagnant foreign investment. For this objective to be attained, nothing less than the total convertibility of the *renminbi* over the whole country will be required. But China is not yet ready for such full-blooded liberalization at one stroke. If China does go ahead with the SEZ currency scheme, the most likely result will be the emergence of yet another black market in the new currency. The reason is that, as long as the *renminbi* remains inconvertible, there will be strong incentives for people outside Shenzhen to exchange their *renminbi* for the new currency. Given its heavy dependence on the rest of China for the supply of goods, manpower, and finance, it is virtually impossible for Shenzhen to be cut off entirely from the hinterland, even with the completion of the so-called 'second line'.

A more feasible and effective alternative, in my view, is a two-stage stabilization and liberalization plan. The first stage should consist of a package of interim measures, of which the most important is the abolition of the FECs. The FECs have proved to be a fiasco that add to the confusion in the financial system without performing any real function. The retirement of outstanding FECs should be a technical operation without any adverse effect on the economy. The second stage should then see the implementation of a comprehensive reform of the whole financial system, comprising principally the development of domestic financial markets, and the gradual deregulation of interest rates and exchange rates, coupled with a tightening of monetary and fiscal policies. One reason for the rapid depreciation of the *renminbi* is that the persistent fiscal deficit has been largely covered by pure money creation. Even though the fiscal deficit cannot be eliminated overnight, a less inflationary method should be used by issuing government debt to a revitalized capital market. In short, what is needed is a sustained programme of 'financial deepening' already referred to in the text.

Y. C. JAO
9 May 1985

Notes

1. The contemporary view on the relationship between financial deepening and economic growth is developed in R.I. McKinnon, *Money and Capital in Economic Development* (New York, The Brookings Institution, 1973); and E.S. Shaw, *Financial Deepening and Economic Development* (New York, Oxford University Press, 1973). A recent review of the relevant literature is given in Y.C. Jao, 'Financial Deepening and Economic Growth: Theory, Evidence and Policy' (Hong Kong, Department of Economics, University of Hong Kong, November 1982), Discussion Paper No. 4.
2. See *Economic Reporter*, 17 January 1983.
3. *Asian Finance*, 15 August 1983.
4. See *The Banker*, February 1981, pp. 15–16. Although some modern office buildings have begun to appear in Beijing and other major cities, rents are as high or higher than any in New York, London, Paris, or Hong Kong. See *South China Morning Post*, 20 April 1984.
5. For recent accounts of the operations of China-controlled banks in Hong Kong, see Y.C. Jao, 'Hong Kong's Role in Financing China's Modernization', in A.J. Youngson (ed.), *China and Hong Kong: The Economic Nexus* (Hong Kong, Oxford University Press, 1983), pp. 12–76; and Leo Goodstadt, 'Banking Tuition in Hong Kong is Never Free', *Asiabanking*, October 1983, pp. 75–83.
6. See *The Banker*, February 1981, pp. 15–16; and P.D. Reynolds, *China's International Banking and Financial System* (New York, Praeger, 1982), pp. 83–4.
7. *Ta kung pao*, 8 October 1983. The same complaint was made by Mr Michael Sandberg, chairman of the Hongkong and Shanghai Banking Corporation. See A. Rowley and M. Lee, 'Peking Ducks the Issue', *Far Eastern Economic Review*, 22 November 1984, pp. 102–3.

8. *Economic Reporter*, 20 February 1984, p. 25.

9. *South China Morning Post*, 14 November 1983, and 5 April 1984.

10. See Economist Intelligence Unit, *Hong Kong: Economic Prospects to 1987* (London, The Economist, 1983), p. 46: and D. Mukerjee, 'China Oil Financing: BP Accepts China's Stiff Terms for Offshore Oil Contract', *Asian Finance*, 15 June 1983, pp. 88–90.

11. The other official logistic bases are Zhanjiang and Guangzhou in Guangdong province and Sanya on Hainan Island. However, the Zhuhai SEZ, because of its geographical proximity, is also likely to become another logistic base.

12. See interview with Mr Graham Harris, area manager for China and Hong Kong, Lloyds Bank International, *Ming pao*, 10 February 1984; Vigor Fung, 'Foreign Bankers See Promise in Peking', *Asian Wall Street Journal*, 9 February 1984; and Qin Xiaoli, 'US Bankers Await Lending Requests', *China Daily*, 28 April 1984.

13. See Bill Brown, 'It's Being So Conservative That Makes China Attractive', *Far Eastern Economic Review*, 26 April 1984, pp. 94–6. The author is area general manager of the Chartered Bank, Hong Kong, and the current chairman of the Hong Kong Association of Banks. See also S. Imai, 'China's Foreign Reserves', *China Newsletter*, No. 49, 1984, pp. 5–8.

14. Fu Wen, 'Zhongyin jituan — cujin Gangao yui neidi jingji guanxi de qiaoliang' ('The Bank of China Group — the Bridge for Promoting Economic Relations between Hong Kong, Macau, and the Hinterland'), *Economic Reporter*, 2 April 1984, pp. 5–6. See also 'BOC Plays an Active Role in Shenzhen SEZ', *China Economic News*, 25 June 1984, pp. 7–8.

15. Liu Kanshuo, Fang Minzhi and Xu Wan, 'Xiamen jinrongye de fanzhan yu qianjing zhanwang' ('Prospects and Outlook for Xiamen's Banking and Finance'), *Zhongguo jingji tequ nianjian* (*Yearbook of China's Special Economic Zones*) (Hong Kong, Yearbook of China's Special Economic Zones Publishing Co., 1983), pp. 339–41.

16. Jao (1983), pp. 29–30.

17. According to the methodology of the Banking Commissioner's Office, liabilities to and claims on banks outside Hong Kong are analysed by the country of the branch making or accepting the deposits, and not by the country of that branch's head office; for example, a claim on the London branch of a US bank is shown against the United Kingdom, and not against the United States. Similarly, the Bank of China's branch and or subsidiaries in Hong Kong are treated, for statistical purposes, as Hong Kong entities.

18. *Zhongguo jinrong* (*China Banking and Finance*), November 1983, pp. 2–3.

19. See Jao (1983), p. 32; and J.A. Cohen, 'The Bank of China Clears Up its Legal Status', *Euromoney*, December 1980, pp. 108–13.

20. See A.W. Samansky, 'China's Banking System: Its Modern History and Development' (New York, Federal Reserve Bank of New York, 1981), Research Paper No. 8108.

21. For a more detailed discussion of banking reforms, see Liu Hongru, *Shehuizhuyi hobi yu yinhang wenti* (*Monetary and Banking Problems of Socialism*) (Beijing, China Finance and Economics Publishing House, 1980), Chapter 10; C.H. Chai, 'Domestic Money and Banking Reforms in China', *Hong Kong Economic Papers*, No. 14, 1981, pp. 37–52; Zhang Enhua, 'On Banking Reform', *Beijing Review*, July 1981, pp. 24–7; 'Banking Reform Favours Centralization', *Beijing Review*, 9 April 1984, pp. 16–18; and W. Byrd, *China's Financial System* (Colorado, Westview Press, 1983), Chapters 4 and 5.

22. See Reynolds (1982), Chapter 2; Leo Goodstadt, 'Bank of China Lending', *Asian Banking*, March 1983, pp. 64–8; Robert Delfs, 'A Lender Dwarfing All Competitors', *Far Eastern Economic Review*, 5 May 1983, p. 72; and Teresa Ma, 'A Test of the Water', *Far Eastern Economic Review*, 1 September 1983, p. 108.

23. *South China Morning Post*, 25 November 1983.

24. *South China Morning Post*, 18 August 1983.

25. In China, for example, individuals can only hold savings and fixed deposits, but not demand deposits (checking accounts). Financial services more or less taken

for granted in developed countries and Hong Kong, such as home-ownership mortgages, hire purchase, and other forms of consumer loans, are virtually unknown in China, though discussions about their feasibility have begun to appear in the Chinese press. Deng Xiaoping is reported to have favoured the introduction of home-ownership mortgages as early as April 1980. See *Renmin ribao* (*People's Daily*), 15 May 1984. A limited form of demand deposits was recently introduced, however, by a bank in Shanghai. See *China Daily*, 29 October 1984.

26. For a more detailed discussion of the modernization and expansion of the Bank of China Group in Hong Kong, see Jao (1983), pp. 30–8.

27. Yuan Shibang, *Guanyu faxing tequ huobi de jianyi* (*On the Proposal for an SEZ Currency*) (Guangzhou, Institute of Southeast Asian Studies, Jinan University, 1981) (hereafter cited as Yuan 1981a).

28. Qian Jiaju, 'Economics of SEZs', *Intertrade*, January–February 1984, p. 56.

29. *Ming pao*, 20 November 1983, and 27 December 1983. An independent newspaper published in Hong Kong, *Ming pao* is widely respected for the reliability of its news and features about China.

30. *Ming pao*, 10 February 1984.

31. The literature on seigniorage is too large to be cited here. For an especially illuminating and relevant analysis, see R.A. Mundell, 'The International Distribution of Money in a Growing World Economy', in R.A. Mundell, *Monetary Theory* (California, Goodyear, 1971), Chapter 15.

32. Zhao Tong, 'Sheli tequ huobi' ('On the Creation of an SEZ Currency'), *Wen wei po*, 28 May 1984.

33. According to the official retail price index, the inflation rate in China was 6 per cent in 1980, 2.4 per cent in 1981, 1.9 per cent in 1982, and 1.5 per cent in 1983. However, it is widely agreed that the official price index measures only 'repressed inflation', but not 'open inflation', which has been estimated at over 10 per cent on average during the 1980s by Western economists. See G. Peebles, 'Inflation in the People's Republic of China 1950–82', *The Three Banks Review*, June 1984, pp. 37–57. For Hong Kong the average annual rate of consumer price inflation in 1980–3 was about 13 per cent.

34. It is well-known that in the USSR and other Soviet-bloc countries, both the non-commercial and black-market exchange rates are much higher than the basic official rates. See J. Wilczynski, *Comparative Monetary Economics* (London, Macmillan Press, 1978), Chapter 11; and J. Wilczynski, 'The Rouble versus the Dollar', paper presented to the Second World Congress on Soviet and East European Studies, 30 September to 4 October 1980.

35. Yuan (1981a), p. 3.

36. See Yuan (1981a); Yuan Shibang, 'Jingji tequ de houbi wenti' ('The Currency Question of the Special Economic Zones'), *Gangao jingji* (*Hong Kong and Macau Economic Digest*), No. 4, 1981, pp. 40–4 (hereafter cited as Yuan 1981b); Yuan Shibang, 'Guanyu faxing tequ huobi yu chengli tequ yinghang de wenti' ('On the Question of Issuing an SEZ Currency and Establishing an SEZ Bank'), *Xueshu yanjiu* (*Academic Research*), No. 1, 1983, pp. 3–10; Yuan Shibang, 'Jingji tequ de liutong wenti' ('The Question of Circulation in the SEZs'), *Gangao jingji*, No. 2, 1984, pp. 58–61; Zhang Yuanyuan and Yan Xianyu, 'Shenzhen tequ huobi wenti de tantao', *Guangdong jinrong yanjiu* (*Guangdong Financial Research*), No. 1, 1982, pp. 21–9; Xie Guoxuan, 'Shenzhen tequ xuyao faxing tequ huobi' ('Shenzhen Special Zone Needs a Special Currency'), *Gangao jingji*, No. 1, 1982, pp. 63–5; and Zhang Yuanyuan, 'Tantan Shenzhen tequ de huobi wenti' ('On the Currency Question of the Shenzhen Special Economic Zone'), *Zhongguo jingji tequ nianjian* (1983), pp. 673–5.

37. Xie (1982), pp. 63–4.

38. Yuan (1984), pp. 59–60. Since Yuan quotes from the Chinese edition of *Das Kapital*, the symbols in the text are all derived from the German original. Thus G stands for *Geld* (money), and W stands for *Ware* (commodity), while G' and W' stand for G and W increased by surplus value respectively.

39. Liu Guangdi, 'Muqian faxing tequ huobi de tiaojian bu chengshu' ('The

Time Is Not Yet Ripe for Issuing an SEZ Currency'), and Zhou Shengye, 'Buyi guoji faxing tequ huobi' ('The SEZ Currency Should Not Be Issued Prematurely'), both in *Guangdong jinrong yanjiu*, No. 12, 1982, and summarized in *Guangdong jingji tequ yaolan* (*A Compendium on the Guangdong Special Economic Zones*) (Guangzhou, Guangdong Research Centre for Special Economic Zones, 1982), pp. 192–3; Tang Huai, 'Faxing tequ huobi shi "weiyi de chulu" ma?' ('Is Issuing an SEZ Currency the "Only Way Out"?'), *Gangao jinji*, No. 6, 1981, pp. 42–4.

40. Yuan (1983), pp. 3–5.

41. Qiu Yongyi, 'Dui Shenzhen tequ juirong zhidu de tantao' ('A Discussion on the Financial System of the Shenzhen Special Economic Zone'), *Guangdong jinrong yanjiu*, No. 1, 1982, pp. 12–20. See also the views of Qiu Yongyi, Wang Zunhu and Lin Hongqian as summarized in *Guangdong jingji tequ yaolan* (1982), pp. 193–4.

42. Verbal report by Qiu Yongyi, of the Finance Research Institute, Guangdong provincial branch of the People's Bank of China, to the seminar on 'China's Special Economic Zones' held in Zhuhai, 12–13 June 1984.

43. *Wen wei po*, 28 May, 8 June, and 16 June 1984.

44. Verbal report by Qiu, see note 42.

45. As reported in *South China Morning Post*, 15 June 1984.

46. Verbal report by Qiu, see note 42.

47. For a perceptive analysis of China's post-Mao reforms, see Harry Harding, 'The Transformation of China', *The Brookings Review*, Spring 1984, pp. 3–7.

48. Contemporary economic theory emphasizes the importance of property rights and the costs of transactions as determinants of economic efficiency. For an application of this approach to China, see Steven N.S. Cheung, *Will China Go 'Capitalist'*? (London, The Institute of Economic Affairs, 1982), Hobart Paper No. 94.

Appendix A

China's Foreign Exchange and Gold Reserves

End of Year	Foreign Exchange (US$ million)	Gold (million troy ounces)
1979	2,154	12.80
1980	2,262	12.80
1981	4,773	12.67
1982	11,125	12.67
1983	14,342	12.67
1984 (first quarter)	15,690	12.67
(second quarter)	16,481	12.67

Source: Zhongguo jinrong (*China Banking and Finance*).

Appendix B

Net Financial Transactions Between China and Hong Kong[1] (HK$ million)

Date	Licensed Banks	Deposit-taking Companies	Total
31 March 1979	+4,725	+96	+4,821
30 June 1979	+5,231	+102	+5,333
30 Sept. 1979	+5,266	+116	+5,382
31 Dec. 1979	+5,701	+32	+5,733
31 March 1980	+5,386	+190	+5,576
30 June 1980	+4,676	+445	+5,121
30 Sept. 1980	+4,617	+390	+5,007
31 Dec. 1980	+5,352	+445	+5,797
31 March 1981	+5,984	+588	+6,572
30 June 1981	+4,291	+487	+4,778
30 Sept. 1981	+3,343	+64	+3,407
31 Dec. 1981	+2,567	−597	+1,970
31 March 1982	−100	−613	−713
30 June 1982	−2,010	−641	−2,651
30 Sept. 1982	−2,677	−404	−3,081
31 Dec. 1982	−4,933	−525	−5,458
31 March 1983	−5,468	−1,446	−6,914
30 June 1983	−5,366	−1,803	−7,169
30 Sept. 1983	−7,001	−1,868	−8,869
31 Dec. 1983	−7,333	−1,822	−9,155
31 March 1984	−9,710	−694	−10,404
30 June 1984	−12,473	−1,235	−13,708
30 Sept. 1984	−12,670	−1,114	−13,784

Note: 1. A negative sign denotes net liabilities to China, while a positive sign denotes net claims on China.

Source: Underlying data from *Hong Kong Monthly Digest of Statistics*.

10. Foreign Investment in the Special Economic Zones: A Management Perspective

T.W.C. Lo

Trends and Developments in Industrial Co-operation in the Shenzhen Special Economic Zone

Types of Industrial Co-operation

For the purpose of this chapter, 'foreign investment' is defined to include the following types of industrial co-operation:[1] processing trade, compensation trade, the contractual joint venture, the equity joint venture and the wholly owned foreign subsidiary.

In the early phases of the opening up of China, industrial co-operation was restricted to processing trade and compensation trade. Gradually, new forms of industrial co-operation, such as the equity joint venture and the contractual joint venture, came into play. More recently, wholly owned foreign subsidiaries have been allowed in the special economic zones (SEZs), and the idea has spread to other parts of China.[2]

It should be pointed out here that, especially in the early stages, many academics and businessmen in the Western world were often bewildered by the different types of industrial co-operation and their method of operation. This is understandable because of the new, evolving and complicated nature of the activities involved. Nevertheless, a clear understanding of these activities is essential to an analysis of industrial co-operation ventures between China and the West. Basically, the main types of industrial co-operation are as follows.[3]

(a) Processing trade: The processing trade consists of the processing and assembly of supplied parts and components. Under this type of arrangement, a foreign firm supplies materials, while the Chinese enterprise processes or assembles them into finished products according to the foreign contractor's designs, specifications and quality requirements. The material inputs supplied by the foreign firm can consist of all or part of the raw materials or semi-finished products and subsidiary materials, parts or components, and even packing and packaging materials, if necessary. All the products are passed on to the foreign contractor or his agent, who is normally required to sell them outside China. The Chinese enterprise receives a processing or assembly fee.

(b) Compensation trade: Under compensation trade, the Chinese partner is normally responsible for providing factory buildings and labour, while the foreign investor supplies production equipment, technology and possibly technical and supervisory personnel. Part of the raw materials may also be supplied by the foreign investor when necessary. The foreign investor is paid directly in instalments, by means of the goods produced in the project, for the cost of the technology, equipment and other materials supplied by him. If repayment in this form is difficult, the foreign firm is paid indirectly by means of other products or by a combination of other products and cash as agreed upon by both parties.

(c) The contractual joint venture: Under a contractual joint venture, the Chinese partner provides land, natural resources, labour, services, buildings, and equipment or facilities. The foreign partner provides either capital or technology, key equipment, and materials. The liabilities, rights and obligations of both parties are stipulated in the contract signed by them. The proportions in which products, revenue and profits are distributed are decided by both parties according to the terms of the contract.

The contractual joint venture differs from the equity joint venture primarily in that the capital contributions of the parties may not necessarily be expressed in terms of money and, therefore, profits will not be distributed in proportion to their equity shares, but in accordance with the agreed investment forms and proportions stipulated in the contract.

(d) The equity joint venture: An equity joint venture takes the form of a limited liability corporation with the status of a legal entity. The parties to the venture decide through consultation on the equity share of each party. Equity investment may be in the form of equipment, cash, rights to the use of a site, factory buildings and industrial property rights, and profits are distributed to the parties concerned in proportion to their equity share. According to the Law of the People's Republic of China on Joint Ventures Using Chinese and Foreign Investment, the share of foreign participants shall in general be not less than 25 per cent. Under this form of venture, both Chinese and foreign investors operate the venture jointly and share risks, profits and losses.

(e) The wholly owned foreign subsidiary: The wholly owned foreign subsidiary is, as the name suggests, a subsidiary of a foreign company which is wholly owned by that company.

Patterns of Development

The relative distribution of various types of industrial co-operation in Shenzhen (excluding Shekou) in August 1981 is given in Table 10.1.

As of August 1981, the total number of agreements stood at 814 and the total value of pledged investment in the Shenzhen SEZ exceeded HK$2,760 million, of which Hong Kong contributed 91 per cent, other overseas Chinese 5.5 per cent, and other foreign partners only 3.5 per cent.[4] Thirty-six of the agreements signed had an investment of over HK$10 million each, amounting to 80 per cent of the total pledged investment. Eight agreements had a pledged investment of over HK$100 million each.

In 1981, most agreements were in the manufacturing industries (66 per

Table 10.1 Industrial Co-operation in the Shenzhen SEZ by Type (as at August 1981)

	No. of Agreements	%	Pledged Investment (HK$ thousand)	%	Average Unit Value (HK$ thousand)
Processing trade[1]	504	62.2	57,450	2.3	114
Compensation trade[2]	5	0.6	44,700	1.8	8,940
Contractual joint ventures[3]	73	9.0	1,420,730	56.8	19,461
Equity joint ventures[3]	8	1.0	71,190	2.8	8,899
Wholly owned foreign subsidiaries[3]	15	1.8	824,815	33.0	54,987
Co-operation in agriculture and other related activities	206	25.4	83,950	3.3	407
Total	811	100.0	2,502,835	100.0	3,086

Notes: 1. Valued in terms of processing and or assembly fees.
2. Valued in terms of machinery, equipment and know-how compensated.
3. Foreign share of investment.

Source: Underlying data in *Economic Reporter*, 11 November 1981, p. 8 (excluding Shekou).

Table 10.2 Industrial Co-operation in the Shenzhen SEZ by Industry (as at August 1981)

	No. of Agreements	%	Pledged Investment (HK$ thousand)	%
Manufacturing	537	66.1	450,200	16.9
Agriculture	211	26.0	114,105	4.3
Services	12	1.5	217,650	8.2
Tourism	20	2.5	781,930	29.2
Real estate	23	2.8	1,090,220	40.8
Transportation	7	0.9	6,485	0.2
Others	2	0.2	10,140	0.4
Total	812	100.0	2,670,730	100.0

Source: Underlying data in *Economic Reporter*, 11 November 1981 (excluding Shekou).

cent) and agriculture (26 per cent). However, the highest pledged investment occurred in real estate and tourism development (see Table 10.2).

Trends in Overall Industrial Co-operation Agreements in the Shenzhen SEZ

The total number of agreements as at the end of 1983 stood at 2,512, with pledged investment amounting to HK$13,224 million and actual investment amounting to HK$2,970 million. During the five-year period from 1979 to 1983, the number of agreements increased each year. However, 1982 showed only a small increase over 1981. Nevertheless, growth continued from 1982 onwards (see Table 10.3).

Up until 1982 the amount of pledged investment continued to rise each year, 1981 being especially healthy with pledged investment in that year surpassing the combined total of previous years. However, the pledged amount dropped sharply in 1982 due to the world economic recession, the slump in Hong Kong's property market and the difficulties encountered in industrial co-operation by foreign partners in Shenzhen. Nevertheless, the actual amount of investment showed an upward trend each year over the same period. It may be noted that actual investment amounted to 22.5 per cent of pledged investment in 1983.

Table 10.4 shows industrial co-operation by industry in Shenzhen as at the end of 1983. In terms of the percentage of the number of agreements, when compared with Table 10.2, the manufacturing sector showed an increase. The manufacturing sector accounted for 43.6 per cent of actual investment as at December 1983 compared with 16.9 per cent of pledged investment as at August 1981. The number of agreements concluded in the manufacturing sector in 1983 stood at 714, that is, 81.3 per cent of the total number of industrial co-operation agreements concluded in that year, which was 878. The amount of investment pledged in the manufacturing sector in 1983 surpassed the total amount pledged in the previous three years.[5] Tourism and real estate accounted for 31.6 per cent of actual investment as at December 1983 compared with 70 per cent of pledged investment as at August 1981. Thus, the relative importance of the manufacturing sector appeared to have increased whereas that of real estate and tourism had decreased.[6]

Contractual joint ventures, equity joint ventures and wholly owned subsidiaries, compared with processing trade and compensation trade, generally represent higher forms of involvement of resources by a foreign company. Table 10.5 compares the number of agreements for contractual joint ventures, equity joint ventures and wholly owned subsidiaries for the years 1979 to 1983 as a proportion of the total number of industrial co-operation agreements. The data indicates that there was a rapid increase of 106 per cent and 263 per cent respectively in the number of contractual joint-venture and equity joint-venture agreements in 1983 as compared with the total for the previous four years. This sudden increase may have been due to new preferential terms introduced in that year. Table 10.5 also shows that, as far as the number of agreements is concerned, contractual joint ventures, equity joint ventures and wholly owned subsidiaries together (S) occupied a larger percentage of the total (T) in 1983 (28.9 per cent) than in previous years.

Table 10.3 Industrial Co-operation in the Shenzhen SEZ, 1979–83

	1979	1980	1981	1982	1983
No. of agreements:					
by year	170	303	578	583	878
cumulative total	170	473	1,051	1,634	2,512
Pledged investment: (HK$ million)					
by year	235	2,136	6,800	1,419	2,634
cumulative total (1)	235	2,371	9,171	10,590	13,224
Actual investment: (HK$ million)					
by year	120	250	590	880	1,130
cumulative total (2)	120	370	960	1,840	2,970
Cumulative total (2) as a percentage of cumulative total (1)	51.1	15.6	10.5	17.4	22.5

Source: Underlying data in *Renmin ribao* (*People's Daily*), 29 March 1984.

Table 10.4 Industrial Co-operation in the Shenzhen SEZ by Industry (as at December 1983)

In Terms of No. of Agreements		
	No. of Agreements	%
Manufacturing	1,847	73.7
Services	132	5.3
Transportation	28	1.1
Real estate	59	2.4
Tourism	16	0.6
Agriculture	423	16.9
Total	2,505	100.0
In Terms of Actual Investment		
	Actual Investment (HK$ thousand)	%
Manufacturing	1,299,010	43.6
Services	224,650	7.5
Transportation	37,040	1.2
Real estate	789,350	26.5
Tourism	150,800	5.1
Agriculture	44,790	1.5
Others	435,170	14.6
Total	2,980,810	100.0

Source: Underlying data in *Renmin ribao* (*People's Daily*), 29 March 1984.

Table 10.5 Contractual Joint Ventures, Equity Joint Ventures and Wholly Owned Foreign Subsidiaries in the Shenzhen SEZ (as at December 1983)

	No. of Agreements						
	1979	1980	1981	1982	1983	1979–82	1979–83
Contractual joint ventures	30	24	39	47	147	140	289
Equity joint ventures	7	4	13	11	92	35	127
Wholly owned foreign subsidiaries	—	5	18	8	13	31	44
Subtotal (S)	37	33	70	66	254	206	460
Total (T)	170	303	578	583	878	1,428	2,512
S as a percentage of T	21.8	10.9	12.1	11.3	28.9	14.4	18.3

Source: Underlying data in *Renmin ribao* (*People's Daily*), 29 March 1984.

In 1983, the production value of equity joint ventures and wholly owned subsidiaries accounted for 37 per cent of total production value in the Shenzhen SEZ.[7]

As shown in Table 10.6, Shenzhen accounted for about 60 per cent of all contractual joint ventures and 88 per cent of all equity joint ventures in China in 1983. In respect of the cumulative total, Shenzhen accounted for nearly 28 per cent of all contractual joint ventures, 68 per cent of all equity joint ventures, and 80 per cent of all wholly owned subsidiaries. Shenzhen's strategic role in China's industrial co-operation strategy is thus extremely significant.

Problems Encountered by Chinese and Foreign Partners

In order to understand the mechanism of industrial co-operation ventures in Shenzhen, it is useful to examine the problems experienced by both foreign and Chinese partners. An attempt is made here to summarize the views of both sides, so that the lessons drawn from their experience may give some directions and indications to existing and potential Western partners, which may in turn help to enhance the performance and growth of industrial co-operation between China and the West.

Problems Encountered by Chinese Partners

The concept of the SEZ is a fairly recent development in China and this is to some extent reflected in the problems that Chinese partners in industrial co-operation face. Based on a survey conducted by a group of Chinese experts on Shenzhen[8] and the author's personal interviews in China, there appear to be seven main areas within which problems are encountered.

First, a Chinese partner may in some cases fail to consider the overall impact on the whole country of the agreement in which he is involved because the agreement appears to be beneficial to his particular region. In one case, for example, a Chinese partner in Shenzhen signed a processing trade contract which appeared to be beneficial to Shenzhen. However, he failed to notice that China had already been exporting similar labour-intensive products from other parts of China. Thus, the result was two different export prices for the same kinds of products, thereby causing unnecessary competition. In some cases, processing ventures have actually disturbed the country's existing overseas distribution channels.

Second, given the fact that some discretion is granted to local authorities in the SEZs in accepting industrial co-operation agreements, a Chinese partner may take on a project which goes against the country's established policies. This may in turn sometimes cause embarrassment. In one case, a Chinese partner was negotiating on a certain entertainment project with a foreign partner when it was discovered that the project contained 'contaminating ideas' which were unacceptable to the central government.

Third, in some instances, the Chinese partner in a venture has been taken advantage of by the foreign partner through, for example, misrepresentation,

Table 10.6 The Number of Agreements for Contractual Joint Ventures, Equity Joint Ventures and Wholly Owned Foreign Subsidiaries in the Shenzhen SEZ and China

	1983 (by year)			1983 (cumulative total)		
	Shenzhen SEZ (S)[1]	China (C)	S/C (%)	Shenzhen SEZ[1]	China	S/C(%)
Contractual joint ventures	149	248[2]	60.1	289	1,040[3]	27.8
Equity joint ventures	92	105[4]	87.6	127	188[4]	67.6
Wholly owned foreign subsidiaries	13	n/a	n/a	44	55[3]	80.0

Note: n/a = not available.

Sources: 1. *Renmin ribao* (*People's Daily*), 29 March 1984.
2. Obtained by subtracting the figure 792 (the cumulative total of contractual joint ventures in 1979–82) from 1,040. See *Intertrade*, October 1983, p. 68.
3. *Economic Reporter*, 25 June 1984, p. 20.
4. *Economic Reporter*, 20 February 1984, p. 20.

the import of obsolete equipment and machinery, unreasonably low processing fees, or inflated import prices. This has been mainly due to the Chinese partner's ignorance of the foreign partner's business operations and the world economic climate.

Fourth, the Chinese partner's lack of knowledge of modern business practices, such as concepts of depreciation, costs and accounting procedures, tends to weaken his bargaining position when negotiating a contract.

Fifth, industrial co-operation agreements tend to be quite brief and usually do not have provisions for instances of non-performance, delays in payment, and so on.

Sixth, there appears to be very little co-ordination among the various state-operated organizations (such as banks, customs bureaux, insurance commissions, trade commissions, and town planning committees). As a result there is no consensus on the assessment of the credibility of foreign partners or on the suitability of proposed projects.

Finally, existing laws are insufficient to deal with the wide variety of legal problems that are coming to light.

Problems Encountered by Foreign Partners

As mentioned previously, industrial co-operation agreements involving Hong Kong partners account for a large percentage of all industrial co-operation activities in Shenzhen. It is thus useful to know what problems Hong Kong partners have encountered in their respective ventures. Based on personal interviews conducted by the author with top-level decision-makers and business executives of companies in Hong Kong, and published data of other researchers or practitioners in this field,[9] problems commonly encountered by business investors in Shenzhen may be summarized as follows.

(a) The lack of a comprehensive legal framework: The number of laws and regulations on foreign investment in the SEZs is limited, there being, for example, no legislation covering bankruptcy cases. And those SEZs laws that do exist are vague and leave many important issues, such as tax, and land and labour costs, open to negotiation. In addition, the negotiation process may be very time-consuming due to a lack of precedents. The inadequate legal system may therefore lead to confusion and frustration on the part of both parties.

As an illustration of this inadequacy, during the first seven months of 1984 more than 90 cases of dispute were reported between foreign investors and their Chinese partners over profit-sharing and the implementation of contracts in joint-venture projects in the Shenzhen SEZ. Many of the disputes concerned property development projects involving Hong Kong businessmen.[10] The disputes were often settled by internal mediation or negotiation as there is no comprehensive judicial system for commercial arbitration in the SEZ. It has been reported that foreign investors are usually in an unfavourable position in such circumstances.

In many cases, the Chinese have adopted a very flexible attitude in interpreting the laws and regulations.[11] Likewise, some of the laws and regulations are for internal guidance only and are not made available to the public.[12] This poses problems of interpretation and gives rise to unnecessary confusion amongst outsiders and even amongst Chinese personnel. It follows that the negotiation process is crucial in establishing and ascertaining each party's rights and obligations, since the laws do not cover adequately the various situations that may arise and are in any case subject to interpretation by the Chinese partner.

(b) The complex administrative structure and inconsistent policies: Given the complicated administrative structure and prevailing bureaucracy in government departments, a foreign investor often does not know which department he should approach, and at what level, to discuss a particular venture. The situation becomes worse when Chinese officials are frequently transferred, for this disrupts established personal relationships and understandings that have developed between foreign investors and the Chinese officials.

The complicated administrative structure and inadequate delegation of decision-making power may give rise to longer negotiations than are normally required. Moreover, due to the complicated administrative structure, a Chinese partner may have difficulties in performing obligations which involve the participation of another Chinese organization which was not consulted when the contract was drafted.[13]

The inadequate channelling and communication of information between government officials and organizations in China may sometimes lead to inconsistent policies, especially when the rules and regulations are vague and are subject to interpretation. As an illustration, it has happened that a businessman has been directed by one department not to undertake a certain task, but has been strongly encouraged by another state organization to do so. Such inconsistent policies, of course, lead to confusion and sometimes frustration amongst foreign partners.

(c) Labour quality and administration: The quality of labour employed in any venture is an important consideration as it will affect productivity. In a number of instances in ventures in Shenzhen it has been found that many workers do not possess the necessary experience and are insufficiently educated to be able to adapt to a change in environment and to absorb new concepts. In some areas of specialization there is still a shortage of labour in Shenzhen but the overall situation has improved in recent years. Although the Chinese government is now providing its workers with some training before they take up jobs in the SEZs, these workers still need time to adjust themselves, both physically and mentally. In addition, the wage level is determined by the Chinese authorities, and the system provides very little incentive for hard work and increased productivity. The 'iron rice-bowl' attitude that many workers have towards their jobs gives rise to a general lack of initiative and enthusiasm. Thus many foreign investors have indicated that they would like to be given the power to recruit and sack workers.

Under the SEZ Labour and Wage Regulations, enterprises enjoy the right to dismiss employees who have become redundant as a result of changes in production and technical conditions, or who fail to meet the requirements of the enterprises. However, dismissal is only permitted if the affected worker, after training, cannot be transferred within the enterprise to other types of work. SEZ enterprises are also required to provide severance pay to dismissed employees, the amount of each payment being determined on the basis of the length of employment.[14] Such requirements add to the complexity of labour administration in the Shenzhen SEZ. In addition, the local labour bureaux have been empowered to approve wage levels for workers and rule on dismissal cases, such that foreign investors' decisions may often depend on the interpretation of the laws, and the attitudes and policies adopted by these local labour bureaux,[15] thus leaving the foreign investor with very little room for manoeuvre.

(d) The lack of management experience and understanding of international practices: Foreign investors who are required to supply machinery and raw materials to their Chinese partners have to go through cumbersome procedures every time goods are imported. They also face such problems when manufactured products are exported out of the zone. The red tape involved in the import and export of goods often causes unnecessary delays.

(e) The lack of planning: The poor infrastructure and lack of many amenities in Shenzhen pose problems for large-scale industrial development. However, there are signs that more funds are now being spent to improve the overall infrastructure of the zone.[16] Still transportation is a headache for many investors.

(f) The lack of information: Due to the general lack of comprehensive published information and official statistics, and the difficulties in conducting research, foreign partners may have to resort to other sources for information. However, such information may be superficial, partial and piecemeal, often leading to misunderstandings or misconceptions on the part of foreign investors, which may in turn result in the formulation of incorrect strategies or even in the definition of the wrong objectives.

(g) The lack of access to the domestic market: Some investors express the wish that the Chinese market be opened up to allow for the internal consumption of products manufactured in the SEZs. This would attract more foreign investment, even though the market has been opened up in some selected cases already. Nevertheless, the suggestion involves the fundamental concept of the centrally planned economy and is outside the scope of the present discussion.

The above list of problems is not meant to be exhaustive. Nevertheless, illustration of the problems mentioned will shed some light on the practical difficulties encountered in conducting industrial co-operation ventures in Shenzhen. In fact, these problems are by no means peculiar to the SEZs: many of them occur in the general context of industrial co-operation between China and the West.

Notwithstanding such problems, efforts have been made by the Chinese government to institute improvements in organization and procedures. In addition, more laws and regulations are to be enacted for the benefit of foreign investors (some of them focusing on the SEZs and Shenzhen in particular) and attempts are being made to improve the infrastructure within the zones. To a large extent, all these moves will help to create a more favourable investment environment in the SEZs.

A Strategic Approach to Industrial Co-operation in Shenzhen

An understanding and analysis of the major strategic issues and functions are useful for the efficient and effective operation of an industrial co-operation venture in Shenzhen. This section is devoted to a discussion of some of the key issues, which include: the choice of the form of industrial co-operation adopted, the choice of a partner, negotiation, and the planning, organization and control of industrial co-operation ventures.

Forms of Industrial Co-operation: The Western Perspective

Assuming that a certain Western company has decided to engage in industrial co-operation in Shenzhen instead of in the traditional import and export business, then it will have to decide on the form of industrial co-operation which it adopts. Generally speaking, of the options available, processing trade requires the minimum involvement of resources by a foreign partner while the wholly owned subsidiary requires the maximum commitment. The other alternative forms of industrial co-operation lie between the above two extremes.

The criteria that influence a company's decision on the choice of a certain form of industrial co-operation can be roughly divided into those that are external and those that are internal to the company.[17] For each project, the feasible alternatives will have to be sorted out and compared as to profitability and the consequences for achieving the company's long-term goals. External factors may include: China's policies and controls on the SEZs; the availability of suitable partners; the competitive situation in the SEZs and the hinterland; and the foreign partner's home country's policies regarding, for example, the export of strategic goods to China, tax policies, and investment-guarantee programmes. Internal factors may include: the characteristics of the company's technology and products/services; the availability of adequate financial and other managerial resources; the degree of operating experience that the company can command for a new and different situation; the speed with which the company wishes to initiate new projects for competitive or other reasons; the company's willingness to assume risk; and long-term corporate goals.

The above are some of the decision variables that may determine the possible forms of industrial co-operation adopted. However, it should be noted that the pros and cons associated with the various options are very fluid at present, hence companies must monitor the situation closely in order to make an optimal choice. As an illustration, in the past foreign partners often preferred the contractual joint venture to the equity joint venture as it was easier to enter into an agreement on the former. However, over time some of the problems of the contractual joint venture came to light while the regulatory framework associated with the equity joint venture became clearer, and this, coupled with the improvement in the approval process for equity joint ventures, resulted in a relatively more rapid increase in the number of equity joint ventures concluded in 1983.

The Choice of a Chinese Partner for Industrial Co-operation

Except in the case of a wholly owned subsidiary, a foreign partner needs to choose a Chinese partner or partners for an industrial co-operation venture. Even for processing trade activities in which the foreign partner has 'limited' commitments, a badly chosen Chinese partner may lead to problems. However, foreign partners are in many instances rather 'passive' in their choice of partner and often pay insufficient attention to the matter. This is probably due to a lack of information upon which a foreign partner can base his decision. Thus, in many circumstances, a foreign company accepts whoever is 'recommended' to it as the counterpart in the venture.

Nevertheless, it is important to realize that a good Chinese partner is, among other factors, crucial to the success of an industrial co-operation venture. As explained previously, Western investors often complain about their Chinese partners' lack of knowledge concerning Western business practices. Therefore if the top Chinese officials involved in the industrial co-operation venture are more open-minded, innovative and ready to accept new ideas, they will be able to communicate and work with the Western partner more effectively. Such qualities on the Chinese side will also help to minimize possible conflicts and to resolve more smoothly those problems which do arise in the course of the industrial co-operation project. At the same time, since Chinese laws and regulations are subject to interpretation, the system works to the advantage of an industrial co-operation venture whose Chinese partner is powerful and has favourable connections because these will help to get things done faster and more easily. Thus the choice of a Chinese associate is of great importance.

A Chinese partner may be chosen by formulating a strategy for locating the partner and establishing criteria for selection, which in turn depend on the external and internal factors mentioned previously, as well as the type of industrial co-operation involved. The process of selecting a suitable partner should be carried out carefully and as much information as possible should be gathered before a final decision is made. In cases of doubt, it is advisable to adopt a 'wait-and-see' approach or alternatively to opt instead for a lower form of industrial co-operation or a smaller amount of investment, so as to limit the level of commitment in order to 'learn' more about the partner before investing further resources. All in all, it is safer to spend a little more time or resources in locating and selecting a good partner than to find out later that one's partner does not meet one's expectations or requirements.

Negotiation

Negotiation is a very important process before the signing of an industrial co-operation agreement. Generally speaking, the negotiating process differs according to the parties concerned and the form and content of the venture. Negotiation is especially significant in China because, as explained previously, China's laws and regulations are often subject to interpretation. In addition, given the fact that industrial co-operation between China and the West is relatively new, there is a general lack of precedents to which the Chinese partner can refer.

Negotiation is complicated by the inexperience of the Chinese partner, the bureaucratic structure of the Chinese system and the desire on the part of some Chinese partners and or negotiators to avoid risks. As far as the difficulties encountered in the negotiation process are concerned, four important gaps appear to be crucial and warrant special attention by foreign investors. These are the culture gap, the information gap, the legal gap and the enforcement gap.[18]

In the process of negotiations, a foreign partner must be able to understand the circumstances which his counterparts face. Since Chinese negotiators are not generally in a position to change their environment and the institutions within which they must operate, complaints that the Chinese are bureaucratic or inefficient are not very helpful. The foreign partner should realize that many of the problems probably do not arise from personal negligence or wilful sabotage but are systemic in nature. In these circumstances, a way out must be found for the Chinese negotiators.[19] At the same time, the foreign partner should set a limit as to how far he can go during a negotiation. He should be seen to be firm, but must remain patient, since a good working relationship is essential for long-term co-operation.

The Planning, Organizational and Control Aspects of Industrial Co-operation Ventures

(a) Planning: A lack of planning and an inadequate understanding of the business environment of the host country are often reasons for failure in international business investments. Good planning is crucial since it will to a large extent affect the success or failure of the industrial co-operation venture, which will in turn have long-term strategic implications in China. This is because in China past performance and experience are often used as evaluative criteria for future co-operative ventures.

Nevertheless, for a Western partner, planning is often difficult because of the limited amount of information available, which may also at times be biased or superficial. Moreover, the fluid nature of the environment prevailing in China poses another problem in planning. Hence a Western partner has to adopt a cautious approach and build in some flexibility into his plans in order to allow for the unexpected. Feasibility studies should be carried out to examine the viability of the project as well as to gather more information which a foreign investor can use for planning at later stages.

It is also to the Western investor's advantage if he can involve his Chinese counterparts and the related Chinese organizations in the planning process as much as possible. The 'inputs' from the Chinese side should be invaluable because these people are more familiar with the environment within which the co-operation venture is to operate. Furthermore, involvement of the Chinese partner and the other participants in the planning process will enable the Western partner to solicit their support more readily at later stages.

(b) Organization: Organization is crucial at various stages in the life of an industrial co-operation venture. Once a contract has been signed, a foreign investor should decide who is to be responsible for assisting the firm in implementing the industrial co-operation venture. Of course, the question of staffing and administration will very much depend on the form of co-operation. It is quite obvious that relatively little staffing is required for a processing trade contract, whereas for an equity joint venture the parent firm may have to send a suitable number of staff to supervise and assist in order to give the necessary back-up on technological know-how or management expertise. Very often, a foreign partner may need to 'educate' and train his Chinese counterparts in accepting new ideas or methods. This is a time-consuming process but, if successfully carried out, will give rise to many fruitful returns.

(c) Control: Many foreign partners engaging in industrial co-operation ventures have reported that they have encountered a lot of 'unexpected' problems. This is not surprising because of the many 'unknowns' in the Chinese environment. As pointed out by Professor N.T. Wang, there are too many actors, institutions and issues involved.[20] When coupled with the inexperience and misconceptions of both foreign and Chinese partners, there are bound to be a number of unforeseen circumstances which may give rise to difficulties and problems. Hence, very close control has to be exercised to monitor the progress and results of the programmes, and to make various adjustments whenever necessary.

Given the fluid nature of the subject, a foreign partner should continuously assess those factors which are internal and those which are external so as to formulate effective strategies for solving problems, and control should be properly exercised at various stages of the industrial co-operation venture. Top officials on the Chinese side ought also to be given some role in management control, so that both parties can co-operate to achieve their common objectives. Such a concept should also be communicated down the hierarchy, since co-operation at even the lowest level is integral to the success of the venture.

Conclusion

To sum up, it is evident that industrial co-operation ventures in the Shenzhen SEZ have numerous short- and medium-term problems, and their overall performance to date has not met the expectations of either the Chinese or foreign partners. In fact, some of the problems are basically related to culture. For example, the concept of 'my word is my bond' is prevalent in the traditional Chinese business community, and little emphasis is placed on established principles and contracts as is the case in the West. In addition, foreign partners (including the Hong Kong Chinese) have little understanding of the mentality of the Chinese bureaucracy and labour force or of the economic system and environment under which these groups of people work.[21] Problems described above may actually have been caused by a communication gap or a failure to understand or appreciate the motives behind an industrial co-operation agreement. Nevertheless, it is encouraging to see that the Chinese government is sincere in initiating various improvements and reforms, and is drawing lessons from its experiment in Shenzhen. At the same time, foreign investors should spend more time on planning and control. To this end, the service of independent consultants may provide more expertise in tackling some of the more difficult problems, as well as in providing a better overall plan.

Finally, whilst the Chinese government has accelerated various reforms that will lead to a more favourable environment for business investors and has placed more emphasis on the education of officials and managers, it is also of the utmost importance that the information gap, which has been a great barrier to both Chinese and foreign partners, be bridged. For successful co-operation requires the mutual understanding of both parties and their respective business environments.

Prospects

The generally more flexible attitude to foreign partners' requirements currently prevailing in the SEZs increases the potential for more fruitful ventures in the future. In the long term, the speed of development of the SEZs will depend on the extent to which the problems described above are solved. It seems that, with the recent visit of Deng Xiaoping to Shenzhen and the other SEZs and the official announcement of the opening up of 14 coastal cities in China to foreign investment, the open-door policy on the SEZs has been confirmed and various developments have been accelerated.

Notwithstanding the fact that there have been a number of economic reforms, it should be recognized that it takes time for the system to change and for the people involved to become familiar with the system. At the same time, the opening up of 14 coastal cities in China for foreign investment may pose a threat to the SEZs, because they will have to face competition from those cities. Nevertheless, the potential and prospects for industrial co-operation in the SEZs will be considerable because of their greater flexibility. Having said that, the overall open-door policy will, by and large, depend on a stable political system and consistent policies.

Notes

1. As Marer and Miller have pointed out, there is no internationally accepted standard definition of industrial co-operation beyond the convention that it must encompass more than simple, arms-length, import-export transactions, and each Eastern country has employed its own definition. Industrial co-operation is a very new phenomenon in China and, for the purpose of this chapter, is defined so as to include processing trade, compensation trade, the contractual joint venture, the equity joint venture and the wholly owned foreign subsidiary. For a discussion of industrial co-operation, see Paul Marer and Joseph Miller, 'US Participation in East-West Industrial Co-operation Agreements', *Journal of International Business Studies*, Fall – Winter 1977, pp. 17–29; C.H. McMillan, 'Trends in East-West Industrial Co-operation,' *Journal of International Business Studies*, Fall 1981, pp. 53–67; and F. Levcik and J. Stankovsky, *Industrial Co-operation between East and West* (White Plains, NY, M.E. Sharpe, 1979), pp. 3–8

2. In the past few years, only a handful of wholly owned foreign ventures have been approved, and only in China's SEZs. Now the Chinese seem eager to attract major foreign companies to set up subsidiaries elsewhere in the country. One of the trail-blazers is 3M Co., which, in November 1983, reached an agreement in principle with the Chinese to set up a small factory in Shanghai. For details, see 'The Problems of Doing Business in China', *Business Week*, 7 May 1984, p. 53.

3. *Guidebook on Trading with the People's Republic of China* (New York, United Nations, 1983, second edition), pp. 167–9. See also *Economic Reporter*, 6 August 1984, pp. 28–9.

4. *Economic Reporter*, 11 November 1981, p. 8. Note that Tables 10.1 and 10.2 only show the breakdown of 811 and 812 agreements respectively.

5. *Economic Reporter*, 20 February 1984, p. 20.

6. *Economic Reporter*, 20 February 1984, p. 20.

7. *Renmin ribao (People's Daily)*, 29 March 1984.

8. *Xueshu yanjiu (Academic Research)*, No. 6, 1981, pp. 42–6.

9. See, for example, *Economic Reporter*, 23 April 1984, pp. 5–9.

10. *Sing tao wan pao*, 13 August 1984.

11. Based on personal interviews conducted by the author. See also M.J. Moser, 'Law and Investment in the Guangdong Special Economic Zones', in M.J. Moser (ed.), *Foreign Trade, Investment and the Law in the People's Republic of China* (Hong Kong, Oxford University Press, 1984), p. 159.

12. S.B. Lubman, 'China Should Make More Laws Public', *Asian Wall Street Journal*, 5–6 August 1983.

13. Moser (1984), p. 101.

14. Provisional Regulations of the Special Economic Zones in Guangdong Province Governing Labour and Wages for Business Enterprises, Art. 16, adopted by the Thirteenth Session of the Standing Committee of the Fifth Guangdong Provincial People's Congress on 17 November 1981 (hereafter cited as the Labour and Wage Regulations).

15. Moser (1984), pp. 158–9.

16. *Renmin ribao*, 29 March 1984.

17. S. Robock and K. Simmonds, *International Business and Multinational Enterprises* (Homewood, Ill., Richard D. Irwin, Inc., 1983, third edition), pp. 294–9.

18. N.T. Wang, *China's Modernization and Transnational Corporations* (Lexington, Mass., Lexington Books, 1984), pp. 113–22.

19. Wang (1984), pp. 126–7.

20. Wang (1984), pp. xxxi.

21. Thamis Lo Wing-chun and Ho Suk-ching, 'Going International: Set Your Steps Right', *The Hong Kong Manager*, August 1982, pp. 20–1.

11. Managerial Reform and Enterprise Performance: Assessing the Experiment in Shenzhen and Zhuhai[1]

K.K. SHUM AND L.T. SIGEL

Introduction

Since 1979, the leaders of the People's Republic of China have attempted to make fundamental alterations to the nation's approach to economic development. The key to the success of China's revised strategy is the ability to switch from the extensive growth pattern of the past to one of intensive growth. Instead of being based largely on quantitative increases in the factors of production, intensive growth depends mainly upon increases in the productivity of the factors of production. This emphasis of current policy is evident in the stress placed on realizing the full potential of existing plants and on making the most effective use of capital stock built up in the past. To attain this major objective, China must rely on qualitative factors such as superior product standards, technological change and organizational reforms. Better management is, therefore, a crucial aspect of the present economic programme.

Managerial reform has long been one of the principal areas of concern to Deng Xiaoping, the dominant figure in the Chinese political leadership. In the 1981 resolution 'On Questions of Party History', the contributions of various Party figures are enumerated. This highly significant document presents the official interpretation of past events. In it, Deng is given credit for his early awareness of the need for managerial reform. During China's first decade of 'socialist construction', 1956–66, he held 'that industrial enterprises should be consolidated and their management improved and strengthened'.[2]

The importance of improving the organization and administration of enterprises again emerges in Deng's talks and speeches in 1975 when he assumed authority for the day-to-day work of the Party and state. Changing the manner in which factories and other units of production were run was an essential component in overcoming the problems of the Cultural Revolution and in combating the 'Leftist' policies of the Gang of Four.

During this period, Deng was appalled at the waste and inefficiency he encountered as he sought to bring order to industrial management. He repeatedly cited the need for appropriate rules and regulations to be re-established and enforced. Calling upon cadres in positions of authority to arouse a sense of organization and discipline within their units, he encouraged them to exert strong influence. He particularly advocated the development of a 'responsibility system' within enterprises, challenging the factory leaders to be bold and daring in their approach to duty.[3]

As part of his 1975 drive to achieve intensive growth through managerial reform, Deng also emphasized the importance of technical transformation and greater production quality. The managers of the basic units of production in China had lacked the power and incentives to decide for themselves on changes in the way work was conducted. This defect was inherent in the Soviet-style centrally planned economic system, but Deng saw that it would inhibit future growth. Greater productivity and efficiency could be achieved only through encouraging the initiative and inventiveness of responsible managerial personnel.[4] Since the end of 1978, when he consolidated his position within the Chinese Communist leadership, Deng Xiaoping has renewed his efforts to improve the operation of industrial enterprises.

To this end, the special economic zones (SEZs) established within the context of the current reform policies have a special role in that they serve as living laboratories of economic change. The Chinese authorities have repeatedly underlined this function in contrast to the foreign emphasis on the introduction of outside investment. These areas provide a training-ground for Chinese cadres. Modern techniques and scientific methods of management can be learned at first hand. These units can also serve as experimental workshops for the testing and evaluation of economic reforms. Within them, the means to modernize can be adapted and perfected and then introduced into enterprises outside the zones.

In this sense, the SEZs of China, especially Shenzhen and Zhuhai, which are more developed, represent a necessary and unique environment. In these small enclaves, foreign investment rather than Chinese state investment is the decisive factor in determining the pace, nature and direction of economic growth. The enterprises utilizing foreign capital are of necessity oriented primarily toward production for competitive export markets. Except under special circumstances, only a limited portion of their output is allowed to be sold on the domestic market.

The new business undertakings established in the SEZs generally function outside the planned economy. In contrast to foreign investment projects elsewhere in China, where investment, raw materials and output are included in the State Plan, the SEZ enterprises using foreign investment must make provision for their own needs. They must procure their own financing and supply their own input requirements. As well as arranging for any domestic distribution, they must also secure and assure their markets outside China.

The differences that set these zones apart are also evident in managerial areas. There is considerably greater autonomy in the zones than in the rest of China in hiring and firing staff and in staff discipline, and far greater leeway in differentiating wages according to individual work responsibility, job performance, and enterprise profitability. In Sino-foreign joint ventures elsewhere in China, management is more restricted. Standard Chinese practice and industrial regulations limit the management's scope in recruitment, labour relations and material incentives, since all the workers are considered to be employees of state enterprises.

The remarkable rapid growth witnessed in Shenzhen and Zhuhai is directly related to the much greater flexibility that they have been granted. The low level of economic efficiency, serious loss and waste, and the failure to achieve productive potential which generally plague industry and commerce in China are attributed to excessive state control, rigid regulation, and bureaucratic barriers which have characterized Chinese socialism. Although change is essential, the urban economy remains largely unreformed and past errors continue to be repeated. The system suppresses enterprise vitality by denying opportunities and incentives for improvement. The recent momentous decision of the Party Central Committee on economic reform admits: 'Our urban reform is only in the initial stage, however, and defects in the urban economic structure that seriously hinder the expansion of the forces of production are yet to be eradicated'.[5]

While optimistically committing China to the basic accomplishment of radical transformation in about five years,[6] the Chinese Communist leaders stress that caution and prudence must be exercised in making reforms that affect the entire economy.[7] Many of the changes which the Chinese authorities are hoping to achieve are already underway or exist in the SEZs. Exploratory and pilot reforms, therefore, can be assessed within the particular economic context of these zones.

A complementarity exists between the wide latitude granted the SEZs in pioneering structural reform and institutional change and the scope they offer for greater interaction between China and foreign businessmen. The SEZs should be seen as one end of a spectrum of far more extensive international economic co-operation and technical exchange fostered by the open-door policy. Within the local zone economies, an export-led growth strategy is being pursued. Market forces are being allowed to act as the dominant rather than the auxiliary or supplementary determinant. The emerging economic structure is to a large degree dependent upon the initiatives of foreign investors in promoting the kinds of factories and enterprises they desire. The SEZs are oriented toward foreign trade and foreign investment. Experience since 1979 has shown that superior results can be achieved through significantly less state intervention in such markets. Shenzhen and Zhuhai have demonstrated the improved performance that is possible when the economic dysfunctions associated with government intervention are reduced.

As the most open area of a more open China, the SEZs have had to become China's vanguard in restructuring economic policies and methods. Foreign investors have focused upon the details of the package of incentives and concessions offered to encourage their participation, but the more significant benefit for China rests with the use that can be made within China of the lessons of the zone. It is these aspects of the more advanced zones of Shenzhen and Zhuhai that, according to Xu Dixin, one of China's most authoritative economists,[8] make them suitable 'as experimental units in economic structural reform and as schools for learning the law of value and the regulation of production according to market demands'.

Xu's attitude is widely held within influential political and intellectual circles in China. At a major conference on the SEZs held in 1981, Qian Junrui forcefully supported this viewpoint. He called upon the central authorities actively to support the work of the SEZs, and said that it was imperative that the government ministries assist and co-operate with the zone authorities and recognize the special nature of the zone economies. He argued that reform proposals for China should first be tried out in the SEZs. In order to make this possible, the leaders of the SEZs had to be trusted and allowed a free hand in carrying out their special tasks. Real flexibility had to be permitted in accordance with the special character of the zones.[9]

More recently, in a speech delivered to the Sixth Chinese People's Political Consultative Conference at its Second Plenary Session, Qian Jiaju cogently pointed out that structural reform could not be separated from the open-door policy. He praised the rapid growth enjoyed in Shenzhen and indicated that Shenzhen's success was due to the much greater autonomy allowed there. Enterprise efficiency and labour productivity compared favourably with those in China particularly because of the greater stimulus the more open economy of the zone could exert. As China's 'window' for modernization, Shenzhen was able to acquire instructive experience from which the rest of the country could profit. The lessons offered by reforms of the price and wage system were highlighted as particularly appropriate.[10]

Mayor Liang Xiang, the head of the Shenzhen Municipal People's Government, noted the singular obligation placed upon the SEZ in his speech at the inaugural session of the Shenzhen People's Assembly in 1983. He indicated that Shenzhen bore a grave responsibility to pioneer institutional change and that Shenzhen's experience would play an important part in China's future development. Elaborating eight areas of structural reform as particularly essential in Shenzhen, Liang warned that the way ahead would be complicated and difficult, and that perseverance would be necessary as the whole nation would follow the zone's example.[11]

The evidence of the significance of the SEZs as a model for reform within China has already been demonstrated. In the middle of 1984, the *Renmin ribao* gave extensive coverage to a proposal for the total separation of the government from enterprises. Citing the positive results of four years of reform in the Shekou Industrial Zone, the article recommended the implementation of this change. It suggested that Shekou was a good example of the prosperity possible when state enterprises (in this case, China Merchants' Steam Navigation Co.) assumed control of local affairs in place of the political bureaucracy. The conclusion to be drawn was that even the development of large and medium-sized cities should be left in the hands of big state corporations.[12]

From this perspective, a closer examination of enterprise reform in China's SEZs is presented in this chapter. We focus on the course these reforms have taken in several specific joint ventures, and provide a fairly detailed account of the measures adopted in these enterprises. Information obtained in structured interviews with leading managerial personnel and government officials during two field trips to Shenzhen and Zhuhai forms the basis for the discussion. This has been supplemented with informal discussions with workers and local residents and with actual and potential foreign investors. The information contained in journalistic and academic accounts has also been consulted. After surveying these examples, the authors explore some of the problems of the transferability of the experiments in Shenzhen and Zhuhai.

Case Studies

The Jialo Mattress and Furniture Factory

The Jialo Mattress and Furniture Factory (Jialo zhuangju jiasi chang) of Shenzhen is one of the successful manufacturing enterprises set up early on in the zone's development. It initially operated under an intermediate processing contract with a Hong Kong bedding company. The terms of this agreement came into force in September 1979. The Shenzhen Municipal Houseware Co. would make available land, a factory and labour. The Hong Kong investor would supply raw and semi-finished materials, designs and the main machinery for producing mattresses and other bedding products according to the Hong Kong businessman's specifications. All the output was for export, distribution being in the hands of the foreign investor. With the establishment of the Jialo Mattress and Furniture Factory, the Chinese firm started to receive a service charge or labour fee for the finished products. The Jialo factory was granted a three-year tax exemption on the original seven-year contract. The contract was later extended to 15 years. The Hong Kong businessman would retain ownership of the main machinery he provided and would bear responsibility for its maintenance with no deductions being made from the service charges paid to China.[13]

The satisfactory operation of this preliminary arrangement led to expanded co-operation in the form of a joint venture agreement. This was for the production of sofas and was signed in November 1981. The two sides each invested HK$300,000 to purchase the necessary new equipment, and the Chinese agreed to provide the factory site for which they would receive rent. The joint venture would be assessed at the regular tax rate of 15 per cent on profit with an additional 5 per cent levy in the form of a products tax on imported materials used in the manufacture of goods distributed on the domestic Chinese market. This contract would remain in force for five years during which time profits would be distributed to the two parties equally. At the end of this period, the factory and new machinery would revert to the Chinese side.

In addition, reflecting the growing competence and enterprise of the management of the Jialo factory, the Shenzhen municipal authorities granted approval for the firm to undertake production and distribution on its own initiative in August 1981. As an autonomous state enterprise it could arrange for the supply of materials for processing from Hong Kong or elsewhere in China to produce bedding and wooden furniture according to its own plans. In this undertaking, it purchased some new machinery, but since it was in part utilizing the original machinery of the factory, which still belonged to the Hong Kong contractor, Jialo was obliged to pay him rent for its use amounting to 5 per cent of the gross value of output. As in the case of the joint venture operation, the factory was also obliged to pay a 5 per cent tax on imported materials used in making products sold within China.

The management of the Jialo company is firmly in Chinese hands. As a joint venture, ultimate authority is vested in a five-member board of directors, the Chinese partner having a majority of three appointees to the board.

The head of the board is the Chinese factory director, and all the Chinese board members concurrently occupy administrative positions within the enterprise. With the exception of the executive director, who was recruited and appointed by the municipal government and entrusted with full responsibility, the rest of the small executive staff was selected and assigned by the Shenzhen Municipal Houseware Co. It has been proposed that this method of selection be altered in 1985. A contractual arrangement is not anticipated in the immediate future, but the director of the factory is to become subject to election by the workers' congress subsequent to his assignment. He is to have the authority to appoint other members of his managerial team. Accountability for the performance of the activities under his jurisdiction can then be more carefully assessed.

The managerial structure of Jialo's operations has been kept simple despite the remarkable growth in its short existence. The managerial staff in 1984 numbered only 14, and the young and dynamic director who oversaw its spectacular expansion from 1981 maintained that a streamlined leadership format with fewer people making decisions was essential for speed and efficiency. A clear division of labour and distinct lines of command fostered initiative and the conscientious application of talents for co-operation under unified control.

This successful executive also stressed the need to integrate the economic benefits of the managerial staff with those of the workers, so that the two were united. In this way, the enthusiasm of both could be aroused to co-ordinate their efforts and a collective spirit of independence could be cultivated. The vitality instilled in the enterprise would enable it to tap the firm's great potential.

In 1983, the incomes of the Jialo management were tied to those of the workers in a rather mechanical way. The monthly salary of the director of the factory was set at 15 per cent more than the average monthly wages of the workers; their incomes, in turn, were largely determined on a piece-work basis. During 1983, when average monthly wages for the Jialo work-force were about 170 *yuan*, the director received about 195 *yuan* each month. The rest of the small technical and administrative staff received salaries according to a 10-point scale, with the director fixed at 10 points and the deputy directors, heads of departments, and other supervisory personnel graded below this. The difference between the top and bottom scales was only about 10 *yuan* or roughly 1 *yuan* per point. Not only was this system of executive remuneration out of accord with the principle of linking wages with responsibility and achievement, but it also failed to give due regard to technical competence. More fundamentally, it ignored the linking of the wages and bonuses of the management with enterprise performance, their primary responsibility. Instead, their material interests were related solely to the labour contribution of the production workers. These defects were perceived at the time, and a new system by which managerial incomes would rise by 20–30 per cent was under consideration.

In 1984, this new salary scheme for the Jialo management became fully operational. The pay of managers is now made up of a graded basic wage component and a profit-sharing component amounting to a percentage of the firm's net annual profit. The basic wages of Jialo staff are arranged into four levels with the director receiving 270 *yuan* per month, the deputy director and chief engineer 250 *yuan*, the heads of departments and offices 230 *yuan*, and general management 210 *yuan*. The profit-based portion of the managers' incomes is to be the same for all at a percentage to be decided upon by the Shenzhen Municipal Houseware Co. By this method, the defects of the earlier system have been overcome.[14]

The director of the Jialo Mattress and Furniture Factory in 1983 commended the practice of adjusting the salary of workers according to their job performance and saw the piece-rate remuneration system as most appropriate for his firm. Not only was it in conformity with the socialist principle of 'more pay for more work', but he also felt it effectively brought out the enthusiasm of workers, especially the younger ones. It raised productivity, lowered the cost of production, and generally helped tap the full potential of the work-force. The piece-work was carried out on a small group basis with collective accounting of products completed by each group. The members of the group could earn a 15 per cent bonus if a set level of output was exceeded and an even larger bonus for higher levels. Individual workers could also earn bonuses for inventions and useful suggestions on improving production. With a work-force of 152 in 1983, the average monthly wage was 170 *yuan*, with 30 per cent of workers earning 200 *yuan* or more and 20 per cent receiving incomes higher than the managerial salaries. (By comparison, the average monthly wage in Shenzhen in 1983 was 131 *yuan*.) In 1984, the level of employment increased to 170 with an average monthly wage of 200 *yuan*; 40 per cent of the workers earned 230 *yuan*, and 20 per cent received higher incomes than the management. The best workers in the factory in 1984 earned more than 300 *yuan* per month. (The Shenzhen average monthly wage in 1984 was 174 *yuan*.)

The work-force in the Jialo factory is recruited through public advertisement. The personnel department of the company assesses the applicants in open competition with written examinations. It submits its selection to the municipal labour bureau for approval. With care used in the selection of workers, training provided within the firm, and suitable incentives and adequate remuneration arranged, the management seldom finds it necessary to resort to the disciplinary sanctions it possesses. Only three or four workers have had to be fired for poor work performance and absenteeism, and another one or two have resigned; between January 1983 and July 1984 none had been fired or had left.

As seen in Table 11.1, the Jialo enterprise grew rapidly in the early 1980s with higher productivity and larger profits accompanying the increase in its output. As it has become bigger, the firm has been invigorated by the stimulus of market forces to adapt and diversify its activities. On the supply side, production was at first almost totally dependent on raw materials from Hong Kong and periodically experienced difficulties in importing what it required. With more experience, it has been able to arrange for the use of domestic sources of wood, bedding material, nails, shredded coconut shell for stuffing, and so on, so that by the middle of 1984 approximately 50 per cent of the value of its raw materials came from China. In terms of

Table 11.1 The Jialo Mattress and Furniture Factory[15]

Year	Gross Value of Production (*yuan*)	Productivity (*yuan*)	Net Profit (*yuan*)
1980	2,650,000	35,800	190,000
1981	3,050,000	38,000	310,000
1982	7,200,000	52,000	540,000
1983	8,530,000	56,000	750,000

marketing, the firm has found a ready demand for its products on the local market; it has also met with success in arranging its own distribution in Hong Kong and is planning to expand these operations.

In order to exploit its growing expertise in the design and manufacture of home furnishings as well as its popular brand name in China, the Jialo Mattress and Furniture Factory has undertaken a major programme of diversification. In the middle of 1984, it was proceeding with official approval to establish an affiliate to produce door frames and windows for the booming construction industry. It was also working to establish a domestic joint venture with the Nanjing Eastern Machinery Co. for the manufacture of gas heaters to be set up in August of that year. In addition, it was in the midst of negotiations with firms from Shaoguan and Beijing for the setting up of domestic joint ventures to make various household furniture and decoration products.

The Jianian Printing Co. Ltd.

The Jianian Printing Co. Ltd. (Jianian yinshua yuxian gongsi) of Shenzhen is another pioneering undertaking in the development of the SEZ. The plant, manufacturing commercial packaging materials, was set up in 1979 on the basis of a compensation trade contract between the Good Year Corporation of Hong Kong and the Shenzhen Municipal Textile and Light Industry Co. The Hong Kong company agreed to provide HK$15 million of the HK$25 million to be invested in plant and equipment for an advanced printing works. Good Year assumed responsibility for transport and technical staff and undertook to provide orders and the necessary raw materials. China would compensate the Hong Kong company for the principal and interest on the finance provided in the form of deductions from the service charges earned on the orders negotiated by Good Year. It was anticipated that the debt would be fully repaid within six years and, with this obligation discharged, the facility would then be owned by China.[16]

The terms of the original agreement for the Jianian works proved to be unsuitable for both sides. They had been adopted partly because the legislation for the SEZ had not yet been finalized at the time. In attempting to operate the new establishment, however, Good Year discovered that it would need a relatively long period to train the Chinese work-force because of the advanced level of technology involved and the high level of skills required. The Chinese side also found the arrangement unsatisfactory because of its total dependence upon Good Year for orders and raw materials. The fluctuations in Good Year's ability to solicit orders meant that work was irregular. Without orders, the plant could not pay compensation to the Hong Kong company and it still had fixed costs to meet when there was little or no work. For these reasons, intermediate processing was considered an improved form of co-operation and, in 1982, the contract was revised along these lines. The printing plant could now accept other orders to assure a steady workload.

Finally, at the beginning of 1983, the relationship between the two sides was restructured into an equity joint venture. This alteration was considered preferable with respect to supply, production, and distribution for it tied the benefits of both parties to improved handling of all phases of the plant's operations. Both contractors committed themselves to a HK$24-million share in the reorganized project and agreed upon a 50:50 division of net profits for a period of 20 years. On the expiry of the contract whichever side wants the machinery can purchase it at a depreciated price or the joint venture can be renewed and extended. With increased involvement of the foreign investor's interests since 1983, the Good Year Corporation has become more concerned with upgrading the plant's technology, improving the level of training provided for the plant's employees, and in diversifying the plant's activities to encompass all types of printing. The Chinese have involved themselves to a greater degree in soliciting domestic orders although limitations have been imposed on the share of the plant's production that can service the Chinese market. The performance of the reorganized operations has improved considerably, with better quality, higher productivity and larger profits being achieved since the change.

The highest executive authority of the Jianian Printing Co. is vested in an eight-man board of directors. The Chinese and Hong Kong contractors each have the power to recommend four directors, the head of the board being chosen from the Chinese delegation. This board holds the decision-making power with regard to personnel, finance, property, and policy. In the case of Jianian, none of the four directors are involved in the day-to-day work of the enterprise. The board of directors appoints the managers with the stipulation that the chief manager should be nominated by the Hong Kong partner. The chief manager is to concentrate on marketing, price-setting and general business aspects, such as conducting market research, arranging agents, handling advertising, and preparing development plans for the plant. The Hong Kong chief manager also undertakes the handling of the direct import of raw materials from abroad as Japanese sources have been found to be preferable to the previous sole reliance on Hong Kong. In this, he is aided by an assistant manager in charge of purchasing and supply who also comes from the Hong Kong side. While overall supervision of Jianian on behalf of the board is in the hands of the Hong Kong-recruited chief manager, the day-to-day running of operations is entrusted to three Chinese deputy managers — those in charge of production, finance and administration.

According to the deputy manager in charge of production, 'to establish a factory you must first establish the workers'. In an interview he emphasized the need for the careful recruitment of individuals by the enterprise on its own, extensive training of those hired to provide them with adequate skills, and the adjustment of salaries in accordance with the quantity and quality of work done. He is firmly opposed to the excessive egalitarianism found elsewhere in China and the lack of incentive to do a better job or acquire more skills. Stress on production is the major obligation of management in his view, and he feels that units should be penalized if they fail to fulfil their output targets; egalitarianism between units as well as between individuals within units has to be discouraged. Finally, he considers the clear division of labour in the management system of Jianian an important asset. Distinct lines of control and accountability for specific tasks are a necessary part of the responsibility system and have helped achieve the superior efficiency displayed by workers at the plant.

The Jianian Printing Co. is able to decide on how to recruit, who to employ and how to use its work-force as a joint venture operation. This autonomy in personnel affairs is one of its principal advantages over Chinese state enterprises. The management openly advertises job vacancies at the plant and makes its own selection from those who apply. This procedure has met with no difficulty because of the numerous people seeking jobs, especially youths accompanying parents transferred to Shenzhen from elsewhere. The greater freedom of choice in employment in Shenzhen reinforces the higher level of job commitment.

Upon selection, workers at Jianian are given eight months' training to prepare them. Teaching staff at Zhongshan University, as well as advanced printing technicians, conduct the programme to provide the new workers with the necessary skills. Two young workers who demonstrated particular aptitude were selected to undertake two years of special studies in accounting and financial planning at Zhongshan University. Workers within the enterprise also have available to them a variety of classes in greater technical expertise. Annual assessment by written examination as well as actual production results are used to choose those who should be promoted, with a general success rate of 10 per cent achieved.

The readjustment of the wage system at Jianian is an important facet of its success in arousing workers' enthusiasm, inspiring them to work more productively, and motivating them to become better qualified. Initially, as a state enterprise with foreign contracting arrangements, the work-force was paid according to an eight-grade system similar to the standard practice which still prevails in enterprises elsewhere in China. When Jianian became a joint venture, the salary structure changed to introduce a greater linkage between remuneration and job accomplishment. The grading in early 1983 is given in Table 11.2.

This basic wage payment was divided into two parts: a fixed component amounting to 60 per cent of the basic wage and a variable component amounting to 40 per cent of the basic wage which was adjusted according to performance. For example, for an ordinary worker in 1983, the set portion of his salary was 60 per cent of 91.00 *yuan*, or 54.60 *yuan*. With an average 26-day month, a worker received 2.10 *yuan* per work-day or about 0.26 *yuan* per hour. He could earn 0.52 *yuan* for each hour of overtime worked. The work-force was guaranteed receipt of this segment of the monthly wage even

Table 11.2 Salary Levels, Jianian Printing Co., 1983 (in *yuan*)

Deputy manager	164.50
Assistant manager	154.00
Supervisor	143.50
Group leader	136.50
Machine operator	115.50
Skilled labourer	101.50
Ordinary worker	91.00

during leave allowed for sickness, child birth, marriage or funerals. No payment was made for unauthorized absences.

The 40 per cent adjustable element in the monthly wage was calculated on a point basis. Each worker commenced the month with 100 points, and certain deductions were assessed for specified behaviour. A one-point deduction would be levied for being 15 minutes late, more after 30 minutes, and a maximum of three points for missing a full work-day without permission. Misconduct like reading the newspaper, eating, or chatting on duty would warrant reductions in the monthly total, with more serious matters such as disobedience and mistakes meriting greater penalties. For ordinary workers, the sliding constituent of their monthly income was 40 per cent of 91.00 *yuan*, or 36.40 *yuan*, which they would receive only if they could retain a perfect 100-point slate, so each point lost cost them about 0.36 *yuan*. In addition to the basic pay, the workers and staff at Jianian received certain monthly subsidies and could earn annual bonuses depending on their overall work performance.

The performance of the Jianian Printing Co. during its first year as a joint venture was impressive. At the start, in January 1983, annual net profits of around 600,000 *yuan* had been anticipated. At year-end, the firm made a profit of 970,000 *yuan*, earning a 15 per cent return on estimated capital of 6,500,000 *yuan*. All the production targets were fulfilled, and labour productivity (measured in terms of the value of output per worker) of 32,000 *yuan* was achieved. Employment increased from 228 to 280. The managerial personnel from Hong Kong were withdrawn and the Chinese deputy manager in charge of production assumed authority for all areas of responsibility under a renewable annual contract concluded with the board of directors.

On the basis of this successful first year, the labour contracts with workers and staff at Jianian have been revised. Not only have the salary levels been raised to an average of 175 *yuan* per month, but the wage system has also been restructured. The positions within the company have been arranged in nine grades with the Chinese director in the first, earning a monthly wage of 262 *yuan*, while new workers are designated to the ninth grade during their six-month probationary period, with their basic pay set at 140 *yuan*. A differential of approximately 16 *yuan* separates each grade. To arouse the enthusiasm of the employees more effectively, the entire monthly wage has been made adjustable on a point system. For example, in the case of a worker's base monthly pay of 150 *yuan*, 100 points represents the full payment of 150 *yuan*. Each point penalized from his total points costs the worker 1.50 *yuan*. As an additional incentive, workers who do not leave their post during working hours, who do not arrive late or depart early and who do not claim any sick or other leave are awarded a supplementary 10 *yuan* for achieving full marks for the month. Furthermore an extra 10 *yuan* can be claimed for scoring the full 100 points in three consecutive months. This system has proved effective and has been popular with the workers, judging by the record of 1983 when 90 per cent of the work-force earned full marks throughout the year.[17]

With the 1983 production and profit quotas surpassed, all the workers and staff of Jianian have become entitled to an annual bonus based upon a year-end assessment of their competence and application. Bonuses are awarded according to three grades. First-class workers earn a bonus equivalent to three months' salary; second-class workers two months; and third-class workers one month. Second-class bonuses were standard in 1983 with only those who had been sick receiving third-class bonuses.

The firm has been able to develop a fair and effective system of promotion based on performance record. This has also spurred the enthusiasm and initiative of the workers. Nearly 30 per cent of the ordinary workers became qualified skilled labourers in 1983, and several have been promoted to positions as group leaders. A further 10 have risen to the level of machine operator in different units of the plant. They have been able to advance because of their talent and effort, unhampered by the stultifying effect of seniority that plagues most Chinese enterprises. This internal ladder of promotion has proved to be an additional means of 'unifying the interests and benefits of the workers and staff members with those of the company.'

The Pepsi Soft Drink Factory

As the nation's vanguard in assessing reforms and economic restructuring, the SEZs have provided negative as well as positive lessons. Continuing difficulties experienced at the Pepsi Soft Drink Factory (Baishi yinliu chang) in Shenzhen, for example, have been closely linked to the lack of autonomy in decision-making in several key areas of operation. In large part, the excessive regulation of this Pepsi-Cola bottling plant has resulted from the terms of the contractual arrangement and the organizational limitations they have imposed on the joint venture. These institutional weaknesses have limited the management's ability to hire and discharge workers, to arrange the standards and conditions of work, and to devise appropriate wage and bonus systems.[18]

The Pepsi Soft Drink Factory was established in 1981 under a joint-venture agreement between Pepsico and the Shenzhen Municipal Food and Beverage Co. In establishing the bottling plant, however, Pepsi functioned as a subsidiary of an existing state enterprise — a cannery which was one of the affiliates operated under the auspices of the Food and Beverage Co. The cannery had operated a small brewery whose facilities comprised the bulk of the Chinese investment in the joint venture. This administrative subordination of the joint venture to a state enterprise severely hampered the management's scope of activity.

In the recruitment of the work-force, for example, the Pepsi enterprise was still obliged to resort to the labour bureau. The bureau often failed to pay sufficient attention to the suitability and qualifications of the individuals referred to the plant for employment. Not only did Pepsi fail to gain the right to advertise job vacancies openly and to examine applicants carefully, but the management also met with obstructions when it sought the dismissal of poor workers. In four instances, recommendations by the Pepsi joint management with the support of the cannery management for the removal of workers with poor attitudes and poor performance were overruled by the labour bureau. It suggested, instead, disciplinary action and a reduction in pay, and the most it would allow was the transfer of these shirkers to the cannery. From the beginning the managers at Pepsi also encountered difficulties when they attempted to limit the size of the work-force and increase the amount of work expected from each employee.

The salary system was also a source of problems in the operation of the bottling plant. According to the provisions on labour and wage management for joint ventures in the SEZs, the enterprise was to pay a labour service charge for all Chinese staff and workers employed at levels stipulated in the labour contracts. This labour service charge was to be apportioned so that 70 per cent was paid directly to the employees as their income, 5 per cent was retained by the enterprise for a collective welfare fund, and 25 per cent was paid as compulsory social labour insurance and as compensation for state-provided subsidies. On average, the labour service charge per worker at the bottling plant was about HK$1,000 per month; but, with an average monthly salary of 150 *yuan*, the workers at Pepsi were being given only about 50 per cent. The management appealed to the labour service authorities to be allowed to raise the personal earnings of the workers and staff to the 70 per cent level stipulated in the regulations, arguing that limitations on giving greater personal remuneration had a deleterious effect on the workers' enthusiasm. Even when the workers' congress within the enterprise passed a resolution to increase salaries to 70 per cent of the labour service charge, the local authorities refused, stating that monthly salaries had to be kept within recent guidelines of between 80 and 150 *yuan*. They were apparently worried that other potential investors might be discouraged if they felt labour costs were too high. Not only were the wages of the staff and workers relatively low, they were also determined according to a fixed wage grade system as rigid as those in state enterprises and devoid of bonuses and adjustable performance-linked components. These factors were held to be responsible for the plant's mediocre record in terms of profitability and schedule fulfilment.

In the course of 1983, the Pepsi management was able to make some modifications in the wage system, and these changes have helped to reduce costs and increase efficiency. A 20 per cent increase in the average monthly wage has been allowed even though the contract only stipulates a 10 per cent annual rise. This level, however, still falls considerably short of the 70 per cent labour service charge. The monthly wage has become slightly less automatic with the introduction of a monthly 30 *yuan* bonus award. This payment depends on the immediate supervisor's view of how well a worker has performed during the month. This variable portion, amounting to only about 17 per cent of the total monthly salary, is considered to be inadequate, and the management is still persevering in attempts to expand the achievement-linked share of earnings.[19]

The Shijingshan Tourist Centre

From the outset, tourism has been designated as the leading economic sector in the growth of the Zhuhai SEZ, and the Shijingshan Tourist Centre (Shijingshan lüyou zhongxin) is one of the pioneering undertakings in the development of Zhuhai's tourist industry. A key aspect of the early success and expansion of the joint venture was the care devoted to personnel matters since people are the crucial element in a service enterprise. Starting operations in October 1980 with a work-force of 100, Shijingshan was the first tourist joint venture in China. It has been steadily enlarged because of the thriving trade it has enjoyed. Employment had increased to 260 by the beginning of 1983 and stood at 338 in the middle of 1984.[20] There has been keen competition for advertised vacancies. Some 700 graduating high-school students sat for the first examination set by the joint venture and 60 were chosen. Since that time, vacancies at Shijingshan have continued to be desirable, and hiring has continued to be selective, with only about one in every ten applicants being successful.[21]

Once selected through this open recruitment system, workers and staff members are given three to six months' training in etiquette, personal hygiene, service and language. The Cantonese-speaking hotel and restaurant personnel have instruction in standard Chinese as well as English and Japanese. The initial training programme has been extended to 70 per cent of the work-force and includes regular classes of two to four hours a week in language, accounting, computer use and management techniques. Employees are given the opportunity and encouragement to acquire greater technical knowledge so that they can secure advancement within the enterprise.

As a new and growing concern, the Shijingshan Tourist Centre has been able to provide scope for internal promotion for workers demonstrating initiative and dedication. Unhindered by entrenched veteran staff with seniority-based security, younger members of the Shijingshan work-force have been able to rise to positions as supervisors and even as department managers on the basis of ability and performance. The manager of the room service department in 1983, for example, was a 19-year-old youth who had started working at Shijingshan when he was 17; and in the hotel restaurant, a young woman of 23 has risen to become manager, working closely with an experienced Hong Kong advisor who has helped upgrade restaurant operations. All of the 20-odd supervisors in 1983 were in the 17–21 age bracket.[22]

One of the most notable examples of the internal promotion of capable youths at Shijingshan is Ms Gao Xiang, who, at the age of 22, is the manager of the shopping centre of Shijingshan. As the head of the most profitable section of the Shijingshan complex, she occupies one of the most important positions under the Chinese assistant general manager. Ms Gao had been granted a transfer from the motor service department in 1981, soon becoming a supervisor in the hotel gift shop. In this capacity, she demonstrated a strong drive to improve her understanding of sales, merchandising and pricing techniques. She sought advice and suggestions from visiting businessmen and endeavoured to familiarize herself with the tastes and interests of tourists passing through Shijingshan. In 1983, Gao Xiang was selected to manage the expanded shopping complex at Shijingshan; this modern emporium boasts a selling area of over 3,000 sq m in floor space, carries an inventory of almost 3,000 types of goods and takes in daily revenue of approximately 100,000 *yuan*.[23]

Workers and staff members alike at Shijingshan are subject to a system of rewards and punishments. Not only can outstanding employees expect recognition and career advancement, but negligent and unfit personnel can anticipate disciplinary action and even dismissal. Up to the beginning of 1983, 2 of the 12 departmental managers had been dismissed for poor performance. In addition, an experienced restaurant worker from Hong Kong recruited by the foreign investor to serve in a supervisory capacity in improving food service at Shijingshan was discharged for playing chess on duty, and a supervisor in the transport department was forced to leave for unauthorized absences during his working hours.

The work-force at Shijingshan is thus highly motivated. The staff of the enterprise are mindful of their privileged economic status as the fortunate holders of much sought-after positions. Performance-based job tenure with positive and negative reinforcements helps engender a sense of pride and initiative that taps their greater human potential.

In conjunction with the wage and bonus system progressively developed at Shijingshan, the personnel policies have effectively integrated the benefit and interest of the workers and staff members with those of the joint venture. In the system for determining monthly wages in use in 1980, there was only a small adjustable component in the wage-fixing process. Workers received a graded basic wage to which was added a monthly border subsidy of 15 *yuan* and a commodity price subsidy of 5 *yuan* which together comprised about half of personal monthly earnings. In addition, staff members received small graded supplementary allowances according to their ranking in the administrative hierarchy. These payments ranged from 5 *yuan* for a small work-group leader, 10 *yuan* for a supervisor, and 15 *yuan* for a department head up to 20 *yuan* per month for the Chinese deputy general manager. Workers and staff were also granted fixed supplementary monthly allowances in accordance with technical skills in various fields, such as cooking, machine operations, translation, and electrical work. Because of the stress placed on cleanliness and hygiene and the need to make a good impression on foreign visitors, all Shijingshan workers were paid a further monthly allowance for the care and maintenance of their personal appearance and uniforms. All these stable elements in their monthly income made up

75–80 per cent of the total in 1980, leaving a dynamic element of only about 20–25 per cent.[24]

This smaller adjustable component, the bonus award, was determined on a monthly basis by the department heads subject to the approval of the Chinese deputy general manager. Employees were divided into three categories — superior, average, and poor — according to clearly specified criteria. A gap of approximately 30 per cent was set between the value of the bonus awards paid to those in each group. Although this aspect of the payment structure gave some encouragement for improvement, it was too small in relation to the predetermined portion of remuneration and did not relate the material interests of the Shijingshan work-force directly to the profitability of the joint venture.

For these reasons, the wage system was altered in 1981. While Shijingshan personnel continued to receive a graded basic wage, a graduated occupational supplement, a skill allowance and a border subsidy as before, this guaranteed portion of their monthly income was revised to constitute only about 50 per cent of the average monthly salary. In addition to the bonus award, the board of directors of Shijingshan introduced a joint-venture subsidy, and the value of both the bonus and the joint-venture subsidy were determined monthly in accordance with the enterprise's operating profits. As with the bonus, workers were allotted three classifications which entitled them to differing amounts of payment.[25]

In addition, the manner of administering these flexible pay elements at Shijingshan has avoided some of the defects encountered with bonus payments in Chinese state enterprises since their reintroduction in 1978. First of all, the assessment of the workers is done daily by their immediate superiors, and the daily assessments are compiled monthly by department heads in a confidential recommendation submitted to the Chinese deputy general manager. The social pressures and interpersonal tensions of the public evaluation and comparison meeting are thus avoided. Before and after the Cultural Revolution these had inhibited the merit-based allocation of bonuses. Furthermore, once the Chinese deputy general manager has assented to the advice from the department head, he notifies the pay office and the worker receives the appropriate amount. In contrast to standard Chinese practice, salaries at Shijingshan are not publicly disclosed.

Further adjustments in the operation of the wage system at Shijingshan were made in 1982 thereby increasing its variable nature. There continued to be three classifications for the awarding of bonuses, but evaluation for bonuses came to be based largely upon an assessment of the worker's attitude, and payment was made only in the case of first- and second-grade bonuses. If a worker was judged to have a poor work attitude, he was not entitled to any bonus money. Five grades of selection were introduced for the determination of the joint-venture subsidy, and the criterion for assessment of this subsidy was performance. Workers assigned first- to fourth-grade subsidies received appropriate rewards for achievements with a large enough differential to provide an effective work incentive. A fifth-grade classification was allocated to workers who violated the enterprise's disciplinary regulations and no subsidy was paid under these circumstances.[26]

Finally, in January 1983, the wage system was again improved by increasing the accountability of each worker. Instead of calculating the value of the bonus and joint-venture subsidy for the entire work-force on the basis of the accounts of Shijingshan as a whole, the calculation is made separately for each department of the tourist complex. Individual departments of Shijingshan's operations are assigned performance quotas, and the value of the graded bonus and joint-venture subsidy payments made to each worker varies according to how well his unit meets its target.[27] In this way, a clear and direct relationship binding the personal interests of employees with those of the enterprise is retained. The problem of the diffusion of responsibility within the larger group is avoided despite the considerable expansion of employment, and the dynamics of small-group pressure are effectively incorporated. This evolution of superior wage mechanisms at Shijingshan, furthermore, has primarily occurred since the departure of the foreign managerial staff.

Qualifications on Reform

While the SEZs bear a major responsibility in that they function as China's vanguard in socialist modernization, the unique nature of the zone environment poses some problems in terms of the applicability of the knowledge gained in developing new management systems. The structural and enterprise reforms in Shenzhen and Zhuhai cannot be separated from the open-door policy since external economic forces have served as the 'engine of growth' in the spectacular development that has occurred there. Such an atmosphere does not exist anywhere else in China. The advantages that have made the zones so successful are part of what is so special about them. As the first half of the principle for zone administration acknowledges, 'new things require new ways of handling and special things require special ways of handling'. The special conditions of the laboratory mean that it is often difficult to reproduce laboratory results under more normal circumstances.

The SEZs possess something of the character of 'green field sites' for the growth of industry in China. This is particularly true in Shenzhen and Zhuhai, where a predominantly rural population depended upon farming and fishing for its livelihood prior to 1979. Because they are establishing new enterprises, management has enjoyed unparalleled freedom in deciding upon types of wages and systems of bonuses, subsidies and other kinds of payments for staff and workers. For instance, depending upon the firm's business requirements, payment can be made on an hourly, daily, monthly or piece-work basis. New labour policies can aim at incentives to spur worker effort without concessions to past practices that were of a more egalitarian and less efficiency-oriented nature. There are no vested interests to consider. Although the Chinese leaders are trying to bring about these kinds of changes in the rest of the country, the beneficiaries of the status quo have been able to frustrate the speedy adoption of these measures.

The joint ventures in the Shenzhen and Zhuhai SEZs have considerable advantages over existing enterprises in the state economy not only in terms of policies and institutions, but also with regard to the behaviour of managers in implementing reforms. Continuing difficulties in state enterprises elsewhere in China have been experienced since 1978, for example, with the reintroduction of bonuses. Despite the suggested official guidelines in favour of the linkage of bonuses to job performance and enterprise profitability, numerous instances of divergent conduct have become evident. In the press and in official reports, leading economic officials have reported indiscriminate granting of bonuses in factories regardless of the profits earned and even in instances where the unit has been running at a loss. Another common problem in existing enterprises has been the egalitarian distribution of bonuses to workers within an enterprise. The workers have come to see these as automatic pay supplements to which they are entitled rather than as special rewards for superior labour contributions. These actions serve to mitigate the intentions of the wage reforms. Managers sometimes feel obliged to curry favour with the workers in these ways despite the effect on productivity. The official Chinese press reports reveal that managers have been subjected to physical threats and even beatings if workers have considered them to be overzealous in their critical assessment of a worker's bonus entitlement. Such incidents attest to the difficulty of coping with public sentiment in factories used to running in a lax and lackadaisical manner.

In Shenzhen and Zhuhai, the managers of joint ventures as well as of new state enterprises have the distinct advantage of being able to adopt reforms and of being remarkably unencumbered by past practice. There are no veteran workers conditioned to the old ways and reliant on their seniority for preferential status. The workers within the Shenzhen and Zhuhai SEZs are generally youths involved in their first enterprise employment. Some have been recruited as school-leavers, locally or regionally. Others have been recruited from the rural areas within the municipality or from neighbouring counties. As they are making their initial entry into the urban labour market, they can more readily accept the more meritocratic industrial environment of the zones' enterprises. The high income levels and general desirability of employment in the SEZs engenders an achievement-oriented enthusiasm that would be difficult to arouse elsewhere in Chinese industry.

The enterprises in Shenzhen and Zhuhai have been able to capitalize on the human resources available locally and regionally. Shenzhen and Zhuhai both constituted part of the more backward fringe areas of the economically prosperous Zhu Jiang Delta region prior to 1979. While the region is one of China's leading centres of light industry and is relatively urbanized, Shenzhen and Zhuhai lacked urban development of any significance before acquiring their SEZ status. Zhuhai was a relatively better-off rural area only marginally affected by its advantageous location bordering Portuguese-controlled Macau. There was virtually no tourist industry in Zhuhai before 1979 in spite of its scenic beauty and inherent appeal as the native district of numerous members of the Hong Kong, Macau and overseas Chinese communities. As a consequence, opportunities were very limited. Given China's lack of labour mobility, Zhuhai school-leavers could expect to join the labour surplus on the land, estimated to constitute about 40 per cent of the rural population. The favoured few might secure places in the small-scale industries set up by their commune or brigade.

The new tourist and industrial enterprises in Zhuhai have offered the most desirable job prospects for local talent. Managers can expect enthusiasm and motivation on the part of their employees, and pay and promotion policies can be developed on this basis. The opportunity to provide the means of advancement for upwardly mobile, talented and ambitious workers and staff cannot be easily allowed in the large and overmanned state sector.

The rapid economic growth experienced in Shenzhen and Zhuhai has largely depended upon joint equity enterprises and co-operative ventures set up with foreign businessmen. As in export-processing zones and free trade zones in other developing Asian economies, 'most of the foreign investors are either small- or medium-size entrepreneurs', and they tend to set up small- to medium-size enterprises in the standard factory sites provided for them in the zones. 'Huge multinational companies seldom seek out such zones for investment'.[28] In the case of Shenzhen and Zhuhai, moreover, this investment has come overwhelmingly from Hong Kong and Macau. These investors are more likely to enter the kind of joint-venture arrangements favoured by China and also to utilize intermediate technology appropriate to the conditions of China's developing economy. However, these foreign businessmen generally lack experience in running major industrial establishments and, if they do, are not building huge industrial complexes in Shenzhen and Zhuhai that will apply this expertise. For this reason, the management systems emerging in the small-scale projects in the SEZs, where close supervision is possible, may prove inadequate for reform of the large enterprises that constitute the core of China's industrial economy.

One area of divergence between managerial reform within China and in the Shenzhen and Zhuhai SEZs is the emphasis on democratic management in domestic Chinese enterprises. The major institutional innovation for implementing workers' participation in work-place decision-making is the system of workers' and staff congresses. Workers' congresses have become a necessary part of Chinese state enterprises since 1982 after experimental trials were conducted. They embody the socialist principle of the working people as masters of the enterprises. Directors and managers assuming full responsibility for the administration of an enterprise are now legally accountable and subject to the supervision of the workers' congress, although in practice these rights are often more theoretical than real. Enterprise directors are obliged to submit production plans, disciplinary rules and regulations, as well as proposals for bonus systems and the expenditure of collective welfare funds, to the workers' congress for examination and discussion. Along with this growing obligation of managerial staff to secure a vote of confidence to stay in office, workers' congresses are gaining increased rights to assess the performance of managers. In numerous instances, the workers' congresses are playing a direct role in the election of top enterprise staff.

In the case of joint ventures in the SEZs, on the other hand, workers' congresses are relatively rare. Where they do exist, they have little or no role in decision-making. When queried about this, one Chinese deputy manager of a newly opened tourist resort replied that the enterprise was supposed to have one. They had not yet got around to setting one up, although they would in the future.[29] When visited 18 months later, the large and growing work-force of this now well-established enterprise still had no workers' congress to represent its rights and interests.[30] In a neighbouring tourist centre, the Chinese deputy manager indicated that he did not intend to adopt the system of a congress of workers and staff members, adding that in any case he did not see it as appropriate for his operations because of the youthfulness and inexperience of his employees. Although workers' congresses have been instituted in enterprises with foreign investment only with the acquiescence of foreign businessmen, workers' congresses do exist in some joint ventures and even existed in the Xinnanxin Printing and Dyeing Plant (Xinnanxin yinran chang) when it was a sole proprietorship.[31] The workers' congress there remained unrepresented on the board of directors, however, and had none of the supervisory powers vested in the workers' congresses by Chinese legislation. The workers' congress is nowhere seen to be significant in managerial practices in the SEZs. To a large extent, this is due to the fact that large areas of decision-making in which workers' congresses are involved within China are already determined in the contracts concluded prior to the start of the enterprises. In addition, the newness of the enterprises and the workers' lack of familiarity with them and with one another favours postponement of a congress to represent their interests. The Chinese managerial staff and the trade union are there to provide for them.

Taxation is another area of divergence between the rest of China and the SEZs. Within China, one of the most significant changes made in the process of ending the overregulation of enterprises and the egalitarianism prevailing in the relationship between enterprises and the state has been the introduction of the *ligaishui* reform. This is a company profit tax replacing the system of remitting annual profits to the government as revenue. In the past, since the state appropriated the economic benefits of improved enterprise performance and subsidized the losses of poorly administered units, there was little incentive for workers and staff to be concerned about doing a better job. Reform efforts since 1979 have focused on ways of combining responsibility and authority with benefit, so that the interests of the state, the unit of production and the individual can be unified. Experiments to arouse entrepreneurship within state enterprises centred on giving managers access to funds and scope for decision-making as an adjunct to operating within the narrow confines of the production targets set by the planned economy.

On the basis of the results of the trials with various mechanisms carried out in this period, the Chinese leadership decided that the use of taxes based on net profits was most promising. They directed that from 1 June 1983 most state enterprises would become liable to the new levy. The after-tax earnings of enterprises were to be retained and could be used for expansion, technical transformation, or product innovation, for collective welfare benefits and for individual bonuses. As implemented in the initial phase, adjustments were to be incorporated into the tax structure to guarantee a certain level of retained profits. From 1 June 1984 the second phase was to commence with the security adjustments eliminated and enterprises not only responsible for their profits and losses but also dependent on their own initiative for earning development financing and collective and personal material incentives.

Although cited in the context of the *ligaishui* reform,[32] the enterprise taxes in the Shenzhen and Zhuhai SEZs serve a different purpose because of the very different economic environment. Within China, where there is a large and comprehensive economic base, the net profit taxes are meant to provide a degree of financial autonomy for existing enterprises linking economic rewards for the unit and its workers with improvement and initiative. In contrast, the progress of the Shenzhen and Zhuhai SEZs depends on new enterprises with foreign investment. This foreign investment inherently enjoys financial autonomy and is guaranteed broad scope in decision-making by regulation and by contract. Foreign investors are subject to a fixed 15 per cent corporate profit tax, with preferential tax concessions of up to a maximum of 100 per cent exemption for the first three years and 50 per cent exemption for the next two years being allowed. While assisting undertakings to achieve satisfactory economic results and providing a strong inducement to foreign investors, the preferential tax treatment is not appropriate for a government concerned about a balanced budget and dependent upon its share of the profits of state-owned enterprises for revenue. New enterprises in the SEZs are not dependent upon performance-linked after-tax profits to provide the means of promoting their creativity and initiative, while existing enterprises within China are.

One unexpected and somewhat ironic area of reform in China where the SEZs provide useful experience, however, is the separation of the Party from direct involvement in the day-to-day operation of enterprise management. The reason for the unanticipated nature of this element of the SEZ experience is that during our interviewing we were frequently given the stock official answer that there are no Party committees in joint ventures. It was said that there might be a Party branch within a Sino-foreign enterprise if the number of Party members warranted one but that it would deal only with their personal ideological education and would have nothing to do with the running of the establishment. Within China, in contrast, the reform of separating the Party from the enterprises means that all enterprises will continue to have Party committees and that the Party secretary within the enterprise will have an important role to play within the technocratic personnel comprising the chain of enterprise management.[33] While Party cadres are to cease interfering in decision-making and day-to-day administrative matters, the Party is to continue to play a major role. It will concentrate on the promotion of proper ideological understanding and a correct political orientation, that is, ensuring that policies and practices conform to the guidelines set by the central Party leadership. In this way, the Party can assist in building solidarity between workers and staff and help in generating a high level of morale within enterprises for achieving better economic results.

In the SEZs, the absence of an enterprise Party committee in joint ventures has been strongly emphasized to allay the apprehensions of foreign investors about the intrusion of the Party and its ideology into business matters. It has been the municipal Party committees in Shenzhen and Zhuhai, however, that have been in the forefront of reform efforts. It has been the boldness and flexibility of Chinese managers selected from within Party ranks, moreover, that have led to the successful development of many of the joint ventures. In citing the favourable experience at Shijingshan, the Xiangzhou Yarn Mill (Xiangzhou maofang chang) in Zhuhai and the Bamboo Garden Hotel (Zhuyuan binguan) in Shenzhen, the importance of Party work for enterprise performance has been recognized.[34] Party branch organizations are to be established wherever possible; in joint ventures, however, this will not lead to the setting up of enterprise Party committees. Through the carrying out of Party policy and the observance of Party regulations, Party members can enhance the smooth running of the enterprise; in practice, they can be mutually reinforcing. The realization of this has recently been noted by one foreign investor, who remarked: 'I've come to realize the importance of harmonious relations between higher and lower levels. To integrate Hong Kong management with Chinese ideological work is the secret of success in the joint ventures'.[35]

Finally, in terms of structural reform, the SEZs have progressively subjected their local economies to the influence of market forces through far greater price reform than has been allowed within China. Although the Party Central Committee has agreed that 'reform of the price system is the key to reform of the entire economic structure',[36] it is also acknowledged to be the most difficult to implement. In the case of the SEZs, however, a significant portion of goods and raw materials is imported from abroad, and local production of agricultural commodities as well as of consumer goods is primarily for export markets. For this reason, reference to world market prices has had to be introduced. These pressures are absent from most of the Chinese domestic market, which remains fairly closed. Caution and prudence will continue to cause price reform in China to lag behind that in the SEZs, but the economic performance of enterprises cannot be accurately gauged without a meaningful price system.

Conclusion

The purpose of the SEZs in China is to accelerate the pace of national economic development. Although the excessively narrow self-reliance of the past has been replaced by the 'open door', the necessity of relying primarily on her own resources and of depending principally on the development of the domestic market remain basic tenets of Chinese economic thinking. In contrast to the export-processing zones and free trade zones in other Asian economies, the SEZs of China are not part of a range of policies that see direct foreign investment and export trade as the dominant engine of economic growth. The model of an externally orientated open economy along the lines of Singapore and Hong Kong is rejected as inappropriate and not feasible, as well as ideologically repugnant, for China.

The immediate benefits of greater foreign investment, expanded foreign exchange earnings and job creation are already being realized in the Chinese SEZs. These tangible results, although major components in the rationale and evaluation of export-processing zones elsewhere in Asia, remain incidental advantages in the Chinese case. Narrow, short-term factors in themselves are considered an inadequate justification for the creation of the Chinese zones. Benefits such as helping Chinese goods to become more competitive in export markets and perfecting terms of foreign capital introduction are secondary considerations. China's foremost expectation of these zones is that they spearhead essential economic reform.

In this context, the most important way in which the SEZs can promote China's growth is as experimental workshops for the formulation of reforms that can be adapted for use within the planned economy outside the zones. Despite an impressive record of quantitative expansion, the Chinese economy is very poorly run; severe problems of waste, inefficiency, low productivity, lack of creativity and poor quality continue to characterize the state enterprises constituting the core of Chinese industry. The future course of the whole economy will be determined by the degree to which improvements can be made in the performance of these state enterprises. The main role of the SEZs is to provide useful lessons on the changes this entails.

Nevertheless, considerable argument remains as to how far the lessons of reform in the SEZs can be applied to the rest of China. Obvious distinctions exist between relatively detached enclaves such as the SEZs and the urban growth centres embedded in the Chinese polity. Shenzhen and Zhuhai have been granted almost complete fiscal autonomy, for example, while the revenue generated in China's leading cities is required to finance the national budget.

Reforms in the administrative regulation of the economy, mechanisms governing enterprise management, and means of motivating workers have been allowed a greater degree of evolution within enterprises in these zones than in the rest of China. The impact of these adjustments must, therefore, be closely assessed in order to find the correctives necessary to overcome the serious defects in Chinese industrial management. This will facilitate the effort being made to rationalize the allocation of China's limited assets, to reverse the stagnation in technology and productivity that has emerged and to assure that output corresponds to the needs and wants of the people.

To fulfil this function, the SEZs have become the 'showplaces' of modernization. Managers, officials and scholars from all over China have visited Shenzhen and Zhuhai in the past few years to study their experiences and achievements at first hand. Managers from Shenzhen and Zhuhai joint ventures have been sent on lecture tours within China to inform domestic enterprises about the operation of personnel practices and incentive schemes; they have also served as management consultants to advise state-owned firms within China on the implementation of reform. In the SEZs, domestic joint ventures are being actively encouraged and they have been a significant aspect of Shenzhen's development in 1983 and 1984. Domestic joint ventures are co-operative undertakings between local companies and enterprises from other parts of China, sometimes with a foreign investor as well. This kind of arrangement can effectively relay reform experiences as well as material rewards to the internal partners. In a more general way, the developments taking place within the zones are widely communicated in extensive newspaper coverage, and study of the zones has become a major focus of academic research and debate.

China can succeed in its commitment to socialist modernization in the 1980s and 1990s only if it can overcome its inability to generate intensive growth. It can no longer continue to depend almost exclusively on increased accumulation of capital and expansion of the labour force for economic growth. The SEZs are meant to assist in finding other means to alter the economy qualitatively, so that more substantial, sustained and suitable quantitative change can follow.

Notes

1. The authors wish to express their gratitude to the Australian Research Grants' Commission for financial support of the field-work on which this chapter is based.
2. 'On Questions of Party History', *Beijing Review*, Vol. 24, No. 27, 6 July 1981, p. 18.
3. *Selected Works of Deng Xiaoping* (Beijing, Foreign Languages Press, 1984), pp. 15, 21, 39, 40 and 45.
4. *Selected Works of Deng Xiaoping* (1984), pp. 39–40 and 44–6.
5. 'Decision of the Central Committee of the Communist Party of China on Reform of the Economic Structure'. *Beijing Review*, Vol. 27, No. 44, 29 October 1984, p. iii.
6. 'Decision of the Central Committee' (1984), p. viii.
7. 'Decision of the Central Committee' (1984), p. xv.
8. Xu Dixin, 'China's Special Economic Zones', *Beijing Review*, Vol. 24, No. 50, 14 December 1981, p. 16. Xu is the vice-president of the Chinese Academy of Social Sciences and director of its Institute of Economics.
9. 'Xue Muqiao Xu Dixin Qian Junrui tongzhi zai Guangdong Fujian liangsheng ho jingji tequ huiyi de fayan yaodian' ('Summaries of the Speeches of Comrades Xue Muqiao, Xu Dixin and Qian Junrui at the Conference on Guangdong and Fujian Provinces and the Special Economic Zones'), *Diaoyan ziliao* (*Investigation Materials*), No. 12, 20 June 1981, pp. 15–16 (*neibu cankao*, internal reference material).
10. *Renmin ribao (People's Daily)*, 23 May 1984, p. 1.
11. *Shenzhen tequbao* (*Shenzhen Special Zone Post*), 14 March 1983, p. 1.
12. *Renmin ribao*, 28 May 1984, p. 5
13. Interview, Jialo Mattress and Furniture Factory, Shenzhen, 2 February 1983.
14. Interview, Jialo Mattress and Furniture Factory, Shenzhen, 29 June 1984.
15. Interviews, Jialo Mattress and Furniture Factory, Shenzhen, 2 February 1983 and 29 June 1984.
16. Interview, Jianian Printing Co., Shenzhen, 2 February 1983.
17. Interview, Jianian Printing Co., Shenzhen, 29 June 1984.
18. Interview, Pepsi Soft Drink Factory, Shenzhen, 2 February 1983.
19. Interview, Pepsi Soft Drink Factory, Shenzhen, 29 June 1984.
20. Interviews, Shijingshan Tourist Centre, Zhuhai, 25 January 1983 and 6 July 1984.
21. Interview, Shijingshan Tourist Centre, Zhuhai, 26 January 1983.
22. Interview, Shijingshan Tourist Centre, Zhuhai, 25 January 1983.
23. *Yangcheng wanbao (Rams City Evening News)*, 25 November 1983, p. 2.

24. *Zhongguo jingji tequ nianjian* (*Yearbook of China's Special Economic Zones*) (Hong Kong, Yearbook of China's Special Economic Zones Publishing Co., 1984), p. 247.

25. *Zhongguo jingji tequ nianjian* (1984), p. 245.

26. Interview, Shijingshan Tourist Centre, Zhuhai, 25 January 1983.

27. Interviews, Shijingshan Tourist Centre, Zhuhai, 24 January 1983 and 6 July 1984.

28. J.N. Lane, 'A Businessman's View of Export Processing Zones: Their Problems', in N. Vittal (ed.), *Export Processing Zones in Asia: Some Dimensions* (Tokyo, Asian Productivity Organization, 1977), pp. 109–12.

29. Interview, Zhuhai, 24 January 1983.

30. Interview, Zhuhai, 5 July 1984.

31. Interview, Shijingshan Tourist Centre, Zhuhai, 25 January 1983; and interview, Shenzhen Municipal Labour Servicing Co., Shenzhen, 2 July 1984.

32. *Shenzhen tequbao*, 14 March 1983, p. 1.

33. 'Decision of the Central Committee of the Communist Party of China on Reform of the Economic Structure', *Beijing Review*, Vol. 27, No. 44, 29 October 1984, p. xiv.

34. Cao Zilu *et al.*, 'Jiaqiang dang de lingdao ho jianshe shi banhao jingji tequ de genben baozheng' ('Strengthening the Party Leadership and Structure is the Basic Guarantee for Building the Special Economic Zones Well'), *Lilun jiaoxue* (*Theoretical Studies*), No. 8, 15 August 1982, pp. 12–18 (*neibu cankao*, internal reference material); and interview, Bamboo Garden Hotel, Shenzhen, 30 June 1984.

35. 'Reports from Shenzhen (3): Labour Relations Smooth in Special Zone', *Beijing Review*, Vol. 27, No. 51, 17 December 1984, p. 28.

36. 'Decision of the Central Committee of the Communist Party of China on Reform of the Economic Structure', *Beijing Review*, Vol. 27, No. 44, 29 October 1984, p. viii.

12. Industries in Shenzhen: An Attempt at Open-door Industrialization

VICTOR F.S. SIT

Introduction

China caught the attention of the world when, in 1979, the creation of four special economic zones (SEZs) was announced. These zones are 'special' in the sense that they are the first areas within Communist China to be developed on the basis of active foreign participation and to be run in ways different from the rest of the country. The zones are to have special characteristics: first, their economy will be mainly based on the free-market system; second, foreign investment will be actively promoted to become the dominant source of investment within the zones; and third, the zones will constitute open systems of high technology and management skills and as such will serve as China's nodal points for the transfer of technology.[1]

As the creation of the SEZs probably marks a turning point in the overall development strategy of China, especially with regard to the use of foreign capital and technology, and the modification of the centrally directed system of managing the Chinese economy, the world has been watching their development with great interest.

Of the present four SEZs (Shenzhen, Xiamen, Zhuhai and Shantou), Shenzhen was the first to be founded and has developed the fastest. In many ways this zone has served as a pace-setter for China's new 'open-door' approach in economic development. In early 1984 a further step forward in this direction was made when 14 coastal cities were designated as 'economic open cities'. These are to enjoy some of the special privileges and economic autonomy of the SEZs. Shortly after the announcement, officials from the 14 cities were reported to have assembled in Shenzhen to learn from its experience.[2] It is believed that these cities will emulate Shenzhen, with modifications to suit local circumstances, as they open up. The development of Shenzhen since 1979 has thus provided a useful basis for the Chinese to assess the merits and demerits of the SEZ approach. Its widely publicized and reasonably documented experience over the past five years has also enabled foreigners to reach a better understanding of what is behind the Chinese mind in the creation of the SEZs. In the present chapter we will first explore Chinese intentions and then examine the strategies Shenzhen has used to attract industries. A study of industrial development in Shenzhen up until the end of 1983 will follow. Finally, the chapter will compare the SEZs with export-processing zones (EPZs) elsewhere and will discuss Shenzhen's future prospects in industrial development.

The Origins of the SEZs

Before 1976, the People's Republic of China was known for its ardent anti-capitalist stance and adopted a closed-door attitude towards foreign investment and business participation. China's international trade was small, amounting to less than 10 per cent of its national income, and was largely accounted for by trade with Hong Kong. The country only started to open up again after the fall of the Gang of Four in 1976. This 'thaw' in China's economic relations with foreign countries first became evident with the adoption of the regulations on joint ventures in 1979, and was confirmed in the same year by the creation of the SEZs in the provinces of Guangdong and Fujian.[3]

Why has a country like China, which is fairly industrialized and self-sufficient in terms of market and range of products, and which has long emphasized self-reliance in development, now been pushed, firstly, into putting its labour force up for hire on the international market, and, secondly, into risking the possibility of social and political disruption by allowing foreign capitalism within its territory? Initially, foreigners saw the creation of the SEZs as the result of China's desire to admit foreign investments in a limited way by restricting them to some carefully selected, sealed-off, and tightly controlled coastal locations. Such a move also perhaps reflected China's uneasiness, as well as an underlining unwillingness to play host to foreign capitalists. The development of the SEZs, in particular the Shenzhen SEZ, and the recent designation of 'economic open cities', however, have dispelled much of this suspicion. It seems more and more likely that the SEZs are the vanguard of sweeping economic and institutional reforms which will affect the whole Chinese economy and which the present leaders have long cherished as necessary for the modernization of the country.

The theoretical justifications for allowing expanded co-operation with foreign capital and the exercise of market forces are currently focal themes in debates regarding China's economic development and planning, as witnessed by a large number of articles written by influential officials and leading economists in the country's main journals.[4] A few salient points have emerged from these debates. First, China needs to promote economic and technical exchanges with foreign countries. Second, in achieving such exchanges, some price has to be paid which may take the form of capitalist exploitation and the 'adverse' social influence of capitalism. Third, to allow successful implementation, a few convenient areas have to be singled out for concentrated development, effective promotion and easy control.

The Chinese leadership feels that it can minimize the ideological ill-effects and overcome the practical problems arising from such innovations in two ways: first, by upholding Chinese sovereignty and hence the sole right to legislate, to control and to regulate daily life within these special zones; and, second, by adhering to the principles of mutual benefit and joint consultation in all dealings with foreign participants.[5] The SEZs may therefore provide China with safe and carefully guarded locations in which to venture into economic and technical exchanges with the West on an unprecedented scale. At first the Chinese leadership was cautious and only a small piece of land about 1 sq km in area in Shenzhen (Shekou) was marked out as an export-processing zone to facilitate joint ventures and co-operative production between China Merchants' Steam Navigation Co. (CMSN) and foreign investors.[6] Less than a year later, the formation of three SEZs in Guangdong was announced. The largest, Shenzhen, which includes Shekou, was designated for comprehensive multi-sector development encompassing manufacturing, agriculture, commerce, transport and communications, property development and tourism. Thus the notion of promoting economic and technological co-operation had gained substantial breadth through the concept of the SEZs.

In 1982, Shenzhen was given another boost. For it was announced that the zone is to be developed into a new type of border city. Shenzhen will, in the future, be mainly financed by foreign capital. It will possess its own set of laws and its economy will be based on the market mechanism. It will also adopt a new approach towards development and management that emphasizes economic incentives and professionalism. In addition, Shenzhen has become physically separated from the rest of the mainland by a newly completed (1984) border fence so that the flow of goods and people between it and the rest of the country is strictly controlled. However, Shenzhen is still closely linked with the rest of the country in a different sense. It serves as a laboratory where Chinese officials can observe and learn from the outside world through direct participation in different types of joint production and business operations or by watching such activities at very close quarters.[7] It also provides a testing ground for new reforms in enterprise management, finance and labour matters which are part of the modernization drive of the country; and these reforms in the SEZs, if found useful, will be applied to the rest of China. Indeed, Chinese officials now consider Shenzhen as the instrument whereby 'China will be able to gain an understanding of modern capitalist economies, accumulate experience in the formulation of regulations for economic development programmes, cooperate with overseas businesses, and obtain access to advanced technology and management techniques'.[8] Apart from foreign capital, well-established Chinese enterprises are also being wooed into Shenzhen so that they can participate in the learning process. Many organized visits of non-SEZ officials have been arranged by the Shenzhen SEZ authorities so that the 'reforms' and 'advancement' of Shenzhen can be learned at first hand. The SEZ may therefore be seen as a sub-system within China separated from the main system by a semi-permeable membrane, which takes the physical form of a new fence and the legal and administrative form of special SEZ rules and policies.[9] This protective membrane shields the zone from the rest of China, providing it with a special economic, political and institutional set-up, while allowing what are considered to be beneficial elements, such as technology, management skills and well-tested reforms, to filter through and spread to the rest of the country, as is shown in Fig. 12.1.

The four SEZs are all located along the South China coast and are each close to a long-established trading port. Thus they all have easy access to existing port facilities and are conveniently located for international trade. Shenzhen and Zhuhai share a border with Hong Kong and Macau respec-

Fig. 12.1 The SEZs as a Sub-system within China

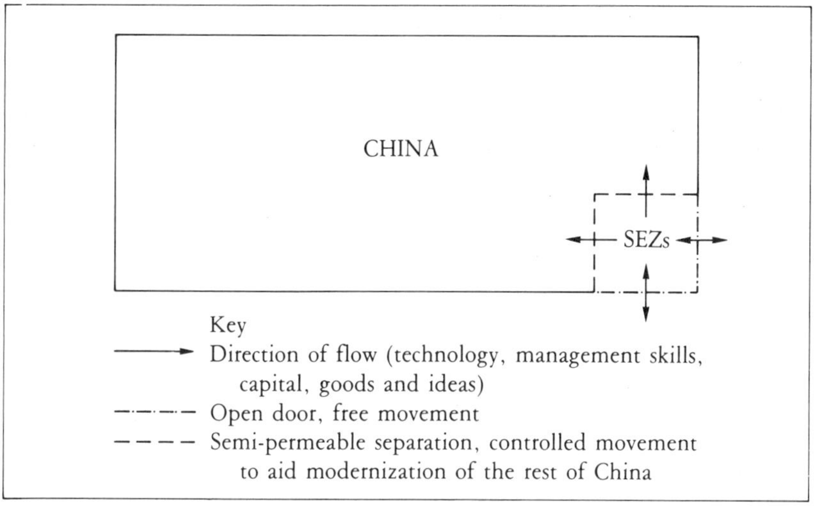

tively. Shantou and Xiamen, though more remote from Hong Kong, are connected with it and South-east Asia ethnically. For they are the native towns of many overseas Chinese in the region. Such geographical and ethnic ties offer the SEZs an edge in terms of foreign relations. Therefore the first efforts in promoting the SEZs were aimed primarily at overseas Chinese as possible clients. The natural endowment of these SEZs, in terms of their harbours, port facilities and other geographical features, has been examined in detail in Chapter 2. We shall now discuss how Shenzhen, the earliest and most developed of the SEZs, has thrived since its creation in 1979 by examining one vital aspect of its development, that is, its industrial growth.

Industrial Development, 1978-83

Before its designation as an SEZ, Shenzhen was basically a small border town, with some market-town functions but very little industrial development.[10] It contained small-scale manufacturing enterprises, engaged mainly in the production of fertilizer, small farm tools and a number of small daily consumer items (Table 12.1). Total industrial employment was estimated to be around 5,000 and the sector generated a gross output value of about 61.5 million *yuan*. By the end of 1983 (Table 12.1), the number of enterprises had risen to 433 and production in the sector had reached 720 million *yuan*, more than tenfold its 1978 value. Employment in the sector over the same period had risen to 25,000 persons, a fourfold increase. The rapid growth of manufacturing can be seen from the changing proportions of the agricultural and industrial sectors in Shenzhen's gross agricultural and industrial output value (GAIOV). In 1978, industry's contribution to GAIOV was 34 per cent, but it shot up to 83 per cent in 1983. Manufacturing thus had

Table 12.1 The Industrial Growth of Shenzhen, 1978–83, and Planned Growth, 1981–2000 (year-end figures)

	1978	1981	1983	1981–2000
No. of establishments	26	267	443	1,500
No. of workers	5,000	12,000	25,000	160,000
Total investment (million *yuan*)	n/a	n/a	n/a	3,700
Gross output (million *yuan*)	61.5	241	720	9,600
Profit before tax (million *yuan*)	4.4	n/a	75	n/a
Labour productivity (*yuan*)	6,000	n/a	26,681	n/a

Note: n/a = not available.

Source: Computed from *Economic Reporter*, 7 September 1984, p. 26 (Chinese weekly).

become the dominant sector, a reversal of the situation before Shenzhen was made an SEZ. According to the Shenzhen SEZ's 20-year plan, the present emphasis on industrial growth will be maintained, with an annual rate of increase of 29.9 per cent in industrial output and 12.6 per cent in employment over the period 1981–2000 (Table 12.1). By the year 2000, Shenzhen will be a medium-sized industrial city employing 160,000 persons in manufacturing and producing an annual gross industrial output of 9,600 million *yuan*. As far as spatial arrangements are concerned, the plan envisages the development of 10 industrial districts with a total gross area of 15 sq km. Three of them — Shekou, Shahe and Shangbu — are already burgeoning industrial districts. Another three — Nantou, Bagualing and Shuibe — are under construction. The seventh, Futian, is planned as an industrial science park. The other districts include Lintang, a textile centre, and a heavy industrial district on the coast of Shenzhen Wan based on oil-related industries.[11] However, the pace of industrial development in Shenzhen over the past five years has been fairly erratic, largely reflecting a lack of experience in the initial two or three years and a misguided concentration of effort on property development.[12] Fortunately, this mistake was realized in 1982–3, a hard fact forced upon Shenzhen SEZ officials by the Hong Kong property slump during that time. Since then it has become quite evident that the SEZ ought to shift its development priority back to industry. Early in 1982 the SEZ amended its incentive package in order to make itself a more attractive place for foreign investment in manufacturing.

As a place for foreign investment in manufacturing, Shenzhen is fairly similar to export-processing zones of the Third World. This may be substantiated by reference to the Regulations on the Special Economic Zones in Guangdong Province which spell out the investment environment and the incentives offered to foreign investments in the SEZs:

(a) Certain areas are delineated to form SEZs in order to develop external economic co-operation and technical exchange and to promote the socialist modernization programme (Article 1).

(b) Products of the enterprises in the special zones are to be sold on the international market (Article 9).
(c) Investors can operate their enterprises independently and employ foreign personnel for technical and administrative work (Article 10).
(d) Machinery, spare parts, raw materials, vehicles and other means of production for the enterprises are exempted from import duty (Article 13).
(e) The rate of income tax levied on enterprises is to be 15 per cent. Special preferential treatment will be given to enterprises established within two years of the promulgation of these regulations, with an investment of US$5 million or more, and involving higher technology or having a longer cycle of capital turnover (Article 14).
(f) Legitimate after-tax profits of investors, and salaries and other earnings of foreign workers and staff members of the enterprises can, after deduction of personal income tax, be remitted out of China (Article 15).
(g) Investors who reinvest their profits for five years or longer may apply for exemption from income tax on profits for such reinvestment (Article 16).
(h) Entry and exit procedures will be simplified for the convenience of foreign personnel (Article 18).[13]

The SEZs themselves provide formed sites with developed infrastructure including power supplies, means of communication, residential quarters and other living facilities for workers and management personnel.

Table 12.2 summarizes the incentive package as at August 1981. The development of industries in Shenzhen up to this time, however, was less than satisfactory as foreign investment was largely being put into property and tourist developments (Table 12.3). Industrial contracts comprised 67.9 per cent of all contracts with foreign participation, but represented only 10

Table 12.2 The Incentive Package of the Shenzhen SEZ, 1981[1]

Item	Details
Corporate profit tax	15 per cent
Tax holiday	One to five years
Labour wage	Minimum US$100 per month (30–50 per cent lower than in Hong Kong)
Duties	All imported goods tax-free except tobacco and liquor; all exports tax-free
Land rent (industrial)	US$3.3–10 per sq m per year (lease 20–50 years)
Land utility cost (industrial)	US$0.33–0.67 per sq m per year
Management autonomy	The right to hire foreign technical and management staff, and to hire and fire local staff and workers
Repatriation of profits	All profits after tax can be repatriated, as can the income of foreign personnel

Note: 1. See text for an up-to-date picture.

Source: Economic Reporter, August 1981, p. 14 (English monthly).

Table 12.3 Foreign Investments by Sector in Shenzhen

	1980[1]					1983 (cumulative)				
	Contracts		Investment[3]		Average Investment per Contract	Contracts		Investment[3]		Average Investment per Contract
	No.	%	HK$ million	%	(HK$ thousand)	No.	%	HK$ million	%	(HK$ thousand)
Industry	395	67.9	160	10.0	405	1,847	73.7	1,299	43.6	703
Property	7	1.2	530	33.1	75,714	59	2.4	789	26.4	13,376
Tourism and recreation	15	2.6	540	33.8	36,000	16	0.6	151	5.1	9,437
Commerce, restaurants and services	14	2.4	190	11.9	13,571	132	5.3	225	7.5	1,704
Transport and communications	—[2]	—[2]	—[2]	—[2]	—	28	1.1	37	1.2	1,321
Agriculture and fisheries	140	24.1	120	7.5	857	415	16.6	45	1.5	108
Others	10	1.7	60	37.5	6,000	8	0.3	435	14.6	54,375
Total (cumulative)	581	99.9	1,600	99.8	2,754	2,505	100.0	2,981	99.9	1,190

Note: 1. Data as at the end of August; other figures are as at year-end.
2. Most likely included under 'Others'.
3. Planned investment.

Source: See Tables 12.1 and 12.2.

per cent of all investments involved. Such a bias towards property and tourism in the first phase of the SEZ's development was caused by two factors. The first was the significant influence of Hong Kong businessmen in the SEZ. At this early stage, most SEZ investments came from Hong Kong and the investment decisions of Hong Kong businessmen were to a very large extent based on what they perceived to be the safer bet, that is the utilization of the resources of Shenzhen to satisfy urgent Hong Kong market demands. A very logical and important consequence of this influence was the spilling over of the property boom in Hong Kong into Shenzhen. One official in charge of such matters even believed that the SEZ should aim at producing 10,000 residential flats per year, or about half of the average annual supply produced by the private sector in Hong Kong. Lack of recreation space at weekends and for short holidays in Hong Kong was another demand factor leading to a flow of investment into hotels, holiday resorts and related facilities during the initial years of the SEZ.[14] Industrial projects at the time consisted mainly of those emphasizing cheap labour and labour-intensive types of light manufacturing, such as garments, radio assembly and furniture-making, or land-intensive obnoxious industries, such as dyeing and other textile-finishing industries. The average investment per industrial contract was only HK$405,000 (see Table 12.3).

These early mistakes soon led to serious problems as the property market in Hong Kong plunged into a deep recession in 1982. The amount of contracted investment in the SEZ dropped from HK$6,800 million in 1981 to HK$1,420 million in 1982, which was lower than the amount signed in 1980 (that is, HK$2,136 million). It was at this time that the need to redirect the development strategy of the SEZ back to the promotion of manufacturing was recognized. In the 20-year plan for the SEZ, released in 1982, the emphasis on manufacturing has been reaffirmed and reiterated.[15] Realizing that Shenzhen had so far not succeeded in attracting foreign investments in high-technology industries, several new approaches were adopted to create a better investment environment for such industries. These have included an improvement in the incentive package and the offer of competent local partners in joint ventures. These new methods were encapsulated at the time in a slogan: 'Enticing outsiders and building relations with locals'.[16]

The methods used in 'enticing outsiders' included cutting down on red tape, improving the physical infrastructure and offering new ingredients in the incentive package. In 1982, a northern fence was begun to separate the Shenzhen SEZ from the rest of Bao'an county. This was seen as a vital measure to facilitate easy import and export as well as the convenient movement of foreign personnel into and out of the SEZ. The new fence extends for 81.2 km. It was completed in 1984 and put into use in 1985. To instill business confidence and improve management efficiency, the Chinese authorities also drew up many new business laws, some of which are specific to Shenzhen. In October 1981, four major laws specific to the SEZs and covering land management, enterprise registration, labour and wages, and entry and exit were enacted. In 1983, a law on the management of commercial properties in the SEZs was passed, with two new laws on economic contracts with foreign interests and technology transfer added to the list at the beginning of 1984.[17] These laid down in some detail the rights and responsibilities of both local and foreign parties involved in joint ventures, and procedures on the acquisition of land, business registration, entry and exit, labour recruitment, imports and exports, and so on in the Shenzhen and other SEZs.

Shenzhen's physical infrastructure was further improved with the completion of a network of 29 roads totalling some 54 km at the end of 1982. In 1983, a further 27 roads were completed, adding 60 km to, or doubling the kilometerage of, the network. Sea transport in Shenzhen is largely dependent on Shekou where a cargo- and passenger-handling pier for ships of up to 3,000 d.w.t. has been constructed. The building of a new port to serve as a base for exploration in the South China Sea oilfields was completed in Chiwan recently. The electricity supply has also been improved with the completion of the first two phases of the Hong Kong – Guangdong grid. Telecommunication links with the major cities of China and Hong Kong are now available, and international telephone calls can be made through Beijing and Shanghai via satellite. The new telephone exchange of the SEZ was also completed at the end of 1983, with 10,000 automatic lines and 300 long-distance call lines. The Shenzhen SEZ therefore now possesses a good physical framework to support rapid industrial development. In addition, the 10 industrial districts, with their phased construction programmes, provide formed and serviced sites for factories at convenient locations.[18]

In order to boost Shenzhen's attractiveness to foreign capital and to direct investments back on to the 'proper track' at a time of world-wide recession, a number of new promotional measures have been taken since 1982.[19] First, the annual rent for industrial land has been brought down by between 10 and 20 per cent. For industries using high-level technology, the land rent has been further reduced by between 20 and 30 per cent during the plant's first three to five years of operation. Similarly, for these industries the tax holiday has been extended to between two and five years after the commencement of production. In addition, joint ventures or foreign-owned enterprises may sell a proportion of their products on the Chinese domestic market subject to prior approval. The proportion of products allowed is to be decided by the relevant ministries.

In order to build up 'relations with locals' joint ventures between foreign investors and established Chinese industrial enterprises are to be promoted. In addition, Chinese enterprises are encouraged to set up branch plants in the SEZs so as to take advantage of the established infrastructure and lack of duty on imports. In doing so they will benefit from the transfer of technology, and will be able to use foreign partnership as a springboard for exploiting possible export markets. In 1982 alone 43 branch factories of mainland enterprises, with a total planned investment of HK$530 million, were set up in the SEZ.[20] Of 878 contracts signed in that year, 153 involved these branch factories. Industrial investments in the SEZ from this internal source accounted for about one-fifth of total planned investments covered by contracts involving foreign interests. Thus the participation of Chinese enterprises has added a new impetus to industrial development in Shenzhen.

The success of the new drive may be seen from the increase in the number of industrial contracts with foreign participation signed in the SEZ in 1982–3. Investments in industrial projects had also overtaken property investments by the end of 1983 and had become the dominant sector of foreign investment (Table 12.3). The average investment per contract also increased from HK$405,000 in 1980 to HK$703,000 in 1983. In the first half of 1984, it was reported that the industrial sector accounted for 82 per cent of all contracts and 60 per cent of all planned investment involved in joint ventures with foreign interests in the zone. This marks a continuation of a trend that has been evident since 1982.[21] Therefore foreign investments in the SEZ do seem, after 1982, to have returned to the original emphasis on industrial growth, and new efforts have clearly been made in improving both the physical and economic investment environment.

The Extent and Forms of Foreign Participation

By 1983, total foreign capital invested in industrial projects in the SEZ stood at HK$1,290 million, or 43.6 per cent of all actual foreign investments in Shenzhen since 1979. Over 90 per cent of the money originated from Hong Kong and Macau, of which a substantial amount involved third parties outside these two neighbouring areas of the SEZ. In 1983, 19 establishments were identified as having received direct investments from 12 countries and regions other than Hong Kong and Macau. In the first half of 1984 alone, 12 investment projects were concluded with foreign parties other than Hong Kong and Macau and these had an aggregate total planned investment of HK$220 million.[22] This trend of increasing foreign investments from countries other than Hong Kong and Macau in the SEZ seems to be continuing.

Shekou took the lead in Shenzhen in putting emphasis on industrial promotion as the main thrust of development. Of the 47 contracts concluded in Shekou up to June 1983, 31 involved industrial projects, 9 of them relating to heavy industries and 22 to light industries. The total investment of these contracts amounted to HK$700 million, of which 70 per cent was contributed by foreign partners. Only 7 out of 47 were solely owned investment projects of CMSN or 100 per cent equity plants set up by mainland Chinese enterprises.[23] The role of foreign capital in the whole of Shenzhen, though not as overwhelming as in Shekou, is very significant. The contribution to gross industrial output by firms with foreign interests amounted to HK$374 million in 1983, 52 per cent of Shenzhen's total gross industrial output in that year.[24] That amount was over 150 per cent of the SEZs' total gross industrial output in 1981 (HK$240 million). The share contributed by private sole ownership and joint-venture enterprises formed 37 per cent of the total gross industrial output, illustrating the interests of foreign capital in these forms of partnership, while processing contracts only accounted for 15 per cent of the SEZ's gross industrial output. Why do foreign partners prefer one form of partnership over another?

The Regulations on the Special Economic Zones in Guangdong Province provide the legal framework for the setting up of foreign-owned private

Table 12.4 Industrial Contracts Signed between 1979 and 1983

Year	No. of Industrial Contracts Signed (those with foreign participation)
1979	112
1980	243
1981	321
1982	457
1983	714

Source: Xinhua News Agency and New Evening Post, *Zhongguo jingji tequ shouce* (*Handbook for China's Special Economic Zones*) (Hong Kong, New Evening Post, 1984).

enterprises and different forms of foreign participation in the SEZs. In short, there are five forms of foreign participation, ranging from the least independent, from the point of view of the foreign investor, to the completely independent sole proprietorship. These forms are given below.[25]

Processing Agreements

Most processing agreements consist of small-scale investments. They take one of two forms. In the first form the Chinese provide the factory premises and equipment and the foreign partner supplies the required raw or semi-finished materials for processing or assembly. The job is specified in the contract with a fixed delivery date. The Chinese side has no control over the processed or assembled product. It receives a processing fee to cover wages, water and electricity supplies, and rent. In the other form of co-operation, the foreign partner supplies the Chinese side with the necessary equipment at an agreed price. The Chinese side repays its costs in instalments through reductions in the processing fees.

Compensation Trade

In this kind of co-operation, the foreign partner provides the necessary equipment and technology in the form of a loan to be repaid by the Chinese side in instalments in terms of output. The main purpose of such co-operation is to transfer advanced technology to existing Chinese enterprises.

Co-operation Production

This form of co-operation is more popular in property and tourism development projects. The foreign partner provides the equipment and working capital, whereas the Chinese side contributes land and labour. The project or business is co-managed, and the profits are shared, according to an agreed ratio. The Chinese side will sell to the foreign partner a fixed ratio of the products or services produced as repayment of capital and interest for the latter's contribution of equipment and working capital. After complete repayment of the foreign party's investment and interest therefrom, the enterprise will be solely owned by the Chinese.

The Joint Venture

The foreign partner in this type of co-operation participates by taking up a proportion of shares in the joint venture through the provision of construction fees and equipment. The Chinese shares are paid in the form of land, factory premises, or office space. The two parties co-manage the enterprise and are jointly responsible for its profits and losses. This type of co-operation is often sizeable in scale and employs advanced technology and management methods provided by the foreign partner under the supervision of foreign personnel. Both the duration and potential profitability of the contract are longer and higher than in other forms of co-operation. Thus foreign investors find this the most appealing of the different types of co-operation.

The Foreign-owned Sole Proprietorship

This last type is self-explanatory. The foreign investor has full control of, and responsibility for, the enterprise. The SEZ benefits from it by collecting land rent and corporate profit tax, and enjoying added employment.

An examination of Table 12.5 shows an obvious difference between 1981 and 1983 in the distribution of the different types of co-operation. In 1983, most contracts and investments were of the last three types specified above. By that year, 96 per cent of cumulative foreign investments were in these forms of co-operation. The table also shows that the investment size of the average contract tended to increase between 1980 and 1983. Figures in Table 12.5 cover foreign investments in all sectors. However, evidence of an increasing foreign preference for industrial projects in joint ventures and sole proprietorship types of co-operation may be gleaned from other sources. In 1979, all foreign involvement in industrial projects in the SEZ took the form of processing agreements. By the end of 1983, only 87 per cent of all industrial contracts involved processing agreements which accounted for 42 per cent of total foreign investment in industries in Shenzhen. The balance, that is, 13 per cent of the contracts and 58 per cent of planned investments, were joint ventures or sole proprietorship businesses.

The increasing average size of planned investment in foreign industrial contracts has been highlighted in Table 12.3. The latest figures available give further support to such an observation. Of the 123 contracts signed between 1979 and June 1984 with a planned investment exceeding HK$10 million, 39 were industrial, 30 were in property, 15 were in commercial and residential projects, with the balance of 16 in others.[26] Therefore the thesis that foreign interest in industrial projects involving larger investment values and possibly higher technology after 1982 has grown may reasonably be sustained.

The Level of Technology

Proximity to Hong Kong was the chief reason for the initial success of Shenzhen, though we have noted its early bias towards property and tourism development. As indicated by Table 12.3, the number of industrial contracts

Table 12.5 Foreign Investments by Type of Co-operation in Shenzhen (cumulative)

	1980			1981[1]			1983		
	No. of Contracts Signed	Investment Involved (HK$ million)	Average Investment per Contract (HK$ million)	No. of Contracts Signed	Investment Involved (HK$ million)	Average Investment per Contract (HK$ million)	No. of Contracts Signed	Investment Involved (HK$ million)	Average Investment Per Contract (HK$ million)
Processing agreements	336 (63.0)[2]	33.6 (2.1)	0.09	710 (87.5)	141.4 (5.6)	0.20	2,047 (81.5)	558.3 (4)	0.27
Compensation trade	4 (0.1)	33.6 (2.1)	8.56	5 (0.1)	44.7 (1.8)	8.94			
Co-operative production	199 (34.3)	1,400.0 (88.4)	7.16	73 (9.0)	1,420.7 (56.8)	19.46	289 (11.5)	13,400.0 (96)	28.8
Joint ventures	6 (1.0)	38.4 (2.4)	6.40	8 (1.0)	71.2 (2.8)	8.89	133 (5.3)		
Sole proprietorships	6 (1.0)	80.0 (5.0)	13.33	15 (1.8)	824.8 (32.9)	54.98	43 (1.7)		
Total	581 (99.4)	1,600.0 (100.0)	2.75	811 (99.4)	2,502.8 (99.9)	3.09	2,512 (100.0)	13,958.3 (100)	5.56

Notes: 1. Up to August and excluding Shekou (about 40 contracts with HK$600 million worth of investment); others are year-end figures.
2. Bracketed figures are percentages.

Sources: *Economic Research* (Beijing), No. 8, 1981, p. 56; and *Economic Reporter*, 17 September 1980, pp. 19–20; 11 November 1981, p. 8; and 19 March 1984, p. 25.

signed by the end of 1980, just a year after the creation of the SEZ, amounted to 395. The majority, 336 in number, were processing contracts. Obviously, the initial reaction of the outside world towards the SEZ was that it was just another cheap labour haven. Some Hong Kong industrialists, being hard-pressed by labour shortages and rising wages in 1979 and 1980, saw the SEZ as a new opportunity to bring down their costs through the decentralization of low-skill, labour-intensive processes into Shenzhen. Indeed the SEZ's first wave of industrial investments (1979–81) were mainly concentrated in types of manufacture that bear at least one if not all of the following characteristics: first, activities in Hong Kong which moved to Shenzhen because of comparative advantages in land and wage levels; second, activities for which Hong Kong provided the market for the final or semi-manufactured product; or, third, activities that faced difficulties in continuing operation in Hong Kong because of environmental considerations.[27]

However, land costs are traditionally a small component in the total costs of an average Hong Kong factory operation (2.9 per cent as revealed by the 1971 manufacturing census); hence the low cost of land in Shenzhen is not particularly attractive to Hong Kong industrialists in general. They worry more about labour quality and its supply; time and efficiency in the transport of raw materials, parts and finished products; and industrial services and linkages. Shenzhen still lags far behind Hong Kong in such crucial production considerations and this comparatively disadvantageous position is unlikely to improve sufficiently in the near future. Thus not only the low cost of land, but even lower labour costs may not be sufficient incentives to pull Hong Kong manufacturers into Shenzhen. What had taken place up to 1981 was therefore minimal when one considers that Hong Kong then had over 40,000 industrial enterprises and an industrial work-force of about one million persons.[28] Nevertheless, industries which require a large amount of space, or industries which are obnoxious, or consist of simple types of assembly jobs that demand little skill, such as weaving, dyeing, printing and other textile-related industries, as well as the assembly of simple electrical goods, plastic flowers and utensils, may still find the SEZ attractive as an alternative location. It is precisely for this reason that there is a danger that Shenzhen may become the dumping ground of Hong Kong for its lower-rung, labour-intensive and obnoxious industries.

With the shift of investment emphasis back to manufacturing, Shenzhen attempted to institute new ways and means of attracting the right sort of industrial investments that would bring in modern technology. New incentives for industrial investments became all the more necessary as the total foreign capital inflow shrank substantially after the 1981–2 property slump in Hong Kong, a decline that had crippling effects on the SEZ.

The types of manufacturing Shenzhen wishes to attract are contained in a list issued in September 1982 and are summarized in Table 12.6. The industries that the SEZ wants are clearly not the simple processing and assembly types but the more sophisticated modern industries facing a rising demand in the Chinese domestic market. CMSN even categorically stated in the official *Investor's Handbook* (revised edition, 1981) that the following industries are not welcome in Shekou:

(a) those causing severe pollution;
(b) those with outmoded or worn-out equipment;
(c) those whose products for overseas markets have to be covered by China's export quotas;
(d) those in the nature of compensation trade; and
(e) those involved in assembly and processing activities.

It has completely ruled out small processing types of agreements. While the Shenzhen authorities have not taken such a rigid line, they too are trying to attract more advanced modern industries.[29] In its 1984 *Investor's Handbook to the Chinese SEZs*, the Shenzhen SEZ Development Co., one of the three major industrial promotion agents of the SEZ, listed nine high-priority promotion items for 1984, all of which belong to the high-technology electronics industry. The Shenzhen Municipal Industrial Development Co., the second of the three agents, listed 58 promotion items which cover almost the same items as those in Table 12.6. The third agent, the Shenzhen Municipal Electronics Co., listed 31 items in the handbook for promotion. With the exception of two, all required an ultimate investment of over US$10 million, one even of US$200 million. The size of the capital and the nature of the products involved point very clearly to high-technology projects. In addition, the newly formed special agent, the Shenzhen Municipal Petrochemical Co., is inviting investments in 34 different items covering the full range of petrochemical industries.

Table 12.6 Preferred Industrial Groups in Shenzhen

Light industries	Paper products, pressure-cookers, lamps, printing ink, cigarettes, soap, plastic sheets and bags, glassware and carpets
Textiles	Weaving, knitting and towels
Electrical goods and electronics	Colour televisions, refrigerators, washing-machines, telephones, electrical calculators, integrated-circuit parts, hi-fi parts, cassette-recorders, transformers, electronic games, photostat machines, cameras, electronic precision equipment, household electrical goods and injection parts
Food and beverages	Composite food factories, biscuits and confectionery, noodles, preserved vegetables, beverages and beer
Metal and machinery	Freezing equipment, air-conditioning equipment, stainless steel cutlery, metal tools and aluminium products
Furniture and daily household goods	Daily metal goods, stationery, steel and wooden furniture, and rattanware
Crafts and garments	Jewellery, art pottery, leather goods, toys and embroidery
Others	Electro-plating, pottery and ceramics

Source: Economic Reporter (Hong Kong), September 1982 (English monthly).

The opening up of the Chinese domestic market to some existing and potential SEZ enterprises serves as an important stimulus to the expansion of existing enterprises, such as Sanyo in Shekou, and to many foreign investors who now assess the SEZ in a rather different light than previously. A new deal with a large US firm was concluded in the summer of 1984 for the setting up of a modern plant to manufacture glass plates largely for the China market.[30] The new project involves an investment of US$200 million. Efforts to encourage Chinese ministries and state enterprises to set up independent, branch, or joint-venture plants in the SEZ have provided another impetus to the move towards high-technology industries. These two are very important factors and the resultant change induced in the structure of manufacturing in Shenzhen is becoming tangible.

In 1978, not only was Shenzhen's industrial structure undeveloped (see Table 12.1), but it was also concentrated in the traditional village industries as indicated in Table 12.7. Although similar statistics for 1983 are not available, there is other evidence of a shift towards a modern industrial structure. One such pointer lies in the development of electronics in the SEZs. There was only one electronics assembly factory in 1978 in the zone, employing about 300 workers (Table 12.8). By the end of 1983, electronics had become Shenzhen's largest industry. It generated a gross output of 320 million *yuan* or 45 per cent of the gross industrial output of the SEZ, and employed 15,000 workers or 60 per cent of the total industrial work-force. This rapid growth seems only to have started in 1982. Of the 60 factories found at the end of 1983, 30 were set up by the Ministry of Electronics, 15 were joint ventures and 15 were owned by other Chinese enterprises.[31] The growth of the electronics industry therefore demonstrates the rapid success of the new approach of the SEZ both in boosting industrial development, and in effecting a shift of the industrial structure towards the SEZ's original basic objective of technology transfer.

Table 12.7 The Industrial Structure of Bao'an County,[1] 1978

Type of Industries	Value of Production (%)
Light industries:	
food products	63.7
building materials	4.8
forestry products	3.7
paper	2.3
textiles	2.1
others	6.3
Heavy industries:	
machinery	10.2
chemicals	6.9

Note: 1. Former administrative unit of the SEZ.

Source: Wu and Yi (1981) quoted in K.Y. Wong (ed.), *Shenzhen Special Economic Zone* (Hong Kong, Hong Kong Geographical Association, 1982), p. 48.

Table 12.8 The Development of the Electronics Industry in Shenzhen (year-end figures)

	1978	1982	1983
No. of establishments	1	12	60
Employment (no. of persons)	300	4,700	15,000
Floor area (sq m)	1,000	110,000	280,000
Gross output value (million *yuan*)	700	n/a	320,000

Note: n/a = not available.

Source: Economic Reporter, 17 September 1984, p. 28.

Evaluating the SEZ

A Comparison with the Export-processing Zones

In many ways the SEZs seem to resemble the export-processing zones (EPZs) set up in other Asian countries in the 1960s and 1970s as a means of promoting foreign investments in manufacturing activities. Most of these zones, such as the Kaohsiung EPZ in Taiwan, the Masan EPZ in South Korea and the Bataan EPZ in the Philippines, provide cheap labour havens to multinational companies interested in exploiting the benefits of international subcontracting. The EPZs share the common characteristics of a separate, well-developed and integrated physical infrastructure and a centralized bureaucracy, and offer attractive incentives in the form of very low rates of taxation and cheap and disciplined labour.[32] Through these special arrangements and privileges, the EPZs hope to provide local employment and earn foreign exchange for the governments concerned without upsetting or changing existing tax, labour, import-export and other laws and policies that currently apply to the rest of the country. The first few EPZs, that is those in Taiwan and South Korea, seem to have been quite successful. They have been able to grow to their designed size and have become viable industrial communities. These EPZs also seem to have become integrated with the industrial system of the rest of the country concerned, and the level of industrialization and the infrastructure for industrial development of the rest of the country have also been developed to the same extent as in the EPZs. The other EPZs of Asia are, however, less successful. As most of them possess the same objectives, aim at the same clients and use the same approach, they have created among themselves intense competition, a situation that more established EPZs such as Kaohsiung were fortunate enough not to experience. Besides competing among themselves, other factors that have contributed to a less than satisfactory performance by the newer EPZs in Asia are the poor quality of labour, a lack of efficiency in management, and a lack of industrial and supply and demand links with other areas of the host country.

The Shenzhen SEZ was modelled on the EPZs in terms of its incentive package, and in the provision of a separate and 'special' physical infrastructure, economic management, and legal environment to attract foreign investments. However, it differs markedly from Asia's EPZs in a number of ways, reflecting the differences in goals as well as the likelihood of those goals being realized. First, Shenzhen is pursuing multi-sector development and is attempting to build up a modern border city which contains modern industries as well as advanced development in science research, financing and tourism. The ultimate purpose is to provide a laboratory for the testing of new ways to develop and reform the management of the Chinese economy. Second, Shenzhen benefits from the new policy of allowing products of its joint ventures and enterprises with foreign interests to enter the Chinese domestic market. This in itself is a very attractive inducement to foreign investments as the potential of the Chinese market is becoming more and more appreciated. Third, the new policy to woo local Chinese enterprises to enter the SEZ and to make use of Shenzhen as one of the major locations for the transfer of technology gives a tremendous boost to industrial development there. Thus the SEZ is, in essence, quite different from the EPZs. In the area of industrial development, it is clear that Shenzhen is performing a very interesting, and indeed significant, role as a matchmaker between foreign partners and Chinese industrial enterprises, as is shown in Fig. 12.2.

The SEZ provides the physical location and infrastructure, and acts as the matchmaker in bringing together a foreign and a Chinese partner, each contributing its best in the production of competitive products. The foreign partner's contribution consists mainly of capital, marketing techniques, technology and management. The Chinese side, sometimes also strong in technology but more often experienced in production with slightly backward technology, provides, with strong support from its ministry, skilled and low-paid labour and supplies of materials that make the transfer of technology efficient and that, with the factors contributed by the foreign partner, permit the production of improved products. Such intensive co-operation and linkages with local industries are of course not possible and rarely seen in the EPZs. But there is no doubt that the SEZ provides a new dimension to the EPZ concept.

Fig. 12.2 Shenzhen's Matchmaker Role

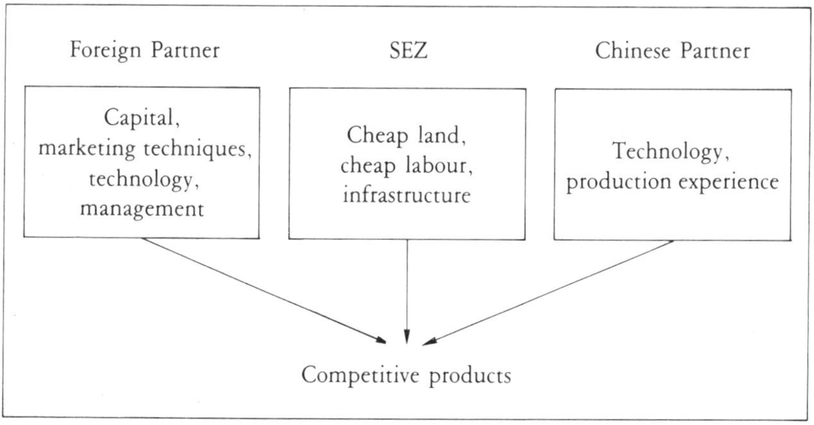

Future Prospects

It is very clear that the Chinese want to make use of their newly formed SEZs to transfer high-level technology and successful management experience. The way in which Shenzhen has moved back to the original emphasis on industrial development seems to support the thesis that the Chinese have found in the SEZs an 'open-door' type of industrial modernization strategy that matches very well Chinese circumstances, for the country has a substantial industrial base and is fairly advanced in certain types of technology, though still lacking in modern market knowledge and marketing techniques. The Chinese domestic market too is among the best in the developing world. The potential of the new strategy for enhancing future economic and technological exchanges between China and the West within the SEZ is certainly great.

The creation of 14 open cities in 1984 indicates the Chinese leadership's further commitment to the new open-door policy. These 14 cities are currently busy planning the strategies for exploiting their newly granted status. The new privileges include an upgrading of their administrative status to the provincial level such that, with the exception of Shanghai (which is a centrally administered city), they have all gained a much larger degree of freedom and autonomy in matters of foreign trade and investment. These cities are also allowed to develop industrial zones and science parks in which the corporate profit tax and import and export duties and formalities will be as generous as in the SEZs. As with the SEZs, these zones provide formed sites and completed infrastructure for industrial growth. They may, therefore, possibly draw some foreign investments from the SEZs. Foreign investors are now in fact presented with more site alternatives in considering joint ventures in China. However, the new open cities are no threat to the SEZs as some may tend to think. Their addition to the 'special zone' category is merely a welcome extension of the 'open-door' strategy to the major coastal ports of China, where opportunities were previously untapped. The new open cities will certainly help the modernization and economic development of these cities and their hinterlands by offering existing enterprises new venues to modernize and by giving the local economy new stimulus. But these new zones are likely to serve different clients as they do not possess some of the attributes of the SEZs. First, multi-sector development occurs in the SEZs. Second, the SEZs constitute new border cities managed under different laws and regulations where the market mechanism is allowed to work in a much wider range of decision-making. Third, the SEZs are regarded as more 'special' than the 'special zones' of the open cities; they are of national significance in the transfer of management and technology and a test-laboratory for related reforms. As such they are given ministerial support and supervision.

Shenzhen, in addition to the above, enjoys the advantage of being next door to Hong Kong. Thus, the zone is better placed than the open cities for those joint projects that require a high level of input from foreign personnel, information, machinery and equipment.

China has just started to venture into more co-operation with foreign interests in its 'open-door' modernization. Although Shenzhen has progressed fairly well in the past five years, there is still much scope for further development. In future the division of labour between the SEZs and the 14 open cities may work out spontaneously through the force of comparative advantages, and Shenzhen's role as a pioneer in the modernization drive will continue in the coming decade.

Notes

1. See Regulations on the Special Economic Zones in Guangdong Province announced in August 1981, and published in *Zhongguo jinji nianjian* (*Almanac of China's Economy*) (Hong Kong, Modern Cultural Co., 1982), pp. 263–5.
2. *Ta kung pao*, 7 April 1984, p. 1.
3. The full title of the joint venture regulations is the Law of the People's Republic of China on Joint Ventures Using Chinese and Foreign Investment. For details see *Zhongguo jinji nianjian* (1982).
4. Many of these debates are contained in articles in *Jingji yanjiu* (*Economic Research*) and *Gangao jingji* (*Hong Kong and Macau Economic Digest*).
5. These points are stressed in 'Xuexi ''jueyi'', jiaqiang jingji tequ yanjiu' ('Study the ''Resolution'' and Strengthen Research on the Special Economic Zones'), and 'Xuexi Liening youguan zurangzhi di lilun' ('Study Lenin's Theory Regarding the Leasing System'), *Gangao yanjiu*, No. 4, 1981, p. 1, and No. 4, 1982, p. 35, respectively.
6. See China Merchants' Steam Navigation Co. (CMSN), *Shenzhen jingji tequ Shekou gongyequ touzi shouce* (*Investor's Handbook: The Shekou Industrial Zone in Shenzhen*) (January 1980), p. 1.
7. This laboratory role is discussed in some detail in V.F.S. Sit, 'The Special Economic Zones of China: a new type of EPZ', in *Developing Economies*, Vol. XIII, No. 1, March 1985.
8. Chi Fu, 'China's Newborn SEZs and their Strategic Significance', *Economic Reporter*, August 1981, p. 14.
9. For the geographic details of the SEZs, see Chapter 2.
10. See K.Y. Wong (ed.), *Shenzhen Special Economic Zone* (Hong Kong, Hong Kong Geographical Association, 1982), for the necessary background.
11. 'Shenzhen jingji tequ gongye fazhan jihua' ('Industrial Development Plan of the Shenzhen Special Economic Zone'), *Economic Reporter*, 6 September 1982, p. 19.
12. See V.F.S. Sit, 'Shenzhen's Potential Contribution to Hong Kong's Growing Land Demand', *Economic Reporter*, July 1981, pp. 17–21.
13. See note 1.
14. See Sit (1981), p. 19.
15. 'Jiantao jingji tequ di gongye fazhan qianjing' ('Re-examining the Prospects of Industrial Development in the SEZs'), *Economic Reporter*, 28 March 1983, pp. 25–6.
16. 'Jiantao jingi tequ di gongye fazhan qianjing' (1983), p. 26.
17. The new laws can be found in Xinhua News Agency and New Evening Post, *Zhongguo jingji tequ shouce* (*Handbook for China's Special Economic Zones*) (Hong Kong, New Evening Post, 1984).
18. Xinhua News Agency and New Evening Post (1984), pp. 9–38.
19. 'Shenzhen jingji tequ jiaqiang xiyin touzi renshi' ('Shenzhen SEZ Gives Investors More Incentives'), *Economic Reporter*, 1 October 1984, p. 33.
20. 'Yi ge xiandaihua chengshi di xingjian: Shenzhen di juda zhuanbian' ('A New City Is Being Build: Big Changes in Shenzhen'), *Economic Reporter*, 9 January 1984, p. 25.

21. 'Shenzhen gongye xiangjuang ji fazhan qianjing' ('The Present Situation and Future Prospects of Shenzhen's Industries'), *Economic Reporter*, 17 September 1984, p. 19.

22. 'Shenzhen gongye xiangjuang ji fazhan qianjing' (1984), p. 19.

23. 'Shekou — yige zonghe fazhan di gongyequ' ('Shekou — A Comprehensive Industrial Development Zone'), *Economic Reporter*, 9 July 1984, p. 26.

24. See *Economic Reporter*, 17 September 1984, p. 19.

25. For details, see 'Youguan jingji tequ xingzhi di tantao' ('Comment on the Nature of the Special Economic Zones'), *Jingji yanjiu*, No. 8, 1981, p. 56.

26. See note 24.

27. See Sit (1981).

28. See Sit (1981).

29. CMSN, *Investor's Handbook (Revised and Enlarged Edition): China Merchants' Shekou Industrial Zone* (Hong Kong, September 1981).

30. Personal interview with CMSN, July 1984.

31. 'Shenzhen di fazhan sudu — dianziye di fazhan gaikuang' ('The Speed of Shenzhen's Development — the Current Situation of the Electronics Industry'), *Economic Reporter*, 17 September 1984, p. 28.

32. There have been a number of attempts to compare the SEZs with EPZs. See V.F.S. Sit, 'Cong Yazhou di chukou jiangongqu kan Zhongguo jingji tequ di qianjing' ('From the Export Processing Zones of Asia to the Prospects of China's Special Economic Zones'), *Dousou*, Vol. 42, January 1981, pp. 1–10; K.Y. Wong and David K.Y. Chu, 'Export Processing Zones and Special Economic Zones as Generators of Economic Development: the Asian Experience', *Geografiska Annaler*, Vol. 66B, No. 1, 1984, pp. 1–16; and Sit (1985). These works have also described and discussed the nature of the EPZs and their effectiveness as a development tool.

Index